PASSING

the

Heavenly

Gift

BY DENVER C. SNUFFER, JR.

Mill Creek Press
Salt Lake City, Utah

Published in the United States by Mill Creek Press.

MILL CREEK PRESS is a registered trademark of Mill Creek Press, LLC

Library of Congress Control Number

ISBN-13: 978-0-615-52896-0

Printed in the United States of America on acid-free paper

Mill Creek Press website address: www.millcreekpress.com

First Edition

Cover design by David Christensen

For those willing to take counsel and flee from Babylon.

Jer. 50: 45-46.

TABLE OF CONTENTS

PREFACE

-x-

Chapter 1

BOOK OF MORMON, THE CHURCH

-1-

Chapter 2

HISTORY AND TRUTH

-38-

Chapter 3

SUCCESSFUL SUCCESSION

-69-

Chapter 4

SUFFICIENT TIME

-96-

Chapter 5

SLAY HIM FOR THE OATH'S SAKE

-120-

Chapter 6

SEVEN WOMEN SHALL TAKE HOLD OF ONE MAN

-147-

Chapter 7

PROPHETS, PROFITS AND PRIESTCRAFT

-185-

Chapter 8

THE CHILDREN OF CAIN WERE BLACK

-213-

Chapter 9
FOLLOW THE (CURRENT) BRETHREN
-240-

Chapter 10
THE TEMPLE AT NAUVOO
-265-

Chapter 11
THE PRIESTHOOD WAS TAKEN FROM ISRAEL
-288-

Chapter 12
PROPHECY VS. THE TRADITIONAL NARRATIVE
-318-

Chapter 13
CORRELATION: CONTROLLING AND CURTAILING
-347-

Chapter 14
GENTILES SHALL REJECT THE FULLNESS OF THE
GOSPEL
-376-

Chapter 15
A CHURCH OF DESTINY
-400-

Chapter 16
FINDING HOPE
-425-

Chapter 17
INDIVIDUAL SALVATION
-446-

Chapter 18
WRAPPING UP
-472-

Selected Bibliography
-500-

About the Author
-509-

Colophon
-510-

SUMMARY OF ABBREVIATIONS USED:

The following abbreviations will be used for the authorities frequently cited in this work:

History of the Church of Jesus Christ of Latter-day Saints, 7 Volumes, published by the Church of Jesus Christ of Latter-day Saints; will be cited as *"DHC"* followed by volume number and page (i.e., *DHC* 6: 23).

Teachings of the Prophet Joseph Smith, arranged by Joseph Fielding Smith, published by Deseret Book Company; will be cited as *"TPJS"* followed by the page number (i.e., *TPJS,* p. 23).

The Words of Joseph Smith, compiled by Andrew F. Ehat and Lyndon W. Cook, published by the Religious Studies Center, Brigham Young University; will be cited as *"WJS"* followed by the page number (i.e., *WJS* p. 23).

The Journal of Discourses, 26 volumes, will be cited as *"JD"* followed by the volume and page number (i.e., *JD* 6: 23).

Lectures on Faith, compiled by N.B. Lundwall, published by Bookcraft; will be cited as *"Lectures"* followed by Lecture Number, paragraph and page number (i.e., *Lectures, Fourth Lecture,* paragraphs 50-54, pp. 90-91).

The Second Comforter: Conversing With the Lord Through the Veil, Denver C. Snuffer, Jr., published by Mill Creek Press, Salt Lake City, 2006; will be cited as *The Second Comforter.*

Nephi's Isaiah, Denver C. Snuffer, Jr., published by Mill Creek Press, Salt Lake City, 2006; will be cited as *Nephi's Isaiah.*

References to the Bible are to the King James Version.

All other authorities are cited at length.

All spellings in quotes have been left as in the original. To prevent the frequent repetition of "[sic]" we take note of that here, and will not otherwise acknowledge antiquated spellings within the text.

PREFACE

History is comprised of pretty rough stuff. The neat contours we tell one another after the events are not actual history, but myth attempting to explain what happened in hindsight. The more important the historical topic, the greater the tendency to replace the rough, contradictory, failings of the past with an overall message of triumph or redemption.

Whether it is the life of Alexander, the Renaissance, the Inquisition, Cortez' conquest, the American Revolution, or World War II, the accounts we regard as "history" are mythical attempts to smooth together the broken confluences to make a tale worth retelling. Mormonism is particularly "smooth" in all the official history retold by the church I belong to: The Church of Jesus Christ of Latter-day Saints. More and more, however, among friends of mine there is an increasing unease with official accounts of the history of the church. They have grown impatient, and some have left Mormonism because they find too many fanciful insertions into the story of our faith.

I have been waiting for someone to write this book. It needs to be written. No one has stepped forward to do so. Therefore, I have decided I am to write it. It explains why I remain a loyal member, despite the rough stuff from which the modern church arises.

This book does not include the traditional account. It only responds to it. Therefore, this is not intended as an introduction to Mormon history. If you are not acquainted with the claims made in basic Mormon history, you may want to read those first.

In this book, the account leaves many of the rough contours in a rough, contradictory form. It will not pretend to answer all the questions. That would require a much longer book. This is an honest effort to give a forthright account of the Mormon faith, but in the end it is only a beginning to the story. This explanation of events is not based on personal preferences, but it instead conforms with prophecies about Mormonism. The result is a story unlike the familiar one. There is no reassuring, no declarations of success in facing the challenges within our new religion. If you are a faithful Latter-day Saint, as I am, you will need to be open-minded as you go through this book. Some conclusions are very different from what you are used to. A great deal of what is regarded as "well settled" is, upon close investigation, merely a series of inconsistent leaps of faith unwarranted by the record. Alternatively, they are simply inaccurate, incomplete or untrue. In the traditional story written and told by Mormons to one another, there has been a great deal of revising, or explaining events from hindsight.

I have found ideas that I once considered renegade are, in fact, an accurate explanation of events at the time they happened. Later ideas tend to creep backwards, offering explanations that do not belong in the story until later changes were adopted. It is very important to know that some events regarded as original are changes which were made at a later date. They do not belong in the account as part of the first, unfolding establishment of the religion.

For Mormon readers, therefore, it will be necessary to keep an open mind about our history until you have finished reading.

I do not make any apologies for believing Joseph Smith's assertion that he was a prophet. I accept the idea. I believe he was at least that. He may have been much more. I will touch upon that in this book.

I appreciate Mill Creek Press most because they exercise no censorship over the things I write. This is uncommon among publishers of Latter-day Saint materials. Therefore, I want to acknowledge this valuable freedom given me. The result is that I alone am responsible for the content of this book. Not only does it not represent any official view of The Church of Jesus Christ of Latter-day Saints, but it offers a very different view of many of the claims made by the church about its history.

I also want to recognize my family's contribution to getting this book done. My wife has become my editor, correcting language, grammar, sentence structure, and requiring me to make clarifications and expansions where needed. Her considerable efforts have required a great deal of sacrifice and work on her part. I am very grateful for that. Completing a book has become more of a family affair of late, with my son Christian helping to check citations and quotes, and my daughters Kylee and Lindsay reading galley proofs. Others aid as well, and I am grateful to them even if they do not want to be mentioned in this preface.

This is the eighth book I've written on Mormon topics. I've deferred any treatment of history until now. But this history will give context to what I have written previously, and I hope help establish the importance of the doctrine already explained in the earlier books. This is not really a change in subject from what I've already written, but a further explanation of why it is important to understand the Gospel as it was originally restored through Joseph Smith. To do that, we need to know how it has been changed. But the changes cannot be divorced from other topics, including the concurrent causes. The result is this book.

Some terms are not clarified in this book. For example, "the fullness of the Gospel" and "the fullness of the priesthood" are not synonymous terms. But they are related. The objective of the fullness of the Gospel is to bring people back to Christ's presence. When in Christ's presence, the fullness of the priesthood is bestowed. The one leads to the other. But they are not the same. Terms are not clarified unless it is necessary to the book.

Finally, it would be a disservice to discuss the problems with traditional accounts of Mormon history and leave the reader with the impression I believe there has been a complete compromise of the faith. Therefore this book also will explain why Mormonism is still the center of God's involvement with religion today.

Denver C. Snuffer, Jr.
Sandy, Utah
June 27, 2011

Chapter 1

BOOK OF MORMON, THE CHURCH

I am a member of The Church of Jesus Christ of Latter-day Saints. I have never belonged to any other church. I came to this faith as a 19 year old convert, while on active duty with the US Air Force. When I joined in September, 1973, the church was led by President Harold B. Lee. Less than a month after my baptism I attended the October 1973, Semi-Annual General Conference and was struck by how dignified a man he was. When he died in December 1973, I learned for the first time about succession, and how seamlessly the transition of church presidents had become through tradition and custom.

My initial impression of President Spencer W. Kimball was not favorable. Since I joined the church while in the Air Force, stationed in New Hampshire, and then transferred to Texas, President Kimball remained to me only a disembodied voice heard on radio broadcasts for the first two years of his presidency. His post-surgery, raspy voice was unpleasant to hear. I grew, however, to respect him. I admired him from afar, then later on a more personal level as I attended law school at Brigham Young University where his son, Professor Edward Kimball taught. I sometimes shared an elevator ride with him in the J. Reuben Clark

Law School. He was diminutive in size, kindly and loving, almost always provoking a smile by his demeanor.

My early memories of belonging to the church are marked most by the flood of doctrines I learned. The church's top leadership was then filled with proponents of doctrine like Marion G. Romney, LeGrand Richards, Mark E. Peterson, Bruce R. McConkie and Boyd K. Packer. LeGrand Richard's *A Marvelous Work and Wonder* was the guide used for the missionary discussions taught to me. Everywhere you looked the books which were sold, read and discussed were doctrinal. The local Seventies Bookstores were filled entirely with doctrinal or historical works. The saints all seemed to know doctrine, and to be able to inform me of deeper insights wherever I turned to learn more.

From those days in the 1970's to now, there has been a remarkable transformation within the church and its culture. Today inspirational stories, divorced from doctrinal expositions, are the norm. I miss the times when doctrines were the rallying point which brought the saints together. That has been replaced by a less vibrant culture, in which now some of the earlier discussions involving deeper meanings are considered inappropriate, now often being termed "mysteries" to be avoided. There has been a great transformation I have experienced in only 38 years as a Mormon.

In those few years I have experienced the disappointment of seeing too many close friends leave the church. There are many reasons for their departures, but increasingly I have heard complaints about the church's failings and its dishonesty about its history. With the coming of the Internet, there is a tidal wave of complaints from disaffected saints available to read, hear or watch. The chorus of criticism does not only include the wayward and disobedient searching for a reason to leave. It includes people of honest intent leading good lives who have learned something about the church they cannot reconcile. Many of these people leave with broken hearts, and would have retained their faith if only candid explanations had been given them. They believe the church to be dishonest.

I have taken assignments as a home teacher, gospel doctrine teacher, ward mission leader and high counselor in which I have dealt with disaffected or languishing members' criticism of the church. As a result, I have had to research, and confront a wide variety of critical issues that have persuaded people to question or abandon their faith. My own faith has been unaffected by the many criticisms I have heard, researched and addressed. The new anxieties from Internet surfing for many saints are issues I confronted many years ago in both callings and discussions with friends.

I have reached the conclusion that faith is never strengthened by sheltering members from problems in church history, mistakes made in the past, or difficult doctrinal issues. In the end, unless we as members, are willing to search deeply for the underlying truth, we avoid what will save us. From all I have read, learned, heard and experienced, I remain of the view the Gospel of Jesus Christ was restored through Joseph Smith and it is resilient enough to take any criticism aimed at it, and remain intact. However, I have also come to see church history much differently than I once did. It is far more nuanced, complex, and in many ways more wonderful than the "faith promoting" versions. The official "faithful" version distorts some things in an attempt to insulate people or events from criticism. I have come to value more honest accounts, even when they caused initial anxiety. Mormonism's history is filled with human failure, divine mercy, foolish enthusiasm, but most importantly the claim of a modern appearance of God's hand again in the affairs of men. It mirrors the greatness and foolishness on display by men every time His presence has intruded into history. Our time is the equal of the time of Abraham or Moses, or the mortal lifetime of Jesus Christ. Our days are filled with sacred events just as happened anciently on Sinai, and in Judea, Jerusalem and Corinth. When a person's study only searches deeply enough to raise questions, but fails to then press on to find an answer to the question, they have neglected their responsibility. We *should* search and discover questions about Mormonism. An unexamined faith is little more than foolishness. But questions deserve answers. I've let people share with me their doubts. I am grateful to hear them. Then, if I do not have an answer, I undertake a search to learn.

Our own time is offered a Divine opportunity, and we join those in history who were witnesses of the peculiar treasure of God's handiwork among frail mortality. The opportunities given to modern man are as electrifying as anything involving Elijah, Isaiah, Peter or Paul. We can understand these ancient figures better by studying our own time than by the limited historical record available about their lives. Everything they experienced is here, unfolding again. The tensions between a prophet claiming to have spoken with God and his skeptical audience, the angry persecution and killing of the prophet have been reenacted. Like the Old Testament, the modern "chosen people" also forsake truth, make compromises with their surrounding culture, adopt lower values and struggle with the consequences. Just like the Deuteronomists in the post-Babylonian period, modern Mormonism is rewriting the original faith given them.

This book will examine the glory, foolishness, wonder, failure and triumph of the Restored Gospel. This is my view of the events. It is not an official account—far from it. In many respects this book will contradict the church's preferred narrative. It is the product of years of study, and an honest desire to understand events, even when the events are so ugly or alarming I would prefer they never occurred. I have not turned from these moments, but have instead tried to put them into a context which gives a fair measure to those involved, and how they are best understood.

I am a lawyer, not an historian. This book is a view of the events as I have come to understand them. Any historian will offer only his editorial opinion dressed in an academic discipline to pretend it is more than mere opinion. But history written by the academics suffers from all the bias, blindness and foolishness of the one who writes. History is too spontaneous and powerful a flow of events for any man to be able to capture it in words alone. History can be felt as it is experienced. Times and events all have their "spirit" and life. The history of The Church of Jesus Christ of Latter-day Saints has not yet been captured and adequately explained by any writer, no matter how they've labored over their attempt. In histories written to date, important context given by God through revelation has been ignored. In contrast, this book will let the prophetic descriptions of our day frame the discussion. By "prophetic descriptions" I refer to those found in scripture, primarily the Book of Mormon, Doctrine and Covenants, Old Testament, and Joseph Smith's writings.

The truth of this dispensation remains an enigma beyond existing explanation, despite all efforts to offer one. I am adding my effort to account for events. It is honest. It is what I think. It is how I have kept myself loyal to the faith despite its many twists, and why I will not draw back when uncomfortable topics arise.

Sometimes people are best understood by their mistakes. It is a person's follies as well as their triumphs that define who they really are. This book will not shy away from those awkward, foolish and dubious moments of Latter-day Saint history. These things also define our faith. They are necessary. If ignored, we lose some of the truth.

In no area of study should the range of discussion be more open than in the study of religion. Yet the level of tolerance for differing views or new ideas is often limited the most when the topic turns to matters of faith. When Elder Pelatiah Brown was called before the Nauvoo High Council because he was allegedly teaching "false doctrine," Joseph Smith defended the man's right to believe as he liked:

> I did not like the old man being called up for erring in doctrine. It looks too much like the Methodist, and not like the Latter-day Saints. Methodists have creeds which a man must believe or be asked out of their church. I want the liberty of thinking and believing as I please. It feels so good not to be trammelled. It does not prove that a man is not a good man because he errs in doctrine. (*DHC* 5:340.)

We have come a long way since Joseph Smith and the case of Elder Brown. In the intervening years, we have restricted our willingness to openly discuss ideas outside narrowly defined topics. Mormonism has not only become part of the larger self-censoring "politically correct" world culture, but it now engages in central doctrinal control through the Correlation Department. Refusing to openly discuss ideas does not make them go away. Censorship instead drives the discussions into places where the church cannot control, and sometimes where it cannot even provide input. The church's effort to exercise control and compulsion results in many people leaving the church. Some leave the church, but retain the faith. Departure from the church does not always signal that a person no longer accepts Joseph Smith as a prophet. People who leave sometimes resent the limitations on their freedom to believe, others because they presume there are no adequate answers to their inner questions. I do not believe in self-censorship. Nor do I think the church should protect a person's fragile faith by shielding it from learning answers about reasonable questions. The Church of Jesus Christ of Latter-day Saints has undergone tremendous changes from the time of Joseph Smith until today. This book candidly discusses those changes, why they happened, and what they say about our religion.

If Joseph Smith received an authentic revelation from God, and restored an ancient religion as I believe, then the first two centuries of the religion should be studied by every person interested in how religions develop. Those who try to understand Historic Christianity know it is critical to understand the changes to Christianity in the two centuries following Christ's death. The records of that time period are woefully inadequate. Even if a person does not accept Mormonism as their faith, studying a new religious tradition in its first two centuries is a valuable opportunity to see history in motion. Mormonism is an example of how all religions move, change alter, and reform.

Christianity was so completely altered from 33 a.d. to 324 a.d it was given a new name. The New Testament tells about a faith now called "Primitive Christianity." But when the council at Nicea concluded, things had so changed a new name was needed. We now refer to this new version as "Historic Christianity" because it so completely replaced the earlier version. Without Apostles, an expanding scriptural canon, revelation, heavenly visitors, or miraculous prophetic power, the heavenly gift was gone. Historic Christianity proceeded with the assumption God was still in control of events. His miraculous presence may have departed, but the religious leaders claimed He still spoke through ecumenical councils. The decisions made in church councils, the creeds and outcomes of meetings, were regarded as the product of the Holy Ghost. Any other alternative would be unthinkable to them because it implied they had apostatized.

It is possible we could learn more about the transition of Primitive Christianity into Historic Christianity by studying Mormonism than by studying the Ante-Nicean Fathers. Even the skeptic may find Joseph Smith's work to restore a religion a rare historic event, worthy of intense scrutiny. And for believers like me, we can appreciate and understand the faith most by noting its many changes.

From the time Mormonism[1] sprang into existence until today, the faith founded by Joseph Smith has been in constant flux. Today the LDS Church claims over 14 million members. My denomination accepted Brigham Young's claim that upon Joseph's death, the Quorum of the Twelve were entitled to preside, and Brigham

---

[1] "Mormonism" was originally used as a term of derision to mock those who accepted the Book of Mormon as scripture. Over time it became accepted by church members. In 2002 The Church of Jesus Christ of Latter-day Saints objected to the term and requested it not be used. Subsequently, however, the church has developed websites such as "Mormon.org" and "Mormon Times" as well as putting "Mormon Messages" on YouTube. Therefore, I will use it unapologetically throughout this book to refer to my faith.

Young as senior Apostle presided over the Twelve. He was later elected president.

The Reorganized Church of Jesus Christ of Latter Day Saints changed its name to The Community of Christ on April 6, 2001. This name change was made, in part, to distance that church and its members from Joseph Smith, the Book of Mormon, and other "Mormons." The name change took place during the administration of W. Grant McMurray, the seventh President of Reorganized LDS Church.[2] He was the first president who was not a descendant of Joseph Smith. The original premise of succession for the Reorganized LDS Church was the belief it was necessary to have a lineal descendant of Joseph Smith lead as President, an idea now abandoned by that sect. The RLDS (or Community of Christ) claims to have 250,000 members.

Other splinter groups who accept the Book of Mormon have been dubbed "Fundamentalists" to distinguish themselves from "Mormons." Many of them claim they more closely follow Joseph Smith's original teachings than do Latter-day Saints. Indeed, they claim they exist to preserve, or return Joseph Smith's original teachings. Each splinter group has leveled criticism at other forms of Mormonism because they claim errors justify their break-off. There are dozens of splinter groups, some of which still exist, and many that have disappeared. The first splintering included groups

---

[2]After Joseph Smith's death, followers of this faith claim the church fell into disorganization until its "Reorganization" in 1860 under the leadership of Joseph's son. The successor RLDS presidents beginning with that son have been Joseph Smith III (1860-1914), Frederick M. Smith (1915-1946), Israel A. Smith (1946-1958), W. Wallace Smith (1958-1978), W. Grant McMurray (1996-2004), and today Stephen M. Veasey (2005-present). The first six were descendants of Joseph Smith, the last two were not.

led by such early dissidents as Sidney Rigdon, William McClellen, David Whitmer, James Strang, and James Emmett. Current splinter groups have been established by Ervil LeBaron, Alexander Joseph, Eldon Park, Loren C. Wooley, and John Y. Barlow. Fundamentalist splinter groups have often degenerated into violence and internal strife, causing still further fragmentation.

In spite of the concern regarding the term "Mormon," it is used throughout this book to identify The Church of Jesus Christ of Latter-day Saints as the faith restored through Joseph Smith which accepts the Book of Mormon as scripture. That church accounts for the overwhelming majority (approximately 97%) of Joseph's followers. The term Mormonism was first used after the Book of Mormon was published. But the religion's foundation began in 1820 when Joseph Smith first experienced a revelation from God. Whenever other groups are referred to as "Mormon," I will clarify that use.

From its very beginning, Mormonism has undergone constant change. It has yet to assume a final form. It has undergone at least four distinct phases to date.[3] The first was during Joseph Smith's lifetime. The second began with Brigham Young and lasted until Wilford Woodruff changed the practice of plural marriage. Wilford Woodruff began the transition into the third phase, but Joseph F. Smith actually ended the practice of plural marriages and is therefore also responsible for ending the second phase. With the abandonment of the practice of plural marriage, Mormons were welcomed into the United States through Utah's statehood, and the

---

[3] Arguably President Gordon B. Hinckley's public relations focus could be a fifth, however, it is my view this was only a continuation of what marks the fourth phase and therefore do not believe it necessary to distinguish it as another distinct phase.

faith entered a third phase. That phase lasted through George Albert Smith's administration in 1951. After many years of incubation, the administration of David O. McKay marks an entrance into a fourth phase in which modern Mormonism was born.[4] Today's version of the religion is institutionally tied to constant change.

The chief distinction between the first phase, involving Joseph Smith, and all other subsequent phases, is the nature of changes. During the Joseph Smith era, changes were additive and innovative. The faith was rapidly added upon. The greatest challenge for Joseph's followers were the new things: the expanding canon of scripture, the increased complexity of the church organization structure, the expanded body of doctrine, and the additions of new ordinances.

In contrast to the first phase, all subsequent phases have reduced or deducted from the religion. After Joseph Smith's death it was a while before the canon of scripture stabalized. When it did, the only expansion made to it was by adding four items: one of Joseph Smith's previously uncanonized revelations, two proclamations, and a personal vision received by Joseph F. Smith as he privately studied and pondered the scriptures.[5] Notwithstanding these four

---

[4]The book, *David O. McKay and the Rise of Modern Mormonism* is aptly titled. The church's fourth and current phase began with President McKay. Prince, Gregory and Wright, Robert. *David O. McKay and the Rise of Modern Mormonism*. Salt Lake City: University of Utah Press, 2005

[5]The Doctrine & Covenants added Section 137 (an 1836 vision of Joseph Smith's), Section 138 (a 1918 revelation to Joseph F. Smith), and Official Declarations 1 (Wilford Woodruff's 1890 Press Release ending plural marriage) & 2 (Spencer Kimball's 1978 announcement permitting priesthood ordination of those of African descent); all were added in 1979 when the new scripture footnoting system was released.

canon additions, the subsequent phases have reduced or abandoned doctrine, and reduced or eliminated portions of temple ordinances. In contrast with the deductions from teachings, in all the subsequent phases church membership has grown, wealth and political influence has expanded, temple building has increased, and scholarship defending Joseph Smith has flourished. The underlying faith is, however, continually reducing what is taught, trimming away doctrine, cutting temple rites and abandoning past positions on many issues.

Mormonism began because of Joseph Smith's uncertainty about which Christian religion was the right one. Joseph's mother, brothers Hyrum and Samuel, and sister Sophrina joined the Presbyterian faith. (JS-H 1: 7.) Joseph was partial toward the Methodist faith, but not convinced. (JS-H 1: 8.)

Joseph Smith, anxious to know what church to join, came to the conclusion he must ask God (as James 1: 5 instructed him), and made the attempt in 1820. (JS-H 1: 13-14.) God answered his inquiry. Coming out of a grove of trees, after obtaining an answer, he understood the visit with God to be a personal experience. His first explanation of the vision was given to his mother, "I then said to my mother, 'I have learned for myself that Presbyterianism is not true.'" This first explanation of the event shows how he initially viewed his revelation. It applied only to him.

By 1823 enough time had passed from his first encounter with God that Joseph wanted to know his standing before Him. (JS-H 1: 29.) In response to his prayer, Joseph was visited by an angel who told him of a book deposited in the ground. This book was an account of former occupants of the American continent. (JS-H 1: 34.) More than any other event in Joseph Smith's life, the translation of the Book of Mormon altered his course. Through it he became acquainted with new and surprising doctrines that revolutionize Christian faith. Jesus Christ is shown to have a pre-birth ministry, and a post-resurrection, global ministry previously unknown. Translation of the book sent Joseph back to God for information about priesthood and practices which would change history.

By 1830 the Book of Mormon was translated and published. Although there was an informal Church of Christ led by Joseph before April 6, 1830, on that day, Joseph formally organized a legal entity according to his understanding of the law in New York State. (D&C 20: 1.)

Twelve years after the First Vision, and two years after the formal organization of a church, Joseph wrote a new account of his expanding understanding of his first encounter with God. He wrote, ". . . while in the attitude of calling upon the Lord in the 16th [sic] year of my age a pillar of light above the brightness of the Sun at noon day come down from above and rested upon me and I was filled with the Spirit of God and the Lord opened the heavens upon me and I saw the Lord and he spake unto me saying, 'Joseph my son thy sins are forgiven thee. Go thy way walk in my statutes and keep my commandments behold I am the Lord of glory I was crucified for the world that all those who believe on my name may have Eternal life.'" (Backman, Milton V. *Joseph Smith's First Vision.* Salt Lake City: Bookcraft, 1980, 2nd Edition, p. 157; punctuation and spellings corrected.) In 1832, Joseph Smith still understood the First Vision to be a personal, conversion experience. The primary meaning to Joseph was that his sins were forgiven.

In 1835 Joseph again related the First Vision which Warren Cowdery recorded, ". . . I called on the Lord in mighty prayer. A pillar of fire appeared above my head; which presently rested down upon me, and filled me with unspeakable joy. A personage appeared in the midst of this pillar of flame, which was spread all around and yet nothing consumed. Another personage soon appeared like unto the first: he said unto me thy sins are forgiven thee. He testified also unto me that Jesus Christ is the son of God. I saw many angels in this vision. I was about 14 years old when I received this first communication." (*Id.*, p. 159; punctuation and spellings corrected.) Joseph's understanding remained personal, and the meaning of God's visit with him, individual forgiveness.

The next account was written by Joseph in 1838. This is the familiar account found as *Joseph Smith-History* in the Pearl of Great Price. It is Mormonism's canonized account, and here the meaning of the First Vision changes to something broader. It no longer stands as a personal conversion experience, but instead is a cosmic event intended to benefit all mankind. It includes the following, "I was answered that I just join none of them, for they were all wrong; and the Personage who addressed me said that all their creeds were an abomination in his sight; that those professors were all corrupt; that: 'they draw near to me with their lips, but their hearts are far from me, they teach for doctrines the commandments of men, having a form of godliness, but they deny the power thereof.'" By 1838 Joseph Smith understood his experience to be universal, not personal. The meaning had expanded. Instead of focusing on Joseph Smith's personal forgiveness, it is about the state of all religions. They are "all wrong." Joseph was instructed he "must join none of them." This is because "all their creeds were an abomination."

Richard L. Bushman made this observation regarding the changes in Joseph's accounts of his First Vision:

In the 1835 account and again 1838, the balance of the two parts of the story-personal forgiveness as contrasted to the apostasy of the churches-shifted. Joseph's own salvation gave way to the opening of a new era of history. The promise of forgiveness through faith in Christ was dropped from the narrative, and the apostasy of Christian churches stood as the central message of the vision. (Bushman, Richard L. *Rough Stone Rolling.* New York: Alfred A. Knopf, 2005, p. 40.)

Between 1820, when the first encounter with God occurred, and 1838, when Joseph understood it to have cosmic significance, Joseph's world had been reshaped by experience. He had eighteen years of persecution, pondering, preaching, and progression between the event and the canonized account. This progression of understanding is common for prophets. Nephi, the first prophet/author in the Book of Mormon took forty years between his visionary encounter with Christ and writing his two volumes of scripture. He explained that in that forty years his mind worked to assign the correct meaning to the things he witnessed, "Behold, my soul delighteth in the things of the Lord; and my heart pondereth continually upon the things which I have seen and heard." (2 Nephi 4: 16.) After forty years of continual pondering, Nephi was finally ready to write scripture about the things of God. (See also, 2 Nephi 4: 15.)

Often, Prophets do not understand what God shows them the instant it is revealed. Sometimes unlocking the vision takes time and care, together with careful, solemn, ponderous thought, before they are understood.[6] Moses saw a vision which so befuddled his

---

[6] In an 1839 letter written from Liberty Jail, Joseph explained: "The things of God are of deep import; and time, and experience, and careful and

mind he was able only to report, "And he beheld also the inhabitants thereof, and there was not a soul which he beheld not; and he discerned them by the Spirit of God; and their numbers were great, even numberless as the sand upon the sea shore. And he beheld many lands; and each land was called earth, and there were inhabitants on the face thereof." (Moses 1: 28-29.) When he pressed the Lord for an explanation of what he saw, the Lord would not explain the vision, but instead gave an account of the earth's creation, Adam and Eve, the Fall of man, and Adam and Eve being cast out of the Garden of Eden with the resulting struggles of mortality. For the rest of mankind's history shown him in the vision, Moses could only wonder at the vision and briefly summarize its contents.

It should be expected for Joseph Smith to gain understanding of his first encounter with God the same way as other prophets. With more experience and reflection, it became the First Vision of a new dispensation of the Gospel. It was no longer just personal.

In his 1838 account, Joseph explained that a few years following the vision he wanted to confirm God would again forgive his sins. He wrote, "I betook myself to prayer and supplication to Almighty God for forgiveness of all my sins and follies, and also for a manifestation to me, that I might know of my state and standing before him; for I had full confidence in obtaining a divine manifestation, as I previously had one." (JS-H 1: 29.) In response Joseph received a visitor who greatly expanded Joseph's role. He was no longer an individual convert. He was the voice of God, calling for all mankind to repent.

---

ponderous and solemn thoughts can only find them out." (*TPJS*, p. 137.)

Quoting the angel, Joseph wrote, "He called me by name, and said unto me that he was a messenger sent from the presence of God to me, and that his name was Moroni; that God had a work for me to do; and that my name should be had for good and evil among all nations, kindreds, and tongues, or that it should be both good and evil spoken of among all people." (JS-H1: 33.) God had a work for Joseph to do. All nations, kindreds and tongues would come to know of it. Joseph was also promised priestly authority, "Behold, I will reveal unto you the Priesthood, by the hand of Elijah the prophet, before the coming of the great and dreadful day of the Lord." (JS-H 1: 38.) Most important of all, there was a new volume of scripture containing the fullness of the Gospel of Jesus Christ, which was written upon gold plates. Joseph would be given that book.[7]

It would be four years before Joseph would obtain possession of the ancient book.[8] During those four years, Joseph married,[9] and his wife accompanied him the evening he obtained possession of

---

[7]"He said there was a book deposited, written upon gold plates, giving an account of the former inhabitants of this continent, and the source from whence they sprang. He also said that the fulness of the everlasting Gospel was contained in it, as delivered by the Savior to the ancient inhabitants; Also, that there were two stones in silver bows--and these stones, fastened to a breastplate, constituted what is called the Urim and Thummim--deposited with the plates; and the possession and use of these stones were what constituted 'seers' in ancient or former times; and that God had prepared them for the purpose of translating the book." (JS-H 1: 34-35.)

[8]JS-H 1: 53.

[9]JS-H 1: 57. His wife was a necessary companion the night he obtained the plates.

the book.[10] Soon afterwards Joseph began to translate the text, his wife Emma acting as the initial scribe.

Oliver Cowdery came to Joseph Smith on April 5, 1829 to investigate the rumors he had heard about Joseph's work. He became Joseph's scribe two days later.[11] By May 15, they had translated the portion of the text that explained the need for baptism. Accordingly, Joseph and Oliver went into the woods to pray concerning baptism. This was the first great result of Joseph's translation of the Book of Mormon. After asking about baptism, Joseph and Oliver were visited by another angel who "said that his name was John, the same that is called John the Baptist in the New Testament." (JS-H 1:72.) The angel laid his hands on Joseph and Oliver, and ordained them, saying, "Upon you my fellow servants, in the name of Messiah, I confer the Priesthood of Aaron, which holds the keys of the ministering of angels, and of the gospel of repentance, and of baptism by immersion for the remission of sins; and this shall never be taken again from the earth until the sons of Levi do offer again an offering unto the Lord in righteousness."

---

[10]Emma's presence was required. Her first child, Alvin, was born June 15, 1828, nine months after the September 22, 1827 date on which the plates were given into their care. Before beginning his ministry as a prophet-translator, legally authorized to hold the incidents of Nephite kingship including the Urim and Thummim, it is likely more was done to commission Joseph's work than we have available in our current records. Though it would be years before the eternal marriage covenant could be explained to his followers, Joseph and Emma may not have departed the Hill Cumorah on September 22, 1827 without first being introduced to eternal covenant making.

[11]JS-H 1: 66-67.

(JS-H 1: 69.)[12] The First Vision connected Joseph to the cosmic will of God and Jesus Christ. The visit of the angel four years later connected him with former residents of the Americas. The visit of John the Baptist connected Joseph with New Testament Christianity. He was becoming the point of intersection between lost understanding, lost scripture, lost authority, and a restored connection to sacred history and heaven. Past dispensations were converging in the work of this obscure frontier farmer.

By May 15, 1829, Oliver Cowdery joined Joseph as his scribe and second eye-witness to his work. This additional witness would testify angels ministered to support the work they were doing. He could confirm Joseph was translating a new volume of scripture. Now two people could jointly testify that priestly authority once lost, was returned. Joseph was not the only one in possession of knowledge that the heavenly gift had returned. God's hand was once again operating in man's history. The heavens were open again, just as they were anciently.

The day the power to baptize was restored, Joseph and Oliver immediately baptized one another. This began the establishment of a church. By June 1829 David Whitmer was baptized.

In June 1829 David Whitmer explained, "In this month I was baptized, confirmed, and ordained an Elder in the Church of Christ by Bro. Joseph Smith. Previous to this, Joseph Smith and Oliver Cowdery had baptized, confirmed and ordained each other to the office of an Elder in the Church of Christ. I was the third person baptized into the church." (Whitmer, David. *An Address to*

---

[12]Oliver Cowdery quotes the angel a little differently: "Upon you my fellow-servants, in the name of Messiah, I confer this Priesthood and this authority, which shall remain upon earth, that the Sons of Levi may yet offer an offering unto the Lord in righteousness!"

all Believers in Christ. Richmond, Missouri, 1887, in Part Second, Chapter 4.)[13] Whitmer went on to explain that six elders were members of the Church of Christ before April 1830. These included Peter Whitmer, Samuel H. Smith and Hyrum Smith, in addition to the first three.

David Whitmer was critical of Joseph's decision to organize a church on April 6th. He explained there were already three branches of the Church of Christ in existence before April 6, 1830. These were located in Fayette and Manchester, New York, and Colesville, Pennsylvania. He wrote:

> [T]he world had been telling us that we were not a regularly organized church, and we had no right to officiate in the ordinance of marriage, hold church property, etc., and that we should organize according to the laws of the land. On this account we met at my father's house in Fayette, N.Y., on April 6, 1830, to attend to this matter of organizing according to the laws of the land; you can see this from Sec. 17 *Doctrine and Covenants* [now Section 20, verse 1]: the church was organized on April 6th "agreeable to the laws of our country." (*Id.*)

According to Whitmer, there were six elders and about seventy members before April 6, 1830. He did "not consider that the church was any more organized or established in the eyes of God on that day that it was previous to that day." (*Id.*) The only addition was to take the existing church and make it "agreeable to the laws of our country"– but not to create it for the first time.

_____

[13] David Whitmer's account of early events is more important than generally given credit by church sources. When he and his brother left in 1838 his brother John had been an historian for the church, and he took with him many of the earliest records. His 1887 account was likely informed by those early records.

David Whitmer's account of the date a church was established raises the question of the difference between priesthood and a church. Joseph and Oliver began to refer to one another as "elders" in the Church of Christ before the church existed. At the time the term began to be used, the position of an elder was not related to priestly office, but was instead a calling to lead others in the church. When Oliver and Joseph worked together to create the document now known as Section 20 of the Doctrine and Covenants, they described the original church offices of elder, priest, teacher, deacon, and member as comprising the church. These offices were church positions. Everyone, even women held a church office. "Member" was, according to Section 20, an office.[14] They came into existence by virtue of the church's need to have order and authority. They were elected offices, filled by popular vote. When D. Michael Quinn discussed this issue, he resolved these early inconsistencies from later practice by associating the office of elder with the lesser priesthood. Quinn writes: "The office of the elder was at first associated with what would come to be known as the lesser (or Aaronic) priesthood. Joseph Smith and Oliver Cowdery ordained the first elders in mid-1829, shortly after the date they later claimed for the visit of John the Baptist."[15]

Lyndon Cook has grappled with this early question of church authority in his book *A Tentative Inquiry into the Office of Seventy 1835-*

---

[14]The office is identified in verse 38, and the discussion of the member's duties begins at verse 68. Once the member has received the required ordinances, they hold the power to vote, thereby establishing the elders, priests, deacons, and teachers of the church.

[15]See Quinn, D. Michael. *The Mormon Hierarchy: Origins of Power.* Salt Lake City: Signature Books, 1994, p. 27.

1845. (See Cook, Lyndon. *A Tentative Inquiry into the Office of Seventy 1835-1845.* Provo: Grandin Book Company, 2010.) In it he explains:

> The elders were the presiding officers of the church in the beginning, and their authority derived from a physical ordination but not from the conferral of any kind of "priesthood." In June 1831, a seismic ideological shift occurred when the Prophet and Sidney Rigdon redefined ecclesiastical power among the ordained. They introduced the order of the high priesthood, an authority conferred by the ceremonial laying on of hands that was greater than that previously possessed by the elders. (*Id.,* p. 35.)

Originally the church's offices of elder, priest, teacher, and deacon were created by vote, and when created, had the authority to minister in baptism, laying on hands, blessing and passing the sacrament, and teaching. If Section 20 is taken at face value, not considering anything which was later learned to reinterpret its meaning, it becomes apparent elders, priests, teachers, deacons and members are offices belonging to the church—not the priesthood. It is the organization of the entity, the church itself, which necessitates and empowers these positions. The offices fit needs of the church. When you separate "physical ordination" from "conferral of any kind of priesthood" (as Lyndon Cook's analysis shows), then these are church offices, and not priestly offices, much like a relief society president, young women's president, or Sunday school president are all positions in the church which do not require priesthood.

Interestingly, the language of Section 20 also defines the process for salvation and justification. The doctrine is important still. Quoting from the original published version in 1833 (then Section 24):

And we know, that all men must repent and believe on the name of Jesus Christ, and worship the Father in his name, and endure in faith on his name to the end, or they cannot be saved in the kingdom of God. And we know, that Justification through the grace of our Lord and Savior Jesus Christ, is just and true; And we know, also, that sanctification through the grace of our Lord and Savior Jesus Christ, is just and true, to all those who love and serve God with all their mights, minds, and strength, but there is a possibility that men may fall from grace and depart from the living God. Therefore, let the church take heed and pray always, lest they fall into temptation; Yea, and even he that is sanctified also.[16]

These doctrines of justification and sanctification, along with the church offices which allowed ordinances of baptism, laying on hands and administration of the sacrament were established without regard to priesthood. Priesthood and church office were not originally conflated.; they would later become so. But that is a revisionist view of the events.

David Whitmer and his brother left the church in 1838. John Whitmer, the church's historian, took the original records. Joseph Smith began a new history in 1838 to replace the one in Whitmer's possession. The account in the Pearl of Great Price titled *Joseph Smith-History* is the beginning of that rewritten history. When David Whitmer composed his *Address to All Believers in Christ,* he had access to records through his brother which informed his account. Although criticized by later church historians, the account contains

---

[16] Quoting 1833 Book of Commandments, Section XXIV, verses 19-23; the original version of Section 20 from which the present version is a revision.

important information about the beginning of the Restoration. It
is worth reading.

On December 27, 1847, in Winter Quarters, when Brigham
Young became president of the Church of Jesus Christ of Latter-
day Saints, he recorded he was "elected" to the office.[17] The
common consent, or election by church members, was the power
by which the president's office became his. He did not believe he
needed any ordination to the office, only the common consent
through a sustaining vote. He was in fact, never ordained president
of the church, only elected to the position. He explained why it was
unnecessary to have anything other than a vote to ascend to the
office: "If men are elected by this Church, it is by Election-Joseph
was ordained an Apostle- but the Church elected him as a
President, Prophet-Seer and Revelator- But he was never ordained
to that office."[18] Because a sustaining vote was all Brigham Young
thought necessary to assume the president's mantle, it was all he
ever received. If his view is correct, then any person elected to the
position has all authority required by reason of the vote or consent
of the members of the church. The members consent or elect a

intention

_____

[17] In the *Manuscript History of Brigham Young*, Vol. 3, p. 82, it is recorded: "I
was unanimously elected President of the Church of Jesus Christ of
Latter-day Saints. Heber C. Kimball and Willard Richards were in like
manner elected respectively my first, and second counselors[.]" When the
comments were repeated in *The Complete Discourses of Brigham Young*,
beside the word "elected" is inserted the word, in brackets "[sustained]"
both times it appears. (See *The Complete Discourses of Brigham Young*. Edited
by Richard S. Van Wagoner. Salt Lake City: Signature Books, 2009, Vol.
1, p. 273.) However, in the same volume on p. 267 it is correctly
reported, without insertions, as follows: "I was unanimously elected
President of the Church of Jesus Christ of Latter-day Saints[.]"

[18] *The Complete Discourses of Brigham Young*. Edited by Richard S. Van
Wagoner. Salt Lake City: Signature Books, 2009, Vol. 1, p. 259.

person to the position, and the position exists through such consent.

The popular selection of local church leaders was so common during the first years of Mormonism, that as late as 1889 the choice was made entirely by the vote of the congregation. Apostles Francis Lyman and Abraham Cannon went to replace the bishop in Kanosh on November 26, 1889. There were "48 of the ward brethren" who came to the meeting.

> Bro. Lyman asked the brethren to carefully think of those whom they thought would make good Bishops and suggest from six to a dozen men, and we would then nominate from among these or some others the person whom we thought capable of presiding. They were told, however, to suggest only such brethren as were hospitable, kind, sober and loving, and who could be a father to the Ward. Bro. Jesse Hopkinson was suggested and received 24 votes; C[hristian] F. Christensen received 15, and Bro. Gardner 2 votes. Seven of those present did not vote at all. George Crane was suggested but he withdrew his name, which was quite proper as he is an alternate high councillor and we could not in any event have made him bishop without first getting Pres. Woodruff's permission. Bro. Hopkinson was then placed in nomination as bishop and received a unanimous vote. He chose as his counselors Bros. Christensen and Gardner, who were also unanimously sustained. (*Candid Insights of a Mormon Apostle: The Diaries of Abraham H. Cannon, 1889-1895.* Edited by Edward L. Lyman. Salt Lake City: Signature Books, 2010, pp. 30-31.)

The church members *were* the original authority to select leaders. Once elected to office, the office belonged to the one elected.

In 1829, and through the first few years of the church, priesthood as the foundation upon which all authority rested did not exist as a concept in the Mormon religion. Instead, it was the common consent of church members which conferred authority. The later revision to insert priesthood, and in particular, "high priesthood" into the early narrative of the church history was criticized by David Whitmer in his *Address to All Believers in Christ*. His explanation is one of the reasons later church historians are offended by his account. He points out the church revised its story to insert later views into earlier events.

The church Joseph Smith founded had the authority to select its officers through "common consent." All its affairs were to be governed through the "common consent" of the members. This includes revelations or instructions given to the church (D&C 26: 2), conferences where decisions are made (D&C 28: 10, 12), operation of the United Order (D&C 104: 71), and in particular ordaining to the church office of elder. Elders receive a license "by vote of the church to which they belong or from conferences" where a vote could be taken. (D&C 20: 63.) "No person is to be ordained to any office in this church, where there is a regularly organized branch of the same, without the vote of that church[.]" (D&C 20: 65.) Authority in the church was derived from the consent of its members. In this sense, authority was originally widespread and generally conferred upon presiding authorities wherever the church was organized.

When priesthood did become part of the picture, it was understood while many are called to receive this authority, only a few have been or ever will be entrusted with the power of the priesthood. Joseph wrote in 1839 the following revelation by the voice of inspiration while confined in jail in Liberty, Missouri:

> Behold, there are many called, but few are chosen. And why are they not chosen? Because their hearts are set so much upon the things of this world, and aspire to the

honors of men, that they do not learn this one lesson — That the rights of the priesthood are inseparably connected with the powers of heaven, and that the powers of heaven cannot be controlled nor handled only upon the principles of righteousness. That they may be conferred upon us, it is true; but when we undertake to cover our sins, or to gratify our pride, our vain ambition, or to exercise control or dominion or compulsion upon the souls of the children of men, in any degree of unrighteousness, behold the heavens withdraw themselves; the Spirit of the Lord is grieved; and when it is withdrawn, Amen to the priesthood or the authority of that man. (D&C 121:34-37.)

Gentiles always crave authority to preside over one another.[19] Gentile authority in the church is not equal to power in the priesthood. President Boyd K. Packer's April 2010 General Conference address described the difference between the authority present in the church throughout the world, and the lack of power in the priesthood:

We have done very well at distributing the *authority* of the priesthood. We have priesthood authority planted nearly everywhere. We have quorums of elders and high priests worldwide. But distributing the *authority* of the priesthood has raced, I think, ahead of distributing the *power* of the priesthood. The priesthood does not have the strength that it should have and will not have until the *power* of the priesthood is firmly fixed in the families as it should be. (Packer, Boyd K. *The Power of the Priesthood.* Ensign CR, May 2010, emphasis in original.)

The power of the priesthood cannot be controlled by men. It comes from heaven or it does not come at all. There has never

---

[19]See, e.g., Mark 10: 42.

been an institution entrusted with the power of heaven. "That the rights of the priesthood are inseparably connected with the powers of heaven, and that the powers of heaven cannot be controlled nor handled only upon the principles of righteousness." (D&C 121: 36.) A gentile church can convey authority for men to rule over one another throughout the world. But the power of the priesthood comes only one way, and, as the revelation to Joseph Smith states, men do not have any right to either confer it, or prevent it from being conferred. Heaven alone determines if a man will be permitted to act as one of Heaven's chosen high priests. Nephi's younger brother Jacob, for example, was ordained by Nephi to the priesthood.[20] He preached and taught after that ordination. When Jacob became his older brother's replacement as a prophet, however, he explained that he obtained that errand from the Lord.[21] Ordination invites. God alone confers His power.

When the church is established, and officers are put in positions of authority by the vote of the people, they have the unquestioned right to preside until removed. No one other than the duly constituted authorities of the church are allowed to collect tithes, establish wards, stakes, missions and districts, appoint other officers (with the sustaining vote of the members), or conduct church business. The authorities are to be respected and

---

[20]See 2 Ne. 6: 2: "Behold, my beloved brethren, I, Jacob, having been called of God, and ordained after the manner of his holy order, and having been consecrated by my brother Nephi, unto whom ye look as a king or a protector, and on whom ye depend for safety, behold ye know that I have spoken unto you exceedingly many things."

[21]See Jacob 1: 17: "Wherefore I, Jacob, gave unto them these words as I taught them in the temple, having first obtained mine errand from the Lord."

sustained.[22] This was originally internal to the church, did not require priesthood, but nevertheless allowed ordinances to be conducted.

Priesthood and redemption are tied together. And if Joseph Smith's revelations are trusted, then the church does not and cannot control either, because God controls both. Establishing the church was distinct from restoring priesthood. And priesthood has, can and does exist independent of a church. Joseph's revelations and ancient scripture repeatedly teach this.

In the case of Moses for example, although he descended from the chosen line through Abraham, Isaac, Jacob, and Levi, he had no priesthood when residing in Egypt. He fled to the wilderness and entered the household of Reuel, eventually married one of his daughters.[23] Reuel was a descendant of Abraham. But he was not an Israelite. Even though Israel had forfeited the priesthood at the time, Reuel had been ordained to hold priesthood through a line of priests going back five generations. As a result of holding the priesthood, he was known by a new name, as Jethro, the Priest of Midian. (See Exo. 2: 16, 3: 1, 18: 1.) It was from Jethro, the Priest of Midian, Moses obtained priesthood. (D&C 84: 6.) Moses would bring this authority to Israel. Jethro received his priesthood from Caleb. Caleb received it from Elihu, who received it from Jeremy, who received it from Gad, who received it from Esias, who received it from God. (D&C 84: 6-12.)

---

[22]This is particularly true of the First Presidency of the church comprised of "three Presiding High Priests, chosen by the body, appointed and ordained to that office, and upheld by the confidence, faith, and prayer of the church, form a quorum of the Presidency of the Church." (D&C 107: 22.) See also, Hebrews 13: 7 and 1 Peter 5: 5.

[23]The Priest of Midian was named "Reuel." See Exo. 2: 18.

Joseph clarified through revelation that there are two orders of priesthood which reckon from the time of Moses. One is called Aaronic, the other Melchizedek. (D&C 107: 1.) Joseph Smith's revelation also confirms that in the church established through him there are again two kinds of priesthood. (*Id.*) In time, the church would become completely dependent on these two, and all of its male offices became regarded as appendages to the priesthood. (D&C 107: 5.) Therefore, the church now regards itself as entirely dependent on priesthood, but the priesthood still remains independent of the church.

Of the two priesthoods, the lesser is the Aaronic, and the greater is Melchizedek. The Aaronic is only a portion of the Melchizedek, and limited to performing outward ordinances. (D&C 107: 13-14.) Aaronic priesthood has power for angels to minister, but Melchizedek priests may behold God. (D&C 107: 18-20.) It follows, therefore, that when a man has beheld God, as Joseph Smith had done in the Spring of 1820, he necessarily holds this higher priesthood. For without it, no man can see the Father and live. (D&C 84: 19-22.) Since Joseph beheld the Father in the First Vision, it was necessary for him to have this higher priesthood even before the appearance of the angels who later conferred priesthood upon Joseph. It is apparent Joseph was among those who priesthood reckons from before the foundation of this world. (See Alma 13: 3, 5-7.)[24] The church's official explanation is Joseph received Melchizedek Priesthood from Peter, James and John nine

---

[24]I've discussed this priesthood on my blog, found at www.denversnuffer. blogspot.com, which can also be read in the book *Removing the Condemnation*. Snuffer, Denver C., Jr. Salt Lake City: Mill Creek Press, 2011. This is a reprint of the blog mentioned earlier. The discussion of Alma, Chapter 13 explains this subject.

years later. The church's narrative cannot reconcile the appearance of the Father and Son to Joseph Smith in 1820 with the necessary precondition of holding higher priesthood explained in D&C 84: 19-22.

In the case of Esaias, from whom Moses' priesthood would come generations later, we see priesthood ordination can and has been conferred by God directly upon a man: "Esaias received it under the hand of God." (D&C 84: 12.) Joseph Smith taught that all Old Testament prophets who obtained higher priesthood during the Dispensation of Moses, did so by receiving it directly from God.[25] In the Book of Mormon we learn there is a "holy order" which is "without beginning of days" which some obtained "from the foundation of the world" and brought here. (See Alma 13: 1-9.)[26] The higher priesthood does not come from man or men, is without father or mother, and is only given one way: by the voice of God to the individual.[27]

In the Book of Mormon, wicked King Noah assembled a body of priests who would be subject to his leadership. One of them

---

[25]"All Priesthood is Melchizedek, but there are different portions or degrees of it. That portion which brought Moses to speak with God face to face was taken away; but that which brought the ministry of angels remained. All the prophets had the Melchizedek Priesthood and were ordained by God himself." (*TPJS*, p. 180-181.)

[26]See *Removing the Condemnation, supra.*

[27]See, e.g., JST Gen. 14: 27-29: "And thus, having been approved of God, he was ordained an high priest after the order of the covenant which God made with Enoch, It being after the order of the son of God; which order came, not by man, nor the will of man; neither by father nor mother; neither by beginning of days nor end of years; but of God; And it was delivered unto men by the calling of his own voice, according to his own will, unto as many as believed on his name."

eventually rejected his wickedness, went into the wilderness and founded a church. The breakaway church was empowered through common consent to establish Alma as their priest. He initially attracted 240 followers, and it grew from there. (Mosiah 18: 1-16.) If he had an ordination, it was through wicked King Noah. His authority, however, came from those willing to sustain him as their priest-leader.

The concept that priesthood exists apart from the church is the reason so many splinter groups have felt it would be possible for them to separate. They view their separation to have been doctrinally justified, and believe they will suffer no loss of priestly authority as a consequence of leaving.

The LDS Church claims as a matter of history and practice that they alone hold the keys of priesthood. In a recent General Conference talk a member of the First Presidency taught the following: "This is the true Church, the only true Church, because in it are the keys of the priesthood. Only in this Church has the Lord lodged the power to seal on earth and to seal in heaven as He did in the time of the Apostle Peter. Those keys were restored to Joseph Smith, who then was authorized to confer them upon the members of the Quorum of the Twelve." (Eyring, Henry B. *The True and Living Church*. Ensign CR, May 2008.) We know the church is dependent on priesthood, but the priesthood is not dependent on the church. "Just four weeks ago President James E. Faust said to BYU students in their devotional: '[The priesthood] activates and governs all activities of the Church. Without priesthood keys and authority, there would be no church.' . . . I begin tonight with these three brief citations (to which scores of others could be added) to stress emphatically just one point: that the priesthood of God, with its keys, its ordinances, its divine origin and ability to bind in heaven what is bound on earth, is as *indispensable* to the true Church of God as it is *unique* to it and that without it there would be no Church of Jesus Christ of Latter-day Saints." (Holland, Jeffrey R. *Our Most Distinguishing Feature*. Ensign CR, May 2005.)

We will look at this teaching, the history behind it, and whether events can (or should) be understood differently. It is clear the church and the priesthood should not be conflated. Therefore, the question arises whether the church can fill offices without regard to the priestly power, or worthiness of the occupant. In other words, do the church offices of elder, priest, teacher, deacon, and member set out in Doctrine & Covenants 20 exist as a church office, not necessarily dependent upon priesthood? There was a time when they did. Do they still? If so, can the church offices permit baptism, passing the sacrament, laying on hands for the Holy Ghost, preaching, teaching, exhorting, and expounding regardless of whether there is priesthood power involved or not?

Priesthood power is clearly something different than an ordination. But it is clear the only thing an ordination accomplishes is to invite the one ordained to then connect to heaven. It is from heaven alone that priesthood power is obtained. "They may be conferred upon us, it is true; but . . . the rights of the priesthood are inseparably connected with the powers of heaven, and that the powers of heaven cannot be controlled nor handled only upon the principles of righteousness." (D&C 121: 36-37.) Power comes from heaven alone. Therefore, no person who has priesthood conferred upon them has any power prior to having it ratified by heaven. The conferral is only an invitation for a man to go obtain power from heaven, not actual power itself. It confers an office within the church, but an office in the church is not synonymous with the power of heaven. Nor, therefore, is it synonymous with priesthood.

If you follow the ordinances of the restored Gospel of Jesus Christ to their end, you will eventually arrive at the symbolic return to God. In that ceremonial encounter, every person who is endowed with knowledge participates in a ritual conversation with God through a veil. The voice of God declares to the person going through the ceremony how they can receive power in the priesthood. Everything is conditioned upon faithfulness. If men are true and faithful to the covenants they enter into, they are promised the time will come when they will be called up and ordained, whereas now they are only given a conditional promise. The realization of the blessings depends on each person's faithfulness. The church's ordinances teach how to come into God's presence and secure real priesthood power. It is both an invitation and a blueprint for each believer to be saved. But the institution, as we shall see, offers only the invitation.

The connection between heaven and priesthood is set out in D&C 121. The matter becomes even more clear from instructions given to the first Quorum of Twelve at the time they were ordained Apostles for the church. There are two different kinds of Apostles. One is an administrative office in the church. The other is a witness of the resurrection, who has met with Christ. The first group of Twelve Apostles were immediately made administrative Apostles in the church, but were told they needed to go on to become Apostolic witnesses of the resurrection by having Christ lay hands on them. Such an Apostolic witness requires heavenly power. To clarify the matter to those in the first quorum, they were instructed as follows:

> ...You have been ordained to this holy Priesthood, you have received it from those who have the power and authority from an angel; you are to preach the Gospel to every nation. Should you in the least degree come short of

your duty, great will be your condemnation; for the greater the calling the greater the transgression. I therefore warn you to cultivate great humility; for I know the pride of the human heart. Beware, lest the flatterers of the world lift you up; beware, lest your affections be captivated by worldly objects. Let your ministry be first. Remember, the souls of men are committed to your charge; and if you mind your calling, you shall always prosper.

You have been indebted to other men, in the first instance, for evidence; on that you have acted; but it is necessary that you receive a testimony from heaven for yourselves; so that you can bear testimony to the truth of the Book of Mormon, and that you have seen the face of God. That is more than the testimony of an angel. When the proper time arrives, you shall be able to bear this testimony to the world. When you bear testimony that you have seen God, this testimony God will never suffer to fall, but will bear you out; although many will not give heed, yet others will. You will therefore see the necessity of getting this testimony from heaven.

Never cease striving until you have seen God face to face. Strengthen your faith; cast off your doubts, your sins, and all your unbelief; and nothing can prevent you from coming to God. Your ordination is not full and complete till God has laid His hand upon you. We require as much to qualify us as did those who have gone before us; God is the same. If the Savior in former days laid His hands upon His disciples, why not in latter days? (*DHC* 2: 195-196.)

The same admonition was repeated to every new church Apostle until the early 1900's. Because so few had the heavens open to them so as to become Apostolic witnesses ordained by Christ, the instruction was abandoned.[28] Church Apostles now testify oftentimes to "the name of Jesus Christ" with seldom any mention of having seen His presence.

Most of the ordinances of the church are not the real thing. They are types, symbols of the real thing. They are official invitations, authorized by Christ, and extended to any person who will join The Church of Jesus Christ of Latter-day Saints. Any person who has priesthood conferred upon him will need to go into God's presence, and receive it through the veil for power in their priesthood. That is, for any person who has priesthood conferred upon them, they will not gain power in the priesthood until they come to God from whom this power comes through the veil. Not as a mere ceremony delivered by the church, but through contact directly with God. It is the voice of God,[29] through the veil, which activates the dormant power conferred by ordination. With that power activated, the person is able to endure the presence of God.[30] The church and its ordinations and ordinances does not confer power. They invite the recipients to press forward into God's presence and receive Him, where the actual endowment of peace, joy, promises of eternal life, and power are conferred by Him who has the right to bestow them. The keeper of that gate is the Holy One of Israel, and He employs no mortal servant there.[31] If men could confer more than an ordination, there would be

---

[28] Quinn, Michael D. *Mormon Hierarchy: Extensions of Power.* Salt Lake City: Signature Books, 1997, pp. 2-3.

[29] JST Gen. 14: 27-29.

[30] D&C 84: 22.

[31] 2 Ne. 9: 41.

nothing to prevent corrupt, wicked men from selling salvation to their friends, family and those they favor even if unworthy; or from barring salvation to others who are worthy, based on petty jealousies and envy. This idea of men holding God's power is what led to the corruptions of Catholicism.

The church's ordinations and ordinances remain vital to the restored Gospel, and the plan of salvation. Whether or not there is any person in the church with priesthood power, every person who joins the church, and keeps its ordinances will be invited, through those ordinances, to come and receive the Lord. When they do come into His presence, they will find themselves in possession of promises, rights, privileges, power, and covenants for themselves and their posterity, for all generations, and into eternity. They will become one of those whose hearts have turned to the fathers. We will look into that further.

This book will explore what is offered by the restored Gospel, the claims of the church, and the reason we make those claims. It is an interesting subject that has been filled with supposition, some amount of sloppy explanations, and broad institutional claims. The history has been overlain with such emotionally charged disputes that a dispassionate review of the events is almost impossible at this point. When you feel yourself challenged by this book, take a deep breath and press on. Until the story told here is finished, you cannot judge the matter. Understanding is worth some amount of anxiety. I have a testimony of The Church of Jesus Christ of Latter-day Saints, and sustain the church's officers and authorities. It is my hope that if you read to the conclusion, your understanding of Joseph Smith and the faith he returned will be significantly enlarged.

Chapter 2

HISTORY AND TRUTH

*H*istory does not belong to the historians. Their techniques only permit them to offer an interpretation of events. Your own opinion is as valid as theirs.

Winston Churchill quipped "history is written by the victors." In the case of Latter-day Saint history, it has been written by the descendants of Nauvoo. However, their interpretation is not the only one possible from the events. In everything I have written before, I have accepted the traditional narrative. It has not been important for me to comment on church history by challenging the traditional story. In this book for the first time it will be necessary to introduce other ways of viewing events.

Keep in mind that a testimony of church history has never been required of the Latter-day Saints. Assistant LDS Church Historian Davis Bitton gave a talk, later published as an article in the FARMS Review, titled *I Don't Have a Testimony of the History of the Church.*[32] He begins his comments with the statement, "I don't have a

---

[32]The talk was originally delivered at a FAIR conference in Sandy, Utah on August 5, 2003. It was subsequently published in the FARMS Review Vol. 16, 2 at pp. 337-354.

testimony of the history of the church. That is why I can be an historian and also a believing Latter-day Saint." If a respected Assistant LDS Church Historian can make such a statement, and BYU can publish it in their FARMS Review, then it should be safe for any believing Latter-day Saint to have their own view of the church's history, even if it is an alternative view from the official account. It should be possible for a faithful member to view skeptically the success of the Nauvoo saints in keeping their charge.

Brother Bitton's experience as an historian informs his paper and causes me to reflect on how delicate a matter faith is for some individuals. Faith, however, for others can and should be powerful. I am an active Latter-day Saint and I love my fellow saints. When I converted at age 19, it was a homecoming for me. At last I found a body of doctrine I could believe, and a church whose ordinances I trusted, and wanted. Though raised by a Baptist mother, I have only belonged to this one church. I have no intention of abandoning it, or ever joining another. However, I did not come to believe without first needing to be convinced. Joseph Smith was anything but a childhood hero to me. My mother told me he was a fraud and I trusted her judgement. She got her information from Baptist ministers who insisted Joseph Smith was corrupt, even evil. Therefore, when the Joseph Smith history was introduced to me by the missionaries, it required me to suspend judgment based on the criticism I'd heard, and allow Joseph's side of the story to be told.

As I listened to the story the missionaries told, I subjected Joseph Smith's claims to relentless critical, even skeptical review. When, at last, he had been given what I regarded as a full hearing, I concluded it seemed more likely than not his claims were true. I found I could believe them. Therefore, I acted on the invitation to accept his ministry, and join the church founded by him.

Baptism did not end the inquiry for me. Since becoming Mormon I have read, prayed, reflected and troubled over Joseph's life, teachings and record from the time the missionaries introduced the sympathetic accounts of his life until now. In my view something as important as salvation, and knowing God, can never be insulated from critical examination and thinking. I have tried to give the critics' accusations as full a review as the apologists' arguments. I have appreciated the church's decision to release the *Joseph Smith Papers*, and I await release of each volume. I read them from cover to cover to reaffirm what I know, discover what I don't know, and test anew my assumptions about him. To me, Joseph Smith has emerged as a full featured human soul. He had many virtues. He was insecure about his education, he was confident in his testimony, he was patient with the vulnerable, and only impatient with those who should know better. He was at times brash, and at other times too hesitant. I think I understand him as well as any person who has reviewed the written record about him. I've prayed for guidance in reaching a conclusion about him. From my careful examination, I have grown to have such confidence in Joseph Smith's calling as a prophet of God that I willingly base my eternal expectations on the decision. But no other person should trust what I have to say. The issue is too important for anyone to rely on another. Make your own investigation. Reach your own conclusion. As you do you will encounter the miraculous and the Divine.

When Brother Bitton was asked about the relationship between faith and history, he responded, "What's potentially damaging or challenging to faith depends entirely, I think, on one's expectations, and not necessarily history. Any kind of experience can be shattering to faith if the expectation is such that one is not prepared for the experience . . . The problem is not the religion; the problem is the incongruity between the expectation and the reality." (*Id.*, p. 340-41.) This is why a new understanding of history can challenge someone's belief when they are unprepared for it. There are those who have either lost or are losing their faith precisely because they have come across an historical event which decimates their understanding. For them, a candid explanation of the event, along with an analysis about how it fits into a larger plan, presided over by the Lord, can rescue their testimony. Whether it damages or rescues depends upon the expectations of the person. There is an increasing number of saints with unanswered questions, and nagging doubts about the church. In talking with these sincere saints, I have found there is a great deal of comfort in acknowledging the difference between the church, and the Gospel. The imperfect, and sometimes overbearing institution is not the same thing as Christ's Gospel. The frail and imperfect men who guide this church can never be adequate representatives of Jesus Christ. For some, their faith can only return when they set the church into the background, move Christ and His Gospel into the foreground, and seek to know Him. Then the church's explanations can be measured against the larger perspective. Shortcomings are not serious. God remains available and involved with our salvation.

I do not intend to harm anybody's faith. But, as Brother Bitton wrote, sometimes Latter-day Saints just need to "get real" and grow up. "I suppose this is a message to those church members who have such tender eyes and ears that real history of real people comes as a shock. 'Oh, no,' they whine. 'This can't be true.' Or, quick to judge, they attack the historian, accusing him or her of lacking spirituality or coveting the praise of the world. My message in such cases is, 'Please! Don't speak until you know what you are talking about." (*Id.*, p. 342.)

If this book challenges your faith, then stop reading it. Alternatively, I would plead with those who have a testimony of the traditional narrative to have the charity to recognize there are many others who desperately want to remain faithful Latter-day Saints, but find their faith is faltering because of historical issues addressed by this book. Some critics justify their anti-Mormon arguments using historical events the church chooses to ignore or gloss over. A candid discussion of historical events is not necessarily faithless because it discloses new ideas or interpretations of events, nor are those who have a different view of events in Mormon history weak in faith. You do not need to accept what I have written or what I believe to be true of the restoration. I readily concede most histories written by other active Latter-day Saints disagree with the view explored in this book. I am not unacquainted with traditional histories. I have spent many years reading, and believing them. However, I am also acquainted with the struggle some saints have with the traditional story. The longer I have reflected on these events, the more nuanced and informative our history becomes. Although I have a testimony and believe to my core Joseph Smith was at least what the church claims him to be, the transitions following his death do not always reconcile the way traditional Mormon histories assert. Critical events in Mormon history require careful and prayerful thought. All of the difficulty encountered in the history of The Church of Jesus Christ of Latter-day Saints has been in accordance with prophecy from Joseph Smith, Book of Mormon prophecy and Divine will.

History attempts to tell a unified story. But events are lived through individual lives. As soon as the discussion shifts from individuals to groups, the complexity of how things happened becomes nearly insurmountable. This is why history is rarely the same story two generations after events as it when it happened. It takes time and later occurrences to define meaning. The early attempts to explain our history will be the most partisan. Writers who knew those involved have personal connections with the events. For example, John Taylor's explanation of the slaying of Joseph and Hyrum found in Section 135 of the Doctrine & Covenants cries out with his love for the dead, bitterness at the mob, and conviction God's work would continue. His eyewitness account is important and true, filled with emotion and yet still inadequate to tell the whole of the matter.

Part of the problem with Mormon history comes from unwillingness of the church to open its archives. Some of what is found in this book is only now possible because of recently published diaries of church leaders. As more information leaks out, a still more accurate history will become possible. In the final analysis, however, telling the complex story of group events is most accurate when insight is inspired from a higher source.

Speaking of the First Vision, Brother Bitton quotes from a University of Utah professor who covers the subject as part of his Utah history class. Brother Bitton relates that after reciting the account of Joseph Smith, Professor David E. Miller would say, "Now you can't prove things like this by historical evidence. You also can't disprove them." (*Id.*, p. 344.) That is always the case. "If we as Latter-day Saints have a testimony of their historicity, it is not because of the kind of evidence that would stand up in a courtroom. It is because we believe other witnesses. It is because we have our own spiritual confirmation. We are not required to let historians determine for us what we will believe." (*Id.*)

I have great empathy for those saints who lived our difficult history. As I read the various attempts to tell their story, I identify with them. It is not "their" history any longer, but "our" history - my history. I am a part of the current of events that are moving forward from Joseph's time to the future. We all are hoping to contribute to an outcome that will please the Lord through redemption of many of His children. I agree with Brother Bitton that when it comes to the saints' history, and those who have lived it, "You don't have to agree with them, you don't have to consider them inspired or vested with God's authority. That is a separate question. But in the face of such history you simply cannot portray them as evil or as simpletons." (*Id.*, p. 349.)

Richard L. Bushman delivered the opening remarks at the conference on Joseph Smith, sponsored by the Library of Congress and Brigham Young University. He made this point about understanding history, "[O]ur histories are detachable. Every nation, every institution, every person can be extricated from one history and attached to another, often with perfect plausibility. Each of us has many histories. The histories I refer to are not the events of our lives, but the various cultural contexts that produce us and explain who we are– our many different pasts." (Bushman, Richard L. *Joseph Smith's Many Histories*, found in *The Worlds of Joseph Smith: A Bicentennial Conference at the Library of Congress*. Edited by John Welch. Provo: BYU, 2006, p. 3.)

The phases Mormonism has passed through have such different conditions in each of them that they deserve separate attention. Joseph Smith's phase was innovative, forward moving, and additive. The second was dominated by issues arising directly from the practice of plural marriage. The practice was offensive to the nation. The national opposition to plural marriage resulted in political, legal, economic, and religious pressure on the church and its leaders. The political, and legal defeat of the practice resulted in a doctrinal change which marked the transition into a third phase. The third phase was unlike any of those before it. In the third phase, prior practices and teachings were abandoned, and outright rejected. Those who would not accept the change, who wanted to continue practicing what had been taught in the preceding phases, were subject to excommunication. The third phase was a radical shift. It set the stage for a final phase that is currently underway. Mormonism has now adopted tools of business management to institute changes based on unfolding events in the larger population. A social science infrastructure has now been hard-wired into The Church of Jesus Christ of Latter-day Saints. This method of institutionalized management not only guards against repeating a serious conflict with political, social and legal forces, it also leads the church to social conformity with the larger American political, social, economic and cultural values. How these transitions fit into a larger, sacred narrative is the focus of this book. The first step to understanding is to recognize these phases exist. Rather than a seamless progression from Joseph to the present, there have been distinct, separate phases. Inside of these phases, Mormonism has looked very different during the past to those involved from what it looks like to us today.

In addition to the other changes, Mormonism has become increasingly less mystic, less miraculous, and even less tolerant of "gifts" of the Spirit. Although it retains an emphasis on personal revelation, there is no continuing expectation of new scripture, new commandments, or Divine visitations. The concepts are retained, but the expectations are gone. The idea of angels, visions and visitations are regarded as "magical thinking" belonging to an earlier, primitive people. D. Michael Quinn's book, *Early Mormonism and the Magic World View*,[33] bears a title that reflects skepticism about the miraculous origin of Joseph Smith's work.[34] Quinn was the first Mormon insider[35] to take earlier events, and recast them into a radically different world view. His book accepts the idea of a great cultural separation between the church today and the church when Joseph Smith was alive. Quinn writes in the *Introduction* about source material he examined to reach his conclusions:

> These sources give evidence of the Smith family's participation in treasure-digging; the possession and use of instruments and emblems of folk magic by Smith, his family members, and other early LDS leaders; the continued use of such implements for religious purposes in the LDS church for many years; and the sincere belief of many Mormons in "the magic world view." This magic world view has as many variations as does "the" scientific world view.
>
> These sources express a perspective of the world different from twentieth-century perceptions. I have tried to approach this earlier world view through the lenses of two groups: those who clearly shared it and those who may

---

[33] Quinn, D. Michael. *Early Mormonism and the Magic World View*. Salt Lake City: Signature Books, 1998.

[34] The term "magical thinking" is used to mean primitive or unsophisticated thinking akin to the child's imagination.

[35] D. Michael Quinn was on the BYU faculty, trusted in the LDS Church archives, and regarded as an important LDS historian at one time. Although today he is criticized, the fact remains his research work was done from inside the church, and with its full cooperation.

have shared it. For readers today, this process resembles Thomas S. Kuhn's description of changes that periodically confront scientists: "It is rather as if the professional community had been suddenly transported to another planet where familiar objects are seen in a different light and are joined by unfamiliar ones as well.

By adopting a different perspective, I present familiar events in unfamiliar ways and introduce evidence previously not recognized as significant. My analysis is by no means conclusive.[36]

The first phase of Mormonism was dominated by visions, angels, and direct involvement by God. Those experiences are still celebrated and taught. However, they are only used as a legitimizing credential for a demystified church. The current phase of Mormonism is missing the direct appearance or involvement of God, angels, and visions. There is a disconnect between the miraculous events upon which Mormonism is based, and current church events.

Joseph Smith became a significant religious figure as soon as he had an encounter with God, in the Spring of 1820. Until then, there was no Christian figure,[37] between the close of the New Testament record, and 1820, who was an authentic prophet with a message from God worthy to become scripture. Joseph's entire message of restoration, however, is encapsulated in his First Vision.

---

[36] *Id.*, p. xxi.

[37] Mohammed was not Christian, and his claims are not discussed or treated in this book.

The trigger for Joseph's experience was a verse in the New Testament book of James.[38] Joseph reflected again and again[39] on the promise God would give liberally to those who ask of Him. At length, he asked.[40] In response to the inquiry, God answered him.[41] This event defines the entire message of the restoration through Joseph Smith. The restoration itself is individual, personal, and intended as a message for all mankind. The message is succinct: "You may ask of God and get an answer." It is James 1: 5.

Joseph's ministry went on to include translating, and publishing the Book of Mormon. From the publication of that volume in 1830 through today, the Book of Mormon bears a second testimony[42] (in addition to the New Testament) of Jesus Christ's status as

---

[38]James 1: 5: "If any of you lack wisdom, let him ask of God, that giveth to all men liberally, and upbraideth not; and it shall be given him."

[39]See JS-H 1: 12: "Never did any passage of a scripture come with more power to the heart of man than this did at this time to mine. It seemed to enter with great force into every feeling of my heart. I reflected on it again and again, knowing that if any person needed wisdom from God, I did; for how to act I did not know, and unless I could get more wisdom than I then had, I would never know; for the teachers of religion of the different sects understood the same passages of scripture so differently as to destroy all confidence in settling the question by an appeal to the Bible."

[40]See JS-H 1: 13-14.

[41]See JS-H 1: 17-20.

[42]"Wherefore murmur ye, because that ye shall receive more of my word? Know ye not that the testimony of two nations is a witness unto you that I am God, that I remember one nation like unto another? Wherefore, I speak the same words unto one nation like unto another. And when the two nations shall run together the testimony of the two nations shall run together also." (2 Nephi 29: 8.)

Redeemer of mankind, and of His global ministry. The Book of Mormon record tells the account of Israelite exiles who fled Jerusalem under God's guidance, and relocated to the American Continent. They struggled with different levels of faith, remembering their faith, apostasy, rebellion, and success. Their story is an epic of the trials experienced by any religious body. Ultimately, the account reaches a crescendo when in approximately 34 a.d., the resurrected Jesus Christ appears to the survivors of a cataclysmic judgment, and He ministers to them. Reduced to its essence, the Book of Mormon reaffirms the same message as James 1: 5. Whether the account is individual (as in the case of Nephi or his father Lehi), or of an entire population (as when Christ visited a gathering in Bountiful), the message remains the same. The Book of Mormon affirms God's willingness to appear, and give wisdom to those who ask of Him. If that message is lost on anyone reading the account, the final writer in the book ends the record with a promise to any reader of his book that God will answer them. Moroni 10: 4 states: "And when ye shall receive these things, I would exhort you that ye would ask God, the Eternal Father, in the name of Christ, if these things are not true; and if ye shall ask with a sincere heart, with real intent, having faith in Christ, he will manifest the truth of it unto you, by the power of the Holy Ghost." The First Vision account is much briefer in content, but is the same message. That message is the restoration. You (whoever you are) may also ask of God and get an answer. It is universal.

Every convert to the faith restored through Joseph Smith was, and is expected to have a revelation from God affirming to him or her the work is God's. When missionaries from The Church of Jesus Christ of Latter-day Saints teach investigators, they invite the prospective convert to read the Book of Mormon, then to pray and

ask God if the book is true. When the prospective convert receives
an answer, they know for themselves continuing revelation by God
is more than theory. It is His vindicated promise to them.

The purpose of Joseph Smith's work was not to inform people
of revelation as a theoretical possibility, but to instill it as a practical
reality. Revelation is required to bring converts into the religion,
but an audience with God is always the expected culminating
event.

Joseph Smith's revelations include another, even more brief,
restatement of the message of the restoration: "Verily, thus saith
the Lord: It shall come to pass that every soul who forsaketh his
sins and cometh unto me, and calleth on my name, and obeyeth my
voice, and keepeth my commandments, shall see my face and know
that I am[.]" (D&C 93: 1.) It is meeting God face to face, and
knowing Him, that is the aim of the restoration. All mankind are
invited to know God, not an exclusive few.[43] Joseph did not restore
a faith-by-representation, where some approach God for others.[44]

----

[43] As set out in Joel: "And it shall come to pass afterward, that I will pour
out my spirit upon all flesh; and your sons and your daughters shall
prophesy, your old men shall dream dreams, your young men shall see
visions: And also upon the servants and upon the handmaids in those
days will I pour out my spirit." (Joel 2: 28-29.) As foreseen by Jeremiah:
". . . After those days, saith the Lord, I will put my law in their inward
parts, and write it in their hearts; and will be their God, and they shall be
my people. And they shall teach no more every man his neighbor, and
ever man his brother, saying, Know the Lord: for they shall all know me,
from the least of them unto the greatest of them, saith the Lord: for I
will forgive their iniquity, and I will remember their sin no more."
(Jeremiah 31: 33-34.)

[44] See Deu. 5: 27: "Go thou near, and hear all that the Lord our God shall
say: and speak thou unto us all that the Lord our God shall speak unto
thee; and we will hear it, and do it."

Each person should approach Him for themself.[45] This was the primary message of Mormonism's first phase.

The Book of Mormon contains more Second Comforter experiences than any other volume of scripture. In a previous book, *The Second Comforter: Conversing With the Lord Through the Veil*, I used the Book of Mormon as the primary scriptural source for teaching the doctrine of the Second Comforter.[46] Some of the greatest insight into the doctrine can be found in the examples of Nephi, Jacob and Enos. Because of a lack of faith, the doctrine has been nearly forgotten. However, it remains a central message of Joseph Smith's teachings, and the restoration itself. In *The Second Comforter,* I set out how frequently this message appeared as part of the first phase of Mormonism. I would refer you to that volume for a detailed discussion of the doctrine.

The Book of Mormon makes frequent use of the words "belief," "unbelief," "faith," and "knowledge." These words have specific meanings in the Book of Mormon. The word "belief" means to

---

[45]See D&C 84: 19-26.

[46]The term "Second Comforter" describes the return to Christ's presence. The term comes from Christ's reference to "another Comforter" in John 14: 16, 18. The concept involves not merely Christ appearing to His disciples, but also His ministry. The Holy Ghost has a ministry to bring a believer to receive angels and then Christ. Christ, in turn, has a ministry to take the faithful servant and bring him to the Father. The process of coming to receive Christ is described in *The Second Comforter*. The results of His ministry are set out in the closing chapters of *Beloved Enos*. (Snuffer, Denver C., Jr. *Beloved Enos,* Salt Lake City: Mill Creek, 2009.) The events involving the Father are not appropriate to set out except through symbols and allegory. To the extent I have made any effort to do that it can be found in *Ten Parables*. (Snuffer, Denver C., Jr. *Ten Parables*. Salt Lake City: Mill Creek, 2008.)

understand and accept true doctrine.[47] The word "unbelief" means to accept false doctrine, or to have an incomplete, and inaccurate understanding of correct doctrine. Often "unbelief" is used in connection with losing truth, forsaking doctrine, and therefore "dwindling." The phrase "dwindling in unbelief" is the Book of Mormon's way to describe moving from a state of belief, with true and complete doctrine, to a state of unbelief, where the truth has been discarded.[48] Miracles end because men dwindle in unbelief.[49]

The word "faith" is used when an angel has ministered to someone.[50] Going from belief to faith is a natural progression as soon as any person with a firm mind in every form of righteousness has been tried and found committed to the truth.[51]

---

[47]See 3 Nephi 16: 6.

[48]See, e.g., 1 Nephi 4: 13; 10: 11; 12: 22-23; 15: 13; 2 Nephi 1: 10; 26: 15, 17; Alma 45: 10, 12; 50: 22; among others.

[49]"And the reason why he ceaseth to do miracles among the children of men is because that they dwindle in unbelief, and depart from the right way, and know not the God in whom they should trust." (Mormon 9: 20.)

[50]See Moroni 7: 37: "Behold I say unto you... it is by faith that angels appear and minister unto men; wherefore, if these things have ceased wo be unto the children of men, for it is because of unbelief, and all is in vain." Also Jacob 7: 5: "And he had hope to shake me from the faith, notwithstanding the many revelations and the many things which I had seen concerning these things; for I truly had seen angels, and they had ministered unto me."

[51]See Moroni 7: 30: "For behold, [angels] are subject unto [Christ], to minister according to the word of his command, showing themselves unto them of strong faith and a firm mind in every form of godliness."

A person acquires "knowledge" when they have an audience with Christ.[52] The Book of Mormon intends for all those who read it to acquire knowledge of Christ. They are to meet Him; to know Him. Hence the saying by Joseph Smith: "A man is saved no faster than he gets knowledge[.]" (*DHC* 4: 588.) Saving knowledge comes from "knowing" – meeting with and being ministered to – by Jesus Christ. He is the Second Comforter. Although this truth appears in the New Testament,[53] prior Joseph Smith's example and teachings, the idea was not understood or believed. Joseph's example restored the truth of John's Gospel teaching.

The culminating ordinances of Joseph Smith's restoration are a repetition of this same theme. In the symbolism of the temple, ordinances wash, anoint, clothe and instruct Latter-day Saints about the journey back into God's presence. The whole temple message can be summarized in one brief statement: We are to be prepared in all things to receive further light and knowledge by conversing with the Lord through the veil. The ceremony of the temple is not the real thing. It is a symbol of the real thing. The real thing is when a person actually obtains an audience with Jesus Christ, returns to His presence, and gains the knowledge by which they are saved. This was the topic I first wrote about, and has remained the underlying theme of everything I have written.

---

[52]See Ether 3: 19-20: "And because of the knowledge of this man he could not be kept from beholding within the veil; and he saw the finger of Jesus, which, when he saw, he fell down with fear; for he knew it was the finger of the Lord; and he had faith no longer, for he knew, nothing doubting. Wherefore, having this perfect knowledge of God, he could not be kept from within the veil; therefore he saw Jesus; and he did minister unto him.

[53]John 17: 3: "And this is life eternal, that they might know thee the only true God, and Jesus Christ, whom thou has sent."

Joseph Smith restored it as a living reality to the earth. Now it is up to each person to follow in turn. First phase Mormonism is consumed with this teaching.

Joseph's journey saved him, but it did not save you. As Joseph put it:

> You, no doubt, will agree with us, and say, that you have no right to claim the promises of the inhabitants before the flood; that you cannot found your hopes of salvation upon the obedience of the children of Israel when journeying in the wilderness, nor can you expect that the blessings which the apostles pronounced upon the churches of Christ eighteen hundred years ago, were intended for you. Again, if others' blessings are not your blessings, others' curses are not your curses; you stand then in these last days, as all have stood before you, agents unto yourselves, to be judged according to your works. (*TPJS,* p. 12.)

It is also equally true that Joseph Smith's blessings, promises and covenants are not yours. They are his. He obtained them from heaven, and so must you. Joseph has helped in that he shows even in these last days it remains possible for man to reach up to God, and have God respect the search by reaching down to man. God can promise you salvation today just as He did to Paul anciently, and Joseph Smith recently. Anyone who labors to find God can find Him. It is open to any of us on the same conditions as it has always been available.

> And what shall others receive who do not labor faithfully, and continue to the end? We leave such to search out their own promises if any they have; and if they have any they are welcome to them, on our part, for the Lord says that every man is to receive according to his works. Reflect for a moment, brethren, and enquire, whether you would consider yourselves worthy a seat at the marriage feast with

Paul and others like him, if you had been unfaithful? Had you not fought the good fight, and kept the faith, could you expect to receive? Have you a promise of receiving a crown of righteousness from the hand of the Lord, with the Church of the Firstborn? Here then, we understand, that Paul rested his hope in Christ, because he had kept the faith, and loved His appearing and from His hand he had a promise of receiving a crown of righteousness. (*TPJS,* p. 64.)

When Joseph was commanded to organize a church, the resulting organization imposed the duty upon all its members and leaders to seek for, and receive revelation, individually. No person should belong to The Church of Jesus Christ of Latter-day Saints who has not asked God if the Book of Mormon is true, and received an answer for themselves. (Moroni 10: 4-5.) This foundation of communication with God is what defines the restoration of Christ's Gospel. Joseph Smith restored the connection between God and man. He did this by his life and example. He did this through the Book of Mormon and its message. He did it in revelations in the Doctrine and Covenants. He did it in the temple ceremonies. It is the overarching message given to the world through Joseph Smith. God is approachable. God wants you to search for and find Him. God wants you to know Him. You can know Him. You do not need another person to speak to Him for you. You should speak to Him directly.

The ceremonies and ordinances of the church all point to Him. They are not the end of the search but instead teach you how to conduct the search. If all you receive are ordinances, you have nothing of real value. They are dead without a living, personal connection with God. God alone can and will save you. Although some may pretend to have authority to save you apart from Him, there is nothing in Joseph Smith's example or message to warrant that conclusion.[54]

Joseph Smith showed by his example that when men come into contact with the Lord, they gain authority from Him. The Lord's friends and fellow-servants are always endowed with power. This was Joseph's message. Therefore, as we search into the history of the restoration, we need to keep in mind Joseph was to be the father of a nation of priests and priestesses. This has been the Lord's objective since the beginning. (See, e.g., Exo. 19: 16.)

This is the Gospel. This is how salvation is obtained. You are required to obtain for yourself a promise from God, not a man, that you have part in the kingdom of God.

This core message was supported by all the restoration. After Joseph and his brother were slain, John Taylor, who survived the assault, wrote:

> Joseph Smith, the Prophet and Seer of the Lord, has done more, save Jesus only, for the salvation of men in this world, than any other man that ever lived in it. In the short space of twenty years, he has brought forth the Book of Mormon, which he translated by the gift and power of God, and has been the means of publishing it on two continents; has sent the fulness of the everlasting gospel, which it contained, to the four quarters of the earth; has brought forth the revelations and commandments which compose this book of Doctrine and Covenants, and many other wise documents and instructions for the benefit of

---

[54] 2 Ne 9: 41: "O then, my beloved brethren, come unto the Lord, the Holy One. Remember that his paths are righteous. Behold, the way for man is narrow, but it lieth in a straight course before him, and the keeper of the gate is the Holy One of Israel; and he employeth no servant there; and there is none other way save it be by the gate; for he cannot be deceived, for the Lord God is his name."

the children of men; gathered many thousands of the Latter-day Saints, founded a great city, and left a fame and name that cannot be slain. (D&C 135: 3.)

This list composed by John Taylor is modest. A more complete list of what was restored through Joseph would include the following:

Knowledge, and a record of God's dealings with Adam, including teaching him the Gospel of Jesus Christ, and baptism by immersion in the first generation of mankind. (Moses 5: 6-15.)

Knowledge of Enoch's ministry and testimony. (Moses 6: 21-7: 69.)

Restored a record of Abraham. (Book of Abraham.)

Knowledge of baptism for the dead, the manner of conducting the ordinance, how an appropriate font was to be constructed, and that a proper record was necessary. (See D&C 127: 5-12, D&C 128: 1-18.)

Knowledge of Temple building.

Knowledge of John's testimony and record. (D&C 93: 6-18.)

Knowledge that marriage and family relations may continue into eternity. (D&C 132: 19.)

Knowledge that man existed before this world and came here as a continuation of a larger plan for salvation, and elevation of mankind through experience. (Abraham 3: 22-28; Moses 4: 1-3.)

Knowledge that man may become like God. (D&C 132: 20.)

Knowledge that man is co-eternal with God, and has an intelligence within him which is not created and cannot be destroyed. (D&C 93: 29.)

Knowledge that Christ appeared to many scattered, but organized bodies of believers who were removed from Jerusalem because of unbelief, but who kept their faith of Him intact. (2 Nephi 28: 7-14; Jacob 5; 3 Nephi 16: 1-3.)

Understanding of Aaronic or Levitical Priesthood. (D&C 107: 1, 13-16, 20, 69-76.)

Understanding of Melchizedek Priesthood. (D&C 107: 1-12, 17-19, 22-67.)

Knowledge of a third order of priesthood referred to as Patriarchal Priesthood.[55]

Knowledge of Melchizedek's life. (JST Genesis 14: 25-40.)

A greater understanding of the Lord's suffering in Gethsemene as part of His atonement for mankind. (D&C 19: 15-20.)

Knowledge that the original inhabitants of the North American Continent included refugees led by prophets who were of Israelite descent. (Title Page for the Book of Mormon.)

---

[55]"The anointing and sealing is to be called, elected and made sure. 'Without father, without mother, without descent, having neither beginning of days nor end of life, but made like unto the Son of God, abideth a priest continually.' The Melchizedek Priesthood holds the right from the eternal God, and not by descent from father and mother; and that priesthood is as eternal as God Himself, having neither beginning of days nor end of life. The 2nd Priesthood is Patriarchal authority. Go to and finish the temple, and God will fill it with power, and you will then receive more knowledge concerning this priesthood. The 3rd is what is called the Levitical Priesthood, consisting of priests to administer in outward ordinances, made without an oath; but the Priesthood of Melchizedek is by an oath and covenant. The Holy Ghost is God's messenger to administer in all those priesthoods. Jesus Christ is the heir of this Kingdom-the Only Begotten of the Father according to the flesh, and holds the keys over all this world. Men have to suffer that they may come upon Mount Zion and be exalted above the heavens. I know a man that has been caught up to the third heavens, and can say, with Paul, that we have seen and heard things that are not lawful to utter. (Aug. 27, 1843.) (TPJS, p. 323; also found at DHC 5: 554-556.)

Knowledge that a future Zion will be established on the North American Continent. (Article 10, Articles of Faith.)

Laying on of hands for the gift of the Holy Ghost. (D&C 33: 15; 49: 14.)

That all angels who minister to this earth have either lived here, or will live here as mortals. (D&C 130: 5.)

Knowledge that the Gospel was to be restored to gentiles, rather than the Jews, in the last days. (1 Nephi 14: 5-7.)

Knowledge that the gentiles will take the Gospel to the remnant of Israelite inhabitants of the American Continent. (1 Nephi 15: 13.)

Knowledge that the gentiles will ultimately reject the fullness of the Gospel, at which time it will be given to the remnant, covenant people. (3 Nephi 16: 10-11.)

Knowledge that ordinances cannot be changed by men.[56]

An understanding that the Gospel of Jesus Christ has been the same since the days of Adam, and whenever God has interacted with mankind He has offered the same message of redemption, the same ordinances, and the same revelations to mankind. (D&C 130: 20-21.)

Knowledge that God has a body as tangible as man's. (D&C 130: 22.) Indeed, man is made in God's image, and therefore looks in form and feature as a man does. (Ether 3: 15-16.)

Restoration of the practice of anointing with oil. (*TPJS*, p. 229.)

---

[56]"Jesus did everything to gather the people, and they would not be gathered, and He therefore poured out curses upon them. Ordinances instituted in the heavens before the foundation of the world, in the priesthood, for the salvation of men, are not to be altered or changed. All must be saved on the same principles." (*TPJS*, p. 308.)

Knowledge of the afterlife including four different conditions, three of which involve kingdoms of glory. (D&C 76.)

The Book of Mormon bridges the Old and New Testaments, revealing how much has been removed from the Old Testament by the scribes.[57]

He restored prayer circles, altar worship, temple ceremonies, covenant making, priestly rites, dietary instructions, sacrament prayers, baptismal form and prayers, a format for dedication of temples, blessing of children, restrictions on baptism of children, a clearer understanding of the Fall of mankind, prophecy of judgments coming upon all the earth, a clearer account of the Lord's future return, the role North American sites have played in the past, and will play in the future of God's dealing with mankind. He explained the spirit of Elias, Elijah, and Messiah. He explained the various priesthood privileges and rites, and how to obtain them. When he finished, he died as a martyr for the faith he restored, and as a witness of its truthfulness.

All the details of Joseph's contributions, however, are only appendages to the single greatest message. Returning to God's presence is Joseph's witness, message and theme. If you return to His presence, you will learn more in five minutes with Him than you can by reading all that has ever been written on the subject.[58]

---

[57]Margaret Barker's reconstruction of the pre-Deuteronomist faith of Israel shows remarkable affinity with what is found in the Book of Mormon record. Margaret Barker's work includes *The Older Testament, The Lost Prophet, The Gate of Heaven, The Great Angel, The Great High Priest, Temple Theology, Temple Themes in Christian Worship,* among others. All her books are available through her website www.margaretbarker.com.

[58]"Could we read and comprehend all that has been written from the days of Adam, on the relation of man to God and angels in a future state, we should know very little about it. Reading the experience of others, or

Joseph showed us that we like him, can gaze into heaven and gain knowledge. No man or woman has ever, or will ever, be saved in ignorance. All of us are saved only as quicky as we gain knowledge of Him directly from Him.

Today, testimonies of the presiding authorities, including the First Presidency and Quorum of Twelve, assert only vaguely they are "special witnesses" of the Lord. The assertion is based on scripture received during the first phase which imposes this responsibility upon those who are ordained as administrative Apostles in the church. This verse describes the calling of the Twelve Apostles: "The twelve traveling councilors are called to be the Twelve Apostles, or special witnesses of the name of Christ in all the world--thus differing from other officers in the church in the duties of their calling." (D&C 107: 23.) The New Testament account of what qualifies an Apostle included the necessary credential of witnessing Christ's resurrection.[59] A great number of active Latter-day Saints do not notice the careful parsing of words used by modern administrative Apostles. They presume a "witness of the name" of Christ is the same as the New Testament witness of His resurrection. The Apostolic witness was always intended to be based upon the dramatic, the extraordinary. Such visionary experiences make Apostles eye-witnesses of Christ's role in salvation. Without such visionary encounters with the Lord, they

---

the revelation given to *them*, can never give *us* a comprehensive view of our condition and true relation to God. Knowledge of these things can only be obtained by experience through the ordinances of God set forth for that purpose. Could you gaze into heaven five minutes, you would know more than you would by reading all that ever was written on the subject." (*TPJS,* p. 324, emphasis in original.)

[59] Acts 1: 22.

are unable to witness about Him, but only of His name. In a recent General Conference Elder David A. Bednar of the Twelve explained how revelation today is not akin to a light going on in a dark room. Rather it is more akin to the gradual sunrise, in which subtle, gradual increasing appreciation of truth is the means by which God reveals truth. He distinguishes between these two as follows:

> Revelations are conveyed in a variety of ways, including, for example, dreams, visions, conversations with heavenly messengers, and inspiration. Some revelations are received immediately and intensely; some are recognized gradually and subtly. The two experiences with light I described help us to better understand these two basic patterns of revelation.
>
> A light turned on in a dark room is like receiving a message from God quickly, completely, and all at once. Many of us have experienced this pattern of revelation as we have been given answers to sincere prayers or been provided with needed direction or protection, according to God's will and timing. Descriptions of such immediate and intense manifestations are found in the scriptures, recounted in Church history, and evidenced in our own lives. Indeed, these mighty miracles do occur. However, this pattern of revelation tends to be more rare than common.
>
> . . . Most frequently, revelation comes in small increments over time and is granted according to our desire, worthiness, and preparation.[60]

Although this is true, revealed religion is always founded on the dramatic; the light going on suddenly and illuminating the room. Without the dramatic appearances of the Lord after His

---

[60]Bednar, David. A.*The Spirit of Revelation*. Ensign CR, May 2011.

resurrection, the New Testament account would not provide the promise of redemption through Christ. Despite all His profound wisdom, it is the suddenly miraculous return to life which moves Him from teacher of wisdom to Savior of mankind.

It was the dramatic appearance to Saul on the road to Damascus that made Paul an Apostolic witness of the Lord. Paul was "called to be an apostle of Jesus Christ through the will of God." (1 Cor. 1: 1, 2 Cor. 1: 1, Eph. 1: 1.) His Apostolic calling was "not of men, neither by man, but by Jesus Christ." (Gal. 1: 1.) From it Paul became an Apostolic witness of Jesus Christ.

The restoration is marked by the First Vision, the appearance of Moroni, the visit by John the Baptist and return of Peter, James, and John. These events identify it as something quite different from other Christian religions. It is not another sect. It is God's latest work among mankind. When angels stop ministering to the Latter-day Saints, then the original faith has ended among us.[61] At that point we become like any other Christian sect.

In the first phase, priesthood was associated with Divine appearances[62] and the power of heaven.[63] By the time the third

---

[61] "Or have angels ceased to appear unto the children of men? Or has he withheld the power of the Holy Ghost from them? Or will he, so long as time shall last, or the earth shall stand, or there shall be one man upon the face thereof to be saved? Behold I say unto you, Nay; for it is by faith that miracles are wrought; and it is by faith that angels appear and minister unto men; wherefore, if these things have ceased wo be unto the children of men, for it is because of unbelief, and all is vain." (Moroni 7: 36-37.)

[62] "And this greater priesthood administereth the gospel and holdeth the key of the mysteries of the kingdom, even the key of the knowledge of God. Therefore, in the ordinances thereof, the power of godliness is manifest. And without the ordinances thereof, and the authority of the priesthood, the power of godliness is not manifest unto men in the flesh;

phase was fully underway in the early 1900's, the president of the
church denounced either the need, or personal desire on his part
to receive a visitation from Divine or angelic visitors. President
Heber J. Grant, in an address given on October 4, 1942 in the
Tabernacle, stated, "I have never prayed to see the Savior, I know
of men – Apostles – who have seen the Savior more than once. I
have prayed to the Lord for the inspiration of His Spirit to guide
me, and I have told him that I have seen so many men fall because
of some great manifestation to them, they felt their importance,
their greatness."[64] In the first phase, Divine knowledge was the
linchpin of the Prophet Joseph Smith's authority. By the third
phase, knowledge of Jesus Christ was not only unnecessary, it was
viewed by the church president as both negative, and potentially
something leading to pride and a fall from grace.[65] For those who
seek and find the miraculous, however, it becomes the defining
moment of their lives. Over forty years after his encounter with
Christ, Nephi recorded there wasn't a day that passed, but what he

---

For without this no man can see the face of God, even the Father, and
live." (D&C 84: 19-22.)

[63]"That the rights of the priesthood are inseparably connected with the
powers of heaven, and that the powers of heaven cannot be controlled
nor handled only upon the principles of righteousness." (D&C 121: 36.)

[64]Quote taken from *The Diaries of Heber J. Grant, 1880-1945 Abridged*. Salt
Lake City: Privately published, 2010, p. 468.

[65]The reference to Apostles who had fallen, Heber J. Grant apparently
had in mind John W. Taylor and Matthias F. Cowley, both of whom had
been dropped from the Quorum and excommunicated.

meditated on the great visions he had seen, and the things taught him by the Lord.[66]

Even into the fourth phase which began with President David O. McKay, rank and file Mormons are often unaware of any difference between the meaning underlying language used now in contrast to what was meant in Joseph's Smith day. Many assume the language "special witnesses of Christ" to mean continuing visitations by Jesus Christ, angels and visions similar to those in the beginning. But when they learn of Heber J. Grant's 1926 letter declaring there hasn't been an appearance of the Lord since Joseph Smith's day, some of them lose faith in the church. President Grant's letter stated: "I know of no instance where the Lord has appeared to an individual since His appearance to the Prophet Joseph Smith."[67] It is the gap between the misconception held by many Latter-day Saints of Christ's regular appearances to church leaders, and the reality of His absence that creates distress. If their expectations were not misinformed, there would be no disappointment.

By the third phase, and throughout the fourth, the primary authority for the church arises from respect for the office of the president of The Church of Jesus Christ of Latter-day Saints, and the associated teachings regarding his "practical" infallibility. The notion of "infallibility" is denounced in principle, and compared

---

[66] 2 Ne. 4: 15-16.

[67] Heber J. Grant to Mrs. Claud Peery, 13 April 1926, found in First Presidency letterbooks, vol. 72; cited by Quinn D. Michael. *Mormon Hierarchy: Extensions of Power.* Salt Lake City: Signature Books, 1997, at p. 4.

with the false Catholic notion associated with the Pope.[68] However, in contrast to the denial of his infallibility, the church asserts the following about its president: "I say to Israel, the Lord will never permit me or any other man who stands as president of this Church to lead you astray. It is not in the program. It is not in the mind of God." (*The Discourses of Wilford Woodruff*. Edited by G. Homer Durham. Salt Lake City: Bookcraft: 1946, pp. 212-13.) And, "I have a consciousness as I have thought through this responsibility [as prophet] and have been close enough to the Brethren over the years, that one in this position is under the constant surveillance of Him in whose service we are. Never would He permit one in this position to lead this church astray. You can be sure of that." (Lee, Harold B. *Teachings of Harold B. Lee*. Edited by Clyde J. Williams. Salt Lake City: Deseret Book, 1996, pp. 535-536.) Also, "I remember years ago when I was a Bishop I had President [Heber J.] Grant talk to our ward. After the meeting I drove him home.... Standing by me, he put his arm over my shoulder and said: 'My boy, you always keep your eye on the President of the Church, and if he ever tells you to do anything, and it is wrong, and you do it, the Lord will bless you for it.' Then with a twinkle in his eye, he said, 'But you don't need to worry. The Lord will never let his mouthpiece lead the people astray.'" (Benson, Ezra Taft. *The Teachings of Ezra Taft Benson*. Salt Lake City: Bookcraft, 1988, p. 137, citing CR October 1960, p. 78.) This is a

---

[68] See, e.g., *Encyclopedia of Mormonism*, 4 Vols. Edited by Daniel H. Ludlow. New York: Macmillan, 1992, p. 59: "Apostasy may be accelerated by a faulty assumption that scripture or Church leaders are infallible. Joseph Smith taught that 'a prophet was a prophet only when he was acting as such' (*DHC* 5:265). He also declared he 'was but a man, and [people] must not expect me to be perfect' (*DHC* 5:181). Neither the Church nor its leaders and members claim infallibility."

constant theme, which varies in its expression. It results in "practical" infallibility, although the use of the term itself has been rejected.

We are going to examine these transitions, and how they have resulted in Mormonism being quite different from what it was during Joseph Smith's day. That journey is one of the remarkable opportunities to learn how religious movements change, adapt, discard ideas, and make difficult choices. This world is fallen. The environment here erodes everything. Despite this world's corrosive environment, almost all great ideas, movements and societies retain their original vitality, and purity if a careful search is made.

Upon Joseph Smith's death, the First Presidency, and Quorum of the Twelve Apostles were divided. Their roles were unclear. These two groups would vie against one another for leadership. There were some who thought the stake president of Nauvoo should lead. Joseph left a son too young to preside, but who was thought to have been ordained by Joseph to replace him. There were also Quorums of Seventy whose role and rights were uncertain. Then there were the members who were uncertain who was to lead the church. From our current vantage point, now informed by historical hindsight, the outcome seems foreordained. Brigham Young, advocating for the Twelve Apostles, won the argument, and now we accept that as the proper, even inspired outcome. If the question of Joseph's successor was considered the day before his death, the answer would have been Joseph's older brother, Hyrum Smith. As the assistant president and presiding patriarch of the church,[69] and the one upon whom Joseph had

---

[69]See D&C 124: 124.

committed co-equality in holding keys,[70] Hyrum was the designated successor. However, in his final moments, Joseph saw Hyrum die. "Hyrum was shot first and fell calmly, exclaiming: I am a dead man! Joseph leaped from the window, and was shot dead in the attempt, exclaiming: O Lord my God! They were both shot after they were dead, in a brutal manner, and both received four balls" (D&C 135: 1.) Hyrum's death may have been needed to seal the testimony that the Gospel has returned to the earth,[71] but it eliminated the obvious successor. In the instant of Joseph and Hyrum's martyrdom, Mormonism's first phase ended and its course would change.

---

[70]See *Encyclopedia of Mormonism*, 4 Vols. Edited by Daniel H. Ludlow. New York: Macmillan, 1992, p. 1360.

[71]"To seal the testimony of this book and the Book of Mormon, we announce the martyrdom of Joseph Smith the Prophet, and Hyrum Smith the Patriarch." (D&C 135: 1.)

Chapter 3

SUCCESSFUL SUCCESSION

Upon Joseph's death, there was no clear path as to what would happen next for the church. Sidney Rigdon advocated that he would be the caretaker of the church for the deceased Joseph, until Joseph's son (Joseph III) could assume the mantle. Brigham Young advocated for the right of the Quorum of the Twelve to preside. Today Brigham Young's claims are buttressed by subsequent events. At the time, however, uncertainty reigned. The confusion of that moment is hardly appreciated in hindsight.

Brigham Young was with Orson Pratt near Boston, in Peterboro, New Hampshire preaching the gospel when he first heard the news of Joseph's martyrdom. This is what he wrote of his initial reaction to the news: "'The first thing which I thought of' Brigham said in his journal, 'was whether Joseph had taken the keys of the kingdom with him from the earth; brother Orson Pratt sat on my left; we were both leaning back on our chairs. Bringing my hand down on my knee, I said the keys of the kingdom are right here with the

Church."⁷² Apparently all prior information, charges, ordinations, washings, endowments, sealings and instruction were not as clear to Brigham Young at the moment Joseph died as he would later make it appear. It was only as time went on that the accounts of Joseph passing keys to the Twelve grew to add detail and certainty. Eventually it added the transfiguration of Joseph, and other details that were never mentioned as part of the original account of the

---

⁷²*The Complete Discourses of Brigham Young.* Edited by Richard S. Van Wagoner. Salt Lake City: Signature Books, 2009, Vol. 1, p. 38, entry of July 16, 1844; also cited in Arrington, Leonard J. *Brigham Young: American Moses.* New York: Alfred A. Knopf, 1985, p. 111. One LDS commentator has noted, "This reaction is somewhat surprising, considering the anointings and charges given by the Prophet to the Twelve shortly before his death." (Brown, Lisle G. *The Holy Order in Nauvoo.* Copyright by the author: November 1995.) This observation confuses historic hindsight, after the narrative was settled with the actual, earlier events. Now we find it surprising. But at the time Brigham Young really did not initially know.

Nauvoo debate deciding the issue of succession.[73] At the time, no one knew how to proceed.

After returning to Nauvoo on the afternoon of August 7, Brigham Young met privately with the other members of the Twelve, Sidney Rigdon, Nauvoo Stake High Council, and all the high priests who were in Nauvoo. Rigdon advanced his claim to be an ordained "spokesman to Joseph Smith," and even though deceased, Joseph would remain head of the church. "Brigham's response was: 'I do not care who leads the church, even though it were Ann Lee (founder of the Shakers); but one thing I must know, and that is what God says about it.' As president of the Quorum of the Twelve, Brigham said, 'I have the keys and the means of obtaining the mind of God on the subject ... Joseph

---

[73]For example, in a meeting in the Tabernacle on April 7, 1895, Wilford Woodruff stated, concerning Joseph Smith: "shortly before his death, he was transfigured before them, his face shone like amber, and he gave us all the keys of the kingdom." (*Candid Insights of a Mormon Apostle: The Diaries of Abraham Cannon 1889-1895*. Edited by Edward Leo Lyman. Salt Lake City: Signature Books, 2010, p. 636.) The footnote to the entry clarifies, "Cannon gives the impression, although ambiguously, that Joseph Smith might have conferred additional authority on the Twelve Apostles at that time. However, Woodruff's sermon was reported in full in the *Millennial Star* and indicates only that Smith reminded the Twelve of the authority they already possessed. Woodruff mentions this on two other occasions. In April 1893 he said that in Nauvoo, Joseph Smith 'spoke to them for more than three hours' and 'was transfigured before them, that his face shone like amber,' but without mention of authority. In another sermon, this one in June 1894, Woodruff said Smith 'called the Twelve together the last time he spoke to us, and his face shone like amber,' but again without referencing the conferral of additional authority. None of the other apostles mentioned a transfiguration, so this was probably Woodruff's private impression; nor did they claim they were given the right of succession at that time." (*Id.*, footnote 18, citing to Brian H. Stuy, ed., *Collected Discourses* [N.p.: B.H.S. Publishing, 1987], 3: 283, 4: 110, 291.)

conferred upon our heads all the keys and powers belonging to the Apostleship which he himself held before he was taken away, and no man or set of men can get between Joseph and the Twelve in this world or in the world to come."[74]

Section 107 already established a basis to claim equality between the First Presidency and Quorum of the Twelve.[75] Today this idea of equal authority between the two presiding quorums is generally accepted to resolve the question of succession. Now it is the justification for leadership transferring to the Twelve upon the death of a church president. In the 1844 debates, however, none of the parties relied on Section 107 to help resolve the question. Instead, the winning argument made by Brigham Young was based on the claim that he and the Twelve possessed the "keys" previously held by Joseph Smith. Therefore, he argued, they were able to continue on in establishing the kingdom of God without interruption, and with the same Divine authorization as Joseph held.

Today The Church of Jesus Christ of Latter-day Saints views Brigham Young as Joseph Smith's legal successor. This is a revision of history. At the time even Brigham Young did not consider himself the legal successor. Instead, he believed the right belonged to one of Joseph's sons, either Joseph Smith III or David Smith.

---

[74] *American Moses, supra,* at pp. 113-114.

[75] "Of the Melchizedek Priesthood, three Presiding High Priests, chosen by the body, appointed and ordained to that office, and upheld by the confidence, faith, and prayer of the church, form a quorum of the Presidency of the Church. The twelve traveling councilors are called to be the Twelve Apostles, or special witnesses of the name of Christ in all the world--thus differing from other officers in the church in the duties of their calling. And they form a quorum, equal in authority and power to the three presidents previously mentioned." (D&C 107: 22-24.)

"[H]e had never considered himself as Joseph Smith's sole successor, and, second, he had long hoped for the Spirit of God to move either Joseph or David to fill the station Brigham believed their father had appointed to them."[76] Thirteen years after being voted into the presidency, President Young made the following comment in a sermon at the Salt Lake Tabernacle:

> What of Joseph Smith's family? What of his boys? I have prayed from the beginning for Sister Emma and for the whole family. There is not a man in this Church that has entertained better feelings towards them. Joseph said to me, "God will take care of my children when I am taken." They are in the hands of God, and when they make their appearance before this people, full of his power, there are none but what will say— "Amen! we are ready to receive you."
>
> The brethren testify that brother Brigham is brother Joseph's legal successor. You never heard me say so. I say that I am a good hand to keep the dogs and wolves out of the flock. I do not care a groat who rises up. I do not think anything about being Joseph's successor. That is nothing that concerns me.[77]

- he hated Emma

Therefore the reality is that both Sidney Rigdon and Brigham Young were making similar claims. Rigdon directly claimed to be a caretaker until Joseph's son could lead. Brigham Young intended the same thing, but in the August 1844 debates he relied upon possession of keys to assert the right to temporarily lead. It began with Brigham Young as a caretaker, but became permanent.

---

[76]Ehat, Andrew. *Joseph Smith's Introduction of Temple Ordinances and the 1844 Mormon Succession Question.* Master's Thesis BYU, 1981, p. 242.

[77]*The Complete Discourses of Brigham Young, supra,* Vol. 3, p. 1588, morning of June 3, 1860.

Brigham Young's claims to possession of "all the keys" previously conferred upon Joseph by heavenly messengers raised the question of exactly what was included in the conferral. Even today there is no full description of what keys were involved or what rights were included. It was not until after 1879 that Section 110 was adapted to become the lynchpin defining "keys" held by Joseph, and passed on to the Twelve. Today the claim is the keys identified in Section 110 came from Moses to gather again scattered Israel.[78] Elias' keys were passed for the Gospel of Abraham.[79] Elijah's sealing keys were conferred.[80] Those were the final keys to be restored, through visitations of these angelic ministers in the Kirtland Temple on April 3, 1836. That claim is demonstrably incorrect.

Section 110 was written by Warren Cowdery,[81] and is found on pages 192 and 193 of the document now identified as *Journal, 1835-1836*. The material from that 1835-1836 journal appears in Volume 1 of the *Joseph Smith Papers*,[82] and runs from p. 61 through p. 222. The Section 110 entry is written in the third person and appears as the last entry, following which are several blank pages.

---

[78]D&C 110: 11.

[79]D&C 110: 12.

[80]D&C 110: 13-16.

[81]Although the source of the handwriting was controversial, the *Joseph Smith Papers* volume has settled on Warren Cowdery as the hand responsible for recording this event. See *The Joseph Smith Papers, Journals: Vol. 1: 1832-1839*, footnote 465, p. 217. Edited by Dean Jesse, Ronald K. Esplin, Richard L. Bushman. Salt Lake City: The Church's Historian's Press, 2008.

[82]*Id.*

All the contemporaneous records kept by any party fail to record any mention by Joseph Smith of the Kirtland Temple visitation from Moses, Elias and Elijah. It was never taught by Joseph Smith, never mentioned in any sermon delivered by him, and was never mentioned in anything Joseph ever wrote. Nor did Oliver Cowdery mention it, write about it, or preach of it at any time in his life. Church historians have searched the record for nearly two centuries hoping to find some statement about this visitation by either Joseph or Oliver, but have found nothing. So far as any preserved record exists, from April 1836, until their respective deaths in 1844 and 1849, neither Joseph nor Oliver ever mentioned this event to anyone.[83] Only Warren Cowdery's third person handwritten account mentions it.

Joseph referred to Elijah's return as a still future event. The first time it appears, Joseph Smith attributed the promise of Elijah's return to instruction he received from Moroni. This was written in 1838 as he resumed rewriting his history.[84] Oliver Cowdery never

---

[83] A recent Masters' thesis from BYU argues there are hints that suggest there may have been private instructions about the revelation. See Trever R. Anderson, *Doctrine and Covenants Section 110: From Vision to Canonization*. Masters of Religious Education thesis, BYU, August 2010. The hints referred to in the thesis were never subsequently clarified by any of the parties involved, to make it certain the hints really do prove pre-death mention of the Kirtland Temple visitation. Another alternative is that Section 110 has assumed a significance after 1870 which it simply didn't have. It is possible we do not understand what Joseph was teaching about the matter, and our use of Section 110 is a misapplication.

[84] This is now Section 2 of the Doctrine and Covenants. It was composed in 1838, and added to scripture in 1876. It was placed as Section 2 to call attention to it as the earliest revelation, Section 1 being the "preface" to the book revealed by the Lord. (See D&C 1: 6.) Section 2 refers to an event on the evening of September 21, 1823, which was 15 years previous to Joseph Smith writing it down in 1838.

uttered a word about the vision, even in his final written testimony composed on January 13, 1849. Oliver confirmed he saw Moroni (who showed to him the plates of the Book of Mormon), John the Baptist (who ordained him with power to baptize), and Peter, James and John. But he says nothing about Christ, Moses, Elias and Elijah appearing in the Kirtland Temple. It is curious his last declaration would mention Moroni, John the Baptist, Peter, James and John, but omit Christ, Moses, Elias and Elijah. Also noteworthy is that Oliver Cowdery's *Kirtland Sketch Book*, written contemporaneous with these events, concludes the day before the appearances, with no mention of the event. The *Kirtland Sketch Book* had available blank pages, but Oliver records nothing on them about the event. Both witnesses to the appearances leave a glaring absence in their statements, writings, testimony, and preaching.

Warren Cowdery, who inserted the account of the vision in the last pages of the 1835-1836 journal, could have written it at any time. It is the last entry in that book, followed only by several blank pages. Events and the written account of the events are not always contemporary in the church's early records. The written account is sometimes made many years after the fact. For example, the quote attributed to Moroni of September 21, 1823 (D&C 2) occurred 15 years earlier than it was recorded. Therefore, recording and dating did not necessarily correspond in Joseph's journals. After the entry dated April 3, 1836, there were two years before anything further was recorded in Joseph Smith's history. We do not have any reliable way of knowing when Warren Cowdery inserted the account found in the last pages of the journal. Nor, for that matter, do we know what source told Warren Cowdery about the event, since only Joseph and Oliver were present. It is written in the third person, (i.e., "The veil was taken from *their* minds, and the eyes of *their* understanding were opened. *They* saw the Lord standing upon the breastwork of the pulpit" etc.)

Although Joseph and Oliver said nothing about the event, it is perhaps significant that Warren Cowdery wrote an article a year later in March, 1837 about these Old Testament prophets. His article refers to Peter on the Mount of Transfiguration witnessing the appearance of Moses and Elias. The same article also suggests the possibility of salvation for the dead.[85] These ideas are now inseparable to Latter-day Saints. So if Joseph and Oliver failed to mention the appearances of Moses and Elijah, the scribe who wrote the event displayed an interest in the subject and even some appreciation for the potential doctrinal significance such an event might bring.

Although unknown in the 1830's and 40's, Section 110 was finally discovered and published in the *Deseret News* on November 6, 1852.

---

[85]*Messenger and Advocate,* March 1837, Vol. 3, No. 30, p. 470. *Love of God,* by Warren Cowdery. It included the following: "In order to demonstrate the reasonableness of this affection in reference to God, it is only requisite to consider his character and perceptions, and the relation in which he stands to us as the Author of our existence and enjoyments. For, for this cause was the gospel preached to them that are dead, that they might be judged according to men in the flesh, but live according to God in the spirit. FIRST PETER, 4:6. To the apostle who penned these words for our instruction; were committed the keys of the kingdom, altho' he was a fisherman by occupation previously to his being chosen and ordained by his divine Master to proclaim that gospel for which he eventually suffered martyrdom. He accompanied the Savior during his travels and public ministry, almost constantly. He witnessed his transfiguration on the mount, saw and heard him converse with Moses and Elias. He had seen the mighty works which he did while he tabernacled with men in the flesh. He had heard him converse with the Pharisees, Sadducees, and lawyers, and knew that the wisdom and the power of the living God were manifest in all his words and deeds, therefore, he could testify boldly of what he had seen and heard.." (Capitalization in original.)

In a sermon delivered on August 29, 1852, Orson Pratt was the first one to teach that Elijah had returned. Elder Pratt mentions Elijah by name and affirms the sealing keys and power were given to Joseph Smith. In the talk Elder Pratt conflates two concepts that ought to have been separated. His comments included the following:

> . . . So in these days; let me announce to this congregation, that there is but one man in all the world, at the same time, who can hold the keys of this matter; but one man has power to turn the key to inquire of the Lord, and to say whether I, or these my brethren, or any of the rest of this congregation, or the Saints upon the face of the whole earth, may have this blessing of Abraham conferred upon them; he holds the keys of these matters now, the same as Nathan, in his day. But, says one, how have you obtained this information? By new revelation. When was it given, and to whom? It was given to our Prophet, Seer, and Revelator, Joseph Smith, on the 12th day of July, 1843; only about eleven months before he was martyred for the testimony of Jesus.
>
> He held the keys of these matters; he had the right to inquire of the Lord; and the Lord has set bounds and restrictions to these things; He has told us in that revelation, that only one man can hold these keys upon the earth at the same time; and they belong to that man who stands at the head to preside over all the affairs of the Church and kingdom of God in the last days. They are the sealing keys of power, or in other words, of Elijah, having been committed and restored to the earth by Elijah, the Prophet, who held many keys, among which were the keys of sealing, to bind the hearts of the fathers to the children, and the children to the fathers; together with all the other sealing keys and powers, pertaining to the last dispensation. They were committed by that Angel who administered in

the Kirtland Temple, and spoke unto Joseph the Prophet, at the time of the endowments in that house."[86]

The revelation of July 12, 1843 he mentioned is Section 132 of the Doctrine and Covenants. Although it was recorded on that 1843 date, Elder Pratt is mistaken about it having been given to Joseph then. He is also mistaken in dating when Joseph received the sealing power in 1843. Section 132 may have been reduced to writing in 1843, but the revelation was received many years earlier. To understand Section 110, it is necessary to also understand Section 132. They have an important relationship to one another which has been hopelessly intertwined by the church's narrative.

Section 132 is an answer to Joseph's inquiry regarding the practice of a man having plural wives. Fixing a date for the revelation with absolute certainty is impossible because the content was not recorded until 1843. But Joseph Smith took plural wives in the early 1830's. Therefore, the inescapable conclusion is that Joseph received the revelation in Section 132 prior to taking plural wives. But we do not know for certain when.

Richard L. Bushman refers to a conversation Levi Hancock had with Joseph in 1832 where plural wives was taught as a righteous principle. Hancock says Joseph explained it was necessary to create a worthy generation prior to the millennium.[87] LDS historians and writers generally conclude the revelation regarding plural wives came while Joseph Smith was rendering an Inspired Translation of the Bible. I have taken the position Joseph inquired when he

---

[86] *JD* 1: 64. *Journal of Discourses.* www.journalofdiscourses.org/volume-01

[87] See Bushman, Richard L. *Joseph Smith: Rough Stone Rolling.* New York: Alfred A. Knopf, 2005, p. 326.

translated the Book of Mormon. The sermon found in the Book of Mormon at Jacob 2: 23-30 raises the issue. Joseph translated this section of the book in 1829. Assuming he inquired about plural marriage, as he had about baptism, then he would have known about the principle in 1829. Dating it in 1829 is supported by a talk Brigham Young gave in the Salt Lake 14th Ward on July 26, 1872. In his comments he stated the following:

> [W]hile Joseph And Oliver were translating the Book of Mormon, they had a revelation that the order of Patriarchal marriage and the Sealing was right. Oliver said unto Joseph, "Br. Joseph, why don't we go into the Order of Polygamy, and practice it as the ancients did? We know it is true, then why delay?" Joseph's reply was, "I know that we know it is true, and from God, but the time has not yet come." This did not seem to suit Oliver, who expressed a determination to go into the order of Plural Marriage anyhow, although he was ignorant of the order and pattern and the results. Joseph said, "Oliver if you do into this thing it is not with my faith or consent." Disregarding the counsel of Joseph, Oliver Cowdery took to wife Miss Annie Lyman, cousin to Geo. A. Smith.[88]

Brigham Young's comment makes the conclusion inescapable that the original revelation of plural marriage and eternal marriage was provoked during and because of the translation of the Book of Mormon, and not the work done revising the Bible. This means it must be dated earlier than the 1830's. It would have been in the latter part of June 1829.

---

[88] *Complete Discourses of Brigham Young,* Vol 5., p. 2906.

Plural marriage is one subject, the sealing power is another. Both topics are covered in Section 132. But they remain two, distinct subjects.

A great deal of myth, misunderstanding, and mistaken assumptions surround the topic of "sealing power." To understand it correctly requires us to first abandon a good deal of error or, in Book of Mormon vernacular, our unbelief.

The first principle of the sealing power is the condition by which it is conferred on a man. Once again the Book of Mormon is the best source to understand the qualifying condition. Nephi, the son of Helaman, qualified, and his account gives an explanation. The Lord explained to Nephi that He had observed his "unwearyingness declar[ing] the word, which I have given unto thee, unto this people. And thou hast not feared them, and hast not sought thine own life, but hast sought my will, and to keep my commandments." (Helaman 10: 4.) In addition to his willingness to sacrifice his own life following the Lord's will, Nephi was also a man who would "not ask that which is contrary to [God's] will." (*Id.*, v. 5.) Because of these two things, Nephi was entitled to have his calling and election made sure; or as the Lord put it: "behold, I will bless thee forever[.]" (*Id.*)

After proving he would sacrifice his own life, and would never ask something contrary to God's will, Nephi received his calling and election. Calling and election is connected with holding the sealing power:

> Behold, thou art Nephi, and I am God. Behold, I declare it unto thee in the presence of mine angels, that ye shall have power over this people, and shall smite the earth with famine, and with pestilence, and destruction, according to the wickedness of this people. Behold, I give unto you power, that whatsoever ye shall seal on earth shall be sealed

in heaven; and whatsoever ye shall loose on earth shall be loosed in heaven; and thus shall ye have power among this people. And thus, if ye shall say unto this temple it shall be rent in twain, it shall be done. And if ye shall say unto this mountain, Be thou cast down and become smooth, it shall be done. And behold, if ye shall say that God shall smite this people, it shall come to pass. (*Id.*, vs. 6-10.)

The qualifications are universal. No man is permitted to receive this power without meeting the same conditions.[89]

The record in Helaman also explains the kind of man who receives this power. Nephi never used the power contrary to the Lord's will. Even though he had the power to smite the earth, seal on earth, curse and bless, Nephi only did what the Lord commanded. Further, the moment he thought the people repented, he interceded for them with the Lord. Although he had the power to command, he did not. He did not judge, but instead taught repentance. He was meek, in the sense the word is defined in my earlier book *Beloved Enos*.

Nephi's first act using the sealing power was something the Lord required. ". . . I command you, that ye shall go and declare unto this people, that thus saith the Lord God, who is the Almighty: Except ye repent ye shall be smitten, even unto destruction." (*Id.*, v. 11.) Nephi's response was immediate, and never called any attention to himself or the great blessings just conferred upon him: ". . . when the Lord had spoken these words unto Nephi, he did stop and did not go unto his own house, but did return unto the multitudes who were scattered about upon the face of the land, and began to declare unto them the word of the Lord which had been

---

[89]D&C 130: 20-21.

spoken unto him, concerning their destruction if they did not repent." (*Id.*, v. 12.)

When the people did not repent, Nephi approached the Lord in prayer and asked the Lord to impose a famine. Despite having the power to smite the earth with a famine in the land, Nephi asked the Lord, "O Lord, do not suffer that this people shall be destroyed by the sword; but O Lord, rather let there be a famine in the land, to stir them up in remembrance of the Lord their God, and perhaps they will repent and turn unto thee." (Hel. 11: 4.) Nephi's concern was the welfare of the people. He preferred to keep them from killing one another, even at the cost of asking God to impose a famine. It was always in his heart to bless the people. He did not want to curse them. The Lord had respect for Nephi's prayer, and sent the famine. As soon as the people repented, Nephi immediately recognized this and made intercession for them. Again, Nephi had the power to end the famine, but instead he asked the Lord.[90]

---

[90]"O Lord, behold this people repenteth; and they have swept away the band of Gadianton from amongst them insomuch that they have become extinct, and they have concealed their secret plans in the earth. Now, O Lord, because of this their humility wilt thou turn away thine anger, and let thine anger be appeased in the destruction of those wicked men whom thou hast already destroyed. O Lord, wilt thou turn away thine anger, yea, thy fierce anger, and cause that this famine may cease in this land. O Lord, wilt thou hearken unto me, and cause that it may be done according to my words, and send forth rain upon the face of the earth, that she may bring forth her fruit, and her grain in the season of grain. O Lord, thou didst hearken unto my words when I said, Let there be a famine, that the pestilence of the sword might cease; and I know that thou wilt, even at this time, hearken unto my words, for thou saidst that: If this people repent I will spare them. Yea, O Lord, and thou seest that they have repented, because of the famine and the pestilence and destruction which has come unto them. And now, O Lord, wilt thou turn away thine anger, and try again if they will serve thee? And if so, O Lord,

The example of Nephi is the most instructive example of a man entrusted with the sealing power. Such a man would sacrifice his own life for others. He would never ask what is contrary to God's will. He will be meek enough that although he is trusted with God's power, he will defer to the Lord, and petition Him rather than command the elements.[91] He will intercede for others. In short, he will be a man after the Lord's own heart, and have charity for all others.

Joseph Smith met those same requirements. Just like Nephi, Joseph had proven himself by what he had done. "Behold, I have seen your sacrifices, and will forgive all your sins; I have seen your sacrifices in obedience to that which I have told you." (D&C 132: 50.)

Section 132 was dictated in one continuous statement, in July 1843. However, it was not received as one revelation. Reading it makes it apparent there were multiple parts, received at multiple times. The topic of eternal covenants is different from plural wives. Emma's reaction to plural wives is yet another, separate topic. We will go through Section 132 to examine its various parts. Because they are all interconnected, they were all dictated in one statement. The "sacrifices" the Lord refers to are those Joseph made to follow the revelations, including the information on plural wives. Joseph inquired, learned of the plurality of wives, was

---

thou canst bless them according to thy words which thou hast said." (Hel. 11: 10-16.)

[91]This power extends to commanding elements and spirits. It does not extend to commanding, controlling, or dictating men. Men are agents, and free to choose.

commanded to obey it,[92] and did. Far from being an outlet for Joseph's lust, it was a "sacrifice" which proved him willing to obey the Lord, even at the peril of his own life. This commandment was so difficult it proved Joseph's heart before God.

As in the case of Nephi, Joseph's calling and election was also made sure as part of receiving sealing power. "For I am the Lord thy God, and will be with thee even unto the end of the world, and through all eternity; for verily I seal upon you your exaltation, and prepare a throne for you in the kingdom of my Father, with Abraham your father." (*Id.*, v. 49.) Sealing power is always connected to calling and election. The power only comes when the Lord knows it will never be used contrary to His will:

> And verily, verily, I say unto you, that whatsoever you seal on earth shall be sealed in heaven; and whatsoever you bind on earth, in my name and by my word, saith the Lord, it shall be eternally bound in the heavens; and whosesoever sins you remit on earth shall be remitted eternally in the heavens; and whosesoever sins you retain on earth shall be retained in heaven. And again, verily I say, whomsoever you bless I will bless, and whomsoever you curse I will curse, saith the Lord; for I, the Lord, am thy God. And again, verily I say unto you, my servant Joseph, that whatsoever you give on earth, and to whomsoever you give any one on earth, by my word and according to my law, it shall be visited with blessings and not cursings, and with my power, saith the Lord, and shall be without condemnation on earth and in heaven. (*Id.*, v. 46-48.)

Throughout all scripture, this kind of covenant is established between God and man in the first person; never through another. God Himself confers this power. Although Abraham had a

---

[92]D&C 132: 3.

covenant from God, raised Isaac in righteousness, and instructed him in the mysteries of God, Isaac received the power from God directly, and not from his father Abraham.[93] Isaac blessed Jacob, but could not confer this power upon him. Jacob needed to covenant directly with God to obtain it. Esau sold the birthright to Jacob, but that did not confer the power upon him either. It is the Lord alone who knows a man's heart. It is the Lord alone who can determine when a man has proven he will obey even if the sacrifice of his own life is necessary. It is the Lord alone who knows when a man will never ask anything contrary to His will. It was the Lord who covenanted with Jacob,[94] despite the covenants his father, Isaac, and his grandfather, Abraham had with God. Isaac and Jacob had authority conferred upon them by their fathers, but each one of them were individually required to connect with heaven. Only through that personal contact with heaven were their calling and election, sealing power and covenant established.[95] It is for this reason it is written "the God of Abraham, God of Isaac, God of Jacob,"[96] and not the God of Abraham, Isaac, and Jacob. God appeared to and covenanted with each of them.[97] The covenant with one did not allow their chosen son and heir to become qualified without also connecting to heaven. Inheritance from a righteous father will not accomplish it. The power is without father and mother, and comes directly from God. Therefore, the claim

---

[93] Genesis 26: 2-4.

[94] Genesis 28: 10-22.

[95] D&C 121: 36-37.

[96] See Matt. 22: 32; Luke 20: 37; Exo. 4: 5.

[97] See Exo. 6: 3; Lev. 26: 42.

~~made by Brigham Young that Joseph Smith had the capacity to~~ ~~confer such power independent of the Lord's~~ direct involvement is a marvelous, even unprecedented claim. It would be the first time the heavenly gift came from a man, not heaven. It would also be the first time a man who had not had the heavens open to him was given control of sealing keys and the fullness of the priesthood. Of course, this cannot be the case because as we have seen these rights are inseparably connected with the opening of heaven.[98]

In 1847, Brigham Young publicly explained his understanding of the keys he obtained in these words: "an apostle is the Highest office and authority that there is in the Church and Kingdom God on the earth. From whom did Joseph receive his authority? From just such men as sit around me here (pointing to the Twelve Apostles that sat with him.) Peter, James and John were Apostles, and there was no noise about their being seers and revelators though those gifts were among them. Joseph Smith gave unto me and my brethren (the Twelve) all the Priesthood keys, power and authority which he had and those are the powers which belong to the Apostleship." (*The Complete Discourses of Brigham Young.* Edited by Richard S. VanWagoner. Salt Lake City: Signature Books, 2009, Vol. 1, p. 241.) This explanation is misleading because Brigham Young was not ordained an Apostle by Joseph Smith. He was ordained by the Three Witnesses to the Book of Mormon. All three participated in the ordination. There is no indication Joseph Smith joined in the ordination, and some evidence against it. Joseph said, "the first business of the meeting was, for the Three Witnesses of the Book of Mormon, to pray, each one, and then proceed to

---

[98] "That the rights of the priesthood are inseparably connected with the powers of heaven, and that the powers of heaven cannot be controlled nor handled only upon the principles of righteousness." (D&C 121: 36.)

choose twelve men." The three prayed, chose, then "the Three
Witnesses laid their hands upon each one's head and prayed."[99]
Joseph does not include himself as a participant in his description.
No one recorded that Joseph helped to ordain the Twelve. While
it is unknown which of the three ordained Brigham Young to be
an Apostle, it is likely David Whitmer was voice.[100] This ordination
occurred on February 14, 1835, more than a year before the April
3, 1836 appearances of Christ, Moses, Elias and Elijah in the
Kirtland Temple. Therefore, if Brigham Young's possession of
keys reckons from his ordination to the Apostleship as he originally
explained, and if it is related to the "sealing power" given by Elijah
as the current LDS position claims, then the dates contradict the
claim. He could not have received keys in 1835 which the church
claims came into Joseph's possession a year later.

Brigham Young was not kept from obtaining the fullness of
priesthood, including sealing power. He was invited to obtain it, as
set out earlier in this book. After confirming the Apostleship on
the first Twelve, you will recall Oliver Cowdery gave a charge to
the Twelve which included the following:

> You have been ordained to this holy Priesthood,
> you have received it from those who have the power and
> authority from an angel; you are to preach the Gospel to
> every nation. Should you in the least degree come short of
> your duty, great will be your condemnation; for the greater
> the calling the greater the transgression. I therefore warn
> you to cultivate great humility; for I know the pride of the
> human heart. Beware, lest the flatterers of the world lift
> you up; beware, lest your affections be captivated by

---

[99] *DHC* 2: 186-87.

[100] See *DHC* footnote beginning on p. 187.

worldly objects. Let your ministry be first. Remember, the souls of men are committed to your charge; and if you mind your calling, you shall always prosper.

You have been indebted to other men, in the first instance, for evidence; on that you have acted; but it is necessary that you receive a testimony from heaven for yourselves; so that you can bear testimony to the truth of the Book of Mormon, and that you have seen the face of God. That is more than the testimony of an angel. When the proper time arrives, you shall be able to bear this testimony to the world. When you bear testimony that you have seen God, this testimony God will never suffer to fall, but will bear you out; although many will not give heed, yet others will. You will therefore see the necessity of getting this testimony from heaven.

Never cease striving until you have seen God face to face. Strengthen your faith; cast off your doubts, your sins, and all your unbelief; and nothing can prevent you from coming to God. **Your ordination is not full and complete till God has laid His hand upon you. We require as much to qualify us as did those who have gone before us; God is the same. If the Savior in former days laid His hands upon His disciples, why not in latter days?**[101] (Emphasis added.)

The ordination as an Apostle, that Brigham Young incorrectly attributed to Joseph Smith, was by the Three Witnesses, and it contemplated a necessary further ordination to make it complete. But the further ordination was not to come from Joseph, nor the Three Witnesses. It would be directly from Him who had the right to confer the Apostleship with power. Brigham Young never

---

[101]*DHC* 2: 195-196.

claimed such an ordination ever happened. Quite the contrary, he claimed it did not happen.

Twenty-four years later, Brigham Young said he still hoped to have that experience. He made this public report to the saints on his unsuccessful effort to have a meeting with the Lord:

> I have flattered myself, if I am as faithful as I know how to be to my God, and my brethren, and to all my covenants, and faithful in the discharge of my duty, when I have lived to be as old as was Moses when the Lord appeared to him, that perhaps I then may hold communion with the Lord, as did Moses. I am not now in that position, though I know much more than I did twenty, ten, or five years ago. But have I yet lived to the state of perfection that I can commune in person with the Father and the Son at my will and pleasure? No,-though I hold myself in readiness that he can wield me at his will and pleasure. If I am faithful until I am eighty years of age, perhaps the Lord will appear to me and personally dictate me in the management of his Church and people. A little over twenty years, and if I am faithful, perhaps I will obtain that favour with my Father and God.[102]

It was believed the Lord appeared to Moses when he was eighty, which is the reason for the comment "if I am faithful until I am eighty years of age." Brigham died age 77.[103]

Three years later, in 1862, Brigham Young reaffirmed he never had any being, angelic or otherwise, from a higher sphere speak with him. He continued to hope if he lived to eighty it might happen:

---

[102] *JD* 7: 243.

[103] He was born June 1, 1801 and died August 29, 1877.

I think it likely that after a while I may be able to so humble myself and become like a little child, as to be taught more fully by the Heavens. Perhaps, when I am eighty years of age, I may be able to talk with some Being of a higher sphere than this. Moses saw the glory of God at that age, and held converse with better beings than he had formerly conversed with. I hope and trust that by the time I am that age I shall also be counted worthy to eujoy [sic] the same privilege.[104]

Therefore Brigham Young's claim to have received the sealing power when he was ordained an Apostle is completely dependent on the Three Witnesses' ordination in 1835. That ordination came a year prior to the 1836 visit of Elijah. Even if a man can confer this power, the story Brigham Young told cannot support his claim.

The church's teaching connecting Elijah to the sealing power is not justified by Section 110. In the revelation, Elijah does not confer, ordain or set apart anyone to anything. Doctrine & Covenants Section 110 has been interpreted with a conclusion already in mind. With that conclusion, the words are read to mean something different than what they actually say. The problem can be traced to Orson Pratt who reasoned backwards in his August 29, 1852 sermon quoted above. He dated Section 132 when it was recorded in 1843 instead of when it was actually revealed. The result is Brother Pratt (and the church thereafter) assumed Section 110 (Elijah's visit) came first and Section 132 (Joseph's calling and election and sealing power) came later. In fact, Section 132 was in 1829, much earlier than the 1836 Section 110. Pratt incorrectly concluded and taught Section 132 reconfirmed in 1843 that Joseph got sealing power in 1836. Or, in other words, the Lord confirmed

---

[104]*JD* 10: 23.

in Nauvoo that the 1836 Kirtland Temple visits had bestowed sealing power on Joseph. Instead, the opposite is true: The 1836 Kirtland Temple appearance confirmed what had been received by Joseph in 1829. Read the account of Elijah's visit again:

> After this vision had closed, another great and glorious vision burst upon us; for Elijah the prophet, who was taken to heaven without tasting death, stood before us, and said: Behold, the time has fully come, which was spoken of by the mouth of Malachi--testifying that he [Elijah] should be sent, before the great and dreadful day of the Lord come-- To turn the hearts of the fathers to the children, and the children to the fathers, lest the whole earth be smitten with a curse-- Therefore, the keys of this dispensation are committed into your hands; and by this ye may know that the great and dreadful day of the Lord is near, even at the doors. (D&C 110: 13-16, brackets in original.)

Rather than ordaining or conferring something, Elijah made a statement about what Joseph had previously received. Elijah is the punctuation at the end of prior events. The "keys of this dispensation are committed into your hands" is a statement about what was already there. The sealing authority had been given to Joseph earlier. When it was given can be fixed somewhat because Joseph used the power to seal on December 27, 1832.[105] Joseph could not seal up unto eternal life in the celestial kingdom using the

---

[105]The first portion of Section 88 was received on December 27, 1832. It is recorded in Revelation Book 1, and can be found on pp. 292 (holographic) and 293 (typeset) of *The Joseph Smith Papers: Revelations and Translations Manuscript Revelation Books*. Edited by Robin S. Jensen, Robert J. Woodford and Steven C. Harper. Salt Lake City: The Church Historian's Press, 2009.

Holy Spirit of Promise[106] unless he held sealing power. Nor could he give another person membership in the Church of the Firstborn unless he held the power to seal. (D&C 88: 3-5.) Therefore, Elijah did not confer the sealing power upon Joseph, but he did establish that the process of delivering keys had been completed by 1836. At which point Joseph was in possession of all that was to come to him as part of his dispensation of the Gospel.

Brigham Young was correct about who should lead the church after Joseph's death. The Twelve Apostles were entitled to lead the church. Although no one mentioned Section 107, that revelation confirms the Twelve have equal authority in the church with the First Presidency.[107] The church has the right to function as a complete organization, including the offices of patriarch, apostle, seventy, high priest, elder, bishop, priest, teacher, deacon, and member. It has the right to sustain by common consent individuals to those various offices. Once sustained, they form the sole authorized leadership in the church. No one is entitled to displace them. Sidney Rigdon's offer may have recognized Joseph Smith's unique and towering status, but it was not his right to claim leadership over the church in Joseph's absence. That belonged (and still belongs) to the Twelve as soon as the church sustains them to their office.

All of this raises the question of whether Joseph Smith died before he conferred the keys he held upon another. It also raises the question of whether the church lost something vital when

---

[106]The phrase "Holy Spirit of promise" is used in D&C 132: 19. The same phrase is used to seal up to eternal life in D&C 88: 3. Both contexts required the sealing power.

[107]D&C 107: 22-24.

Joseph was taken. It is clear the church was offered the fullness of what Joseph possessed. In the only significant revelation received in Nauvoo, the Lord offered to give the church the fullness. However, it would require the saints to first build a temple. The Lord explained a temple was required[108] for such a transfer of priesthood to take place. And, when the temple was built, the Lord would be the one who would confer priesthood power on the saints, for He expected to dwell there.[109] Had the temple been built, and the Lord come to dwell there, the "fullness of the priesthood" that was promised would have been given by Him to the Saints. However, Joseph Smith died before the temple was completed to the second floor. Joseph Smith conducted no higher ordinances in the Nauvoo Temple. The Lord never visited the building. Nevertheless the church repeats Brigham Young's claim that the fullness was given by Joseph Smith (not the Lord) in ceremonies conducted in the upper floor of Joseph Smith's red brick store in Nauvoo, not in the still incomplete temple. Section 124 declared the only place the fullness could be passed was in the temple. The promised fullness, if it came as the church now claims, was not passed to the Saints in the manner Section 124 commanded. The post-Nauvoo church narrative presumes the keys passed. The claims are made because the church starts with a conclusion. If you proceed from the conclusion that the fullness of the priesthood, and all the keys were passed from Joseph to the Twelve, then the history must be written to support the conclusion. In the traditional narrative, therefore, the fullness and keys passed in Joseph's red

---

[108]D&C 124: 28.

[109]D&C 124: 24.

brick store. If you leave the conclusion open until the end, then you probably reach a different outcome.

It is clear Joseph's death did not end the Lord's plan for Latter-day Saints. The Book of Mormon reaffirms the gentile church[110] will remain part of God's plan from the moment of the restoration until the New Jerusalem is built. No matter what turns we take, the root of the church originates in the heavenly gift. Its destiny will roll forward according to the mind of the Lord, whether the members fully keep, or allow to pass away that heavenly gift.

---

[110]The Church of Jesus Christ of Latter-day Saints is identified with the "gentiles." (D&C 109: 60.) All the prophecies of the Book of Mormon upon the gentiles are references to what the latter-day gentile church will accomplish (or fail to accomplish). There is much left to happen, and The Church of Jesus Christ of Latter-day Saints will be directly involved for some time yet in the Lord's handiwork.

Chapter 4

SUFFICIENT TIME

Central to all phases of Mormonism is the concept of sealing power or keys. Having the power to seal on earth and in heaven is critical to Mormonism's claim to offer salvation, and exaltation for its followers. Brigham Young claimed to have received those keys from Joseph Smith. He initially explained they were inherently part of the Apostleship. Later he would claim the power came at the time of Elijah's visit to the Kirtland Temple.

As we have seen, the sealing power did not originate in the Apostleship, nor when Elijah appeared in the Kirtland Temple. It was originally given by the early 1830's after Joseph received, and lived the law of plural marriage. This law was a terrible test for him. He obeyed even though it required personal sacrifice to do so. As a result, he qualified and received the sealing power. If I am right, this happened in 1829, or if the majority of LDS historians are

right, in 1831.[111] The sealing power is received in connection with
being sealed up to eternal life, having calling and election made
sure, and becoming a son of Abraham, Isaac and Jacob, as
explained to Joseph in the revelation conferring this power.[112]

The conditions for receiving this power are always the same.[113]
Latter-day Saints tend to reason backward on this issue. Since the
church claims the sealing power, then it forces the conclusion that
the power was successfully transmitted from Joseph Smith to
Brigham Young, and so on, to the present time. With questions of
significant importance, however, reasoning backward is not always
advisable.[114]

After Joseph lived the requirement to take plural wives, he was
proven worthy to receive the sealing power, sometime between
1831 and September 1832. However, by 1832 the saints came
under condemnation because of their failure to keep the covenant
revealed in the Book of Mormon.[115] By 1841, the fullness of the
priesthood had been suspended or "lost" from Joseph Smith. He

---

[111]"Though the revelation was first committed to writing on July 12,
1843, considerable evidence suggests that the principle of plural marriage
was revealed to Joseph Smith more than a decade before in connection
with his study of the Bible (see JOSEPH SMITH TRANSLATION OF
THE BIBLE), probably in early 1831." (*Encyclopedia of Mormonism*, p.
1092.)

[112]See D&C 132: 45-50.

[113]See D&C 130: 20-21.

[114]I wrote a chapter on this kind of dangerous religious error in *Eighteen
Verses* discussing Mosiah 12: 15. (Snuffer, Denver C. *Eighteen Verses*. Salt
Lake City: Mill Creek Press, 2007. See Chapter 9, Prospering in the Land,
pp. 162-180.)

[115]See D&C 84: 54-57, received in September, 1832.

was no longer authorized to use that fullness on behalf of the church.[116] The details of how it was taken have not been preserved. But the conduct of the Saints in Missouri, including the vigilante activities of Dr. Sampson Avard,[117] were part of the reason for their condemnation. The church should not ignore our own responsibilities in causing the Missouri violence. Nor should we disconnect it from the condemnation revealed in Section 84.

It is hard to reconsider some points in our history. One terrible, almost incomprehensible moment happened in Missouri, when the saints were expelled by mobs acting with approval from the state. Our pride wants us to be the innocent victims of unrighteous and wicked outsiders. But the events are not so one-sided.

The suggestion there would be further violence came from inside the Mormon community. President Sidney Rigdon began by threatening dissenters from the church. On June 17, 1838 he delivered a sermon which threatened the "apostates" still living in the Mormon communities. Although a complete version of the talk no longer exists, one recent account explains the sermon:

> Mormon Reed Peck, who heard it, claims that the address was rabid and quoted Rigdon as stating that members of the Church who lose the faith are as salt that has lost its savor and "it is the duty of the Saints to trample them under their feet." John Corrill, who also heard the speech, reported: "President Rigdon delivered from the pulpit what I call the 'Salt Sermon:' 'If the salt have lost its savour, it is thenceforth good for nothing but to be cast out and

---

[116]See D&C 124: 28.

[117]The full extent of Joseph Smith's early authorization of this conduct is not known. Even Joseph's journal may have been compromised on that question, because George Reynolds kept the journal and was a Danite supporter. (See Bushman, *Rough Stone Rolling*, pp. 349-353.)

trodden under the feet of men,' was his text; and although he did nto call names in his sermon, yet it was plainly understood that he meant the dissenters or those who had denied the faith. He indirectly accused some of them with crime." (Gentry, Leland H. and Compton, Todd M. *Fire and Sword A History of the Latter-day Saints in Northern Missouri, 1836-1839*. Salt Lake City: Greg Kofford Books, 2011, pp. 99-100. Footnotes omitted.)

A year later, his rhetoric elevated further still. He changed the target from Mormon dissidents to non-Mormons. He first introduced the idea of extermination or violent expulsion from Missouri. Non-believers were targeted for violent expulsion. When the sad expulsion of Mormons came the following winter, the outcome was the very judgment President Rigdon first threatened to impose on outsiders.

Sidney Rigdon gave the talk when the cornerstone for the Far West Temple was set in place on July 4th, 1838. His public sermon at Far West threatened extermination of the non-Mormons, using the phrase "war of extermination."[118] His talk at the religious ceremony laying a temple cornerstone, included these direful warnings:

> We take God and all the holy angels to witness this day, that we warn all men in the name of Jesus Christ, to come on us no more forever, for from this hour, we will bear it no more, our rights shall no more be trampled on with impunity. The man or set of men, who attempts it, does it at the expense of their lives. And that mob that comes on us to disturb us; it shall be between us and them a war of extermination, for we will follow them, till the last drop of

---

[118]*Encyclopedia of Mormonism*, pp. 926, 1235. See also, Bushman, *Rough Stone Rolling*, p. 355.

their blood is spilled, or else they will have to exterminate us: for we will carry the seat of war to their own houses, and their own families, and one party or the other shall be utterly destroyed.[119]

The idea of a war of extermination, taken to the families and homes of participants, would later be borrowed from this threat and adopted by Governor Lilburn W. Boggs in the Mormon Extermination Order issued October 27, 1838. He was only accepting the form of warfare first suggested by President Sidney Rigdon against the non-Mormons. As a result, the saints were expelled from Missouri, Joseph was imprisoned in Liberty Jail from December 1, 1838 until April 6, 1839, and the church was temporarily in disarray. The church relocated to Commerce, Illinois. There they received favorable, even sympathetic treatment from the surrounding communities, and the Illinois State Legislature. Taking advantage of that sympathy they established the city of Nauvoo on the banks of the Mississippi.

In the aftermath of the Missouri difficulties, Joseph approached the Lord to make acknowledgments, and an offer to Him. Joseph acknowledged the failure of the saints to obtain their inheritance and establish Zion, and he apparently offered his life in exchange

---

[119] *Oration, Delivered by Mr. S. Rigdon, on the 4th of July, 1838. At Far West, Caldwell County, Missouri.* Far West, printed at the Journal Office, p. 12.

for another chance.[120] The Lord accepted both his acknowledgment and his offer.[121]

Most significantly, the revelation confirmed there was still the chance for the saints to have another opportunity to gain a fullness of the priesthood, with all that implied. To qualify, they were required to prove they desired it above all else. It is always required for God's people to sacrifice all things.[122] The Lord set a task that allowed the saints to prove they were willing to make the sacrifices required to obtain the necessary faith for His fullness:

> And again, verily I say unto you, let all my saints come from afar. And send ye swift messengers, yea, chosen messengers, and say unto them: Come ye, with all your gold, and your silver, and your precious stones, and with all your antiquities; and with all who have knowledge of antiquities, that will come, may come, and bring the box-tree, and the fir-tree, and the pine-tree, together with all the precious trees of the earth; And with iron, with copper, and with brass, and with zinc, and with all your precious things of the earth; and build a house to my name, for the Most High to dwell therein. For there is not a place found on earth that he may come to and restore again that

---

[120]What was offered is not explained either in the revelation or by Joseph Smith. Subsequent events, however, make it clear what Joseph offered for this additional chance to complete the restoration and have the saints receive the fullness of the priesthood. He offered, and ultimately forfeited, his life.

[121]"Verily, thus saith the Lord unto you, my servant Joseph Smith, I am well pleased with your offering and acknowledgments, which you have made; for unto this end have I raised you up, that I might show forth my wisdom through the weak things of the earth." (D&C 124: 1.)

[122]See Lecture 6, *Lectures on Faith*.

which was lost unto you, or which he hath taken away,
even the fulness of the priesthood. (D&C 124: 25-28.)

The saints were assigned to build a house where the Lord could
come to bestow the fullness. The fullness of the priesthood could
only be given to the saints inside a house belonging to God; a place
He could come. The Lord's presence was necessary for the
fullness. "There is not a place found on earth that he may come to
and restore again that which was lost unto you." It is necessary for
the Lord to come because only He can confer the fullness of the
priesthood. He granted such a fullness to Joseph. He intended all
qualified saints to have it. According to the revelation, until there
was a house for Him to visit, built through the sacrifices of the
saints to whom the fullness was to be passed, it could not be
conferred.

  The language is unequivocal. If the fullness was to be "restored,"
it required the Nauvoo Temple to be completed first. This has a
great deal to do with what the "fullness of the priesthood"
includes. It does not get transferred by men, or the wishes of men,
but by the Lord Himself. For this to happen, sacred space must be
established by those who are worthy to enter the Lord's presence,
and receive from Him the keys to this power through their sacrifice
and obedience. As illustrated by Nephi, in Helaman 10, it is not
given unless a man has proven he will sacrifice everything,
including his own life, to obey the Lord. He must qualify to have
his calling and election made sure. That is the only kind of faith
that allows a man to possess the power to seal on earth, and in
heaven. The Lord first proves the man through sacrifice. The only
acceptable sacrifice is life itself. Only when a man has proven he
will lay down his life to obey God, will he qualify to receive the
power to seal. This guarantees the power will be used solely in

accordance with the will of the Lord. Like Nephi, such a person will never "ask that which is contrary to [God's] will." (Hel. 10: 5.) It involves the kind of trust that even when granted that power, the possessor waits on the Lord to direct how it is to be used.

Even when such a man who has gained the fullness hears the Lord declare to him: "I am God. Behold, I declare it unto thee in the presence of mine angels, that ye shall have power over this people, and shall smite the earth with famine, and with pestilence, and destruction, according to the wickedness of this people," (*Id.*, v. 6.) – even then the man will only ask the Lord, never command in His name using His power. Such men are meek like Moses.[123] Only a meek man can be trusted with such power. The thought of judging or condemning another man to damnation is abhorrent to all meek souls.[124] To obtain it they must necessarily enter into the presence of the Lord. Only there do men find rest.[125] Building the Nauvoo Temple was not an option; it was essential. It was the only environment where it would be possible for the transfer of the "fullness of the priesthood" by the Lord to others, thereby allowing them also to 'enter into His rest.'

The revelation goes on to explain:

> But I command you, all ye my saints, to build a house unto me; and I grant unto you a sufficient time to build a house unto me; and during this time your baptisms shall be

---

[123]Num 12: 3: "Now the man Moses was very meek, above all the men which were upon the face of the earth."

[124]Mosiah 28: 3: "Now they were desirous that salvation should be declared to every creature, for they could not bear that any human soul should perish; yea, even the very thoughts that any soul should endure endless torment did cause them to quake and tremble."

[125]D&C 84: 24.

acceptable unto me. But behold, at the end of this appointment your baptisms for your dead shall not be acceptable unto me; and if you do not these things at the end of the appointment ye shall be rejected as a church, with your dead, saith the Lord your God. (D&C 124: 31-32.)

The revelation required the construction of the Nauvoo Temple. It was a "command" to the saints. There was a set time. If at the end of that time the temple was not constructed, the words are clear: "ye shall be rejected as a church, with your dead, saith the Lord your God."

It is critical to know when the time period of that "appointment" ended. Latter-day teaching assumes the appointment was kept, and the condition met. The presumption is based on the fact that a small group of saints left behind to complete the work on the temple after the church abandoned the site, dedicated it just before they also abandoned the city.

The leadership, along with most of the members, left Nauvoo in early February 1846, but "a special crew stayed behind and completed the temple. Three months later the building was considered complete and was publicly dedicated on May 1, 1846."[126]

Joseph died June 27, 1844. No one claims the Nauvoo Temple was completed by that time. The outer walls of the second floor were not even finished at the time of Joseph's death. The question of whether or not the "sufficient time" for the "appointment"

---

[126] *Encyclopedia of Mormonism*, p. 1002. Note the carefully phrased description: "considered complete." It was never fully completed because although the roof was repaired after a fire, the attic space was not.

ended at Joseph's death is important to answer. In Nauvoo at the time of Joseph's death, there were completed homes built, a Masonic Temple, and manufacturing and retail facilities, but the Nauvoo Temple had been neglected. It was nowhere near completed when Joseph and Hyrum died. It was not possible to dedicate the building until two years following Joseph and Hyrum's death.

The revelation giving an opportunity for the saints to receive a fullness explains:

> For verily I say unto you, that after you have had sufficient time to build a house to me, ... For therein are the keys of the holy priesthood ordained, that you may receive honor and glory. And after this time, your baptisms for the dead, by those who are scattered abroad, are not acceptable unto me, saith the Lord." (D&C 124: 33-35.)

The "keys of the holy priesthood" are "ordained" to be received exclusively in such a "house" belonging to God, and built through sacrifice. The Nauvoo Temple was never complete enough to use for that purpose while Joseph was alive.

Two and a half years after the revelation was given, Joseph reminded the saints they needed to complete the Temple. "He said that he could not reveal the fullness of these things until the Temple is completed[.]"[127] If the saints seemed unmoved by a

---

[127] *The Nauvoo Diaries of William Clayton, 1842-1846, Abridged.* Salt Lake City: Privately Published, 2010, p. 23, entry of July 16, 1843. Clayton's entry for that day can also be found in *WJS*, p. 233; where footnote 11 (found on pp. 293-294) offers an explanation of how this "fullness" was nothing more than "the relationship of the temple endowment and the temple ordinance of marriage for time and all eternity." That explanation, however, is unsupported and unsupportable. It reflects the view which reads into events a favorable outcome, rather than taking the events as they occurred.

fading opportunity to receive what was offered to them, Joseph Smith was not. He returned to the issue again early in 1844, this time warning the saints the opportunity might be lost to them:

> . . . And I would to God that this temple was now done, that we might go into it, and go to work and improve our time, and make use of the seals while they are on earth.
>
> The Saints have not too much time to save and redeem their dead, and gather together their living relatives, that they may be saved also, before the earth will be smitten, and the consumption decreed falls upon the world.
>
> I would advise all the Saints to go with their might and gather together all their living relatives to this place, that they may be sealed and saved, that they may be prepared against the day that the destroying angel goes forth; and if the whole Church should go to with all their might to save their dead, seal their posterity, and gather their living friends, and spend none of their time in behalf of the world, they would hardly get through before night would come, when no man can work; and my only trouble at the present time is concerning ourselves, that the Saints will be divided, broken up, and scattered, before we get our salvation secure; for there are so many fools in the world for the devil to operate upon, it gives him the advantage oftentimes." (*TPJS*, p. 330-331.)

Interestingly, only Wilford Woodruff recorded the content of that talk. Willard Richards reports only that a talk was given, the weather was "somewhat unpleasant," and the subject was "sealing the hearts of the fathers to the children."[128] Joseph's warning that there was a limited time to "make use of the seals while they are on earth" seems to have gone unheard by those in Nauvoo, and later

---

[128]See *WJS* pp. 317-319.

their descendants. Even the leadership of the church at the time were tone deaf to Joseph's alarm.

The importance of the limited time remaining for the "appointment" to be kept is reiterated in the revelation:

> And ye shall build it on the place where you have contemplated building it, for that is the spot which I have chosen for you to build it. If ye labor with all your might, I will consecrate that spot that it shall be made holy. And if my people will hearken unto my voice, and unto the voice of my servants whom I have appointed to lead my people, behold, verily I say unto you, they shall not be moved out of their place. But if they will not hearken to my voice, nor unto the voice of these men whom I have appointed, they shall not be blest, because they pollute mine holy grounds, and mine holy ordinances, and charters, and my holy words which I give unto them. And it shall come to pass that if you build a house unto my name, and do not do the things that I say, I will not perform the oath which I make unto you, neither fulfil the promises which ye expect at my hands, saith the Lord. For instead of blessings, ye, by your own works, bring cursings, wrath, indignation, and judgments upon your own heads, by your follies, and by all your abominations, which you practise before me, saith the Lord. (D&C 124: 43-48.)

The promise and the curse are linked to one another. It is all or nothing. The highest blessings men may attain were offered on the one hand, and "cursings, wrath, indignation, and judgments" were the result of rejecting the offer, on the other hand. Blessings would bring peace, the Lord's favor, a fullness of the priesthood, the power to seal on heaven and earth. With that power, Nephi was able to bring all warfare to an end by sealing the heavens.

Combatants had no choice but to submit.[129] If the saints obtained this fullness, they could have peace. The "blessings" offered were worth the sacrifice of all things.

On the other hand, cursings would bring expulsion, suffering, persecution, forfeiture of property, war and plagues. The revelation promised the Latter-day Saints God's "wrath, indignation, and judgments" in the bitter events following Joseph and Hyrum's death, if the fullness was rejected. Instead of the ability to seal the heavens and bring about peace through the Lord's intervention, they would be vulnerable to being cast out, trodden under foot, and made to wander in the wilderness.

Brigham Young, and those few others who received their "endowments" and "sealings" from Joseph Smith before his death, received them in the red brick store belonging to Joseph. The red brick store was not the house spoken of in the revelation. Nevertheless, Joseph began the Temple endowment ceremonies on May 4, 1842.[130] He began higher ordinances, now regarded as the "fullness of the priesthood," more than a year later, on September 28, 1843.[131] Nine months later he was killed. The church claims the

---

[129]See Helaman 11: 3-8.

[130]*Encyclopedia of Mormonism,* p. 456.

[131]The official LDS understanding of relevant events passing the keys from Joseph to the Twelve is well explained in this excerpt from *The Words of Joseph Smith*: "One of the major milestones, if not the major milestone, of the Latter-day work was to be the restoration of the fulness of the priesthood (D&C 124:28). The Prophet's 'mission...[was to] firmly [establish] the dispensation of the fullness of the priesthood in the last days, that all the powers of earth and hell [could] never prevail against it' (*History of the Church,* 5:140, or *Teachings,* p. 258). What was this fulness of the priesthood? The most concise but inclusive definition of the authority of the fulness of the priesthood was given by Joseph Smith

fullness of the priesthood was conferred by Joseph on a handful of church leaders in the red brick store. The Nauvoo Temple was

---

in his 10 March 1844 discourse when he said, 'Now for Elijah; the spirit, power and calling of Elijah is that ye have power to hold the keys of the revelations, ordinances, oracles, powers and endowments of the fulness of the Melchizedek Priesthood and of the Kingdom of God on the Earth and to receive, obtain and perform all the ordinances belonging to the kingdom of God...[to] have power to seal on earth and in heaven.' However, the Prophet had not as yet administered the ordinances that made men kings and priests. Brigham Young said three weeks before this discourse that no one yet in the Church had the fulness of the Melchizedek Priesthood, 'For any person to have the fullness of that priesthood, he must be a king and priest' (*History of the Church*, 5:527, which is quoted verbatim from the original source kept by Wilford Woodruff, Church Archives). These ordinances were instituted on 28 September 1843 and in the next five months were conferred on twenty men (and their wives, except for those whose names are asterisked): Hyrum Smith, Brigham Young, Heber C. Kimball, Willard Richards, Newel K. Whitney, William Marks, John Taylor, John Smith, Reynolds Cahoon, Alpheus Cutler, Orson Spencer, Orson Hyde*, Parley P. Pratt*, Wilford Woodruff, George A. Smith, Levi Richards*, Cornelius P. Lott, William W. Phelps, Isaac Morley, and Orson Pratt.* As George Q. Cannon later said,

'"Previous to his death, the Prophet Joseph manifested great anxiety to see the temple completed, as most of you who were with the Church during his day, well know. 'Hurry up the work, brethren,' he used to say, 'let us finish the temple; the Lord has a great endowment in store for you, and I am anxious that the brethren should have their endowments and receive the fullness of the Priesthood.... Then,' said he, 'the Kingdom will be established, and I do not care what shall become of me.'"

'"Prior to the completion of the Temple, [Joseph Smith] took the Twelve and certain other men, who were chosen, and bestowed upon them a holy anointing, similar to that which was received on the day of Pentecost by the Twelve, who had been told to tarry at Jerusalem. This endowment was bestowed upon the chosen few whom Joseph anointed and ordained, giving unto them the keys of the holy Priesthood, the power and authority which he himself held, to build up the Kingdom of God in all the earth and accomplish the great purposes of our Heavenly Father.'" (*WJS*, p. 306.)

years away from being finished to the point of performing any ordinance work there when he died.

Although today the keys are understood to have arrived in the Kirtland Temple, and to have been passed along in the red brick store, Brigham Young gave another explanation of how he received keys from Joseph Smith. His earliest explanation, as we already saw, was the Apostleship inherently held all the keys.[132] However, as discussed previously, Brigham Young's ordination to the Apostleship was not performed by Joseph, but the Three Witnesses.

By November following Joseph's death, the *Times and Seasons* associated passing the keys instead to the endowment ceremonies given Brigham Young and others of the Twelve.[133] That position

―――――――――――――

[132] After learning Joseph was killed, Brigham Young reports: "The first thing which I thought of was, whether Joseph had taken the keys of the kingdom with him from the earth; brother Orson Pratt sat on my left; we were both leaning back in our chairs. Bringing my hand down on my knee, I said the keys of the kingdom are right here with the Church." (*The Complete Discourses of Brigham Young, Volume 1: 1832-1852*. Edited by Richard S. Van Wagoner. Salt Lake City: Signature Books, 2009, p. 38.) "Said Joseph, 'Will you insult the Priesthood? Is that all the knowledge you have of the office of an Apostle? Do you not know that the man who receives the Apostleship, receives all the keys that ever were, or that can be, conferred upon mortal man? What are you talking about? I am astonished!' Nothing more was said about it." (*Discourses of Brigham Young*. Edited by John A. Widstoe. Salt Lake City: Deseret Book, 1954, p. 141.)

[133] Writing in support of Brigham Young's right to now lead: "He has not only had much experience with President Smith, but he has proved himself true and faithful in all things committed to his charge, until he was called to hold the keys of the kingdom of God in all the world, in connection with the Twelve: was the first to receive his endowment, from under the hands of the Prophet and Patriarch, who have leaned upon him in connection with the Twelve, for years, to bear off this kingdom in all the world, in connection with the Twelve." (*Times and Seasons*, Nov. 2, 1844.)

perhaps proves too much, because if information in the endowment alone is sufficient to pass keys, then Mormon dissidents Jerald and Sandra Tanner, who have published the various endowment ordinances and versions would hold the keys and could in turn confer them upon anyone who obtains a copy of these ceremonies from them. It cannot be the ceremonies alone which hold the "keys."

Joseph Smith, of course, had the fullness of the priesthood. It included the promise to him by God of eternal life, authority to seal on earth and in heaven, a marriage relationship which would secure for him eternally the right to have children, and a binding seal between him and "the fathers." These gave him power in his priesthood, and the ability to use the power on behalf of others. There is a difference between the power of the priesthood, and the blessings of the priesthood. Joseph's fullness gave him power. Without question he had the right to use that power to confer blessings upon others. It should be clear to everyone Joseph Smith had the right to confer blessings upon others using his priesthood. But for him to be able to transfer that power in a fullness to others seems altogether contrary to the clear conditions set by the Lord. First, it would be unprecedented for the Lord to not be personally involved. Second, the revelation (Section 124) says otherwise. As we saw above, the fullness had been "taken away" from Joseph.[134]

---

[134]The words "lost" and "taken away" as to Joseph Smith should be understood to mean he could not pass it along, not that he forfeited it as to himself. He received it by the Lord's own oath. Further, even after the church fell under condemnation, the Lord told Joseph in 1839: "hold on they way, and the priesthood shall remain with thee." (D&C 122: 9.) Joseph individually is not the same as the church collectively. Therefore what the church "lost" or had "taken away" is different from what Joseph had "remain with [him]."

To "restore again" the fullness, the saints needed to build the Nauvoo Temple. "For there is not a place found on earth that he may come to and restore again that which was lost unto you, or which he hath taken away, even the fulness of the priesthood." (*Id.*) This raises at least these questions:

-If it is the Lord who must "come to and restore again" this fullness, then do we have any record of the Lord "coming to" the red brick store to make this transfer?

-If a temple was required as the "place . . . on the earth that he may come" to make the transfer, how did the red brick store become an adequate substitute?

-If Joseph Smith was able to confer the blessings of the priesthood, using the power of his priesthood, did that extend also to conferring the power itself?

-If Joseph Smith could confer the blessings of the priesthood, but not the power of the fullness, then was the power lost when Joseph died?

-If the fullness of the priesthood ended with Joseph Smith, then Brigham Young, John Taylor, and Wilford Woodruff would have continued to hold the blessings of the priesthood through Joseph Smith's administration of the temple ceremonies to them. But President Snow received all of his temple ceremonies from Brigham Young.

-What is the difference between higher priesthood, and fullness of the priesthood?

These questions have been answered by The Church of Jesus Christ of Latter-day Saints with claims that remove any debate. The church, based on its conclusion, and not a dispassionate review of events, unequivocally affirms Joseph transferred the fullness to the

Twelve, and the keys have continued undiminished from him to the present holder of the office of president of the church.

Ever since the expulsion of church members from Nauvoo, the highest leadership positions in the church have been held by Nauvoo's proud descendants. The interpretation of these events by these proud Nauvoo descendants has become the official view. As a result of this interpretation, by this group of people, the possibility of a general rejection of the fullness by the saints in Nauvoo is never even considered.

The January 1841 revelation never defined the "appointed time." Joseph would live for 3 ½ years after the revelation. During that 3 ½ years, the saints would spread their labor for construction on a number of projects to improve their city. By the time Joseph was killed, work on the temple had only progressed to just starting construction on the second floor. Between the time of the revelation, and Joseph's death, the saints also contributed effort to build a Cultural Hall, a Seventies Hall,[135] and a Masonic Temple. In addition, commercial buildings, like the Post Office and Mercantile, Browning Home and Gunsmith Shop, Boot Shop, Bakery, Tin Shop, and Blacksmith Shop were completed. Wilford Woodruff's home was under construction and completed in 1845. Sarah Granger Kimball's completed home was the place the idea of the Relief Society was conceived. Brigham Young completed a home, and started to construct two wings as additions to it.

After Joseph's death, and his return to Nauvoo, Brigham Young learned for the first time just how important it was to complete the Nauvoo Temple. He stated, "I have learned some things I did not

---

[135]The Seventies Hall was not completed while Joseph was alive, but had been substantially completed. Formal dedication occurred in December, 1844.

know when I came home." He explained the absolute necessity for the saints to remain in Nauvoo, and not scatter. They needed to remain, and build the Temple, or they would forfeit what the Lord offered them:

> ...the counsel of the Twelve is for every family that does not belong to the Pine Company to stay here in Nauvoo and build up the Temple and get your endowments; do not scatter... they cannot give an endowment in the wilderness. If we do not carry out the plan Joseph has laid down and the pattern he has given for us to work by, we cannot get any further endowment... in that case you will not get your endowments but will sink and not rise, go to hell and not the bosom of Abraham. ...We want to build the Temple in this place, if we have to build it as the Jews built the walls fo the Temple in Jerusalem, with a sword in one hand and the trowel in the other. ...would the Lord give an endowment to a people who would be frightened away from their duty? ...if we should go into the wilderness and ask the Lord to give us an endowment, he might ask us, saying, Did I not give you rock in Nauvoo to build a Temple with? ...I want to have the faithful stay here to build the Temple and settle the city. (*The Complete Discourses of Brigham Young*. Edited by Richard S. Van Wagoner. Salt Lake City: Signature Books, 2009, 5 Vols.; Vol. 1, pp. 45-47.)

Even with Brigham Young's new appreciation of the necessity to complete the Nauvoo Temple because of Joseph's January 1841 revelation, the temple was never completed for any endowment given in Nauvoo. Only the attic of the unfinished building was used for those ceremonies. When the attic was sufficiently complete, that area was dedicated on November 30, 1845. It was in the attic of the unfinished temple the Nauvoo Temple ceremonies were offered for two months. From December 10,

1845 until February 8, 1846, more than 5,000 men and women received their endowments in the attic area of the unfinished Nauvoo Temple.[136] None of them reported the Lord came to minister there.

Within a few days of beginning the endowments, the saints were rebuked by Brigham Young for their misconduct. The attic endowments did not have the desired effect on the behavior of the participants, and Elder Young both threatened the participants, and accused them of stealing:

> [T]here are not 6 persons that have gone through these ordinances that can offer them correctly, and some has had the presumption to approach this veil, which is the most sacred ordinances that is performed in this house, and have marked the garments wrong. And levity has been used here which is not pleasing in the sight of the Lord, therefore I have shut down the gate, and came to the conclusion that when we commence again we would make a selection of such persons as are worthy and will give them their endowments first, and when they get their endowments then the remainder may get their endowment. I don't know but what I shall displease some of you, but I don't care if you I do. There are about 200 persons that are dressed today and unless I lay an embargo on the brethren we will not find garments enough to take the company through tomorrow without changing them from one to another. The Seventies have had about 18 garments made and this morning there are not more than 5 or 6 to be found. Some have taken garments and carried them off. I call such conduct stealing and it must be stopped. *(The Complete Discourses of Brigham Young*, 5 Vols.; Vol. 1, p. 114.)

---

[136] See *Nauvoo Endowment Companies, 1845-1846: A Documentary History.* Edited by Devery Scott Anderson and Gary James Bergera. Salt Lake City: Signature Books, 2005.

Still the church claims a fullness was passed to these people who not only neglected the command to build the temple, but who, when the rites became available, were accused by Brigham Young of being thieves. The highest and holiest of heavenly power apparently descended upon the unworthy. This was something which was a hitherto impossibility. Yet the proud descendants of Nauvoo claim this is nevertheless the case.

Washings, anointings, sealings and endowments continued in the Nauvoo Temple attic until the exodus began on February 8, 1846. Although incomplete as a building, its use ended February 8th. Before leaving town, members of the Twelve knelt around an altar in the temple. They asked the Lord to bless their journey, to let the temple be completed, and for the opportunity to have it formally dedicated. The Kirtland Temple dedication was accepted by cloven tongues of fire resting on the building. This was witnessed by many of the Kirtland residents.[137] The Nauvoo Temple, however, had a more physical manifestation of fire after the prayer. February 9, the day after the prayer by the Twelve asking to be able to complete the temple, an overheated stove pipe caused a fire that burned part of the roof and attic before it was extinguished. When Brigham Young returned on February 22nd, he held a meeting in the main floor assembly room. When a large crowd attended, the weight of the assembly caused damage to the floor joists, and the floor dropped between 1 and 3 inches. The cracking and jolt panicked the people, who fled outside. Elder Young was irritated by their reaction, and continued the meeting outside in the grove near the temple. "Br. Brigham spoke also and said he was surprised that

---

[137]See, e.g., *Oliver Cowdery's Kirtland Sketch Book*. Arrington (BYU Studies 23, no. 4, 1983) p. 426.

people did not know any better than to get frightened because the floor of the temple settled a little."[138] As to the fire damage, Brigham Young said, "feed the hands on the Temple- it must be finished and we mean to be in it- even if we have to put on a new roof- I say it in the name of the Lord."[139]

Work continued on the temple until the end of April when it was considered sufficiently finished to be dedicated, and then abandoned. The roof was replaced, but the attic remained unrepaired from the fire. The cracked floor joists on the main floor were never repaired. But private dedication services were nevertheless held April 30, and a public dedication on May 1, 1846. Wilford Woodruff, and Orson Hyde presided at the dedication. Wilford Woodruff thought the dedication proved Sidney Rigdon, and other critics who claimed the temple would never be repaired and completed were all wrong.[140] Orson Hyde, however, explained the real reason was to avoid condemnation under the January 1841 revelation:

> If we moved forward and finished this house we should be received and accepted as a church with our dead, but if not we should be rejected with our dead. These things have inspired and stimulated us to action in the finishing of it which through the blessing of God we have been endable [sic] to accomplish and prepared it for dedication. In doing

---

[138] *The Complete Discourses of Brigham Young*, 5 Vols.; Vol. 1, p. 127.)

[139] *Id.*

[140] *Wilford Woodruff's Journal.* Edited by Scott Kenny. Salt Lake City: Signature Books, 1983, 3: 38.

this we have only been saved as it were by the skin of our teeth.[141]

This assumption of Elder Hyde – which has been taught by all the proud descendants of Nauvoo ever since– is that what was done in Nauvoo completed the temple enough to satisfy the appointment given in the revelation. The "appointed time" apparently extended for as long as it took to get the temple to a point it could be "considered complete," without regard to any other limit set by the actual language of the revelation. This is important because hanging on this question is the continuation of the fullness of the priesthood, including sealing keys, into the institutional care of The Church of Jesus Christ of Latter-day Saints. From Brigham Young through the present, the church has maintained Elder Hyde's assertion that these keys were kept "by the skin of our teeth" by completing the Nauvoo Temple in conformity with the Lord's commandment.

It would be a completely different narrative if it were changed to read significant meaning into Joseph's "offering and acknowledgment."[142] If instead he offered to forfeit his life in exchange for more time that the saints might build an acceptable temple, then ungrateful and oblivious saints squandered a prophet's life. If Joseph died not merely to seal his testimony of the Book of Mormon and Doctrine and Covenants,[143] but also in a vain purchase of a forfeited chance for the saints to receive the Lord's presence, then his life assumes even larger significance. But

---

[141]*Id.*, 3: 43.

[142]D&C 124: 1.

[143]D&C 135: 1.

accepting that view would come at the great expense of reassessing the Nauvoo events. Joseph's name and significance would grow,[144] but the Nauvoo saints and their proud descendants would necessarily diminish. This view is unlikely to ever be accepted by a church whose leadership is filled overwhelmingly by those same proud descendants of Nauvoo. There hasn't been a single church president without Nauvoo ancestors.

As the story moves forward, other subsequent events suggest the traditional narrative has overlooked things. Therefore, we continue by looking at a change in practice and doctrine involving the sealing power claimed to have gone with Brigham Young and the Twelve Apostles in the mid-winter westward flight from Nauvoo.

---

[144]As Moroni put it: "God had a work for [Joseph] to do; and [his] name should be had for good and evil among all nations, kindreds, and tongues, or that it should be both good and evil spoken of among all people." (JS-H 1: 33.) As the Lord put it: "The ends of the earth shall inquire after they name, and fools shall have thee in derision, and hell shall rage against thee; While the pure in heart, and the wise, and the noble, and the virtuous, shall seek counsel, and authority, and blessings constantly from under thy hand." (D&C 122: 1-2.)

Chapter 5

SLAY HIM FOR THE OATH'S SAKE

he 1841 Nauvoo revelation stated the saints were required to build a temple if they expected to obtain the fullness of the priesthood. If the events in Nauvoo discussed in the previous chapter indicate a rejection of the fullness by the Nauvoo gentiles, then Section 124, along with other scriptures predicts a gentile rejection of the Lord's offer to restore a fullness of the priesthood. Christ prophesied in the Book of Mormon the gentiles would reject the fullness of His Gospel nearly two millennia previously.[145] "At that day when the Gentiles shall sin against my gospel, and shall reject the fulness of my gospel, and shall be lifted up in the pride of their hearts above all nations, and above all the people of the whole earth, and shall be filled with all manner of lyings, and of deceits, and of mischiefs, and all manner of hypocrisy, and murders, and priestcrafts, and whoredoms, and of secret abominations; and if they shall do all those things, and

---

[145]Christ prefaces the prophecy by explaining "the Father commanded" Him to deliver it.

shall reject the fulness of my gospel, behold, saith the Father, I will bring the fulness of my gospel from among them." (3 Ne. 16: 10.)

If the fullness was rejected in Nauvoo, then the only surprise is how quickly it occurred. The fact it was to occur, however, should be expected. To decide if the fullness was lost, we do not need to rely exclusively on the events in Nauvoo as evidence. Subsequent events should also disclose if there were "cursings" instead of "blessings."[146] We should also be able to find "lyings... deceits... mischiefs, and all manner of hypocrisy, and murders, and priestcrafts, and whoredoms, and . . . secret combinations" as outlined in Christ's prophecy. If there is no evidence of lyings, deceits, mischiefs, hypocrisy, murders, priestcrafts, whoredoms and secret combinations in post- Nauvoo events, then we can presume the fullness, which "shall" be rejected by the gentiles according to Christ, is yet future.

We need to begin with Joseph Smith, and events that took place some ten years before his death. His example and teaching about violence are relevant to whether "murders" were committed by the gentile church established through him. Joseph Smith, like Moses, was a meek man.[147] He raised an army twice, but never used it to fight a single battle. He was the victim of violence, but not the perpetrator of it.

The first army Joseph raised was dubbed "Zion's Camp." It was organized in 1834 to rescue those Latter-day Saints who were under siege in Independence, Missouri. Zion's Camp marched from May to June, traveling from Kirtland, Ohio to Jackson County, Missouri.

---

[146]D&C 124: 48.

[147]See Numbers 12: 3.

Mormon settlers had been driven from Jackson County the preceding year, and were scattered to the north, in Clay County. Zion's Camp was organized as a militia to rescue the saints, and put them back in possession of their property. However, after a 900 mile march the only battles Zion's Camp fought were with cholera. The only battle the Missourians fought was with the weather. The two sides never fought one another.

Joseph did not use his militia for war. He would not even allow his followers to kill the rattlesnakes found inside their evening encampment. He stopped the men who were about to kill the poisonous snakes, and admonished:

> Let them alone-don't hurt them! How will the serpent ever lose his venom, while the servants of God possess the same disposition, and continue to make war upon it? Men must become harmless, before the brute creation; and when men lose their vicious dispositions and cease to destroy the animal race, the lion and the lamb can dwell together, and the sucking child can play with the serpent in safety. (DHC 2: 71.)

Although an armed militia, Zion's camp never engaged in armed conflicts, poison snake abatement, or the killing of any creature during the 1834 campaign. Joseph explained: "I exhorted the brethren not to kill a serpent, bird, or an animal of any kind during our journey unless it became necessary in order to preserve ourselves from hunger." (Id.)

There were, however, conflicts between Joseph's followers inside the camp. Despite his effort to obtain peace among them, bickering persisted throughout the journey. Joseph warned the saints that "in consequence of their misconduct a scourge would strike the camp. His words proved prophetic when, at the conclusion of their journey on June 23 at Rush Creek in Clay

County, Missouri, cholera struck the camp. Some sixty-eight men were afflicted, and thirteen of them, and one woman died of the disease."[148]

When the opportunity for combat finally came, Zion's Camp did not fire a shot. The Missouri mob came to fight against them, but were instead battered by a nighttime storm. Joseph's diary described it in these words:

> We traveled but a short distance when one wagon broke down, and the wheels ran off from others; and there seemed to be many things to hinder our progress, although we strove with all diligence to speed our way forward. This night we camped on an elevated piece of land between Little Fishing and Big Fishing rivers, which streams were formed by seven small streams or branches.
>
> As we halted and were making preparations for the night, five men armed with guns rode into our camp, and told us we should "see hell before morning;" and their accompanying oaths partook of all the malice of demons. They told us that sixty men were coming from Richmond, Ray county, and seventy more from Clay county, to join the Jackson county mob, who had sworn our utter destruction.   During this day, the Jackson county mob, to the number of about two hundred, made arrangements to cross the Missouri river, above the mouth of Fishing river, at Williams' ferry, into Clay county, and be ready to meet the Richmond mob near Fishing River ford, for our utter destruction; but after the first scow load of about forty had been set over the river, the scow in returning was met by a squall, and had great difficulty in reaching the Jackson side by dark.
>
> When these five men were in our camp, swearing vengeance, the wind, thunder, and rising cloud indicated an

---

[148]*Encyclopedia of Mormonism*, p. 1629.

approaching storm, and in a short time after they left the rain and hail began to fall. The storm was tremendous; wind and rain, hail and thunder met them in great wrath, and soon softened their direful courage, and frustrated all their designs to "kill Joe Smith and his army." Instead of continuing a cannonading which they commenced when the sun was about one hour high, they crawled under wagons, into hollow trees, and filled one old shanty, till the storm was over, when their ammunition was soaked, and the forty in Clay county were extremely anxious in the morning to return to Jackson, having experienced the pitiless pelting of the storm all night; and as soon as arrangements could be made, this "forlorn hope" took the "back track" for Independence, to join the main body of the mob, fully satisfied, as were those survivors of the company who were drowned, that when Jehovah fights they would rather be absent. The gratification is too terrible.

Very little hail fell in our camp, but from half a mile to a mile around, the stones or lumps of ice cut down the crops of corn and vegetation generally, even cutting limbs from trees, while the trees, themselves were twisted into withes by the wind. The lightning flashed incessantly. [sic] which caused it to be so light in our camp through the night, that we could discern the most minute objects; and the roaring of the thunder was tremendous. The earth trembled and quaked, the rain fell in torrents, and, united, it seemed as if the mandate of vengeance had gone forth from the God of battles, to protect His servants from the destruction of their enemies, for the hail fell on them and not on us, and we suffered no harm, except the blowing down of some of our tents, and getting wet; while our enemies had holes made in their hats, and otherwise received damage, even the breaking of their rifle stocks, and the fleeing of their horses through fear and pain. (*DHC* 2: 103-105.)

Those holding the sealing power have, at the behest of the Lord, the elements fight their battles for them. This was the power Moses called upon to defeat the Pharaoh.[149] This was the power that protected Enoch's City.[150] It will be this same power that will defend the New Jerusalem.[151] If the people who build the New

---

[149]"And the Lord said unto Moses, Stretch out thine hand over the sea, that the waters may come again upon the Egyptians, upon their chariots, and upon their horsemen. And Moses stretched forth his hand over the sea, and the sea returned to his strength when the morning appeared; and the Egyptians fled against it; and the Lord overthrew the Egyptians in the midst of the sea. And the waters returned, and covered the chariots, and the horsemen, and all the host of Pharaoh that came into the sea after them; there remained not so much as one of them. But the children of Israel walked upon dry land in the midst of the sea; and the waters were a wall unto them on their right hand, and on their left. Thus the LORD saved Israel that day out of the hand of the Egyptians; and Israel saw the Egyptians dead upon the sea shore." (Exo. 14: 26-30.)

[150]"And so great was the faith of Enoch that he led the people of God, and their enemies came to battle against them; and he spake the word of the Lord, and the earth trembled, and the mountains fled, even according to his command; and the rivers of water were turned out of their course; and the roar of the lions was heard out of the wilderness; and all nations feared greatly, so powerful was the word of Enoch, and so great was the power of the language which God had given him." (Moses 7: 13.)

[151]"And it shall be called the New Jerusalem, a land of peace, a city of refuge, a place of safety for the saints of the Most High God; And the glory of the Lord shall be there, and the terror of the Lord also shall be there, insomuch that the wicked will not come unto it, and it shall be called Zion. And it shall come to pass among the wicked, that every man that will not take his sword against his neighbor must needs flee unto Zion for safety. And there shall be gathered unto it out of every nation under heaven; and it shall be the only people that shall not be at war one with another. And it shall be said among the wicked: Let us not go up to battle against Zion, for the inhabitants of Zion are terrible; wherefore we cannot stand... For when the Lord shall appear he shall be terrible unto them, that fear may seize upon them, and they shall stand afar off and

Jerusalem are not protected by power over the elements, they cannot be a restoration of the ancient order. The City of Enoch, and the New Jerusalem are sister-cities. They must practice the same religion, possess the same power, and be governed the same way. Joseph Smith held the power to enable him to establish that order again. As a result, those who threatened destruction against Joseph's people were not challenged by the men of Zion's Camp. They were instead repelled by the elements.

The second army at Joseph's command was the Nauvoo Legion. This military force marched, paraded, and became an extension of the Illinois State Militia. At one point they numbered 5,000 men, and were the largest military force in the state.[152] Yet when mobs gathered and Nauvoo threatened, and hostilities were already begun, Joseph Smith did not use the Nauvoo Legion to protect Nauvoo; he instead surrendered to the state authorities. Then, upon request from the Governor, he sent an order for the Nauvoo Legion to surrender their arms. To insure the order was carried out, he returned to Nauvoo to oversee the surrender. Joseph Smith sent a letter to Governor Ford stating:

> Dear Sir.-On my way to Carthage to answer your request this morning [for Joseph to surrender], I here met Captain Dunn, who has here made known to me your orders to surrender the state arms in possession of the Nauvoo Legion, which command I shall comply with; and that the same may be done properly and without trouble to the state, I shall return with Captain Dunn to Nauvoo, see that the arms are put into his possession, and shall then return

---

tremble. And all nations shall be afraid because of the terror of the Lord, and the power of his might." (D&C 45: 66-70, 74-75.)

[152]*Encyclopedia of Mormonism*, p. 998.

to headquarters in his company, when I shall most cheerfully submit to any requisition of the Governor of our state. (*DHC* 6: 556.)

Joseph then went back to Nauvoo, supervised surrender by the Nauvoo Legion he commanded of all arms belonging to the state, and returned to be imprisoned by the Governor at Carthage. He was killed three days later, while in state custody.

When his people were threatened, he disarmed them. When his life was threatened, he surrendered, and was killed. His example was meek. Although he held the sealing power which can change the course of events, he instead submitted to abuse, imprisonment and death. He did not call on his army to fight, or invoke the power of heaven for protection.

The first phase of Mormonism had opportunities for organized violence. In the two instances which involved Joseph Smith directly, the only violence was inflicted on Joseph and the saints. None was returned.

When Joseph Smith died, Brigham Young incorporated an oath to avenge the killings of Joseph and Hyrum Smith as part of the temple rites. Despite the oath of vengeance, no action was ever taken against those directly involved in Joseph's murder. They were identified, tried and acquitted, but no Latter-day Saint vengeance was taken on any of them. A fanciful book about their terrible fate at God's hands was enjoyed by Mormons for years.[153] It was later replaced by a more historically competent account[154] that showed

---

[153]Lundwall N. B. *The Fate of the Persecutors of the Prophet Joseph Smith*. Salt Lake City: Bookcraft, 1952.

[154]Oaks, Dallin H. and Hill, Marvin S. *Carthage Conspiracy: the Trial of the Accused Assassins of Joseph Smith*. Urbana: University of Illinois Press, 1979.

these men, after their acquittal for the murders of Hyrum and Joseph, for the most part, lived successful lives. No one acted on the temple oath of vengeance, and no one directly responsible for killing Joseph Smith died. In fact, no one was punished for the murders of Joseph and Hyrum. Years later, however, Brigham Young's oath of vengeance would take the lives of innocent victims.

The saints left Nauvoo under threats of violence, mobbing, and pressure from the State of Illinois. Rather than fight, the saints withdrew. The second phase of Mormonism began just as the first had concluded - without revenge, violence or retaliation by the saints against their persecutors. It would not remain that way.

The second phase of Mormonism began at Joseph's death. Within two years, the saints abandoned Nauvoo for the wilderness. The trek west was difficult. The suffering and sacrifices of the saints during the western movement has been the subject of books, general conference sermons, artwork, statuary, songs and plays. The expulsion from Nauvoo has become an epic tale.

During the exodus, Brigham Young aspired to be more than the chief Apostle. He wanted to reconstitute the First Presidency, and be elected the new president. This would give him the same office as Joseph. But his ambition was opposed by some of the Apostles. At one point he publicly complained about two Apostles who opposed his ambition to ascend. In a talk at Winter Quarters on November 16, 1847, Brigham Young stated:

> ...[Like Joseph I will not be trammeled– I would rather have to be shot in Carthage Jail than to be under the necessity of having to run to my brethren before I can speak before the public[.] ...If my lot is to preside over the

Church and I am the head of the Quorum– I am the
mouthpiece and you are the belly–[155]

The two Apostles who opposed him acting as a "President" over
the church were Parley Pratt and John Taylor. Concerning them,
he threatened in the same talk, "I shall never have any rest until I
get in that Valley and Parley Pratt and John Taylor bow down and
confess they are not Brigham Young. They are devoid of the
authority–"[156]

By early December, 1847 Brigham had his fill of the Twelve
sharing control with him. On December 5th in a meeting with the
other Apostles, he proposed to reorganize the First Presidency,
making himself President. Pratt, Taylor and Lyman Wight (another
opponent of his) were not at the meeting. After 5 hours of debate,
he obtained a favorable vote of those who were present. Woodruff
claimed the church needed a revelation before the First Presidency
could be reorganized. During the meeting he was persuaded to
abandon his view.

> ...There was no explicit revelation as Woodruff
> thought would be required, but a general feeling that this
> was right. Orson Hyde offered the motion for this
> organization of the First Presidency on 5 December 1847.
>
> Years later Hyde and Young said the vote occurred
> because of a divine manifestation. In April 1860 Young
> told the apostles: "At O. Hyde's the power came upon us,
> a shock that alarmed the neighborhood." He added that
> the previously hesitant Pratt "believed when the
> Revaluation] was given to us." Hyde expanded on that at
> the October conference by affirming that the apostles

---

[155] *The Complete Discourses of Brigham Young*, Vol. 1, p. 255.

[156] *Id.*

organized the First Presidency because the voice of God declared: "Let my servant Brigham step forth and receive the full power of the presiding Priesthood in my Church and kingdom." By contrast, Woodruff later said he did "not remember any particular manifestations at the time of the organization of the Presidency." His diary mentions nothing unusual about the 5 December meeting, and the minutes mention nothing extraordinary.[157]

The vote of the Apostles was not enough to make Brigham Young the church's president. He needed the vote of a conference of the church. This was the only way to satisfy the requirement of common consent. To accomplish this, he called a Special Conference and asked for a vote on December 27, 1847. Before the vote his remarks included the following:

> –it is contemplate [sic] we shall organize a First Presidency– we have proved to God, Satins [sic] and all manner of sinners and devils that we can carry the kingdom off triumphant– ...
>
> I realize my enjoyments today– my soul is happy and can cry aloud– and shout Hallelujah– the privilege of seeing the people of God – it fills be [sic] with fire– and my soul with consolation – that this is the best day I have seen in my life– this is a heavenly day — a day of Zion – the air is impregnated with peace– and feel as ready to go to heaven if I am wanted– I am at peace with all heaven, all earth, and all hell if they will keep out of my road– but if they wont [sic] I have waged war with them right straight...[158]

---

[157] Quinn D. Michael. *The Mormon Hierarchy: Origins of Power.* Salt Lake City: Signature Books, 1994, p. 249.

[158] The Complete Discourses of Brigham Young, Vol. 1, p. 271-272.

His remarks were favorably received and he got the vote he needed to prove there was common consent. Brigham Young became the church's president. He was never set apart or ordained to the office. He considered the vote of the Special Conference, called by him for this purpose, sufficient to confer the right upon him.

Under President Brigham Young's leadership the saints continued to relocate to the Great Basin where they would encounter years of difficulty and suffering. Food and money were scarce, and faith faltered. In the malaise that followed the migration, Brigham Young determined the saints must have lost God's favor. To stop the punishments from an angry Almighty,[159] he concluded the saints needed a "Reformation." He began a formal, mandatory re-baptism program for all church members, and started preaching the need for more strict, and godlike conduct. Despite this, the distresses continued, and multiplied. An Assistant LDS Church Historian co-authored a book that includes this description of the afflictions imposed on the proud refugees from Nauvoo:

> By the mid-1850's, Mormon leaders believed their kingdom was not going well. The harvest of converts in American and Great Britain had fallen off. The Saints faced bad weather, insect plagues, poor crops, and near famine. Young sensed a spiritual lethargy among his people, perhaps because of their decade-long focus on pioneering but also because of the growing number of apostates and dissenters. Many immigrants to Zion were proving to be

---

[159]The possibility that this was the fulfillment of God's prophetic warning to them if they rejected the fullness offered to them in Nauvoo was never considered. "For instead of blessings, ye, by your own works, bring cursings, wrath, indignation, and judgments upon your own heads, by your follies, and by all your abominations, which you practise before me, saith the Lord." (D&C 124: 48.)

indigestible chaff. To Young, Mormons were not living up
to the standard of their mission.[160]

The Reformation began in earnest in 1856, and took on a
revivalist flavor. "[A] policy was established to have two home
missionaries assigned to each ward. Equipped with a twenty-seven-
question catechism to help measure the worthiness of the Saints,
the home missionaries assisted families with everything from
hygiene and church attendance to obeying the Ten
Commandments."[161] The reaction to the Home Missionary
program was not always favorable because of the coercive nature
it assumed.

> A "home missionary" program was established in the hope
> that systematic preaching might stir "the people to
> repentance and a remembrance of their first love" – the
> gospel. When these programs failed to achieve full reform,
> Young called for sterner measures. "Instead of ... smooth,
> beautiful, sweet ... silk-velvet-lipped preaching," he said,
> the people needed "sermons like peals of thunder."[162]

It was during this Reformation that Brigham Young's fiery
rhetoric included the doctrine of "blood atonement," and
vengeance for enemies of and apostates from the faith. Today there
is no question this rhetoric resulted in tragedy. But at the time it

---

[160]Walker, Ronald, Turley, Richard Jr., and Leonard, Glen. *Massacre at
Mountain Meadows: An American Tragedy.* Oxford: Oxford University Press,
2008, p. 24, footnotes omitted. Richard Turley is Assistant Church
Historian for The Church of Jesus Christ of Latter-day Saints. Glen
Leonard is the former Director of the LDS Museum of Church History
and Art.

[161]*Encyclopedia of Mormonism*, p. 1197.

[162]*Massacre at Mountain Meadows, supra,* p. 24, footnotes omitted.

was used to inspire religious fervor and intimidate "sinners." The following is from a sermon given on September 21, 1856 at the Salt Lake City Bowery:

> We need a reformation in the midst of this people; we need a thorough reform, for I know that very many are in a dozy condition with regard to their religion; I know this as well as I should if you were now to doze and go to sleep before my eyes.
>
> You are losing the spirit of the Gospel, is there any cause for it? No, only that which there is in the world. ...
>
> There are sins that men commit for which they cannot receive forgiveness in this world, or in that which is to come, and if they had their eyes open to see their true condition, they would be perfectly willing to have their blood spilt upon the ground, that the smoke thereof might ascend to heaven as an offering for their sins; and the smoking incense would atone for their sins, whereas, if such is not the case, they will stick to them and remain upon them in the spirit world.
>
> I know, when you hear my brethren telling about cutting people off from the earth, that you consider it is strong doctrine; but it is to save them, not to destroy them. ...
>
> I do know that there are sins committed, of such a nature that if the people did understand the doctrine of salvation, they would tremble because of their situation. And furthermore, I know that there are transgressors, who, if they knew themselves, and the only condition upon which they can obtain forgiveness, would beg of their brethren to shed their blood, that the smoke thereof might ascend to God as an offering to appease the wrath that is kindled against them, and that the law might have its

course. I will say further; I have had men come to me and offer their lives to atone for their sins.[163]

In his zeal to reform the saints, President Young even equated the taking of the sinful saint's life with the love of Jesus Christ. On February 8, 1857, he instructed the audience in the Salt Lake City Tabernacle as follows:

> Brother Cummings told you the truth this morning with regard to the sins of the people. And I will say that the time will come, and is now nigh at hand, when those who profess our faith, if they are guilty of what some of this people are guilty of, will find the axe laid at the root of the tree, and they will be hewn down. What has been must be again, for the Lord is coming to restore all things. The time has been in Israel under the law of God, the celestial law, or that which pertains to the celestial law, for it is one of the laws of that kingdom where our Father dwells, that if a man was found guilty of adultery, he must have his blood shed, and that is near at hand. ...
>
> Now take a person in this congregation who has knowledge with regard to being saved in the kingdom of our God and our Father, and being exalted, one who knows and understands the principles of eternal life, and sees the beauty and excellency of the eternities before him compared with the vain and foolish things of the world, and suppose that he is overtaken in a gross fault, that he has committed a sin that he knows will deprive him of that exaltation which he desires, and that he cannot attain to it without the shedding of his blood, and also knows that by having his blood shed he will atone for that sin, and be saved and exalted with the Gods, is there a man of woman

---

[163] *The Complete Discourses of Brigham Young,* Vol. 2, pp. 1169-1170; see also *JD* 4: 52-54.

in this house but what would say, "shed my blood that I may be saved and exalted with the Gods?"

All mankind love themselves, and let these principles be known by an individual, and he would be glad to have his blood shed. That would be loving themselves, even unto an eternal exaltation. Will you love your brothers or sisters likewise, when they have committed a sin that cannot be atoned for without the shedding of their blood? Will you love that man or woman well enough to shed their blood? That is what Jesus Christ meant.[164]

These teachings have been used by critics to accuse Mormons of pioneer era murders as part of Brigham Young's implementation of "blood atonement." The criticism has been utterly rejected by the church. In a book devoted to defending plural marriage, and rejecting any wrongful "blood atonement," Elder Joseph F. Smith stated the following:

Did you not know that not a single individual was ever "blood atoned," as you are pleased to call it, for apostasy or any other cause? Were you not aware, in repeating this false charge, that it was made by the most bitter enemies of the Church before the death of the Prophet Joseph Smith? Do you know of anyone whose blood was ever shed by the command of the Church, or members thereof, to "save his soul?"[165]

This rejection of any provable instance of "blood atonement" is the official position of the church. However, in *The Encyclopedia of*

---

[164]*The Complete Discourses of Brigham Young,* Vol. 3, pp. 1228-1229; see also *JD* 4: 219-220.

[165]Smith, Joseph F. *Blood Atonement and the Origin of Plural Marriage.* Salt Lake City: Deseret News, 1905, p. 15.

Mormonism the wording rejecting the idea is more carefully phrased than Elder Smith's 1905 denial. In the 1992 *Encyclopedia*, an artful distinction is made based upon "Church-sanctioned" blood atonement, rather than any outright denial it happened.[166]

The subject of Mormon acts of blood atonement has been discussed by two opposing camps who are equally zealous in accusing and denying actual killings. Anti-Mormon critics have vastly overstated the case as a basis to damn Mormonism. In

---

[166]The entry on *Blood Atonement* reads: "The doctrines of the Church affirm that the Atonement wrought by the shedding of the blood of Jesus Christ, the Son of God, is efficacious for the sins of all who believe, repent, are baptized by one having authority, and receive the Holy Ghost by the laying on of hands. However, if a person thereafter commits a grievous sin such as the shedding of innocent blood, the Savior's sacrifice alone will not absolve the person of the consequences of the sin. Only by voluntarily submitting to whatever penalty the Lord may require can that person benefit from the Atonement of Christ. Several early Church leaders, most notably Brigham Young, taught that in a complete theocracy the Lord could require the voluntary shedding of a murderer's blood-presumably by capital punishment-as part of the process of atonement for such grievous sin. This was referred to as 'blood Atonement.' Since such a theocracy has not been operative in modern times, the practical effect of the idea was its use as a rhetorical device to heighten the awareness of Latter-day Saints of the seriousness of murder and other major sins. This view is not a doctrine of the Church and has never been practiced by the Church at any time. Early anti-Mormon writers charged that under Brigham Young the Church practiced "blood atonement," by which they meant Church-instigated violence directed at dissenters, enemies, and strangers. This claim distorted the whole idea of blood atonement-which was based on voluntary submission by an offender-into a supposed justification of involuntary punishment. **Occasional isolated acts of violence that occurred in areas where Latter-day Saints lived were typical of that period in the history of the American West, but they were not instances of Church-sanctioned blood Atonement.**" (*The Encyclopedia of Mormonism*, p. 131, emphasis added.) The truthfulness of the words used hinges on the qualification, "Church-sanctioned" and not on whether anyone was killed.

response, Mormon apologists have denied (sometimes artfully) any instance of blood atonement ever happening. A neutral examination was hard to find until Polly Aird's recent book, published in 2009.[167]

She explains that the release of two convicts from prison, John Ambrose and Thomas Betts, resulted in Brigham Young targeting them for killing. He suspected they were going through southern Utah en route to California. He worried they would steal church-owned horses sent south for winter grazing. Two letters from President Young suggested these men be disposed of quietly. Aird's account relates the following:

> [H]is letters warning the leaders to watch the two men's activities went much further. After outlining his suspicions about the released prisoners, he wrote: "If any such thing we have suggested should occur we shall regret to hear a favorable report; we do not expect there would be any prosecutions for false imprisonment or tale bearers left for witnesses ... Bro Johnson, you know about these things, have a few men that can be trusted on hand, and make no noise about it and keep this letter safe. We write for your eye alone and to men that can be trusted." The second letter was similarly worded but added another directive: "Be on the look out now, & have a few trusty men ready in case of need to pursue, retake & punish."
>
> In a case of mistaken identity, four other travelers to California were ambushed on the night of February 17 as they camped along the Santa Clara River in southern Utah. The men scrambled out of the firelight, except for one who had been shot in the face. In spite of finding more than fifty bullet holes in their bedding the next

[167] Aird, Polly. *Mormon Convert, Mormon Defector, A Scottish Immigrant in the American West, 1848-1861.* Norman: Arthur H. Clark Company, 2009.

morning, they all survived. It appears that the attackers believed they were pursing [sic], retaking, and punishing the former prisoners according to Young's wishes; but the intended targets of the assault passed through the area unmolested two days later.

President Young's letters had a further, more deadly effect and show that the Reformation had not dissipated. Aaron Johnson, bishop of Springville, to whom the first letter had been addressed, called a series of council meetings. At the first one, held shortly after he received the letter, he spoke of people going away, that they might steal horses, and that he had instructions that they needed to be watched. Before a second meeting, Brigham Young's discourse in the Tabernacle in Salt Lake City on February 8 was published in the *Deseret News.*[168]

This is the same talk quoted earlier in this chapter. It includes the reference to shedding blood of someone whom you love, to secure for them forgiveness for their sins. The instruction to the local bishop was applied to justify the elimination of an apostate. Aird describes the events as follows:

> Within days of this issue of the *Deseret News* reaching Springville, Bishop Aaron Johnson called a second council meeting. In this one, instead of singling out the released prisoners, he called attention to William R. Parrish, a longtime church member. In Nauvoo after Joseph Smith's death in 1844, controversy had arisen over who should succeed him. Parish sided with the Twelve Apostles, declaring he would support them even if it led him to hell. Now a Springville resident, Parrish had become disillusioned and was planning to go to California by the

------

[168] *Mormon Convert, Mormon Defector, supra*, pp. 174-175, footnotes omitted.

southern route with his two oldest sons. When times were safer, he planned to return to get his wife and four younger sons.

At the second meeting the bishop called two men, Gardiner G. "Duff" Potter and Abraham Durfee, to find out when the Parrishes were planning to leave. According to one participant, Bishop Johnson said, "Some of us would yet 'see the red stuff run.' He said he had a letter, and the remark was made by some one that 'dead men tell no tales.'" Bishop Johnson's counselor, John M. Stewart, another witness to this meeting, said that Potter asked for the privilege of killing Parrish whenever he could find "the dammed curse." The bishop had replied, "Shed no blood in Springville." Stewart understood that "blood would probably be shed, not in Springville, but out of it." Following the bishop's orders, Potter and Durfee found Parrish and told him that they too wished to leave Utah. They soon gained his confidence. A third council meeting was called by the bishop, after which events moved quickly. On March 15, 1857, outside the city gates, William Parrish was killed by knife wounds after a hard struggle, and one of his sons was shot dead. Duff Potter was also killed, having been mistaken for the young Parrish son.[169]

In the aftermath of the killings, an official inquest conveniently determined only that the murders were caused by "an assassin, or assassins, to the jury unknown."[170] The Parrish-Potter murders were not investigated by the church, and Bishop Johnson continued as the local bishop, enjoying favor from President Young. The following Pioneer Day, President Young invited

---

[169] *Id.*, pp. 175-176, footnotes omitted.

[170] *Id.*, p. 176.

Bishop Johnson to join him in his important celebration in Big Cottonwood Canyon.[171]

In a separate case, the "Aiken party" of six California men were also killed. First arrested, and accused of being army spies, they were taken to Salt Lake City and imprisoned. Four were taken south, and on November 25th, when crossing the Sevier River south of Nephi, they were shot by the Mormons and the Mormon reinforcements sent by the bishop from Nephi to escort them. Two died immediately. Two survived. The survivors were tended to, then sent back north. On the return trip, they were shot to death on November 28th. A fifth member of the Aiken party was killed near Bountiful. The sixth and final member disappeared.[172]

The Parrish murders, Aiken party murders, and others were not investigated by either the church, or state while Brigham Young was Territorial Governor. Nothing was done until a judge appointed from Washington, DC came to Utah to investigate the matter. Judge Cradlebaugh required the matter to be tried in 1859. So far as church officials had been concerned, the issue did not arouse curiosity or any need to punish.

The greatest violence to occur during the era of preaching "blood atonement" happened at Mountain Meadows. This involved killing over 120 men, women, and children by a confederacy of Mormons and Indians. The killings were locally orchestrated by Mormon leaders, but did not involve President Young's direct authorization or sanction. The evidence shows he sent a letter saying the besieged party should be let go, but his letter arrived after the killings. It is clear enough, however, President Young created the

---

[171]*Id.*, p. 176, see also footnote 17 on that page.

[172]*Id.*, pp. 201-202.

rhetorical and doctrinal environment that contributed to the killings. An LDS Assistant Church Historian has recently conceded that President Young does bear responsibility for creating the atmosphere in which these killings happened. "From Young's perspective, the reformation accomplished a great deal of good, though tough talk about blood atonement and dissenters must have helped create a climate of violence in the territory,[173] especially among those who chose to take license from it."[174]

There is a detail from the history of Mountain Meadows which makes President Young's responsibility in this event more apparent. It's significance has not been adequately appreciated.

We draw from three different Latter-day Saint histories giving credible accounts of the Mountain Meadows Massacre. They all include the same detail. The first is taken from B.H. Roberts, who was an LDS General Authority at the time he wrote an account in *The Comprehensive History of the Church*. In the discussion of the event, he includes the following detail:

> No complaint is made against their deportment as emigrants until they reach Fillmore-a distance of about 150 miles south of Salt Lake City-and at Corn Creek, in Millard county-about 15 miles south of Fillmore. At the former

---

[173]The first three questions asked by the Home Missionaries in the Reformation Catechism were these: "Have you committed murder, by shedding innocent blood, or consenting thereto? Have you betrayed your brethren or sisters in anything? Have you committed adultery, by having any connection with a woman that was not your wife, or a man that was not your husband?" These first questions, if they were answered in the affirmative, were among the offenses Brigham Young taught warranted blood atonement, or the necessity of shedding the sinner's blood to qualify for forgiveness. For a complete copy of the questions, see p. 26 of *Massacre at Mountain Meadows*.

[174]*Massacre at Mountain Meadows, supra.*, pp. 25, 27.

place "they threatened the destruction of the town," says George A. Smith, "and boasted of their participation in the murders and other outrages that were inflicted upon the 'Mormons' in Missouri and Illinois."[175]

Juanita Brooks, in her book, *The Mountain Meadows Massacre*, makes a similar report. Her account includes several references to the Francher Party's claim of involvement in killing Joseph Smith. Thomas Waters Cropper, who was fifteen years old at the time of the event, recalled this:

> "There appeared to be two companies of them joined together for safety from the Indians. One company which was mostly men called themselves the Missouri Wild Cats. I heard one of them make the brag that he helped to mob and kill Joe Smith, and he further said, 'I would like to go back and take a pop at Old Brig before I leave the territory.'"[176]

In the book, *Massacre at Mountain Meadows*, Harold Turley's account is set out. According to Turley, John D. Lee, who was directly involved in the killings, spent the evening talking to his stake president, Isaac Haight, who presided over, and directed the murders. That account states:

> "We spent the night in an open house on some blankets," Lee said, "where we talked most all night." Lee claimed Haight told him terrible things about the emigrants, that they "were a rough and abusive set of men" who "had

---

[175]Roberts, B.H. *The Comprehensive History of the Church*. Salt Lake City: Deseret News, 1930, Vol. 4, p. 142. His account begins on page 139 of that volume. It was in Illinois Joseph was murdered.

[176]Brooks, Juanita. *The Mountain Meadows Massacre*. Norman: University of Oklahoma Press, 1950, new edition 1962, p. 47.

insulted, outraged, and ravished many of the Mormon women." They had heaped abuses on the people "from Provo to Cedar City" and had poisoned water along the road. "These vile Gentiles" had "publicly proclaimed that they had the very pistol" that killed Joseph Smith, and wanted "to kill Brigham Young and all of the Apostles."[177]

Despite the bragging attributed to them, there is no proof any of those killed by the Mormons at Mountain Meadows were actually involved or even present when Joseph Smith was killed. It was their boast of involvement that triggered the response based on their claim.

Prior to killing the emigrants, the Mormons gathered in a circle and prayed. The pre-killing ceremony was explained by Walker, Turley and Leonard as follows: "The men sat in a circle off by themselves and began by praying for 'Divine guidance,' a sacrilege that only the passions of the time could explain."[178] The "passions of the time" was the larger political battle between the Mormon hierarchy, and Washington, DC in which Johnson's Army was sent to suppress the claimed Mormon rebellion. These tensions existed, to be sure, but the reason for Mormons killing over 120 men, women and children stemmed from the religious convictions of the participants, more than in larger political concerns.

After Joseph Smith's death, Brigham Young had instituted the covenant in the temple ceremonies requiring all covenant-makers to swear to avenge the blood of Joseph and Hyrum Smith.[179] Some

---

[177] *Massacre at Mountain Meadows, supra*, p. 143.

[178] *Id.*, p. 187, 189.

[179] As a result of the Reed Smoot Senate Confirmation Hearings, the oath was removed from the temple rites by President Joseph F. Smith.

church officials have denied the oath ever existed. However, the oath, and the seriousness of it was discussed by First Presidency Counselor George Q. Cannon and the church Apostles in a meeting on December 6, 1889:

> Father said that he understood when he had his endowments in Nauvoo [Illinois] that he took an oath against the murderers of the Prophet Joseph as well as other prophets, and if he had ever met any of those who had taken a hand in that massacre he would undoubtedly have attempted to avenge the blood of the martyrs. The Prophet charged Stephen Markham to avenge his blood should he be slain; after the Prophet's death Bro. Markham attempted to tell this to an assembly of the Saints, but Willard Richards pulled him down from the stand, as he feared the effect on the enraged people.
>
> Bro. Joseph F. Smith was traveling some years ago near Carthage [Illinois] when he met a man who said he had just arrived five minutes too late to see the Smiths killed. Instantly a dark cloud seemed to overshadow Bro. Smith and he asked how this man looked upon the deed. Bro. S. was oppressed by a most horrible feeling as he waited for a reply. After a brief pause the man answered, "Just as I have always looked upon it– that it was a d–d cold-blooded murder." The clouds immediately lifted from Bro. Smith and he found that he had his open pocket knife grasped in his hand in his pocket, and he believes that had this man given his approval to that murder of the prophets he would have immediately struck him to the heart.[180]

The oath of vengeance and prayer before killing at Mountain Meadows are directly connected. The Mormons involved may have killed these men, women, and children for the oath's sake.

---

[180] *Diaries of Abraham Cannon, supra,* pp. 34-35.

During the first phase of Mormonism, Joseph Smith twice had opportunities to engage in violence with armed supporters. Both times he declined. In the second phase, preaching about violence, even equating killing to an act of love, actually resulted in murders. President Young did not personally attend or direct the killings. In the case of Mountain Meadows he sent a message to not kill any of the besieged party. It is untrue that he was personally involved in that final act of mass murder. However, he was responsible, through his rhetoric and the oath of vengeance he extracted from the saints, for establishing a climate in which murder by Mormons did happen. Also, he never investigated while he had the governmental authority and responsibility to do so. Nor did the church display any curiosity about who was responsible for the events. It was an interesting transition from the first phase to the second.

Another incident involving the slaughter of Indians left a young boy who survived with a lifelong score to settle. The pre-dawn ambush and slaughter included women and children on Battle Creek above modern Pleasant Grove, and was more of an execution than a battle. Young Black Hawk was still a boy when 44 Mormons led by Dimick Huntington, including Hosea Stout, acting on Brigham Young's authority, slaughtered his people. He lived to avenge the incident in what is now known as The Black Hawk War. That interesting matter, however, is beyond the scope of this book.

Although the gentile church was established by a Prophet upon whom the Lord conferred the fullness of the priesthood, the transfer of that fullness is more presumed in the accounts than proven. It is largely a matter of faith. But subsequent events can help illustrate whether the prophesied gentile lyings, deceits, wickedness, abominations, murders and hypocrisy foretold by Christ[181] have happened.

We turn next to changing marriage practices from the first phase to the third phase of Mormonism.

---

[181] 3 Nephi 16: 10.

Chapter 6

SEVEN WOMEN SHALL TAKE HOLD
OF ONE MAN

*I*n no topic does the contrast between the different phases of Mormonism become more apparent than in plural marriage, or as it became popularly referred to, polygamy. The first three phases are clearly distinguished by this practice. It began as a secret practice in the first phase, then transitioned into being justified and practiced openly in the second phase. Finally, there was complete rejection and intolerance of the practice in the third phase. Clearly, plural marriage is central to recognizing and understanding the early three phases of Mormonism.

Joseph's revelation on eternal marriage included the possibility of a man taking plural wives. However, the first 33 verses of the revelation do not mention plural wives, apart from acknowledging that Joseph asked about the issue.[182] The entire discussion within the revelation about "obeying the law once it is revealed" is referring only of marriage between a man and *one* woman. The

---

[182]D&C 132: 1.

qualification for godhood, and promise of continuation of the family are explained in the portion of the revelation dealing with marriage between a man and *one* woman.[183] Despite this, Section 132 is most often associated with the requirement of plural marriage because the revelation does go on to answer the question Joseph asked about why Abraham, Isaac, and Jacob, Moses, David, and Solomon had many wives and concubines.

The answer to that separate question begins in verse 34 with the case of Abraham: "God commanded Abraham, and Sarah gave Hagar to Abraham to wife. And why did she do it? Because this was the law; and from Hagar sprang many people. This, therefore, was fulfilling, among other things, the promises." (D&C 132: 34.) It was the law at the time of Abraham that a barren wife was required to provide, or allow another wife so the husband's family line did not end because of her infertility. Sarah did this "because this was the law." Instead of this being an endorsement for taking multiple wives, the revelation explains Abraham was *not condemned* for doing it: "Was Abraham, therefore, under condemnation? Verily I say unto you, Nay; for I, the Lord, commanded it." (*Id.*, v. 35.)

As to Isaac and Jacob, they were also *not condemned* because they did what they were commanded to do. (*Id.*, v. 37.) As to David, Solomon, and Moses, the revelation states: "David also received many wives and concubines, and also Solomon and Moses my servants, as also many others of my servants, from the beginning of creation until this time; and in nothing did they sin save in those things which they received not of me." (*Id.*, v. 38.) The revelation

---

[183]The singular ("a wife") is used in verses 15, 18, 19 and 26. Exaltation or godhood and posterity are explained in verses 17, 18, 19 and 20.

explains that when a woman is given to a man under the authorized priesthood authority, then the man "cannot commit adultery" because the woman is given to him. (*Id.*, v. 62.) The man is "justified" in having the wives. These words of the revelation fall short of an outright endorsement for taking multiple wives. The language only permits it in two narrow circumstances: when the Lord commands, or when someone asks who has the right to ask—but not until after the Lord first approves the request. In contrast, the law which must be obeyed, the law "no one can reject... and be permitted to enter into [God's] glory"[184] is the everlasting marriage between a man and one woman.[185] In all the

---

[184]D&C 132: 4.

[185]D&C 132: 13-20.

relevant verses it involves marriage between a man, and "a wife"[186]

---

[186]"And everything that is in the world, whether it be ordained of men, by thrones, or principalities, or powers, or things of name, whatsoever they may be, that are not by me or by my word, saith the Lord, shall be thrown down, and shall not remain after men are dead, neither in nor after the resurrection, saith the Lord your God. For whatsoever things remain are by me; and whatsoever things are not by me shall be shaken and destroyed. Therefore, if a man marry him *a wife* in the world, and he marry *her* not by me nor by my word, and he covenant with *her* so long as he is in the world and *she* with him, their covenant and marriage are not of force when they are dead, and when they are out of the world; therefore, they are not bound by any law when they are out of the world. Therefore, when they are out of the world they neither marry nor are given in marriage; but are appointed angels in heaven, which angels are ministering servants, to minister for those who are worthy of a far more, and an exceeding, and an eternal weight of glory. For these angels did not abide my law; therefore, they cannot be enlarged, but remain separately and singly, without exaltation, in their saved condition, to all eternity; and from henceforth are not gods, but are angels of God forever and ever. And again, verily I say unto you, if a man marry *a wife*, and make a covenant with *her* for time and for all eternity, if that covenant is not by me or by my word, which is my law, and is not sealed by the Holy Spirit of promise, through him whom I have anointed and appointed unto this power, then it is not valid neither of force when they are out of the world, because they are not joined by me, saith the Lord, neither by my word; when they are out of the world it cannot be received there, because the angels and the gods are appointed there, by whom they cannot pass; they cannot, therefore, inherit my glory; for my house is a house of order, saith the Lord God. And again, verily I say unto you, if a man marry *a wife* by my word, which is my law, and by the new and everlasting covenant, and it is sealed unto them by the Holy Spirit of promise, by him who is anointed, unto whom I have appointed this power and the keys of this priesthood; and it shall be said unto them--Ye shall come forth in the first resurrection; and if it be after the first resurrection, in the next resurrection; and shall inherit thrones, kingdoms, principalities, and powers, dominions, all heights and depths--then shall it be written in the Lamb's Book of Life, that he shall commit no murder whereby to shed innocent blood, and if ye abide in my covenant, and commit no murder whereby to shed innocent blood, it shall be done unto them in all things whatsoever my servant hath put

for eternity.

There are two different issues addressed in this revelation on the subject of marriage. The first issue relates to marriage between a man, and one woman. As to that, the revelation *requires* any relationship the parties intend to endure beyond death must originate under the Lord's authority. If it is not done by His authority, it will end with the grave. When partner's marriage ends with the grave, they cannot enter into exaltation because they are limited or damned. They stop - which is what being damned means. They do not increase - which is what being saved means. To be able to increase requires they have a marriage, through which their "seed" or children are created. Otherwise they remain single, in an immortal condition, through all eternity and are servants to those whose seed continues.[187] Heaven's work is familial. It is all about the family of God. Therefore, in the resurrection people are either members of the family as sons and daughters, having their own seed continue, or they support that

---

upon them, in time, and through all eternity; and shall be of full force when they are out of the world; and they shall pass by the angels, and the gods, which are set there, to their exaltation and glory in all things, as hath been sealed upon their heads, which glory shall be a fulness and a continuation of the seeds forever and ever. Then shall they be gods, because they have no end; therefore shall they be from everlasting to everlasting, because they continue; then shall they be above all, because all things are subject unto them. Then shall they be gods, because they have all power, and the angels are subject unto them." (D&C 132: 13-20, emphasis added. It is clear from the single pronouns referencing the wife that the plural "they" means the man and his one wife.)

[187] D&C 132: 16: "Therefore, when they are out of the world they neither marry nor are given in marriage; but are appointed angels in heaven, which angels are ministering servants, to minister for those who are worthy of a far more, and an exceeding, and an eternal weight of glory."

effort as angelic servants. But the family unit is what heaven is all about in this revelation to Joseph Smith.

The second issue addressed by Section 132 involves the direction to take more than one wife. For that second event to happen, the Lord will need to either "command" it be done,[188] or the person must ask, and be permitted.[189] Unless the Lord either commands or gives permission, it is a sin for a man to take additional wives.[190]

From this revelation alone, it is unclear whether Joseph asked or was commanded. There is nothing in Section 132 that tells Joseph anything about whether he should take plural wives. It required another revelation, in addition to Section 132, for Joseph to receive direction on that question. Joseph did receive another revelation, but the event was not recorded nor the language preserved apart from remarks Joseph made in passing to others.

The statements Joseph made to others informs us he did not take additional wives voluntarily. He spoke about an angel that stood by him with a drawn sword, who told him that unless he moved forward and established plural marriages, he would be slain.[191] In the case of Joseph Smith, it was a "command," and not

---

[188]He commanded Abraham. See verse 35.

[189]David asked and received wives from Nathan, the prophet. See verse 39.

[190]For taking additional wives as a sin, read verse 38.

[191]See *Rough Stone Rolling*, p. 438-439 and footnote 3. Eliza R. Snow gives a slightly different account, saying that an angel "stood by him with a drawn sword, [who] told him that, unless he moved forward and established plural marriage, his Priesthood would be taken from him." (Smith, Snow, Eliza R. *Biography and Family Record of Lorenzo Snow, One of the Twelve Apostles of The Church of Jesus Christ of Latter-day Saints.* Salt Lake City: Deseret News, 1884, pp. 69-70.)

"permission" that caused him to take additional wives. Joseph was the head of a dispensation. He became the new "root" of the family tree. He was sealed "to the fathers," and it is to him that any who are subsequently made heirs of the Celestial Kingdom must also be sealed. In the case of Joseph Smith, taking additional wives was a commandment intended to accomplish a larger design involving salvation for the human family.[192] Until his exaltation could be secured, the salvation of others who would follow could not be grafted together. He, like Abraham, would become a father to the righteous who came to this earth after him. Therefore, his family would need to be numerous.

Joseph received this revelation in all likelihood as early as 1829. He began taking additional wives sometime early in the 1830's. When the entire language of the revelation is considered, it is evident Joseph found taking plural wives a bitter personal trial. Nevertheless, he obeyed. He proved he would not withhold anything from the Lord, even if it broke his heart, complicated his life, and disturbed his marriage to Emma. As the Lord states in the revelation: "I have seen your sacrifices in obedience to that which I have told you. Go, therefore, and I make a way for your escape, as I accepted the offering of Abraham of his son Isaac." (*Id.*, v. 50.) The full explanation of Joseph's "sacrifices" are not recorded. Details of Joseph's life involving plural wives were deliberately kept

---

[192]The full import of Joseph's status as Latter-day father of Israel is beyond the scope of this book. However, his plural wives were designed to accomplish a larger pattern involving all the Tribes of Israel. The deliberate nature of the pattern becomes evident with the sealing of Chief Tuva, the Hopi Tribal Chief, to Joseph Smith in the first day sealings were performed in the St. George Temple. In addition to gathering Israel through sealings, the Book of Mormon "remnant" was added by this adoption.

from public notice while he was living. It is clear enough, however, that Joseph took plural wives, and began in the early 1830's. It is also clear Joseph's plural wives were contracted as part of a plan for eternity, and not as a sexual indulgence in this life. Indeed, it appears Joseph did not have marital relations with most of his plural wives.[193] When other leaders were informed about the command to take additional wives, they were equally dismayed at the idea. Even though plural marriage was lived in secret, and denied publicly, as a subplot, it had significant effects on early Mormonism.

Section 132 is not a single revelation, but instead contains several revelations received at different times separated by years between them. Since none of them had previously been reduced to writing, when it was finally written in July 1843, all of them are set out as a single narrative. The first revelation included only the announcement of the possibility of an eternal marriage covenant, and an answer to the inquiry about Abraham, Isaac, Jacob, Moses, David, and Solomon's multiple wives. A subsequent revelation (vs. 45-50) approves Joseph's "sacrifices,"[194] confirms his "exaltation,"[195] and confers the power to "seal on earth... and in the heavens."[196] Between the first portion and the second of these recorded verses, there was another unwritten revelation. In it Joseph had been commanded to take plural wives. He obeyed, and merited the sealing power by his obedience and sacrifice. He had

---

[193] *Rough Stone Rolling, supra,* pp. 439-442.

[194] Verse 50.

[195] Verse 49.

[196] Verse 46.

offered what was necessary to be able to lay hold upon eternal life.[197]

This means Joseph received the revelation on eternal marriage, (verses 1-33) and plurality of wives (34-40 or 44) first. Then later Joseph was told by an angel "with a drawn sword" that he was commanded to practice this form of marriage. The time, place and language of that second revelation concerning plural wives was not recorded. Only after living it did he then obtain the keys to be able to perform such marriages, marking the third revelation set out in verses 45-50.

As to the unrecorded second revelation commanding him to take up the practice, we have several accounts. Eliza R. Snow Smith's account of the sword bearing angel directing Joseph to take additional wives is likely the most accurate. Her account ties Joseph's failure to live the practice to a forfeiture of keys. Through these events we see the evidence of how keys are obtained. When the Lord directs a man to do something, that direction establishes a Divine commission. Following through opens the door to then

---

[197]"Let us here observe, that a religion that does not require the sacrifice of all things never has power sufficient to produce the faith necessary unto life and salvation; for, from the first existence of man, the faith necessary unto the enjoyment of life and salvation never could be obtained without the sacrifice of all earthly things. It was through this sacrifice, and this only, that God has ordained that men should enjoy eternal life; and it is through the medium of the sacrifice of all earthly things that men do actually know that they are doing the things that are well pleasing in the sight of God. When a man has offered in sacrifice all that he has for the truth's sake, not even withholding his life, and believing before God that he has been called to make this sacrifice because he seeks to do his will, he does know, most assuredly, that God does and will accept his sacrifice and offering, and that he has not, nor will not seek his face in vain. Under these circumstances, then, he can obtain the faith necessary for him to lay hold on eternal life." (*Lectures on Faith*, Lecture 6, para. 7.)

obtain possession of keys. Nephi and his brother were commanded to retrieve the brass plates. His brothers murmured. Nephi said he would "go and do the things which the Lord hath commanded,"[198] which led to his subsequent kingship.[199] The same pattern was evident in Joseph Smith's life. Every one who receives their calling and election, and sealing power from the Lord walks the same path. The specific sacrifice required is dependent upon the heart of the one involved.

The revelations regarding eternal marriage, plural wives, Joseph's calling and election, and the conferral of the sealing power upon Joseph were reduced to writing for the first time on the morning of July 12, 1843. These several revelations given over years in separate events are what we now know as Section 132. Joseph dictated it, and included all the prior commandments, and instructions on the subject, with the exception of the incident involving the angel with the drawn sword. William Clayton wrote it down, and Hyrum took it to Emma Smith. William Clayton's journal explains the event:

> [July 12, 1843] This A.M. I wrote a Revelation consisting of 10 pages on the order of the priesthood, showing the designs in Moses, Abraham, David and Solomon having many wives & concubines. After it was wrote Press. Joseph

---

[198] 1 Ne. 3: 7.

[199] 2 Ne. 5: 18. His destiny was fixed when he returned with the brass plates, (word of God) and sword of Laban (emblem of kingship). He also kept the king's orb (Liahona) when he departed into the wilderness, leaving his older brothers. Joseph Smith came into possession of these same implements of kingship during the four years he visited the Hill Cumorah. A full discussion of this subject is beyond this work.

and Hyrum presented it and read it to E.[200] who said she did not believe a word of it and appeared very rebellious. J.[201] told me to Deed all the unencumbered lots[202] to E. & the children. He appears much troubled about E.[203]

Emma neither welcomed, nor even tolerated the revelation. She rejected it outright, and asked for Joseph to transfer property into her name. Apparently, once Joseph reduced the matter to writing, Emma realized he was not going to end the practice as she had insisted. She wanted some security for herself, and her children. Therefore, she wanted the unencumbered building lots moved into her name alone, to prevent other women from claiming they could share in the property.

The following day Joseph and Emma reached a division of property between them. They asked William Clayton to witness the agreement to divide their property:

> [July 13, 1843] This A.M. J. sent for me. & when I arrived he called me up into his private room with E. and there stated an agreement they had mutually entered into. they both stated their feelings on many subjects & wept considerable. O may the Lord soften her heart that she may be willing to keep and abide by his Holy Law. (*Id.*)

---

[200]William Clayton would often identify persons by the first letter of their name. In this case "E." was Emma Smith, Joseph's wife.

[201]"J." was Joseph Smith.

[202]These were the remaining building lots in Nauvoo belonging to Joseph.

[203]*The Nauvoo Diaries of William Clayton, 1842-1846, Abridged.* Salt Lake City: Privately Published, 2010, p. 22.

Two days later William Clayton records making out the deed for Joseph's half interest in the Steamboat Maid of Iowa, transferring it to Emma. "Also a Deed to E. for over 60 city lots." (*Id.*, pp. 22-23.) The "agreement" which Joseph and Emma mutually struck resulted in a property settlement between them.

The division between Joseph and Emma caused by plural wives in the first phase of Mormonism is a harbinger of later divisions among the saints over the same issue.

Joseph Smith began to teach this principle to a limited number of close associates. Just as it had been a terrible trial to him, he used the doctrine to test others.[204] He asked men to give their wives

---

[204] As to Heber C. Kimball, his experience was as follows: "Before he would trust even Heber with the full secret, however, he put him to a test which few men would have been able to bear. It was no less than a requirement for him to surrender his wife, his beloved Vilate, and give her to Joseph in marriage! The astounding revelation well-nigh paralyzed him. He could hardly believe he had heard aright. Yet Joseph was solemnly in earnest. His next impulse was to spurn the proposition, and perhaps at that terrible moment a vague suspicion of the Prophet's motive and the divinity of the revelation, shot like a poisoned arrow through his soul. But only for a moment, if at all, was such a thought, such a suspicion entertained. He knew Joseph too well, as a man, a friend, a brother, a servant of God, to doubt his truth or the divine origin of the behest he had made. No, Joseph was God's Prophet, His mouthpiece and oracle, and so long as he was so, his words were as the words of the Eternal One to Heber C. Kimball. His heart-strings might be torn, his feelings crucified and sawn asunder, but so long as his faith in God and the Priesthood remained, heaven helping him, he would try and do as he was told. Such, now, was his superhuman resolve. Three days he fasted and wept and prayed. Then, with a broken and a bleeding heart, but with soul selfmastered for the sacrifice, he led his darling wife to the Prophet's house and presented her to Joseph. It was enough-the heavens accepted the sacrifice. The will for the deed was taken, and 'accounted unto him for righteousness.' Joseph wept at this proof of devotion, and

to him. If, after a soul searching struggle they agreed, Joseph would inform them they passed the test, and seal the man, and his wife to one another in marriage. It was a brutal test, but one that allowed Joseph to weigh the man's heart in the same fashion the Lord had weighed his. By asking a man to give his wife to Joseph, Joseph was able to accomplish several things in one terrible test: First, it demonstrated if the person was willing to accept the doctrine of plural wives. Second, it proved if the man accepted Joseph's role as the Lord's spokesman. Third, it tore at the heart of the man by asking for his wife; a test akin to the one visited upon Abraham when the Lord proved his heart. Interestingly, the testing did not ask for anyone else to live plural marriage. They had to accept the doctrine as true, because the wife would clearly not be Joseph's first wife. But the practice was nevertheless revealed by this terrible ordeal. If they agreed to give their wife to Joseph, they passed the test. Then Joseph rejoiced at their faithfulness, sealed the faithful husband to his wife in an eternal covenant, and explained it had only been a test of their willingness to obey God. In this manner

---

embracing Heber, told him that was all that the Lord required. He had proved him, as a child of Abraham, that he would 'do the works of Abraham,' holding back nothing, but laying all upon the altar for God's glory. The Prophet joined the hands of the heroic and devoted pair, and then and there, by virtue of the sealing power and authority of the Holy Priesthood, Heber and Vilate Kimball were made husband and wife for all eternity. Heber's crucial test was in part over." (Whitney, Orson F. *Life of Heber C. Kimball*. Salt Lake City: Bookcraft, 1992, pp. 333-335, paragraph indentations omitted.) Joseph required the same test of John Taylor, and others. The John Taylor account can be found at *Deseret Evening News*, December 9, 1879.

he introduced the concepts of eternal marriage and the idea of plural wives in one, single ordeal. Brigham Young would later conflate the two, making plural marriage a required part of eternal marriage itself.

In the first phase of Mormonism, this practice was secret, closely guarded, and involved only a handful of the trusted inner circle. No public teaching, or general practice of plural marriage was begun.

Things changed dramatically in the second phase. After Joseph's death, and the relocation west, the saints began to speak openly among themselves of the practice. They also began to spread it beyond the inner-circle. However, until 1852 it was kept secret, and publicly denied. Elder Orson Pratt was called upon "unexpectedly" to address the subject in a talk before an audience that would be reported in the newspapers. His address acknowledged the practice hadn't been spoken of in public, and would be a challenge to the American and European cultures.[205] Despite that, Elder Pratt

---

[205] He argues this is an extreme minority view, however: "I think there is only about one-fifth of the population of the globe, that believe in the one-wife system; the other four-fifths believe in the doctrine of a plurality of wives. They have had it handed down from time immemorial, and are not half so narrow and contracted in their minds as some of the nations of Europe and America, who have done away with the promises, and deprived themselves of the blessings of Abraham, Isaac, and Jacob. The nations do not know anything about the blessings of Abraham; and even those who have only one wife, cannot get rid of their covetousness, and get their little hearts large enough to share their property with a numerous family; they are so penurious, and so narrow and contracted in their feelings, that they take every possible care not to have their families large; they do not know what is in the future, nor what blessings they are depriving themselves of, because of the traditions of their fathers; they do not know that a man's posterity, in the eternal worlds,

taught, "It is well known, however, to the congregation before me, that the Latter-day Saints have embraced the doctrine of a plurality of wives, as a part of their religious faith."[206] The lid had been lifted. At that point the previously limited practice of plural marriage would thereafter become explained, advocated and spread.

With the public unveiling of plural wives, it became the teaching of the church that plural wives and exaltation were synonymous:

> I wish here to say to the Elders of Israel, and to all the members of this Church and kingdom, that it is in the hearts of many of them to wish that the doctrine of polygamy was not taught and practiced by us. It may be hard for many, and especially for the ladies, yet it is no harder for them than it is for the gentlemen. It is the word of the Lord, and I wish to say to you, and all the world, that if you desire with all your hearts to obtain the blessings which Abraham obtained, you will be polygamists at lest in your faith, or you will come short of enjoying the salvation and the glory which Abraham has obtained. This is as true as that God lives. ...The only men who become Gods, even the Sons of God, are those who enter into polygamy. Others attain unto a glory and may even be permitted to come into the presence of the Father and the Son; but they cannot reign as kings in glory, because they had blessings offered unto them, and they refused to accept them.[207]

---

are to constitute his glory, his kingdom, and dominion." (*JD* 1: 61.)

[206] *JD* 1: 54.

[207] *The Complete Discourses of Brigham Young*, Vol. 4, p. 2357; also *JD* 11: 269.

The practice was so foreign to the sensibilities of the saints that elevated rhetoric claiming it was a vital part of eternal salvation was required to overcome the natural hesitancy to embark on such a family relationship. The rhetoric turned the entirety of the revelation, not merely the eternal marriage covenant, into something absolutely mandatory for exaltation. On September 28, 1856, Heber C. Kimball warned the saints the sufferings they were enduring were nothing compared to what was coming if they rejected plural marriage. This was during the Reformation, as the leadership cast about in perplexity to discover what was causing their afflictions. Elder Kimball taught:

> Many of this people have broken their covenants by speaking evil of one another, by speaking against the servants of God, and by finding fault with the plurality of wives and trying to sink it out of existence. But you cannot do that, for God will cut you off and raise up another people that will carry out His purposes in righteousness, unless you walk up to the line of your duty. On the one hand there is glory and exaltation; and on the other no tongue can express the suffering and affliction this people will pass through, if they do not repent.[208]

Joseph F. Smith taught rejecting the practice of plural marriage would result in the keys being taken away from the saints.

> When the time came to introduce this doctrine to those who were worthy in the church, God commanded the Prophet and he obeyed. He taught it as he was commanded to such as were prepared to receive and obey

---

[208] *JD* 4: 108.

it, and they were commanded to enter into it, or they were threatened that the keys would be turned against them, and they would be cut off by the Almighty. It need scarcely be said that the Prophet found no one any more willing to lead out in this matter in righteousness than he was himself. Many could see it-nearly all to whom he revealed it believed it, and received the witness of the Holy Spirit that it was of God; but none excelled, or even matched the courage of the Prophet himself.[209]

The second phase of Mormonism equated Celestial Marriage with plurality of wives. During this time period, the preaching was so strongly worded concerning the practice that talks from this era continue to persuade even those today who study the transcripts that declare celestial glory cannot be obtained without plural wives. If in the first phase a man could be exalted with one wife, by the second phase he could not. Of the 23 marriages sealed by Joseph prior to his death,[210] other than his own, only one involved a plural

---

[209] *JD* 20: 29. This is consistent with Eliza R. Snow Smith's recollection of the warning to Joseph which equated the failure to practice with the threatened loss of keys.

[210] The 23 marriages Joseph sealed were: James Adams and Harriet Denton Adams, Reynolds Cahoon and Thirza Stiles Cahoon, Alpheus Culter and Lois Thethrop Culter, Joseph Fielding and Hannah Greenwood Fielding, Heber C. Kimball and Vilate Murray Kimball, William Law and Janes Silverthorne Law, Cornelius P. Lott and Permelia Darrow Lott, William Marks and Rosannah Robinson Marks, George Miller and Mary Catherine Fry Miller, Isaac Morely and Lucy Gunn Morley, William W. Phelps and Sally Waterman Phelps, Willard Richards and Jennetta Richards Richards, Goerge A. Smith and Bathsheba W. Bigler Smith, Hyrum Smith and Mary Fielding Smith, John Smith and Clarissa Lyman Smith, Joseph Smith, Jr., and Emma Hale Smith, Orson Spencer and Catherine Curtis Spencer, John Taylor and Leonora Cannon Taylor, Newel K. Whitney and Elizabeth Ann Smith Whitney, Wilford Woodruff and Poebe Carter Woodruff, Lucien Woodworth and Phebe

Which one?

wife) If plural wives was necessary for exaltation, as was taught in the second phase, proof of that cannot be established through Joseph's actions.

By the 1880's, the doctrine that plural wives was *required* for salvation was well established. With that doctrine in place in the church, the United States began a campaign to end the practice. Since the church believed it was a requirement demanded by God and essential to exaltation, it was believed it could not be abandoned by anyone who was to remain true to God. John Taylor succeeded Brigham Young as church president. He prayed about ending the practice. In answer to the prayer he received a revelation on September 27, 1886 which reads in its entirety as follows:

> My son John: You have asked me concerning the New and Everlasting Covenant and how far it is binding upon my people. Thus saith the Lord All commandments that I have given must be obeyed by those calling themselves by my name unless they are revoked by me or by my authority and how can I revoke an everlasting covenant [sic] For I the Lord am everlasting and my everlasting covenants cannot be abrogated nor done away with; but they stand forever. Have I not given my word in great plainness on this subject? Yet have not great numbers of my people been negligent in the observance of my law and the keeping of my commandment, and yet have I borne with them these many years and this because of their weakness because of the perilous times. And furthermore it is more pleasing to me that men should use their free agency in regard to these matters. Nevertheless I the Lord do not

---

Watrous Woodworth, Brigham Young and Mary Ann Angell Young, Joseph Young and Jane A. Bicknell Young. (See Brown Lisle, G. *The Holy Order in Nauvoo*, Appendix 1.)

change and my word and my covenants and my law do not. And as I have heretofore said by my servant Joseph all those who would enter into my glory must and shall obey my law. And have I not commanded men that if they were Abraham's seed and would enter into my glory they must do the works of Abraham. I have not revoked this law nor will I for it is everlasting and those who will enter into my glory must obey the conditions thereof, even so Amen.[211]

You can read this again and again, but you will not find the words "plural wives" or the plural form of "wife" anywhere in this revelation. It is true by 1886 "New and Everlasting Covenant" had acquired a new definition. The "New and Everlasting Covenant" as revealed to Joseph Smith required "a wife" to be sealed to a man. Interpretations and dramatic claims by the church's leaders revised the way the words were interpreted. But this 1886 revelation and the one recorded in 1843 should be read together. If they are, it is clear the requirement for eternal marriage was, is, and will remain a requirement for exaltation. But multiple wives is not, and never has been required. Even if every word of John Taylor's revelation was, and is true, it does not demand plural wives to be taken by the men of the church. However, at the time it was received, and in the context of the meaning assigned to the words at the time, this revelation was thought to stand as a reaffirmation that plural wives was mandatory. They thought the practice could not be abandoned. What is affirmed, however, is a practice involving eternal marriage between a man and "a wife" which

---

[211] See *Unpublished Revelations of the Prophets and Presidents of The Church of Jesus Christ of Latter-day Saints.* Compiled by Fred C. Collier. Salt Lake City: Collier's Publishing Co., 1979, pp. 145-146.

remains an obligation, even in third and fourth phase Mormonism, after plural wives was abandoned.

The pressure applied by the US government in 1886 increased. After being fortified by their interpretation of President John Taylor's revelation, however, church leaders were determined to keep the practice. In a meeting on December 20, 1888, Joseph F. Smith stated that, "he never expected to be required by the Lord to take a position where he would acknowledge to the world that the laws of the land were superior to the laws of God."[212] In the same meeting President Woodruff prophesied, "The Lord will never give a revelation to abandon plural marriage."[213]

By 1889 Wilford Woodruff had succeeded John Taylor, and he was struggling with the issue of continuing or abandoning the practice. On November 24, 1889, President Woodruff received a revelation very similar in word and content as John Taylor's 1886. The words "plural wives" are also absent from the Woodruff revelation. There is no word in the revelation that includes the concept of a plural wife, or anything abrogating the first 33 verses of Section 132 respecting the necessity of marriage between a man and "a wife." After reminding him the destiny of the United States and, "all other nations of the earth are in mine own hands;"[214] the revelation goes on to address the subject of covenants and obligations: "Let not my Servants who are called to the Presidency of my Church, deny my word or my law, which concerns the

---

[212]*Diaries of Heber J. Grant, supra*, p. 89.

[213]*Id.*, p. 90.

[214]*In the President's Office: The Diaries of L. John Nuttall, 1879-1892*. Edited by Jedediah S. Rogers. Salt Lake City: Signature Books, 2007, p. 395. The entire revelation is found on pp. 395-396.

Salvation of the children of men."[215] Interestingly, the revelation gives counsel that became directly applicable to the unfolding events:

> Place not yourselves in jeopardy to you[r] enemies by promise; your enemies seek you[r] d[e]struction and the destruction of my people. If the Saints will hearken unto my voice, and the counsel of my Servants, the wicked shall not prevail. Let my servants, who officiate as your Counselors before the Courts, make their pleadings as they are moved upon by the Holy Spirit, without any further pledges from the Priesthood, and they shall be justified.[216]

The above revelation was received with some enthusiasm by church leaders. At the time, government officials were asking for a pledge from church leaders that plural marriages would no longer be established in the United States. Apostle Abraham Cannon recorded that the church was under pressure to make concessions, and neither counselor to President Woodruff would give any advice on the matter. Left without counsel, President Woodruff took the matter to the Lord in prayer, and, according to Elder Cannon: "The answer came quick and strong. The word of the Lord was for us not to yield one particle of that which He had revealed and established."[217]

Despite this, by June of the following year, negotiations between the church, and government officials resulted in a proposed pledge to renounce further plural marriages. On May 19, 1890 church leaders received a telegram "informing us that the Supreme Court

---

[215]*Id.*, p. 395.

[216]*Id.*, typeset as in original.

[217]*Diaries of Abraham Cannon, supra*, p. 38.

of the United States had decided against the Church and that all of our property Real and Personal was gone."[218] A paper was prepared by the U.S. Secretary of State, James G. Blaine "for the leading authorities of the Church to sign in which they make a virtual renunciation of plural marriage."[219] Elder Cannon's recorded his "feelings revolt at signing such a document."[220]

Twenty-two days later, despite the revelation telling them not to give "any further pledges" the First Presidency adopted a pledge to end plural marriages in the United States. They would continue to be contracted in Mexico, but only if the wife would agree to remain in Mexico after the marriage.[221] It wasn't enough. The US government would at that point would not accept the church leader's pledge and required more if Utah was ever going to obtain statehood. By September 24, 1890, President Woodruff knew the U.S. Supreme Court had found the federal campaign against Mormonism to be constitutional. The church's property was forfeited, trustees had acquired title, and criminal prosecution for bigamy was lawful. In the face of that pressure, the "Manifesto" was issued denying the practice of plural marriage was continuing.[222] The Manifesto was written in response to the Utah

---

[218] *Diary of Heber J. Grant, supra*, p. 114.

[219] *Diaries of Abraham Cannon., supra*, p. 98.

[220] *Id.*

[221] "The resolution of the First Presidency of June 30/90 in regard to plural marriages was read. It is to the effect that none shall be permitted to occur even in Mexico unless the contracting parties, or at least the female, has resolved to remain in that country." *Id.*, p. 104.

[222] The Manifesto appears as Official Declaration 1 in the D&C.

Commission's finding that plural marriages were continuing in Utah even after the U.S. Supreme Court decision. Woodruff's Manifesto denies the report.

The horrified reaction of many saints was immediate and "considerable." The church leaders were caught between two forces, and while wanting to submit to the government to preserve their property and civil rights, they hoped their followers would not overreact. The rationalization for discontinuing plural marriages was purely legal, but the underlying teaching was not disavowed. "In [Pres. Woodruff's] declaration, however, there is no renunciation of principle nor abandonment of families recommended, as some [Latter-day Saint] fault-finders try to make it appear."[223]

The plan was to obtain statehood, become self-governing, and then adopt laws that permitted plural marriage. If pledges were made along the way to obtain statehood, it was worth the temporary difficulties, and compromises. All would be fixed by statehood. The government, however, was aware of this intent, and would not permit it. Before being granted statehood, the church would need to do more than compromise. They would need to utterly repudiate the practice. It was a long time before church leaders came to that realization.

By early October 1890, the First Presidency and Twelve were debating whether to present the Manifesto to the saints in General Conference to sustain it by common consent. It was issued to appease the federal government. "Joseph F. Smith presented the view that it would lack much force and would not bring the desired

---

[223] *Diaries of Abraham Cannon, supra,* p. 135.

results unless accepted by the vote of the people."[224] It was hoped the Manifesto would allow them to negotiate favorable terms, including permission for those already in plural marriages to continue to live openly with their wives.[225] Negotiations continued, and on October 5th, during General Conference, the government's response came back:

> A telegram was read from J. T. Cain concerning an interview with Secretary of the Interior [John W.] Noble. The latter felt that he could not accept Pres. W. Woodruff's manifesto without its acceptance by the Conference as authoritative, against the statements of the Utah Commission and Gov. Arthur] L. Thomas. It was therefore decided to present the matter tomorrow for the vote of the people.[226]

The following day it was presented, and unanimously approved by the saints attending General Conference.[227] However, most of those practicing plural marriage were not in attendance at the conference because of the federal prosecutions underway.

It is clear from the private record the decisions, Manifesto language, and reasons motivating the church to change all were intended to accomplish one end - to bring statehood, and a greater degree of political independence for the church, its leaders and the saints. Later criticism would result in defending the course of events by declaring that the decision was inspired by revelation,

---

[224] *Id.*, p. 141.

[225] *Id.*, p. 142.

[226] *Id.*, pp. 144-145.

[227] The proposal to adopt the Manifesto appears in Official Declaration 1 in the D&C.

and God's will. However, there is no contemporaneous discussion among the church's leaders in any of the available private meetings and personal diaries reporting a revelation. To the contrary, the diaries of those immediately involved report discussions about political compromises, and "pledges from the Priesthood" which President Woodruff's 1889 revelation warned them against. Complaints about the change resulted in President Woodruff explaining in October 1891 that he "never would have issued the Manifesto had it not been for the inspiration of God to [him]."[228]

The position which the church was trying to negotiate with the US Government would have left the existing marriages intact, and permit others to be contracted outside the United States. Eventually both of these hopes would be dashed, and plural marriages would be utterly abandoned. Political pressure, and criminal prosecutions continued to dog the church for years as they struggled to keep the practice after the Manifesto. The legal proceedings that took place in August 1891, to regain church property required testimony under oath about the church's real intent. As they prepared to testify, church leaders reviewed written questions anticipated to be asked of them in the courtroom. According to Abraham Cannon:

> Some of these are very searching, and almost make us, if we answer them the way it is desired, deny the principle of plural marriage for all time. We believe that this suspension is merely temporary, and, that God will open the way for his divine revelation to be established, but judging from a human standpoint plural marriage is forever stopped.[229]

---

[228] *Diaries of Abraham Cannon, supra*, pp. 261-262.

[229] *Diaries of Abraham Cannon, supra*, p. 244.

Church leaders sought legal counsel on how to proceed. After advice from attorneys Franklin S. Richards, and LeGrand Young on the morning of October 12, 1891, there was an afternoon meeting on that same day with attorney William H. Dickson. The church's final position was worked out with the advice of these lawyers, preparing the church leaders to testify. The final position of the church was decided based on William H. Dickson's legal counsel:

> After hearing us testify that polygamy had indeed ceased, he said he believed the best way to meet the thing was to say in substance: We believe God revealed the principle of plural marriage, and hence we practiced and maintained it in the hope that the sentiment of the nation towards it would change when they became convinced that it was a religious principle with us. As the opposition to it increased, however, instead of abated[,] we became convinced that it was useless to further oppose public sentiment. Then the Manifesto was issued and we are relieved of further obedience to this principle.
>
> If any are questioned as to what we should answer if plural marriage were again commanded of God he [Dickson] said we could only reply that we do not know. There was considerable discussion on these matters, but the result was an acceptance of Mr. Dickson's theory.[230]

President Woodruff followed the counsel, testified accordingly, and so far as the public was concerned, the practice at that point came to a complete end. Even cohabitation with already existing wives was to end. Elder Cannon records President Snow's comment on April 1, 1892:

---

[230] *Id.*, at p. 263.

When the Manifesto was issued we had no idea that it was to effect our cohabitation with our wives, but Pres. Woodruff and his brethren who were on the witness stand before the Master in Chancery, were forced to go further in their testimony than we anticipated, or we would have been placed in a worse position than we were before the Manifesto was issued.[231]

Despite the public facade, the church did not abandon the practice as a result of the Manifesto. It continued until 1904 when, in another confrontation with the US Government, the church president was again forced to testify under oath about the practice. In March 1904 he denied such marriages continued,[232] and thereafter issued a letter permanently ending even the clandestine practice of plural marriage. The letter was issued April 6, 1904 stating:

OFFICIAL STATEMENT

"Inasmuch as there are numerous reports in circulation that plural marriages have been entered into contrary to the official declaration of President Woodruff, of September 26, 1890, commonly called the Manifesto, which was issued by President Woodruff and adopted by the Church at its general conference, October 6, 1890,

---

[231] *Id.*, at p. 317.

[232] He testified that church leaders had "heard rumors; such as have been published by the anti-Mormon press, that there were marriages going on, the question has been broached many times in our councils, and invariably it has been resolved in our councils that all such things must stop, if they had not stopped, and so far as we are concerned, we knew of no such things occurring, and if anything of the kind did occur, it was without our knowledge or consent or approval." *(The Mormon Church on Trial: Transcripts of the Reed Smoot Hearings.* Edited by Michael Harold Paulos. Salt Lake City: Signature Books, 2008, p. 133.)

which forbade any marriage violative of the law of the land; I, Joseph F. Smith, President of the Church of Jesus Christ of Latter-day Saints, hereby affirm and declare that no such marriages have been solemnized with the sanction, consent or knowledge of the Church of Jesus Christ of Latter-day Saints, and

"I hereby announce that all such marriages are prohibited, and if any officer or member of the Church shall assume to solemnize or enter into any such marriage he will be deemed in transgression against the Church and will be liable to be dealt with, according to the rules and regulations thereof, and excommunicated therefrom. JOSEPH F. SMITH,
President of the Church of Jesus Christ
of Latter-day Saints.... "

. . . President Francis M. Lyman presented the following resolution and moved its adoption:
RESOLUTION OF ENDORSEMENT

"Resolved that we, the members of the Church of Jesus Christ of Latter-day Saints, in General Conference assembled, hereby approve and endorse the statement and declaration of President Joseph F. Smith, just made to this Conference concerning plural marriages, and will support the courts of the Church in the enforcement thereof.... "

The resolution was then adopted, by unanimous vote of the Conference....[233]

This 1904 letter marked the actual end of the practice of plural wives for the church. This ended any basis for continuing the practice. It threatened excommunication if anyone violated the

---

[233]*Messages of the First Presidency*. Edited by James R. Clark. 6 Vols. Salt Lake City: Bookcraft, 1970, Vol. 4, pp. 84-85, quotes and all as in original.

decree. The threat to excommunicate resulted in two of the Twelve, John W. Taylor and Matthias F. Cowley tendering their written resignations from their quorum on October 28, 1905. Neither of them were willing to abandon their wives or the practice. With the complete abandonment of the practice, the departure of two Apostles as casualties of the fight, and a church committed to excommunicating anyone who continued the practice, the second phase of Mormonism fully ended, and a third was under way.

The concept of plural wives originated in the first phase of Mormonism, but was limited in application. Joseph Smith preached it in private to a few in his inner-circle. Other than his own, there was only one plural marriage sealed by him prior to his death. However, many plural marriages were sealed in Nauvoo by church leaders before the western migration led by Brigham Young. Brigham Young was a vocal, ardent advocate of plural wives.

The second phase transitioned so instead of being private and narrowly confined, it was advocated as necessary for Celestial exaltation. It became an absolute requirement for any man who hoped to be fully redeemed. It was so necessary a doctrine and practice in the second phase, it was believed that abandoning it would cost a man salvation and condemn the church.

When the church traded the practice of plural wives for U.S. approval, the second major splintering of Mormons began. Although not as sizeable as the split when Joseph Smith died, there were nevertheless many groups who continued the practice of plural wives in opposition to the church's decision to abandon it.

"Mormon Fundamentalism" denotes the beliefs and practices of contemporary schismatic groups that claim to follow all the teachings of the Prophet Joseph Smith. They often style themselves believers in the "fulness of the gospel," which they assert must include plural marriage and sometimes the United Order.

The Fundamentalist movement began after the issuance of the Manifesto of 1890, which publicly declared an official end to plural marriage in The Church of Jesus Christ of Latter-day Saints. The period from 1890 to 1904 was one of confusion for some over the application and extent of the ban on new plural marriages in the Church. For example, since the Manifesto referred to "marriages violative of the law of the land," some felt the prohibition did not apply outside the United States. In 1904 the Manifesto was therefore officially and publicly proclaimed to be worldwide in jurisdiction and overall scope.

Following this second pronouncement, unyielding Fundamentalists continued to hold that God requires all "true" believers to abide by the principle of polygamy, irrespective of Church mandate. This insistence has separated Fundamentalists from mainstream Mormonism. In the 1920s, Lorin C. Woolley of Centerville, Utah, claimed God had authorized him to perpetuate plural marriage, saying he received this commission while a young man in 1886 through the ministration of Jesus Christ, John Taylor, and Joseph Smith. His assertion further polarized the Fundamentalists and the Church.

Some Fundamentalists of the 1920s rejected Woolley's claims to authority and went their separate ways. Charles Kingston settled in Bountiful, Utah, and set up a type of united order community that persists as a relatively closed society. Alma Dayer LeBaron moved to Mesa, Arizona, and eventually to Juarez, Mexico, laying the groundwork for the Church of the Firstborn of the Fulness of Times and offshoots such as the Church of the Lamb of God. Other Fundamentalists have broken away through the years, making various religious claims.

Despite these defections, the majority of Fundamentalists remained an organized group, showing small but steady gains in adherents.[234]

The doctrine of plural wives put Mormonism in conflict with the United States. The U.S. won that conflict. After a prolonged struggle, the compromise to gain statehood required a complete abolition. When the practice ended, there was another development in changing Mormonism that would have been unthinkable in the second phase. The second phase church from the least of the members to the top leadership, idealized the first, attempted to perpetuate it, remain true to it, and preserve it insofar as it was possible to do so. But the third phase began by not only rejecting an essential doctrine from the earlier phases, but the church took the dramatic step for the first time of threatening excommunication of any Latter-day Saint who continued to practice a recognized, accepted, previously orthodox doctrine. This development made it possible for Mormonism to entirely change. If even known, accepted and established doctrine could be converted into grounds to excommunicate those who followed it, Mormonism could be redefined to become anything.

This new idea of rejecting and condemning earlier doctrine and practices made it possible to disconnect early Mormonism from everything that was to follow from the third phase onward. It made Mormonism for the first time 'anti-historical,' in the sense that earlier practices were no longer adequate reason to continue anything. Once it was possible to retract and condemn well known doctrines, Mormonism could choose to become Historic Christianity. Even its scriptures were vulnerable to obsolescence.

---

[234] *Encyclopedia of Mormonism, supra*, p. 531.

Temple rites, ordinances, doctrines, teachings, principles, and even church structure were no longer necessarily constant. It would take time before the church management's central infrastructure developed to take advantage of this new opportunity to alter the faith. In the fourth phase, church leadership has recognized this great potential to transform the religion. They now regularly make changes, with increasing rapidity, using the church mantra, "Follow the Prophet," to reinforce the concept of permitted change. The only fixed concept held over from the first phase of Mormonism to the fourth phase is the idea of a living prophet. After the idea there is a prophet in control has been firmly planted in followers' minds, nothing can stop the changes. Further, resistence to change can arouse the institutional ire and, as the third phase has established, risk church discipline, even excommunication.

An additional issue to be considered in connection to the topic of plural wives is Christ's prophecy about the wickedness and abominations that would follow the gentile rejection of the fullness of the Gospel. Jacob equated taking multiple wives to wickedness, abominations and whoredoms. Here is an excerpt from his sermon about taking additional wives by the Nephites:

> [N]otwithstanding the greatness of the task, I must do according to the strict commands of God, and tell you concerning your wickedness and abominations, in the presence of the pure in heart, and the broken heart, and under the glance of the piercing eye of the Almighty God. Wherefore, I must tell you the truth according to the plainness of the word of God. For behold, as I inquired of the Lord, thus came the word unto me, saying: Jacob, get thou up into the temple on the morrow, and declare the word which I shall give thee unto this people. ...[He then rebukes them for seeking wealth and being prideful, which we omit here.] ... And now I make an end of speaking unto

you concerning this pride. And were it not that I must speak unto you concerning a grosser crime, my heart would rejoice exceedingly because of you. But the word of God burdens me because of your grosser crimes. For behold, thus saith the Lord: This people begin to wax in iniquity; they understand not the scriptures, for they seek to excuse themselves in committing whoredoms, because of the things which were written concerning David, and Solomon his son. Behold, David and Solomon truly had many wives and concubines, which thing was abominable before me, saith the Lord. Wherefore, thus saith the Lord, I have led this people forth out of the land of Jerusalem, by the power of mine arm, that I might raise up unto me a righteous branch from the fruit of the loins of Joseph. Wherefore, I the Lord God will not suffer that this people shall do like unto them of old. Wherefore, my brethren, hear me, and hearken to the word of the Lord: For there shall not any man among you have save it be one wife; and concubines he shall have none; For I, the Lord God, delight in the chastity of women.

And whoredoms are an abomination before me; thus saith the Lord of Hosts. Wherefore, this people shall keep my commandments, saith the Lord of Hosts, or cursed be the land for their sakes. For if I will, saith the Lord of Hosts, raise up seed unto me, I will command my people; otherwise they shall hearken unto these things. For behold, I, the Lord, have seen the sorrow, and heard the mourning of the daughters of my people in the land of Jerusalem, yea, and in all the lands of my people, because of the wickedness and abominations of their husbands. And I will not suffer, saith the Lord of Hosts, that the cries of the fair daughters of this people, which I have led out of the land of Jerusalem, shall come up unto me against the men of my people, saith the Lord of Hosts. For they shall not lead away captive the daughters of my people because of their tenderness, save I shall visit them with a sore curse, even unto destruction; for they shall not commit whoredoms, like unto them of old, saith the Lord of Hosts. And now behold, my brethren, ye know that these commandments were given to our father, Lehi; wherefore, ye have known them before; and ye have come unto great condemnation; for ye have done these things which ye ought not to have done. Behold, ye have done greater iniquities than the Lamanites, our brethren. Ye have broken the hearts of your tender wives, and lost the confidence of your children, because of your bad examples before them; and the sobbings of their hearts ascend up to God against you. And because of the strictness of the word of God, which cometh down against you, many hearts died, pierced with deep wounds. (Jacob 2: 10-11, 22-35.)

In the second phase of Mormonism the explanation given to distinguish what Mormonism was doing from what this sermon was saying was to seize upon the phrase, "if I will, saith the Lord of Hosts, raise up seed unto me, I will command my people; otherwise they shall hearken unto these things." This language was claimed as the exception which permitted the rule to be ignored.[235]

---

[235] See, e.g., Orson Pratt's explanation: "Here, then, we perceive that there are things which God forbids, and which it would be abominable for his people to do, unless he should revoke that commandment in certain cases. Because certain individuals among the Nephites, in ancient days, were expressly forbidden to take two wives, that did not prohibit the Lord from giving them a commandment, and making an exception, when he should see proper to raise up seed unto himself. The substance of the idea in that book is that-When I the Lord shall command you to raise up seed unto myself, then it shall be right; but otherwise thou shalt hearken unto these things-namely, the law against polygamy. But when we go to the Jewish record, we find nothing that forbids the children of Israel from taking as many wives as they thought proper. God gave laws regulating the descent of property in polygamic families. Turn to the 21st chap. of Deuteronomy, and the 15th verse, and you have there recorded that 'If a man have two wives, one beloved and another hated, and they

What is clear from Jacob's sermon, however, is if there is any unauthorized relationship where a man takes plural wives, he is guilty of wickedness, abomination and whoredoms. So if there were gentile marriages, even a single marriage, authorized by the church but not authorized by the Lord, Jacob's warning would

---

have borne him children, both the beloved and the hated; and if the firstborn son be hers that was hated, then it shall be, when he maketh his sons to inherit that which he hath, that he may not make the son of the beloved firstborn before the son of the hated, which is indeed the firstborn; but he shall acknowledge the son of the hated for the firstborn, by giving him a double portion of all that he hath; for he is the beginning of his strength: the right of the firstborn is his.' In this law the Lord does not disapprobate the principle. Here would have been a grand occasion for him to do it, if it had been contrary to his will. Instead of saying, If you find a man that has two wives, he shall be excluded from the congregation of Israel, or shall divorce one and retain the other, or shall be put to death, because he presumed to marry two wives, he considers both women his lawful wives, and gives a law that the son of the hated wife, if the firstborn, shall actually inherit the double portion of his property. This becomes a standing law in Israel. Does not this clearly prove that the Lord did not condemn polygamy, but that he considered it legal?" (*JD*, 6: 351-352.) Also George Q. Cannon taught: "[I]nstead of the Book of Mormon being opposed to this principle, it contains an express provision for the revelation of the principle to us as a people at some future time-namely, that when the Lord should desire to raise up unto Himself a righteous seed, He would command His people to that effect, plainly setting forth that a time would come when He would command His people to do so. It is necessary that this principle should be practiced under the auspices and control of the Priesthood. God has placed that Priesthood in the Church to govern and control all the affairs thereof, and this is a principle which, if not practiced in the greatest holiness and purity, might lead men into great sin, therefore the Priesthood is the more necessary to guide and control men in the practice of this principle. There might be circumstances and situations in which it would not be wisdom in the mind of God for His people to practice this principle, but so long as a people are guided by the Priesthood and revelations of God, there is no danger of evil arising therefrom." (*JD* 13: 201-202.)

condemn it as wickedness, abomination and whoredom. Of course, as the numbers of such marriages grew, the risk the church was sponsoring such wickedness, abominations and whoredoms also multiplied.

In 1857, there was an incident that gives pause for considering that not all plural marriages were engaged in with purity of motive or God's approval.

> In Sanpete Valley, Manti bishop Warren S. Snow led a party of men who castrated Thomas Lewis at Willow Creek that winter as he was being escorted to the prison at Great Salt Lake for alleged sexual crimes. The thirty-eight-year-old bishop and his companions took the young man "into the willows" and emasculated him "in a brutal manner Tearing the Chords right out," Samuel Pitchforth said. They left Lewis bleeding and senseless on a "bitter cold night." When found two days later, he was crazed and almost dead.
>
> The unpunished crime prompted Joseph Young to tell his younger brother, Brigham, that he disapproved of this act and "would rather die than to be made a Eunuch." To which Governor Young replied that the day would come when thousands would be made eunuchs "in order for them to be saved in the Kingdom of God." As for Bishop Snow, he said, "when a man is trying to do right & do[es] some thing that is not exactly in order I feel to sustain him & we all should." John D. Lee said that Lewis was castrated because he refused to give up a young woman whom Snow wanted to make one of his polygamous wives.[236]

---

[236]Bigler, David L. and Bagley, Will. *The Mormon Rebellion: America's First Civil War 1857-1858.* Norman: University of Oklahoma, 2011, pp. 113-114, footnotes omitted.

The account given by John D. Lee gave a few different details. According to his recollection, there was no allegation of a sex crime committed by the young man. The attack was motivated by Bishop Snow's desire to make this young man, who was his competition in pursuit of a young woman, no longer acceptable as a marriage partner.[237] The attack occurred in a school house. The severed organs were nailed to the school house wall[238] and, on the next day, Bishop Snow called a meeting to warn residents about disregarding priesthood directions, pointing out the graphic results nailed to the wall to those who attended. The plan worked, and the young lady later became the Bishop's wife.[239] The event was later

---

[237] According to Lee, the young man was called on a mission to remove him as a suitor, but he refused to accept the mission call. "It was then determined that the rebellious young man must be forced by harsh treatment to respect the advice and orders of the Priesthood. His fate was left to Bishop Snow for his decision. He decided that the young man should be castrated; Snow saying, 'When that is done, he will not be liable to want the girl badly, and she will listen to reason when she knows that her lover is no longer a man.'" (Lee, John D. *Mormonism Unveiled, or: The Life and Confessions of John D. Lee.* Albuquerque: Fierra Blanca Publications, reprint 2001, p. 291.)

[238] "He was severely beaten, and then tied with his back down on a bench, when Bishop snow took a bowie-knife, and performed the operation in a most brutal manner, and then took the portion severed from his victim and hung it up in the schoolhouse on a nail, so that it could be seen by all who visited the house afterwards." (*Id.*, p. 292.)

[239] "After this outrage old Bishop Snow took occasion to get up a meeting at the schoolhouse, so as to get the people of Manti, and the younger woman that he wanted to marry, to attend the meeting. When all had assembled, the old man talked to the people about their duty to the Church, and their duty to obey counsel, and the dangers of refusal, and then publicly called attention to the mangled parts of the young man, that had been severed from his person, and stated that the deed had been done to teach the people that the counsel of the Priesthood must be

described to Brigham Young by his brother. The Bishop suffered no consequences.

Clearly there were social as well as spiritual perils stemming from the practice of taking plural wives. Others have written on this topic, and the full extent of the depravity of this form of marital relationship has been denounced not only by church critics, but by the church itself since the practice ended. There is at least some reason to think Jacob's warning regarding abominations and whoredoms resulting from multiple wives may have been part of the church's practice of plural marriages in the years between 1847 and its final abandonment in 1904. If so, there is more reason to think Christ's prophecy about the gentile failure may be past, and not future.

We turn next to the economic development of Mormonism during the second phase, which established a foundation upon which all subsequent phases were built.

---

obeyed. To make a long story short, I will say, the young woman was soon after forced into being sealed to Bishop Snow." (*Id.*)

Chapter 7

PROPHETS, PROFITS AND
PRIESTCRAFT

The religion restored by Joseph Smith made no distinction between temporal and spiritual matters. In an 1830 revelation, any distinction between them was abolished by the Lord: "Wherefore, verily I say unto you that all things unto me are spiritual, and not at any time have I given unto you a law which was temporal; neither any man, nor the children of men; neither Adam, your father, whom I created." (D&C 29: 34.) The effect of this revelation was widespread, and constitutes one of the real distinctions between Mormonism and almost all other churches. Saints were knit together into an economic unit, as well as by a common belief system. At a time when the new religion was struggling to establish a community on the frontier, they also began construction on a Temple in Kirtland, Ohio. The building would require the unthinkable fortune of $40,000.00 to complete.[240] This would have been beyond the ability of any other

---

[240]Arrington, Leonard. *Great Basin Kingdom.* Cambridge: Harvard University Press, 1958, p. 13.

similarly sized frontier population, but the saints were economically unified, making the project possible. The sacrifice of purse and time involved made a powerful statement about the direction Mormonism would take in its first phase.

Joseph led the saints in more than worship. Or, perhaps it is more correct to say the worship Joseph led encompassed community building, feeding, sheltering, educating, and employing his followers. Converts came to the faith from the poorer classes, many arriving in need of immediate assistance. Kirtland was not merely a place to come for religion, but a place where religion helped provide for earthly needs. (Like Nephi of old. See 2 Ne. 5: 13-18.)

Wherever Joseph's followers congregated, there were economic effects. Kirtland, Missouri, and finally Illinois, saw Mormon industry, as well as Mormon worship. To a great extent the organized economic efforts were unnerving to neighbors, who invariably grew to fear Mormon political, social, military and economic clout. In Illinois, the saints were destitute refugees in 1839, but by 1844 they were thriving, growing, and amassing wealth. The accumulation of wealth was a byproduct of the industry, thrift and work-ethic incorporated into principles of the faith. It happened with such rapidity it alarmed observers.

The Mormon ambition was not limited to preaching a new religion, but to also build a kingdom belonging to God. There were economic needs for the kingdom that necessitated some amount of business development by the church, and its leaders.

The kingdom was to be "one" in all things. The result was intended to eliminate poverty,[241] and remove the pride of riches. The United Order, as it was named, contemplated much more than agreement on religious principles. Everything they possessed was part of a larger stewardship, where the best interests of the whole body was most important. No one was to be left behind. The revelation commanded:

> It is wisdom in me; therefore, a commandment I give unto you, that ye shall organize yourselves and appoint every man his stewardship; That every man may give an account unto me of the stewardship which is appointed unto him. For it is expedient that I, the Lord, should make every man accountable, as a steward over earthly blessings, which I have made and prepared for my creatures. I, the Lord, stretched out the heavens, and built the earth, my very handiwork; and all things therein are mine. And it is my purpose to provide for my saints, for all things are mine. But it must needs be done in mine own way; and behold this is the way that I, the Lord, have decreed to provide for my saints, that the poor shall be exalted, in that the rich are made low. For the earth is full, and there is enough and to spare; yea, I prepared all things, and have given unto the children of men to be agents unto themselves. Therefore, if any man shall take of the abundance which I have made, and impart not his portion, according to the law of my gospel, unto the poor and the needy, he shall, with the wicked, lift up his eyes in hell, being in torment. (D&C 104: 11-18.)

---

[241]This was to be a return of the ancient order of Enoch's City of Zion, about which it is written: "And the Lord called his people ZION, because they were of one heart and one mind, and dwelt in righteousness; and there was no poor among them." (Moses 7: 18.)

Initial efforts at this kind of Mormon unity ultimately failed, but the revelation did inspire the construction of "a general store, tannery, printing shop, and steam sawmill ...by the method of joint stewardships of leaders."[242] In fairness, external pressure and problems in the larger American economy contributed significantly to the failure. But the fundamental failure was because the saints were unprepared to accept "oneness" with each other on the level required.

The difficulty of this kind of unity among people who crave independence and self-sufficiency cannot be overstated. The ideal remained just an ideal, with an unrealized potential for changing people into Zion. One early example serves to illustrate the high cost of failing in the attempt to live this ideal. The senior Apostle in the first Quorum of Twelve, Thomas Marsh, left the church over his family's inability to give all that was required of them in this system.

Because he was the oldest of the first group chosen to serve as Apostles, Elder Marsh was designated the senior Apostle on May 2, 1835. After serving a mission in the eastern states, he returned to Kirtland to receive a special anointing as president of his quorum on January 22, 1836. The charge to him as an Apostle led him to make a comment the following day which Oliver Cowdery recorded: "In the evening Elder Marsh called at my house: we talked much upon the subject of visions: he greatly desired to see the Lord. Brother Marsh is good man, and I pray that his faith may be strengthen[ed] to behold the heavens open."[243] Marsh was not

---

[242] *Great Basin Kingdom, supra*, p. 12.

[243] Cook, Lyndon, W. *"I Have Sinned Against Heaven, and Am Unworthy of Your Confidence, But I Cannot Live Without a Reconciliation": Thomas B. Marsh*

alone in this desire, for as the time for dedicating the Kirtland Temple approached, the saints generally anticipated a visitation from the Lord. At the dedication there were many who had visions, saw angels, and beheld the Lord. (See *Opening the Heavens*, Salt Lake City: Deseret Book, 2005, pp. 327-371.)

Elder Marsh returned to Missouri after the dedication. The saints were impoverished by the earlier displacement from the first settlement in Jackson County, and the circumstances there were direful. Elder Marsh helped to build Far West in Clay County, and he initially distinguished himself in his leadership. However, he became embroiled in a leadership dispute in 1838 between the local high council, and local presidency. The local leadership had been organized before the Quorum of Twelve, and at the time, despite Section 107: 22-23, were regarded as superior to an Apostle. The political and ecclesiastical issues were sorted out over the next year. However, an incident involving property, and pride resulted in Elder Marsh leaving the church. The events show just how difficult it is for very good, devout, converted people to live in perfect honesty while sharing earthly goods:

> Sometime in August or September 1838, an incident occurred which would serve as a major factor in Marsh's apostasy from the Church. His wife, Elizabeth, was accused of unfairly taking cream from the daily milking which she shared with another sister, Lucinda Harris. Although the matter was heard by several priesthood courts, all of them found Sister Marsh guilty of promise-breaking. In a final move, Bishop Edward Partridge pleaded with her "to make things right and offered her time to do so," but Sister Marsh adamantly

---

Returns To the Church. BYU Studies, Vol. 20 (1979-1980), Number 4- Summer 1980, p. 391.

claimed she was innocent. When Joseph Smith bluntly told the sister that she had lied to the court and would be disfellowshipped, an indignant Thomas refused to hear of it. George A. Smith, apostle and Church historian, remembering the occasion, detailed the essential facts:

An appeal was taken from the Teacher to the Bishop, and a regular Church trial was had. President Marsh did not consider that the Bishop had done him and his lady justice, for they [the courts] decided the strippings were wrongfully saved, and that the woman had violated her covenant.

Marsh immediately took an appeal to the High Council, who investigated the question with much patience, and I assure you they were a grave body. Marsh being extremely anxious to maintain the character of his wife, as he was the president of the Twelve Apostles, and a great man in Israel, made a desperate defence, but the High Council finally confirmed the Bishop's decision.

Marsh, not being satisfied, took an appeal to the First Presidency of the Church, and Joseph and his Counsellors had to sit upon the case, and they approved the decision of the High Council. This little affair, you will observe, kicked up a considerable breeze, and Thomas B. Marsh then declared that he would sustain the character of his wife, even if he had to go to hell for it. ...

"I became jealous of the Prophet, and then I saw double, and overlooked everything that was right, and spent all my time in looking for the evil. . . . I was blinded, and I thought I saw a beam in brother Joseph's eye, but it was nothing but a mote, and my own eye was filled with the beam. . . . I got mad, and I wanted everybody else to be mad. I talked with Brother Brigham and Brother Heber, and I wanted them to be mad like myself; and I saw they were not mad, and I got madder still. . . . Brother Brigham, with a cautious look, said, 'Are you the leader of the

Church, brother Thomas?' I answered, 'no.' 'Well then,' said he, 'Why do you not let that alone?'"

Embarrassed over the "strippings affair," Thomas Marsh threatened to leave the Church. When Joseph learned of this, Thomas said that "he got me into a tight corner I could hardly evade. He put the questions directly to me, whether I was going to leave." But instead of working for a reconciliation, Thomas Marsh responded with contempt: "Joseph, when you see me leave the Church, you will see a good fellow leave it."

Stunned by these events in his life, Thomas Marsh possessed ambivalent feelings about leaving the Church. He accompanied a group of Saints to Daviess County, Missouri, on 16 October 1838 to abate reported mob activities against the Saints there. But his heart was not in it, and he questioned the legality of their actions. "Pretending there was something urgent at home," [sic] Thomas returned to Far West on 21 October 1838, and encouraged by Orson Hyde he decided to leave the Church. Believing that Joseph should not have allowed the "cream" trial, and being persuaded that the Prophet had directed extralegal activities in Daviess County, Thomas Marsh lost what faith he had left. His great love for the Church and its leaders had now turned to hate, and with Orson Hyde he left Far West on 22 October for Richmond, Missouri.[244]

Until it is attempted, it is not possible to fathom how difficult communal sharing of resources between families tests those involved. Those who imagine they would do better than the early saints are only fooling themselves. The Lord's Sermon on the Mount describes the kind of inner-heart required for those who

---

[244]*Id.*, pp. 394-396.

will establish Zion. He summarizes how it must be approached: "Therefore all things whatsoever ye would that men should do to you, do ye even so to them: for this is the law and the prophets." (Matt. 7: 12.) How easy these words are to read, but how difficult to apply. When we do think to apply them, we generally do so by judging others because we think their actions do not measure up to how we would like to be treated. We hardly ever take time to assess our own fidelity to this standard. Sharing becomes self-sacrifice. And while the burdens of the restored faith, including being mobbed, had been borne by Elder Marsh with heroism, sharing cow's cream was too much. He lost his position as the senior Apostle, and ultimately his membership in the church.

The saints' failure to live the United Order did not arise from some deep malignancy, but from the common weaknesses of human nature. When it comes to such communal sharing of property and resources, human weakness is enough to destroy the required unity. The higher standard is so foreign to normal existence it was beyond their reach. Reflecting on the failure to secure Zion in Jackson County, Lorenzo Snow said:

> There was no one man in the Church that could have bought that land (Jackson County, Missouri); there were no two men, or half a dozen men, or a hundred men that could have bought it. The people as a general thing were poor. There were no rich men that received the gospel in those early days. But by combination and union they could have secured the means to carry out the purposes of the Almighty in regard to the purchase of that country. They failed because of their love for money. In a revelation after this we are told that they failed to give their names as they were commanded. The Lord sent elders throughout the states where there were Latter-day Saints, to collect means for this purpose; and the people in Jackson County were

required to observe the law of consecration. But they failed to do it, and therefore the lands were not secured. The Lord could have sustained the people against the encroachments of their enemies had they placed themselves in a condition where He would have been justified in doing so. But inasmuch as they would not comply with His requirements, the Lord could not sustain them against their enemies. So it will be with us, or with any people whom the Lord calls to comply with His requirements and whom He proposes to confer the highest blessings upon, as He has in reference to us, and as He did in reference to the people in Jackson County.[245]

Zion requires a united people, one in heart and one in possessions. But people associating in any close proximity with one another always encounter fractious disputes. The Lord's formula for resolving them is clear: "And if any man will sue thee at the law, and take away thy coat, let him have thy cloak also. And whosoever shall compel thee to go a mile, go with him twain. Give to him that asketh thee, and from him that would borrow of thee turn not thou away." (Matt. 5: 40-42.) The Lord's formula for Zion is to take offenses inflicted by others, but never impose them. When you think you have taken all the offenses others can carelessly heap upon you, almost always they in turn are feeling just as imposed upon by your selfishness, foolishness, and insensitivity. The road to becoming "one" requires such a journey from where we are at present, the trip is unlikely to ever be taken by this or any like-minded generation. To their credit, the early saints at least

---

[245] *The Teachings of Lorenzo Snow.* Edited by Clyde Williams. Salt Lake City: Bookcraft, 1984, p. 159.

attempted the journey. We are too competitive, too uncooperative to ever try.

After failure in Kirtland and Missouri, there was no attempt to revive the United Order in Nauvoo. The law of tithing took its place. There was also a compact in Nauvoo through which the saints agreed to use private resources for the common good. The temporal needs of the church continued to require communal effort. The Nauvoo Mansion, the Nauvoo Temple, the Masonic Temple, the Seventy's Hall and the Grove were all built with community effort supported by the church. (Canvas purchased to be used in improving the Grove into a Bowery became the covering for covered wagons built for the exodus.) Industry was not merely encouraged by preaching about it, but also by entangling the church's resources with private resources.

The first phase of Mormonism laid a groundwork for a complete interconnection between the church and the economic activities of its members. However, the ideal of common ownership was attempted, failed, withdrawn, and replaced by tithing. Nevertheless, the revelations of the first phase established a framework that took a form in the second phase that was necessary to enable the church to migrate into the Great Basin. By the time the first phase ended with Joseph's death, Joseph's estate, and the church's property were so entwined it was part of the rift between Emma, and the church leadership. It took litigation to finally sort out what belonged to the church, and what was Joseph's (and therefore his widow's).

The forced exodus from Nauvoo left the church in still more direful circumstances. All the accumulated capital and property of Nauvoo was abandoned, or sold in distress. John Taylor estimated the community did not realize even a third of the value of farms, houses and lots.[246] To encourage the saints to move along, mobs burned outer properties, which resulted in a total loss to the owners. When the moment approached for departure, all of the available buyers knew the saints were selling under duress. Therefore, they offered only a fraction of the true value, which the saints were compelled to accept.

Communal efforts were required for the western migration. The doctrinal concept of cooperation in economic enterprises already existed, and the experiences in Missouri and Nauvoo prepared the saints to cooperate in the effort. Although the United Order was a distant goal, the Nauvoo compact was reaffirmed as part of the migration. The resulting successful, group cooperation was singular in United States history. Leonard Arrington observed the closest comparison was the early pre-revolution pilgrims, whose communal efforts also united first for survival, then for greater prosperity.[247] Crops were planted along the migration route, beginning at Winter Quarters. The crops were planted by the first companies, but would be harvested by later migrants. Things were done for the benefit of the group, not the individual. This kind of subordination of self to benefit others was not just to survive, it was believed to be necessary to gain heaven's favor. Revelation would only come to those whose actions mirrored heaven's, which blesses both the good and the bad with sun, and rain:[248] "Nevertheless, in your temporal things you shall be equal, and this not grudgingly, otherwise the abundance of the manifestations of

---

[246] *Great Basin Kingdom, supra*, p. 19.

[247] *Id.*, pp. 4-5.

[248] Matt. 5: 45.

the Spirit shall be withheld." (D&C 70: 14.) When the pattern of heaven was followed, they believed heaven would take notice. When the commandment to be equal is not followed, the "abundance of manifestations of the Spirit" end.

The saints arrived in the Salt Lake Valley in late July 1847. Despite the late start, they attempted to get a crop planted on a thirty-five acre plot. The difficulties of the first two years was harrowing:

> [T]oo many persons had been allowed to join the second contingent which left Winter Quarters in 1847. A food problem emerged. In the fall, the cattle and horses had gotten into the planted acreage and destroyed everything but the potatoes. Later in the winter, the Indians, wolves, and other "destroyers" and "wasters" made away with much of the livestock. ...Controls were placed on the prices of necessities, and a voluntary rationing system was instituted limiting each person to about one-half pound of flour per day. The people tried eating crows, thistle tops, bark, roots, and Sego Lily bulbs – anything that might offer nutriment or fill the empty stomach. One or two persons were poisoned by eating wild parsnip roots. ...All looked forward to the spring harvest. But when the winter wheat and garden vegetables began to show their heads, late frosts injured a considerable portion. And then, in May and June, hordes of hungry crickets moved upon the land and seemed certain to rob the settlers of the last vestige of food.[249]

Things were so bleak, the president of the High Council sent word that no one should part with their wagons or teams because they may need to use them– intimating that abandoning the Salt Lake

---

[249] *Great Basin Kingdom, supra*, pp. 48-49.

Valley for California was under consideration at that time. At this moment of despair the arrival of seagulls that devoured the crickets was a providential sign which "changed [their] feelings considerable for the better."[250]

The difficulties continued, however. The winter of 1848-49 was severe. The saints suffered a cold, heavy snowfall and could not access winter firewood. They also lost livestock to the cold. The cattle deaths cost them both food, and work animals.

> As the winter wore on the food problems became critical. On February 9, 1849, a committee appointed to investigate the food supply reported that there was on hand a little over three-quarters of a pound of breadstuffs per head per day for the next five months – that is, until harvest. A large proportion of the people were having to satiate their hunger, as during the previous year, with rawhides, sego roots, and thistles. None, however, had followed the Indians in eating grasshoppers and crickets. ...Church officials also wrote to leaders in Winter Quarters not to send companies west during the summer of 1849 unless they could depend entirely on their own resources, and unless they could bring with them enough provisions to last the winter of 1849-1850.[251]

It was as if the church was, like the revelation suggested, enduring the Lord's wrath, indignation and judgments upon their heads.[252] To cope with the extremities, the saints were instructed by Brigham Young to divide labor, scout for resources, and organize to overcome the adversities. In addition to agricultural efforts, the

---

[250] *Id.*, pp. 49-50.

[251] *Id.*, p. 59.

[252] D&C 124: 48.

work extended to basic industries, as well. The church turned economic development into "mission" calls:

> It is of great importance to the development of the West that the institution of the mission was applied after 1848 to colonization and economic activity. At the same conferences at which persons were called to foreign and United States gospel missions, others were called, in the same spirit, to mine gold, manufacture iron, raise silk, settle a disagreeable country, and teach Indians the arts of agriculture.[253]

When water was needed to plant, and cultivate, ditch digging was a church duty. Water rights were decided by church authorities, as was the allocation of timber rights. There were 200 families called to develop iron, and coal resources near Cedar City. Several hundred people were called on a sugar mission in the 1850's to establish a sugar beet industry. Men were called to a lead mission in Nevada. There was a cotton mission, a flax mission, a wool mission, and a wine mission. Because these were callings, the production belonged in part to the church. The church founded a newspaper, a retail store chain, and banking ventures. The church's development necessarily involved it in political activities, as well. By the 1880's, meetings of the First Presidency and Quorum of Twelve were predominately devoted to politics, railroad, mining, cattle, and banking discussions. The church's highest leadership became the nerve center for economic development and resource management.

There was a seamless connection between the economy of the Great Basin and the church. In the beginning, it was necessary for

---

[253] *Great Basin Kingdom, supra,* p. 33.

the church to be involved. In short order the church came to dominate all economic interests:

> The church's prime obligation was to forward the building of the Kingdom, and that meant it had positive functions to perform in increasing the production of goods and services. In line with this basic orientation, church funds were used to promote many types of new enterprizes, ecclesiastical officials regulated many phases of economic activity, and positive measures were taken to counteract panic and depression and to improve the welfare of the church and its members.[254]

The US Congress targeted the church's temporal accumulations in the Edmunds-Tucker Act passed in 1887. The legislation disincorporated both the church, and the Perpetual Emigrating Fund, as part of targeting the practice of polygamy.[255] By the late 1880's, the church's economic base was so significant Congress believed it was the single most effective target at which to aim. As the legislation was being considered, church leadership sought ways to influence or delay it. They were willing to spend money to save property. The church's Washington DC lobbyist sent a telegram saying, "Looks like the bill can be killed in conference, but will cost twenty to forty thousand more than we have now, contingent on success."[256] The church was not only willing to make the under-the-table payment, but the response from President John Taylor told President George Q. Cannon that if the church could "come into the Union untrameled by conditions, I would add

---

[254]*Id.*, p. 34.

[255]See *Encyclopedia of Mormonism*, p. 52.

[256]*Diaries of L. John Nuttall, supra*, p. 179.

$10,000.00."[257] As a back-up plan, the church considered ways to avoid the losses the Edmunds-Tucker Act would cause. Tithing property in Salt Lake, and Ogden was transferred to local ownership. The Gardo House was to be moved into trustee's names, real estate at various locations would be put into a local ecclesiastical corporation. The Street Railroad and Gas Company stock was to be bought by Heber J. Grant, Provo and Washington Factories, Zion's Savings Bank, Deseret Telegraph stock was also to be bought by Heber J. Grant. In fact, the plan considered was intended to reduce the church's direct holdings below the $50,000.00 limit set in the legislation.[258]

The attempts to transfer property into friendly hands and avoid the effects of the legislation failed. The act was passed, and the resulting financial distress felt by the church ultimately led them to abandon the practice of plural marriage. As a result of the capitulation by the church, the federal government returned the church's property, and it resulted in a return to business by the church and its leadership.

The result of all this was that after the late 1890's it was possible for church members to spend their entire lives doing business with church-owned or church-leadership owned business entities for everything needed. From retail purchases at ZCMI, cereal from Utah Cereal Food Company, dairy products from Mutual Creamery Company, sugar from Amalgamated Sugar Company or U and I Sugar, food from Grower's Market, beef from Nevada Land and Livestock Company, clothing from Salt Lake Knitting Works or

---

[257] *Id.*, p. 180.

[258] See the entries of December 28, 1886-June 15, 1887, *Diaries of John Nuttall, supra*, pp. 176-187, including footnotes.

Knight Woolen Mills, furniture from Granite Furniture Company, and insurance from Southwestern Fire Insurance Company, the economic horizon was church dominated. These are only a few of the businesses, however. It also included Inland Fertilizer Company, Consolidated Wagon & Machine Company, The Wasatch Land and Improvement Association, Riverside Canal Company, Utah Bag Company, Alaska Ice and Storage Company, Inland Crystal Salt Company, Rexburg Milling and Elevator Company, Deseret Book Company, Utah Construction Company, Utah Power and Light, Mountain States Telephone and Telegraph Company, Lambert Roofing Company, Insulation Manufacturing Company, Utah State National Bank, Ensign Amusement Company, Saltair Beach Resort, Utah Light & Traction Company, Zion's Savings Bank & Trust, Utah Oil Refining Company, Utah Onyx Development Company, Salt Lake Iron and Steel Company, Utah Lime and Stone Company, Emigration Canyon Rock Company, and Union Portland Cement Company, to name only some.[259] The church economic interests mushroomed in the second and early third phase. This growth was in part because of the necessity to be productive in the wilderness, and in part because the successes that came fostered an ambition by the leaders to continue, and do yet more with economic opportunities. When the wealth was threatened by anti-polygamy legislation, the church abandoned the politically unpopular practice to gain statehood, but the leverage used by the US Government to motivate was confiscation of property. When commerce was threatened, the church's business involvement was also put at risk

---

[259]See Quinn D. Michael. *The Mormon Hierarchy: Extensions of Power.* Salt Lake City: Signature Books, 1997, pp. 214-216.

of complete loss. It is hard to lay down the wealth and privileges of this world. Particularly when you believe there is an underlying theological reason to keep hold of them. By the end of the second phase of Mormonism, management of the church's economic interests occupied as much or more time, attention, thought, and care by the church's leadership as any theological shepherding.

As the third phase was beginning, the Salt Lake Temple, after forty years of effort, was at last completed. The first dedication service was conducted in the temple in April with the First Presidency and Twelve all present. The abandonment of plural marriage remained a source of division among church members. Private meetings before the dedication reflected the divisions among even church leaders. The temple dedication was intended to be a moment when they would return at last to unity. As the temple was dedicated, nature and Nature's God responded violently:

> The assembly room was filled to its utmost capacity. Pres. Woodruff offered the dedicatory prayer. Remarks were then made by himself and counselors. During the time of the services the wind outside blew a perfect hurricane, doing considerable damage throughout the city, and in various parts of the country.[260]

An economic storm to match nature's ire on the day of the temple dedication would quickly follow. Shortly after the completion of the Salt Lake Temple, the church and its leaders would be buffeted by the looming national depression that sent the greater national economy into a tailspin. The collapse was so quick, so complete, that by July following the April dedication of the Salt Lake Temple,

---

[260] *Diaries of Abraham Cannon, supra*, p. 382.

the church was unable to pay the Presidency, Twelve, or its employees. Heber Grant, en route east to borrow funds, recorded on May 11, 1893, "Money is so close that I am free to confess that I feel that I am to have a hard task in getting what we need."[261] On June 30, 1893 he recorded:

> This is the end of the month and not a dollar to pay anyone with not even Prest Woodruff and the Twelve. We have sent out or caused to be sent, circulars to the Presidents of Stakes to dispose of anything on hand in their stakes, in the shape of stock-produce or other property, cheap for cash and send the same to us at once. There is nothing doing–no tithing coming in– or means stirring and everybody seems paralyzed as well as business.[262]

The next month he reported:

> For the first time, this month the Church could not pay its employees, not the Presidency and Twelve. Well do not think I have lost hope – for I have not. I believe that Providence has something better in store for us than bankruptcy and ruin, but it will be a close shave in my opinion. May the Lord help us![263]

Things were bad enough that businesses were failing, and banks were closing to prevent runs from depleting all available cash. Apostle Cannon reported a July 1st bank closing in his diary:

> I was in the State Bank this afternoon and was sorry to learn that a run had been made by depositors to the extent of about $30,000, which has run down the finances of the

---

[261] *Diaries of Heber J. Grant, supra,* p. 160.

[262] *Id.*, p. 161.

[263] *Id.*

institution very materially... The National Bank of
Commerce of Provo today closed its doors because of the
run made on it. It is expected that the suspension will be
merely temporary.[264]

The following day, Sunday, July 2, 1893, things were desperate
enough the directors of The State Bank and Zion's Bank held an
emergency meeting. Because the directors of these banks were
church leaders, the meeting was held in the church president's
office:

> At 9 a.m. I went to a called meeting of the directors of The
> State and Zion's Savings Bank, held in the President's
> office to consider our financial condition. We heard a
> statement from both cashiers that were anything but
> reassuring. They cannot stand another run like that of
> yesterday. After some talk it was decided that Zion's
> Savings Bank shall demand the 30 day notice of withdrawal
> on all sums less than $100, and 60 days on more than that
> amount. They are entitled to this time. Heber M. Wells
> desired to state to the Clearing House that the State bank
> could not meet its calls, and ask to be helped. He said that
> The Bank of Commerce in this city had pursued that
> course, and had been helped.[265]

Twenty days later, in a Thursday meeting of the First Presidency
and Twelve, after the opening prayer the business was all about the
precarious financial condition of the church. A solution for the
problem was suggested. But Apostle Cannon thought it would only
further weaken the banks belonging to the church and its leaders:

---

[264] *Diaries of Abraham Cannon, supra*, p. 397.

[265] *Id.*

It was proposed that a hundred or more men of the Church be asked to loan to the Church from one to five thousand dollars apiece to meet the bills which are continually falling due. I felt that this course would be unwise, as such men as have money would draw the same from our needy institutions, and thus cripple them if they agree to loan the money on these terms. I expressed my views and others of the brethren coincided with them. I felt that an appeal for the prompt payment of tithing should be made, and that men be asked to assume the Church debts, instead of asking them to raise the money.[266]

The rallying hoped for in the April temple dedication was dampened by the economic troubles that quickly followed. On Friday, October 6, 1893, Elder Cannon remarked about the opening session of General Conference: "Everything is extremely dull for Conference. The attendance is also very small, there being scarcely more at the meetings than we usually have at our [Salt Lake] Stake Conference."[267]

The financial downturn was reflected in the total tithing receipts during these years, which were as follows:

1889: $782,798.78
1890: $878,394.11
1891: $747,273.30
1892: $723,264.63
1893: $576,583.64
1894: $52,506.52 for the first six months.[268]

---

[266] *Id.*, p. 403.

[267] *Id.*, p. 423.

[268] *Id.*, entry of October 5, 1894, *supra*, p. 557.

It was as if the church labored under Divine disapproval. It was as if the Lord's ire was on display, from nature's reaction to the Salt Lake Temple dedication to the economic distresses experienced by the church and its various business enterprises. The traditional narrative, however, dispenses with such an idea. The church is, wherever it goes, regarded as Zion. And all is and always has been well with Zion.

In the fourth phase, as church doctrines were further curtailed, the church's economic might would grow dramatically as a result of the management and business seeds planted in the second and third phases. The church's ability to build a brick-and-mortar presence became one of the hallmarks pursued in the beginning of the David O. McKay administration. When he began his presidency, there was not a single church-owned chapel in the British Isles.[269] There was a sentiment, originally attributed to Joseph F. Smith, which President McKay acted upon: "a good chapel is worth twenty full-time missionaries as a proselyter."[270] It was only three weeks after becoming president when he told Los Angeles reporters, "that the focus of the Mormon Church today is upon building."[271]

Building did become the church's focus. For the first time there were plans to build temples where stakes were not yet organized. The original model used to justify building a temple was inverted. Instead of building to support an existing body of believers, the

---

[269]Prince, Gregory and Wright, Wm. Robert. *David O. McKay and the Rise of Modern Mormonism*. Salt Lake City: University of Utah Press, 2005, p. 199.

[270]*Id.*, p. 200.

[271]*Id.*, p. 202.

temples were constructed to attract a body of believers.[272] Facilities were built as a missionary outreach. The economics of this approach were not sound. By 1960, building had outstripped tithing revenues, resulting in a projected $20-25 million deficit for the next year. Belt tightening across the board reduced the projected deficit to $17 million, but more cuts were needed. After paring back further still, President McKay was unwilling to reduce the building program. To the consternation of BYU President Wilkinson, President McKay moved $3.6 million from BYU to the Building Committee.[273]

Management of the church was becoming more akin to management of a typical Fortune 500 company. Building projects and budgeting needed to be spread across not only the church's ecclesiastical mission, but also over the legacy of businesses and investments owned by the church. By 1966, President McKay organized the various businesses under one management entity.

In phase four, President McKay consolidated the church's for-profit operations into Deseret Management Corporation. DMC oversees Beneficial Financial Group, Beneficial Life Insurance Company, Bonneville International Corporation, Bonneville Communications, Bonneville Interactive, Bonneville Satellite Company, Deseret Book, Newspaper Agency Corporation, Deseret News Publishing, Hawaii Reserves, Temple Square Hospitality, City Creek Development, Zions Securities, Zion's Utah Bancorp, KSL Broadcast Division, Deseret Digital Media, Deseret Trust Company, Farm Management Company, and other interests. The church owns Laie Resorts, Inc., the Polynesian Cultural Center,

---

[272]*Id.*, pp. 202-203.

[273]*Id.*, pp. 210-211.

and the largest agri-business in Hawaii. The agri-business holdings include not only 7,000 acres in Hawaii,[274] but also 317,000 acres in Florida[275] for cattle, citrus and nut production.

Beginning with the second phase, the business interests of the church have necessitated calling leaders whose business talents are critical to providing and overseeing church service. As a practical matter, leaders needed to have a set of talents that would match the job they are expected to perform. In 1898, President of the Quorum of the Twelve, Lorenzo Snow, observed the kind of men being called to fill positions of leadership in the church: "The Lord does not always select religious men to do His work, but he selects men of strong will and determination."[276] Reed Smoot, for example, had been chosen as an Apostle in 1895. Many were astonished at his call because he had so little of religion about him. When he received the call he confessed: "My past life has been in a business line, and I feel unfit for this position, but if it is the wish of the presidency I will do my best to magnify my calling."[277] He would be the center of a storm from 1903, when he was elected Utah's Senator, until 1907, when the Senate concluded their investigation, and seated him in a divided 42-28 vote. The committee investigating him recommended he not be seated, but

---

[274]Hawaii Reserves, Inc. manages church owned property in Hawaii, including Laie Water Company, Laie Treatment Works, Laie Shopping Center, Laie Park, Laie Cemetery, Hukilau Beach Park, and many residential and commercial properties in Laie. See www.hawaiireserves.com.

[275]See Deseret Ranches webpage, www.deseretranchflorida.com.

[276]*Diaries of Heber J. Grant, supra,* p. 243.

[277]*Diaries of Abraham Cannon, supra,* p. 650.

the two-thirds vote required to disqualify him was not obtained. His service as a US Senator lasted 30 years, and gave the church the political legitimacy it had been seeking since 1850.

Like Smoot, Heber J. Grant also confessed how little he knew about the Lord's dealings with mankind when he was called as an Apostle. As a young missionary, Hugh Nibley heard David O. McKay, like Grant speak about his selection as an Apostle. Brother Nibley remembered:

> His whole talk was about how skeptical he had always been about the gospel. He said he had never believed it for most of his life and was very skeptical. And of course, he was made an apostle, and he was an apostle at that time. He did believe it, we assumed. He showed a side of skepticism, at least different from all the others. I don't think the others had ever been as skeptical as he was... When he was made an Apostle, a lot of people were shocked. "David McKay, an Apostle?" Because he had been quite open and honest in expressing his doubts about things.[278]

By phase four, the church's development was shaped by business management and public administration principles. To accomplish all that is required by a leader in the church's abundant involvement in business, banking, politics, education, communication, and management, the people chosen have proven management talent. Leaders must fit the challenges the church faces. Church leaders at the highest levels are selected from banking, business, law, educational management, and land development, most often with family ties to other church leadership. Almost all Apostles and members of the First Presidency are related by blood or marriage. They are almost

---

[278] *David O. McKay and the Rise of Modern Mormonism, supra*, p. 7.

always drawn from descendants of the Nauvoo saints. The family interrelationships of all 101 general authorities and their wives in 1994 are documented by D. Michael Quinn in Appendix 4, to *The Mormon Hierarchy, Extensions of Power.*[279] Talented business, civic, and education backgrounds, according to leader's own explanations, outweigh religious backgrounds. For example, there is currently only one former seminary instructor included in the First Presidency and Quorum of the Twelve.

The church's goal of being well informed before making decisions has been accomplished by using the business marketing techniques of opinion polling and focus group meetings to test reactions to proposed church actions or policies. Correlation was adopted as a way to control the bureaucracy, but was extended to control teaching. Now, before an idea is taught, it is first tested using scientific means developed to market products. In a recent General Conference address, Elder Jeffrey Holland explained how very well adapted the church's infrastructure is for gathering opinions before acting:

> Not often but over the years some sources have suggested that the Brethren are out of touch in their declarations, that they don't know the issues, that some of their policies are practices are out-of-date, not relevant to our times. As the least of those who have been sustained by you to witness the guidance of this Church firsthand, I say with all the fervor of my soul that never in my personal or professional life have I ever associated with any group who are so *in* touch, who know so profoundly the issues facing us, who look so deeply into the old, stay so open to the new, and weigh so carefully, thoughtfully, and prayerfully everything

---

[279] *The Mormon Hierarchy, Extensions of Power.* Appendix 4, begins on page 731.

in between. I testify that the grasp this body of men and women have of moral and societal issues exceeds that of any think tank or brain trust of comparable endeavor of which I know anywhere on the earth.[280]

The groundwork for intermingling the temporal with the spiritual goes back to the first phase of Mormonism. But its original purpose was to break down inequalities between members of the church. Today's multi-billion dollar management is a legacy of the church's history, tended by church leaders who have accepted responsibility over it as a necessary part of their stewardship. But the economic disparity between the saints has perhaps never been greater. Further, the mixture of spiritual with temporal affairs has skewed the entire trajectory of the church. The church's wealth and influence have never been greater than today. At best, that is only a mixed blessing.

There is a warning in the Book of Mormon about priorities. It cautions: "He commandeth that there shall be no priestcrafts; for, behold, priestcrafts are that men preach and set themselves up for a light unto the world, that they may get gain and praise of the world; but they seek not the welfare of Zion." (2 Ne. 26: 29.) It is not for me to say when such a line was crossed, for only those involved are ever able to weigh all the difficulties involved in each decision as it was made. But those who have been, and are involved in these ancillary activities of the church have certainly been cautioned by the Lord, as recorded by Nephi, to never set themselves up as a light or to seek their own benefit. They are to never try to get gain. They are to avoid this world's praise. And

---

[280]Holland, Jeffrey R. *Prophets in the Land Again.* Ensign CR, November 2006, emphasis in original.

they are always to seek singularly for the welfare of Zion. Cumulatively, when these boundaries are crossed the participants move from priesthood to priestcraft, and the heavenly gift passes away. When that happens rights are lost, lands of possession are forfeited, and then God's judgments and wrath discipline those who will learn in no other way.

Chapter 8

THE CHILDREN OF CAIN WERE BLACK

During the first phase of Mormonism, African slavery was part of the larger American social order. It was a legal institution, protected by the Constitution. Latter-Day Saints were mostly northern non-slave owners whose sensibilities were abolitionist. European converts who joined and migrated to America were similarly opposed to slavery.

Part of the underlying tensions between Mormons and their Missouri neighbors was over the issue of slavery. The Missouri Compromise admitted Maine as a free state and Missouri as a slave state. It kept balance in the US Senate between the opposing sides. However, when abolitionist Mormons began to move to Missouri in large numbers, the large migration of new voters into this frontier state threatened the national and local interests.

The question of how first phase Mormonism viewed black Africans is complex. There were several new scriptures during the first phase that addressed the question. One of them, written by

Oliver Cowdery, was adopted by the church in a conference at Kirtland August 17, 1835, while Joseph Smith and Frederick G. Williams were in Michigan. It included the following statement about how to deal with black slaves:

> We believe it just to preach the gospel to the nations of the earth, and warn the righteous to save themselves from the corruption of the world; but we do not believe it right to interfere with bondservants, neither preach the gospel to, nor baptize them contrary to the will and wish of their masters, nor to meddle with or influence them in the least to cause them to be dissatisfied with their situations in this life, thereby jeopardizing the lives of men; such interference we believe to be unlawful and unjust, and dangerous to the peace of every government allowing human beings to be held in servitude. (D&C 134: 12.)

This statement says nothing about whether "every government allowing human beings to be held in servitude" was good or bad. Merely that, so far as it was allowed by a government, the institution of slavery ought not be interfered with by preaching to bondservants when their masters objected.

Mormons believed, as did other Christian faiths at the time, that black Africans descended from Cain through Ham, one of Noah's sons. There was a general expectation among many faiths that black Africans were destined to slavery because of a curse dating back to Genesis. This idea did not originate with Mormons, but they accepted it as did many other Christians in America and

Europe at the time.[281] The following verses were an often used proof-text to support the belief, and in turn, to justify slavery:

> And Ham, the father of Canaan, saw the nakedness of his father, and told his two brethren without. And Shem and Japheth took a garment, and laid it upon both their shoulders, and went backward, and covered the nakedness of their father; and their faces were backward, and they saw not their father's nakedness. And Noah awoke from his wine, and knew what his younger son had done unto him. And he said, Cursed be Canaan; a servant of servants shall he be unto his brethren. And he said, Blessed be the Lord God of Shem; and Canaan shall be his servant. God shall enlarge Japheth, and he shall dwell in the tents of Shem; and Canaan shall be his servant. (Gen. 9: 22-27.)

This was generally understood by those who accepted slavery to justify the enslavement of the African race. They thought that since Ham and his descendants were cursed to become a "servant" to both Shem and Japheth, they had an assigned destiny which justified enslavement. Though this is an odd concept to phase four Mormons, it was once accepted as true by many faiths. Islamic

---

[281]Concerning the belief Negroes descended from Ham: "Though particularly common in the first half of the nineteenth century this idea was actually very old. Recent studies have traced the association to at least 200 to 600 A.D. Jordan reports that early Jewish writings invoked Noah's curse to explain the black skin of the Africans. Among early Christian fathers, both Jerome and Augustine accepted the Ham genealogy for Negroes, and this belief is said to have become 'universal' in early Christendom. Most recently the association is evident in the earliest English descriptions of Africans in the fifteenth and sixteenth centuries. By the eighteenth century the connection had become common in the New World, where it was not infrequently cited in justification of black slavery." (Bush, Lester E., Jr. *Mormonism's Negro Doctrine: An Historic Overview.* Dialogue 8: Spring 1973, pp. 54, 59.)

traditions also include references to this idea. Al-Tabari, for example, included the following in his writings:

> Noah... prayed that Ham's color would be changed and that his descendants would be slaves to the children of Shem and Japheth.
>
> ...Ham begat all those who are black and curly-haired, while Japheth begat all those who are full-faced with small eyes, and Shem begat everyone who is handsome of face with beautiful hair. Noah prayed that the hair of Ham's descendants would not grow beyond their ears, and that wherever his descendants met the children of Shem, the latter would enslave them.[282]

In the Book of Jubilees (accepted as Jewish scripture by some), the possibility of salvation for Ham's descendants was denied:

> Be careful, my son, Jacob, that you do not take a wife from any of the seed of the daughters of Canaan, because all of his seed is (destined) for uprooting from the earth; because through the sin of Ham, Canaan sinned, and all of his seed will be blotted out from the earth, and all his remnant, and there is none of his who will be saved.[283]

Contrary to other views, Joseph Smith thought the capacity of a Negro slave to be saved was possible beyond any question. In that respect, Joseph Smith was more broad in his view of the potential for redemption of the slaves than many others:

> At five went to Mr. Sollars' with Elders Hyde and Richards. Elder Hyde inquired the situation of the Negro. I replied,

---

[282] *Extracts from Al-Tabari*, found in *Traditions About the Early Life of Abraham*. Compiled and edited by John Tvedtnes, Brian Hauglid and John Gee. Provo: BYU, 2001, pp. 333, 334.

[283] *Book of Jubilees*. Chapter 22, verses 20-21; found also at *Traditions About the Early Life of Abraham, supra,* p. 20.

they came into the world slaves, mentally and physically. Change their situation with the whites, and they would be like them. They have souls, and are subjects of salvation. Go into Cincinnati or any city, and find an educated Negro, who rides in his carriage, and you will see a man who has risen by the powers of his own mind to his exalted state of respectability. The slaves in Washington are more refined than many in high places, and the black boys will take the shine off many of those they brush and wait on.

Elder Hyde remarked, "Put them on the level, and they will rise above me."

I replied, if I raised you to be my equal, and then attempted to oppress you, would you not be indignant and try to rise above me, as did Oliver Cowdery, Peter Whitmer, and many others, who said I was a fallen Prophet, and they were capable of leading the people, although I never attempted to oppress them, but had always been lifting them up? Had I anything to do with the Negro, I would confine them by strict law to their own species, and put them on a national equalization. (*TPJS*, p. 269.)

While Joseph Smith believed in liberating slaves, his comment shows strong opposition to intermarriage between African descendants and other races. His belief in ending slavery was deeply held, and when he ran as a candidate for President of the United States he adopted a platform that would have ended slavery, and avoided the Civil War. He proposed selling public lands to fund repurchasing slaves by the government, then setting them free. The purchase would compensate slave owners for the loss of their property, making it possible to employ the freed African as a wage earner. The compulsory freeing of the slaves after the war bankrupted the South. The Fourteenth Amendment made it Constitutional to leave the slave owners unpaid for the loss of their investment in slave ownership. The resulting collapse of the economy of the South left the freed slaves with limited employment opportunities; mainly "sharecropping." The poorest classes suffered the risks associated with crop failures and price collapse, but white, southern, former slave owners were unable to employ or compensate workers on any other basis because they were destitute from both the war and the confiscation of their property. All the direful effects of the Civil War could have been avoided, and slavery could have ended peacefully, if Joseph Smith's approach had been adopted.

In an article titled *Gen. Smith's Views on the Government and Policy of the U.S.*, published in May, 1844, the following was Joseph's position on abolishing slavery:

> Petition also, ye goodly inhabitants of the slave states, your legislators to abolish slavery by the year 1850, or now, and save the abolitionist from reproach and ruin, infamy and shame. Pray Congress to pay every man a reasonable price for his slaves out of the surplus revenue arising from the sale of public lands, and form [sic] the deduction of pay from the members of Congress. Break off the shackles from the poor black man, and hire them to labor like other human beings; for "an hour of virtuous liberty on earth, is worth a whole eternity of bondage!" ... More economy in the national and state governments; would make less taxes among the people: more equality through the cities, towns & country, would make less distinction among the people; and more honesty and familiarity in societies, would make less hypocrisy and flattery in all branches of community; and open, frank, candid, decorum to all men, in this boasted land of liberty, would beget esteem, confidence, union and love; and the neighbor from any state, or from any country, of whatever color, clime or tongue, could rejoice when he put his foot

on the sacred soil of freedom, and exclaim: the very name of "American," is fraught with friendship! Oh! then, create confidence! restore freedom! break down slavery! banish imprisonment for debt, and be in love, fellowship and peace with all the world!...

Wherefore, were I the president of the United States, by the voice of a virtuous people, I would honor the old paths of the venerated fathers of freedom: I would walk in the tracks of the illustrious patriots, who carried the ark of the government upon their shoulders with an eye single to the glory of the people and when that people petitioned to abolish slavery in the slave states, I would use all honorable means to have their prayers granted: and give liberty to the captive; by giving the southern gentlemen a reasonable equivalent for his property, that the whole nation might be free indeed![284]

There were revelations Joseph received which made the question of how African descendants were to be regarded somewhat problematic. The tradition was that Ham married a woman who descended from Cain. Cain was the first murderer and his line was stricken by Divine decree from association with other lines. In the generations before Ham, the antediluvian descendants of Cain were excluded from some blessings. In one of his revelations, there is a description given of Enoch's Zion. This is the ideal Joseph's restoration was aiming to duplicate in the last days. With respect to the earlier Zion, the revelation states the following:

And it came to pass that the Lord showed unto Enoch all the inhabitants of the earth; and he beheld, and lo, Zion, in process of time, was taken up into heaven. And the Lord

---

[284] *Times and Seasons*, Vol. 5, No. 10. Nauvoo Illinois, May 15, 1844. Whole No. 94.

said unto Enoch: Behold mine abode forever. And Enoch
also beheld the residue of the people which were the sons
of Adam; and they were a mixture of all the seed of Adam
save it was the seed of Cain, for the seed of Cain were
black, and had not place among them. (Moses 7: 21-22.)

This raised the issue of whether the latter-day City of Zion
would, like the former one, exclude those with black skin because
they were the seed of Cain. However, Joseph made no effort to
segregate Kirtland or Nauvoo. Other than to advocate confining
them by strict law to intermarry in "their own species" he made no
effort to otherwise exclude them.

In March 1836, Joseph Smith ordained Elijah Able an Elder. Six
years later Joseph received another revelation which included the
following information:

From this descent sprang all the Egyptians, and thus the
blood of the Canaanites was preserved in the land. The
land of Egypt being first discovered by a woman, who was
the daughter of Ham, and the daughter of Egyptus, which
in the Chaldean signifies Egypt, which signifies that which
is forbidden; When this woman discovered the land it was
under water, who afterward settled her sons in it; and thus,
from Ham, sprang that race which preserved the curse in
the land. Now the first government of Egypt was
established by Pharaoh, the eldest son of Egyptus, the
daughter of Ham, and it was after the manner of the
government of Ham, which was patriarchal. Pharaoh,
being a righteous man, established his kingdom and judged
his people wisely and justly all his days, seeking earnestly to
imitate that order established by the fathers in the first
generations, in the days of the first patriarchal reign, even
in the reign of Adam, and also of Noah, his father, who
blessed him with the blessings of the earth, and with the
blessings of wisdom, but cursed him as pertaining to the

Priesthood. Now, Pharaoh being of that lineage by which he could not have the right of Priesthood, notwithstanding the Pharaohs would fain claim it from Noah, through Ham, therefore my father was led away by their idolatry; (Abr. 1: 22-27.)

This revelation was first published in March 1842. The following year Elijah Able was restricted in his missionary work to other African descendants. Shortly after Joseph's death, Elder Able was told to refrain from any priestly service.

Two sources claim Joseph Smith had Elijah Able quit using priesthood. One was Zebedee Coltrin, who had ironically ordained Elijah a Seventy. The other was Abraham Smoot, who recalled asking Joseph about that matter. Abraham Smoot reported that he asked: "What should be done with the Negroes in the South as I was preaching to them? [The Prophet] said I could baptize them by consent of their masters, but not to confer the priesthood upon them."[285]

There are other revelations, however, which speak about no limit to the gospel's universal offering of salvation. The Lord "inviteth them all to come unto him and partake of his goodness; and he denieth none that come unto him, black and white, bond and free, male and female; and he remembereth the heathen; and all are alike unto God, both Jew and Gentile." (2 Ne. 26: 33.)

As soon as Joseph was gone, the second phase of Mormonism immediately showed a hardened view toward Africans. If the prior statements were insufficient, Brigham Young declared on January

---

[285]Bush, Lester E., Jr. *Mormon's Negro Doctrine: An Historical Overview.* Dialogue 8: Spring 1973, p. 60.

5, 1852 that he knew, by revelation, there was a ban on any Negro receiving priesthood because of the first murder by Cain of Abel:

> If there never was a prophet or apostle of Jesus Christ [that] spoke it before, I tell you, this people that are commonly called Negroes are the children of old Cain. I know they are; I know that they cannot bear rule in the Priesthood, for the curse on them was to remain upon them until the residue of the posterity of Michael and his wife receive the blessings, the seed of Cain would have received had they not been cursed, and hold the keys of the Priesthood until the times of the restitution shall come, and the curse be wiped off from the earth and from Michael's seed. Then Cain's seed will be had in remembrance and the time come when the curse should be wiped off.[286]

There would be a continual reaffirmation of this principle from the second phase of Mormonism until the fourth phase. Black Africans were barred from priesthood. They were not permitted to receive ordination, or in turn to receive temple rites available only to men holding the office of elder. During Brigham Young's lifetime the justification was Biblical. That is, he relied upon the "seed of Cain" idea. Cain was cursed. Cain's curse was preserved through the flood by Ham, Noah's son. Here is another teaching of Brigham Young's from 1854:

> We have this illustrated in the account of Cain and Abel. Cain conversed with his God every day, and knew all about the plan of creating this earth, for his father told him. But, for the want of humility, and through jealousy, and an anxiety to possess the kingdom, and to have the whole of it under his own control, and not allow any body else the right to say one word, what did he do? He killed his

---

[286] *The Complete Discourses of Brigham Young, supra,* p. 468.

brother. The Lord put a mark on him; and there are some of his children in this room. When all the other children of Adam have had the privilege of receiving the Priesthood, and of coming into the kingdom of God, and of being redeemed from the four quarters of the earth, and have received their resurrection from the dead, then it will be time enough to remove the curse from Cain and his posterity. He deprived his brother of the privilege of pursuing his journey through life, and of extending his kingdom by multiplying upon the earth; and because he did this, he is the last to share the joys of the kingdom of God.[287]

The idea that God would curse a posterity for all time as punishment for the first murder, was in Brigham Young's mind a confirmation of how evil murder was. It is odd, however, that he did not regard it as equally evil in all cases. There is some irony about his preaching of "blood atonement" (righteous killing of even the unwilling) when it is juxtaposed against his near everlasting condemnation of Cain and his posterity.[288] Of course, Brigham Young made a distinction between a senseless murder to get gain (by Cain), and murder in furtherance of repentance (blood atonement). Murder was allowed, but only when President Young thought it was needed for the salvation of the victim. But if murder is unforgivable, salvation and eternal cursing get risked when the wrong person is "blood atoned." Given the risk, the doctrine of religious killing seems extraordinary.

---

[287] *JD* 2: 143.

[288] If read carefully, Brigham Young did not assert black Africans were prevented from ever receiving priesthood authority. Only that they would have to await a future time, when after all of children of Adam were resurrected they would at last have the curse removed.

Though his position confined blacks to being a servant, deprived of the church's priesthood, he did not think it proper to abuse Negroes or treat them as animals:

> The seed of Ham, which is the seed of Cain descending through Ham, will, according to the curse put upon him, serve his brethren, and be a "servant of servants" to his fellow-creatures, until God removes the curse; and no power can hinder it. These are my views upon slavery. I will here say a little more upon this point. The conduct of the whites towards the slaves will, in many cases, send both slave and master to hell. This statement comprises much in a few words. The blacks should be used like servants, and not like brutes, but they must serve. It is their privilege to live so as to enjoy many of the blessings which attend obedience to the first principles of the Gospel, though they are not entitled to the Priesthood.[289]

Throughout the second and third phases of Mormonism this teaching was confirmed and expounded. Although Brigham Young did not refer to the revelations given to Joseph Smith in the Book of Abraham and the Book of Moses as justification for the teaching, others would reaffirm the ban on priesthood and cite to these scriptures for support.

Church Patriarch, John Smith, asked a question in 1902 that suggested the possibility of temple blessings one day becoming available for black Mormons. In a meeting of the First Presidency, Twelve and Patriarch on November 13, 1902 he asked the following question, which the meeting of church leaders answered with a postive reply:

---

[289] *Discourses of Brigham Young,* Vol. 2, p. 908.

He said that Black Jane [i.e., Jane Manning James] had called on him and wanted to know when the curse would be taken off that she might have her endowments. Brother John was instructed to tell her to be patient and wait a little longer; that the Lord has his eye on her and would be far better to her than ever she had dreamed.[290]

The whole landscape of America changed from the third to the fourth phase of Mormonism. Between the 1940's and 1970's America was transformed. The larger social change accompanying the Civil Rights movement, Voting Rights Act, and integration resulted in a dramatic shift in attitudes. By the 1960's, the accepted notions of "Negro inferiority," and the propriety of legal segregation was breaking down through federal legislation, and a series of US Supreme Court decisions. American and Mormon attitudes alike were affected. The church's doctrine was becoming an embarrassment to many members. It was also affecting the church's ability to project international growth in areas where the mission field appeared open to conversion. In particular, Brazil was a place growth would be affected because of this doctrine.

The first weakening of the teaching came because of members in Brazil. Exclusion from the priesthood was no longer based on appearance alone. Positive proof of black ancestry was necessary. In the absence of positive proof, ordination was allowed. This permitted church growth despite the silent violation of the proscription regarding ordination of a person with "even one drop of Negro blood."

In the Spring of 1973 an influential article appeared in *Dialogue: A Journal of Mormon Thought*, titled, *Mormonism's Negro Doctrine: An*

---

[290] *A Ministry of Meetings: The Apostolic Diaries of Rudger Clawson.* Edited by Stan Larson . Salt Lake City: Signature Books, 1993, p. 509.

Historical Overview, supra. The article made the case for changing the policy. By attacking presumptions, challenging the adequacy of the historic record, and pointing out weaknesses in analysis, the article made a change seem possible. Nevertheless, the article also conceded the necessity of a revelation to accomplish the change:

> No one, I believe, who has talked with leaders of the contemporary Church can doubt that there is genuine concern over the "Negro doctrine." Nor can there be any question that they are completely committed to the belief that the policy of priesthood denial is divinely instituted and subject only to revelatory change. ...A thorough study of the history of the Negro doctrine still has not been made. In particular, three fundamental questions have yet to be resolved:
>
> First, do we really have any evidence that Joseph Smith initiated a policy of priesthood denial to Negroes?
>
> Second, to what extent did nineteenth-century perspectives on race influence Brigham Young's teachings on the Negro and, through him, the teachings of the modern Church?
>
> Third, is there any historical basis from ancient texts for interpreting the Pearl of Great Price as directly relevant to the black-priesthood question, or are these interpretations dependent upon more recent (e.g., nineteenth-century) assumptions?[291]

Within five years of the article, the doctrine was abandoned. The announcement affirmed a revelation was received, but the content of the revelation has always remained unstated. Only the result was announced. Every person, regardless of race, was permitted to receive priesthood ordination in The Church of Jesus Christ of

---

[291] *Id.*, at pp. 96-97.

Latter-day Saints. To make it a binding change, the matter had to be presented to a conference and sustained by common consent, at which point as a matter of church government it was the replacement doctrine for all that went before. The record of both the announcement and vote to sustain it are found in Official Declaration No. 2, in the Doctrine and Covenants, and states the following:

To Whom it May Concern:

On September 30, 1978, at the 148th Semiannual General Conference of The Church of Jesus Christ of Latter-day Saints, the following was presented by President N. Eldon Tanner, First Counselor in the First Presidency of the Church:

In early June of this year, the First Presidency announced that a revelation had been received by President Spencer W. Kimball extending priesthood and temple blessings to all worthy male members of the Church. President Kimball has asked that I advise the conference that after he had received this revelation, which came to him after extended meditation and prayer in the sacred rooms of the holy temple, he presented it to his counselors, who accepted it and approved it. It was then presented to the Quorum of the Twelve Apostles, who unanimously approved it, and was subsequently presented to all other General Authorities, who likewise approved it unanimously.

President Kimball has asked that I now read this letter:

June 8, 1978

To all general and local priesthood officers of The Church of Jesus Christ of Latter-day Saints throughout the world:

Dear Brethren:

As we have witnessed the expansion of the work of the Lord over the earth, we have been grateful that people of many nations have responded to the message of the restored gospel, and have joined the Church in ever increasing numbers. This, in turn, has inspired us with a desire to extend to every worthy member of the Church all of the privileges and blessings which the gospel affords.

Aware of the promises made by the prophets and presidents of the Church who have preceded us that at some time, in God's eternal plan, all of our brethren who are worthy may receive the priesthood, and witnessing the faithfulness of those from whom the priesthood has been withheld, we have pleaded long and earnestly in behalf of these, our faithful brethren, spending many hours in the Upper Room of the Temple supplicating the Lord for divine guidance.

He has heard our prayers, and by revelation has confirmed that the long-promised day has come when every faithful, worthy man in the Church may receive the holy priesthood, with power to exercise its divine authority, and enjoy with his loved ones every blessing that flows therefrom, including the blessings of the temple. Accordingly, all worthy male members of the Church may be ordained to the priesthood without regard for race or color. Priesthood leaders are instructed to follow the policy of carefully interviewing all candidates for ordination to either the Aaronic or the Melchizedek Priesthood to insure that they meet the established standards for worthiness.

We declare with soberness that the Lord has now made known his will for the blessing of all his children throughout the earth who will hearken to the voice of his authorized servants, and prepare themselves to receive every blessing of the gospel.

Sincerely Yours,
Spencer W. Kimball
N. Eldon Tanner
Marion G. Romney
The First Presidency

Recognizing Spencer W. Kimball as the prophet, seer, and revelator, and president of The Church of Jesus Christ of Latter-day Saints, it is proposed that we as a constituent assembly accept this revelation as the word and will of the Lord. All in favor please signify by raising your right hand. Any opposed by the same sign.

The vote to sustain the foregoing motion was unanimous in the affirmative.

Salt Lake City, Utah, September 30, 1978

With that vote, the doctrine was gone. One of the most outspoken defenders of the prior doctrine denying priesthood to blacks was Elder Bruce R. McConkie. He not only wrote in defense of the teaching, but he edited his father-in-law's[292] books which also reiterated and defended the doctrine. Elder McConkie was a member of the Twelve when the doctrine changed. He was as dogmatic about defending the change as he had been about the earlier teaching. The way he explained his abrupt change is a reflection of how greatly welcomed the change was when it was finally made. He and other church leaders were weary of this topic. His statements after the 1978 change included the following:

> We have read these passages and their associated passages for many years. We have seen what the words say and have said to ourselves, "Yes, it says that, but we must read out of it the taking of the gospel and the blessings of the temple to the Negro people, because they are denied certain things." There are statements in our literature by the early Brethren that we have interpreted to mean that the Negroes would not receive the priesthood in mortality. I have said the same things, and people write me letters

---

[292] His father-in-law was church President Joseph Fielding Smith. The five volume *Answers to Gospel Questions* and three volume *Doctrines of Salvation* taught and justified the earlier doctrine.

and say, "You said such and such, and how is it now that we do such and such?" All I can say is that it is time disbelieving people repented and got in line and believed in a living, modern prophet. Forget everything that I have said, or what President Brigham Young or President George Q. Cannon or whoever has said in days past that is contrary to the present revelation. We spoke with a limited understanding and without the light and knowledge that now has come into the world.

It doesn't make a particle of difference what anybody ever said about the Negro matter before the first day of June 1978. It is a new day and a new arrangement, and the Lord has now given the revelation that sheds light out into the world on this subject. As to any slivers of light or any particles of darkness of the past, we forget about them. We now do what meridian Israel did when the Lord said the gospel should go to the Gentiles. We forget all the statements that limited the gospel to the house of Israel, and we start going to the Gentiles.[293]

The change opened up missionary work in Africa. It also expanded the potential pool of converts in the United States, the Carribean, and South America.

One matter, however, was not officially changed. The idea of intermarriage and mixed race children remained a subject of aversion:

An aversion to miscegenation has been the single most consistent facet of Mormon attitudes towards the Negro. Though the attitudes towards the priesthood, slavery, or equal rights have fluctuated significantly, denunciations of interracial marriage can be identified in discourses in

---

[293] McConkie, Bruce R. *Sermons and Writings of Bruce R. McConkie.* Salt Lake City: Bookcraft, 1989, p. 165.

virtually every decade from the Restoration to the present day. ...The Church viewed miscegenation from the unique perspective of the priesthood policy but was, of course, by no means unique in its conclusions; in fact, the leadership generally invoked "biological and social" principles in support of their conclusions on the subject.[294]

This aversion continued with President Spencer W. Kimball, the church president who announced abandonment of the doctrine. He maintained the church's view that racial intermarriage with whites and negroes was discouraged. He phrased it in universal terms, but the result was the same. He said:

> The interrace marriage problem is not one of inferiority or superiority. It may be that your son is better educated and may be superior in his culture, and yet it may be on the other hand that she is superior to him. It is a matter of backgrounds. The difficulties and hazards of marriage are greatly increased where backgrounds are different. For a wealthy person to marry a pauper promises difficulties. For an ignoramus to marry one with a doctor's degree promises difficulties, heartaches, misunderstandings and broken marriages.
>
> When one considers marriage, it should be an unselfish thing, but there is not much selflessness when two people of different races plan marriage. They must be thinking selfishly of themselves. They certainly are not considering the problems that will beset each other and that will beset their children.
>
> If your son thinks he loves this girl, he would not want to inflict upon her loneliness and unhappiness; and if he thinks his affection for her will solve all her problems, he should do some more thinking.

---

[294]*Mormonism's Negro Doctrine: An Historical Overview, supra,* pp. 89-90.

> We are unanimous, all of the Brethren, in feeling
> and recommending that Indians marry Indians, and
> Mexicans marry Mexicans; the Chinese marry Chinese and
> the Japanese marry Japanese; that the Caucasians marry
> Caucasians, and the Arabs marry Arabs.[295]

It is noteworthy that the subject of black and white intermarriage was so sensitive that Negroes were unmentioned in the "unanimous" view of "all the Brethren" to discourage such marriage. A small sample of the statements made in opposition to those marriages shows the prior historic view did not include intermarriage of races other than the Negro race. It was intermarriage with them, alone, which was discouraged. However, in the current Church Handbook of Instructions, the discouragement is phrased in universal terms. No single form of interracial marriage is discouraged, rather all marriages of people with different racial, cultural, social and other differing backgrounds are targeted. The race-neutral phrasing conceals the primary concern.

There is perhaps no more respected thinker among Latter-day Saint leaders than J. Reuben Clark. He was an attorney in the Department of State, later becoming Under Secretary of State, and US Ambassador to Mexico. As Under Secretary of State, his Clark Memorandum on the Monroe Doctrine was instrumental in changing the use of United States military force in Latin America. He was called into the First Presidency in 1933, and continued to serve there until his death in 1961. The law school at Brigham Young University has been named after him.

---

[295]Kimball, Spencer W. *The Teachings of Spencer W. Kimball.* Edited by Edward Kimball. Salt Lake City: Bookcraft, 1982, p. 303.

It is obvious that the racial tensions in America during his lifetime affected President Clark's thinking. However, some of his actions show how indelible was the view of the curse of black Africans. Even the most broad-minded in church leadership held the view. In response to a newspaper photograph, President Clark met with Deseret News Editor Mark E. Petersen and complained about the integration of races:

> Pres. Clark brought to his attention the article in the Saturday paper, front page, colored child with white child, asked who was responsible for it. ...Pres. Clark thought the News people should be instructed that there should be no pictures with colored people; they are trying to break down the color line, and we will have enough trouble as it is. Pres. Clark said he would not do anything to hurt the Negro, but is very concerned about this growth of Negro tolerance, and he did not want anything done to lead his grandchild to marry a Negro.[296]

Although he did not advocate persecution of black people, like Joseph Smith, he was alarmed at the idea of intermarriage. Another entry shows both his sympathy for Negro dignity, and his strong rejection of intermarriage. The entry concerns local stage depictions of Negroes:

> President Clark said that he asked Mrs. Manning if they were making fun of the Negro, and said he thought they ought [not] to do that, and repeated his attitude toward the intermarriage of races, that he does not like to see things that breaks down the color line ...He repeated he did not think they should make fun of them. He said that he had a deep sympathy for the Negroes, but that did not mean he

---

[296] *The Diaries of J. Reuben Clark, 1933-1961, Abridged.* Salt Lake City: Privately Published, 2010, pp. 155-156, entry for May 1, 1950.

would want one of his children to marry one, and he did not want them to dance with them, and he did not approve of the breaking down of the color line because anything that breaks down the color line leads to marriage.[297]

Despite a willingness to see equality among Caucasian, Japanese, Chinese, and East Indians, President Clark did not want the same for blacks. In advising a church representative attending a National Council for Women in December, 1957, he told her he "thought she should do what she could to keep the National Council from going on record in favor of what in the last analysis would be regarded as Negro equality."[298]

The church's antipathy toward interracial marriage with Negroes started with the first phase, and endured through the fourth. For example, in the first phase, an article written by Oliver Cowdery stated:

> We have travelled in the south, and have seen the condition of both master and servant; and without the least disposition to deprive others of their liberty of thinking, we unhesitatingly say that if ever the condition of the slave is bettered, under our present form of government, it must be by converting the master to the faith of the gospel and then teaching him to be kind to his slave. The idea of transportation is folly, the project of emancipation is destructive to our government, and the notion of amalgamation is devilish! And insensible to feeling must be the heart, and low indeed must be the mind, that would consent for a moment, to see his fair daughter, his sister, or

---

[297] *Id.*, p. 194.

[298] *Id.*, p. 239.

perhaps, his bosom companion, in the embrace of a Negro![299]

In the second phase, discouragement of intermarriage between whites and blacks went beyond mere denunciation. It was accompanied with the threat of required execution to repent of the sin of such a marriage:

> But let me tell you further, let my seed mingle with the seed of Cain, that brings the curse upon me and upon my generations; we will reap the same rewards with Cain.
>
> In the Priesthood, I will tell you what it will do. Were the children of God to mingle their seed with the seed of Cain it would not only bring the curse of being deprived of the power of the priesthood upon them but they would entail it upon their children after them, and they cannot get rid of it. If a man in an unguarded moment should commit such a transgression, if he would walk up and say cut off my head, and kill the man, woman and child, it would do a great deal towards atoning for the sin. Would this be to curse them? No, it would be a blessing to them; it would do them good that they might be saved with their brethren. A man would shudder should they hear us talk about killing folk, but it is one of the greatest blessings to some to kill them, although the true principles of it are not understood.[300]

[handwritten margin note: blood atonement]

In the third phase, a theological course prepared by a General Authority B.H. Roberts touched on the subject. He appealed to then-current scientific views to support the teaching. He instructed:

---

[299] *Messenger and Advocate*, (October 1835-September 1836). Vol. 2, April 1836 No. 19, p. 300

[300] *The Complete Discourses of Brigham Young, supra*, p. 469.

"At this point we hear some one exclaim, 'Not so fast! To sit at table, to mingle freely in society with certain persons, does not imply you would marry them." Certainly not, in every case. We may recognize socially those whom we personally abhor. This matters not, however; for wherever social commingling is admitted, there the possibility of intermarriage must be also admitted. It becomes a mere question of personal preference, of like and dislike. Now, there is no accounting for tastes. It is ridiculous to suppose that no negroes would prove attractive to any white. The possible would become actual-as certainly as you will throw double-double sixes [in dice], if only you keep on throwing. To be sure, where the number of negroes is almost vanishingly small, as in the north and in Europe, there the chances of such misalliances are proportionally divided; some may even count them negligible. But in the South, where in many districts the black outnumbers the white, they would be multiplied immensely, and crosses would follow with increasing frequency. * * * But some may deny that the mongrelization of the Southern people would offend the race notion-would corrupt or degrade the Southern stock of humanity. If so, then such a one has yet to learn the largest-writ lessons of history and the most impressive doctrines of biological science. That the negro is markedly inferior to the Caucasian is proved both craniologically and by six thousand years of planet-wide experimentation; and that the commingling of inferior with superior must lower the higher is just as certain as that the half-sum of two and six is only four."[301]

Two fourth phase statements are cited below. They are attributed to the father-in-law, Joseph Fielding Smith, and the

---

[301]Roberts, B.H. *Seventy's Course in Theology*, Vol. 1. Salt Lake City: Deseret Book, 2009, p. 166.

son-in-law Bruce R. McConkie. Joseph Fielding Smith was a church president, and Elder McConkie one of the Twelve Apostles, in the fourth phase of Mormonism. First President Smith:

> Answer: During the past decade there has arisen in this country, the United States, a wave of "non-segregation," that is, that there should be an equality in all things between the white races and the black or Negro race. This doctrine of social equality and the common mingling of these races is said to be made for the purpose of eventually eliminating the Negro race by absorption through intermarriage. This matter of amalgamation to a great degree has been enforced by the justices of the Supreme Court of the United States. This tendency for "equality" in all things, has brought a flood of correspondence from all parts of the Church asking how it is that The Church of Jesus Christ of Latter-day Saints stands out in opposition and teaches a doctrine of segregation denying the Negro the right to hold the priesthood. Some of these letters border on a spirit of resentment and claim that the Church is guilty of a great injustice, since "all men were created free and equal." This answer is written to place us in the right light before the members.[302]

This is from Elder McConkie:

However, in a broad general sense, caste systems have their root and origin in the gospel itself, and when they operate according to the divine decree, the resultant restrictions and segregation are right and proper and have the approval of the Lord. To illustrate: Cain, Ham, and the whole Negro race have been cursed with a black skin, the mark of Cain,

---

[302]Smith, Joseph Fielding. *Answers to Gospel Questions, Volume 2*. Salt Lake City: Deseret Book, 1963, 5 Volumes, p. 184.

so they can be identified as a caste apart, a people with whom the other descendants of Adam should not intermarry. (Gen. 4; Moses 5.) The whole house of Israel was chosen as a peculiar people, one set apart from all other nations (Ex. 19:5-6; Deut. 7:6; 14:2); and they were forbidden to marry outside their own caste.[303]

Once the change was made, J. Reuben Clark's reluctance to see children of African descent alongside white children depicted in photographs was forgotten. In church publications, magazines, films, and manuals the barrier evaporated. The church's New Era, a magazine targeting teens and young adults, has regularly depicted and advocated race mingling.[304]

Just as other teachings and practices have been in flux over the four phases of Mormonism, so also this doctrine has been changed. Perhaps the two changes which appear most dramatic to the

---

[303]McConkie, Bruce R. *Mormon Doctrine*. 2d ed. Salt Lake City: Bookcraft, 1966, p. 114.

[304]See, e.g., New Era, July 1992 "Family Photo" showing 19 young people, male and female, of various ethnicities. The photo was explained with this caption: "God created the races– but not racism. We are all children of the same Father. Violence and hatred have no place in His family." New Era, August 1995 "Add Spice to Life" showing six different spice jars and six different faces of different races, ages and sexes. The caption read: "Learn to savor the goodness found in so many different people." New Era, October 1998, "Some Assembly Required" showing a black boy in the front and center, with two boys, one white and the other Latin, behind him while they all set out chairs in what appears to be an LDS chapel overflow area. New Era, September 2000 "Look Ahead" showing a white boy whose neck is so twisted to look behind him that only the back of his head is visible; behind him are seated a black boy on the right and a white girl on the left beside each other, all of them seated in school desks while taking an examination. The white boy apparently cheating by looking at the apparently better informed black boy and white girl behind him.

uninformed observer would be the abandonment of plural marriage and the position on blacks of African descent. They are easy to see as changes. However, the two most significant changes are not these, but two others. When Joseph Smith was lost and the first phase came to an end, Mormonism stopped expanding its doctrine and began to contract. This was the most significant change, although its importance has not been appreciated by the Mormon faithful.

The second most important change was the decision at the beginning of the third phase to abandon, and then denounce as apostate, what was an orthodox prior practice. The significance of these two cannot be overstated. The first may have fulfilled an ominous prophecy about latter-day Gentile rejection of the fullness of the Gospel. The second made it possible for Mormonism to make radical changes, enforce those changes, and punish by excommunication those who would not support those radical changes. It made Mormonism capable of transforming into anything, no matter how unlike what went before. It made it possible for the church to still defend itself as a continuation of what Joseph Smith restored even when it lost, abandoned, even condemned what Joseph Smith taught. This is also not adequately appreciated by Mormons as a monumental change to our religion.

Chapter 9

FOLLOW THE (CURRENT) BRETHREN

n the third phase of Mormonism the miraculous wanes. The two revelations given to John Taylor in 1886[305] and Wilford Woodruff in 1889[306] (understood at the time to

---

[305] Although the John Taylor revelation is somewhat controversial, his son John W. Taylor accepted it as an authentic revelation and spoke of having found it, "among my father's papers I found a revelation given him of the Lord, and which is now in my possession, in which the Lord told him that the principle of plural marriage would never be overcome." (See *Diaries of Abraham H. Cannon*, April 1, 1892, p. 319.) The revelation includes, among other things, the statement: "For I the Lord am everlasting and My everlasting covenants cannot be abrogated nor done away with; but they stand forever." (*The Book of the Prophet John Taylor*. Chapter 10, revelation received Monday, September 17, 1886. John Taylor Papers LDS Archives.) A photocopy of the handwritten document is also in my possession.

[306] John Nuttall, secretary to the First Presidency, records the revelation was received on Sunday, November 24, 1889. See *In the President's Office: The Diaries of L. John Nuttall, 1879-1892*. Edited by Jedediah S. Rogers. Salt Lake City: Signature Books, 2007, pp. 395-396.

reaffirm the Lord's direction to practice plural marriage) were discarded. In place of prophecy and revelation, church management focused on an effort to gain uniformity and control. Business ventures that were started in the second phase, and were necessary to support the members, came to dominate the time and attention of the third phase leadership. These legacy business ventures grew to occupy an increasingly greater role in the life of the church and its leaders.

More important, the third phase introduced a new kind of orthodoxy. Third phase Mormonism abandoned, and denounced as heretical, principles and practices that were a vital part of the earlier phases. The denunciation of these new found heresies became so ardent as to justify excommunication. Whereas, the second phase venerated and tried to live all of the first phase's teachings, the third phase did not. In order to accomplish this kind of adjustment to the religion, a cult of personality, comparable to Catholicism's veneration of the Pope, needed to attach to the office of the President of The Church of Jesus Christ of Latter-day Saints. These changes in third phase Mormonism made it possible to create a faith on a distinctly different trajectory than the original.

Mormonism no longer believed persecution was a badge of authenticity,[307] but began to work for acceptance, even popularity.

---

[307]The concept that persecution is the heritage of the righteous still got lip service into the fourth phase. For example, Joseph Fielding Smith wrote: "Tribulation is the heritage of the righteous. It was never intended that those who serve the Lord in faithful obedience to covenants should find a rosy path to eternity. Persecution has been the reward of righteousness. Hatred of those who love the world is usually made manifest against that which is good. 'As many as I love, I rebuke and chasten: be zealous therefore, and repent.' (Rev. 3:19.) Again: 'Behold, happy is the man whom God correcteth: therefore despise not thou the chastening of the Almighty." (Job 5:17.) 'And I said unto him, Sir, thou

Instead of the ambition to be "independent above all other creatures beneath the celestial world,"[308] the new hope was to become mainstream American; accepted, and even admired by as many fellow Americans as possible. This ambition began to shape Mormonism during the second phase, and would eventually be the reason for the end of the second phase. This desire for acceptance would grow throughout the third phase, becoming part of the church's management infrastructure in the fourth phase.

Apostles in the first and second phases of Mormonism were given the same charge as Oliver Cowdery gave the first Twelve. They were cautioned that they were not fully ordained to the Apostleship until they received a visit from Christ. It was a duty not often realized. Elder Orson Pratt, for example, explained his witness was based upon the Holy Ghost:

> Have I seen the face of the Almighty in open vision? No; this is a great privilege that I have never attained to. Have holy angels come down from heaven when I was awake and conversed with me as one man converses with another? No; I have not had so great a privilege-I have not attained to that. But I know by the power of the Holy Ghost shed forth in my heart from time to time; for,

---

knowest. And he said to me, These are they which came out of great tribulation, and have washed their robes, and made them white in the blood of the Lamb. Therefore are they before the throne of God, and serve him day and night in his temple: and he that sitteth on the throne shall dwell among them.' (Rev. 7:14-15.)" (*Church History and Revelation. Being a Course of Study for the Melchizedek Priesthood Quorums.* Salt Lake City: Deseret Book, 1947, Vol. 2, p. 77.) Despite this idea, the overwhelming effort in the fourth phase is to avoid persecution, acquire acceptance, and gain favorable public perception for the church and its members.

[308]D&C 78: 14.

notwithstanding all my faults, all my weaknesses, my imperfections, and failings, through the past thirty years, I do know one fact, and that is that God has from time to time, through his infinite mercy and goodness, shed forth upon me his Holy Spirit, unworthy as I was to receive it, and that has borne testimony, time and again, that this is the work of God: it has given me a knowledge which it is impossible for me to doubt. If I had seen angels, I might doubt, without having the Holy Ghost. I might doubt if I had seen great miracles, without the Holy Ghost accompanying them; and I might doubt if I saw the heavens opened, if I heard the thunders roll; and I might go and build a golden calf and worship it: but when the Holy Ghost speaks to me and gives me a knowledge that this is the kingdom of God, so that I know it just as well as I know anything else, then that knowledge is past controversy. By that knowledge I know this work to be true; by it I know that this kingdom will roll on until it shall attain its high destiny, and the kingdoms of this world become the kingdoms of our God and his Christ. (*JD* 8: 314.)

The charge to see Christ was rarely realized, and that failing gave rise to feelings of inadequacy among Apostles who were never able to obtain such a blessing. Early in the third phase, the Apostolic charge to pursue an audience with Christ was eliminated:

> In the twentieth century, charismatic apostleship changed in several ways. First, the "charge" at ordination no longer obligated apostles to seek visions. Second, the Presidency and apostles began down-playing the importance of these experiences. Third, apostles began speaking of a non-visionary "special witness of Christ" by the Holy Ghost in terms which allowed listeners to conclude that the apostles referred to an actual appearance of deity. Fourth, apostles were reluctant to discuss their

visionary experiences publicly. Fifth, evidence indicates that a decreasing number of apostles experienced visions before or after ordination.

The change in the apostolic "charge" apparently began with the appointment of Reed Smoot as an apostle in 1900. General church authorities had long regarded him as "reliable in business, but [he] has little or no faith." President Lorenzo Snow blessed him to receive "the light of the Holy Ghost" so that he could bear testimony of Jesus Christ and Joseph Smith. This was an extraordinary departure from the apostolic charge as given since 1835.

The lessening of charismatic obligation continued during Joseph F. Smith's administration. In 1903 the "charge" to new apostle George Albert Smith spoke of his obligations to attend quorum meetings, to sustain the First Presidency and Twelve's leadership, to express his views "boldly" in quorum meetings, and to lead an exemplary life. There was no mention of visions. In 1907 Francis M. Lyman instructed newly ordained Anthony W. Ivins: "The Twelve are the Special witnesses of Jesus Christ & should be able to testify that he lives even *as if* he had been seen by them" (emphasis added).

Twentieth-century apostles began applying this "as if" approach to their spoken testimonies. Usually this involved wording their "special witness" of Christ in a way that encouraged listeners to assume the leader has had a more dramatic encounter with the divine than actually claimed. Apostle Boyd K. Packer acknowledges that some Mormons have become impatient with those carefully worded apostolic testimonies and ask: "Why cannot it be said in plainer words? Why aren't they more explicit and more descriptive. Cannot the Apostles say more?" He dismisses this objection as seeking "for a witness to be given in some new and dramatic and different way." (Quinn D. Michael. *Mormon Hierarchy: Extensions of Power.*

Salt Lake City: Signature Books, 1997, pp. 2-3, footnotes and citations omitted, emphasis in original.)

The forces at work in Mormonism's third phase are illustrated and embodied by Heber J. Grant. He was called as an Apostle in the second phase, became church president in the third phase, and helped create the circumstances in which the fourth could follow. Heber J. Grant was the last president to have plural wives. He struggled in his personal family life with the decision by President Woodruff to abandon the practice, but then disagreed with those who wanted to continue the practice once it had been discarded. We look at the third phase of Mormonism through the life of Heber J. Grant.

Heber J. Grant was called to serve as a stake president when he was 23 years old. Less than two years later he was called into the Quorum of the Twelve. A year before he was called as an Apostle, Charles R. Savage suggested to him that he would be called into the Twelve. The night of that conversation he records his reaction to this idea:

> [October 7, 1881] I must confess there is no honor in this world that I consider half so great as to be an Apostle of God, and while it would fill my heart with joy that I can not possibly express to be considered by God as worthy [to] be one of his apostles, I must confess that my past life has not been such as to merit any such honor. I have endeavored to live an honorable and a true life, that I have done many little things wrong, I am free to confess— I think the greatest wrong of my life has been the neglect to study the works of our Father in heaven. I am comparatively speaking ignorant of the principles of truth

and the many things pertaining to the work of God on the Earth.[309]

Despite his desire to be called, his diary and personal comments recorded a lifelong view that he remained in "comparative ignorance" of God's work, which he never overcame. Notwithstanding this personal sentiment that he was unworthy, he accepted the calling when it was offered.

He was told the following as part of his ordination as an Apostle, as recorded in his diary:

> [October 16, 1882] We ordain thee to be a Prophet, a Seer, a Revelator, to have every key of authority connected with this holy Apostleship– it embodying all the power and all the authority that God ever vouchsafed to His children upon the earth.[310] (*Id.*, p. 8.)

Eight years after receiving those keys and authority, Elder Grant recorded his continuing insecurity arising from spiritual limitations. He entertained doubts not only about his capacity to have spiritual experiences, but also about the propriety of such things. He feared they would not contribute to faith, but undermine it. His diary records:

> [May 30, 1890; in apostles' meeting] . . . Heber J. Grant. Stated that he had never had an inspired dreaming his life and that although he had always desired to see his father in dream or vision that he had never been allowed to enjoy this great privilege. He had at all times been afraid to ask for any great spiritual manifestation as he would then be

---

[309] *The Diaries of Heber J. Grant, 1880-1945, Abridged.* Salt Lake City: Privately Published, 2010, p. 5.

[310] This is consistent with Brigham Young's explanation that "all the keys" are embodied in the office of the Apostle and came to him by operation of that ordination.

under greater obligations and he had feared that he might become unfaithful as others had done who had been blessed with great manifestations. He was ready and willing to obey his brethren who preside over him and said that he had never engaged in any kind of business without submitting the same to the First Presidency. I have always felt that I am greatly deficient in spiritual gifts." (*Id.*, p. 115.)

This fear of risking apostasy because of a spiritual manifestation continued to motivate his attitude and approach to spiritual experiences throughout his calling as an Apostle, and later as church president. He would resist any effort to pursue a spiritual manifestation the remainder of his life. He became church president in 1918, serving for twenty-six and a half years; the second longest president in LDS church history. Throughout that time he continued to regard spiritual manifestations as a potential harbinger of apostasy.

Prior to his calling into the Twelve, Elder Grant was obsessive about his business activities. "In addition to selling insurance, he peddled books, found Utah retailers for a Chicago grocery house, performed tasks for the Deseret National Bank, and taught penmanship. With Brigham Young's support, he was appointed an assistant cashier of the church-owned Zion's Savings and Trust Company."[311] Seventeen years into his calling as an Apostle, Elder Grant continued to spend so much time on his personal business activities he felt guilty because of it.

He explains in his diary the reasons underlying his business drive. He replaced Elder Pratt, whose life ended in financial destitution.

---

[311] *Encyclopedia of Mormonism*, p. 565.

Because he regarded it as a personal failing by Elder Pratt, he did not want that to be his experience. He records the following:

> [November 4, 1889] . . . I felt that I had been neglectful of my duty as an apostle in the past and had devoted too much of my time to business affairs. I had deceived myself into feeling that I was doing my full duty because I attended as many if not more meetings in the different wards and stakes of Zion than any of the other members of my Quorum, except Francis M. Lyman. I explained that when I was chosen to be an apostle seventeen years ago to fill the vacancy caused by the death of Orson Pratt that I had not been impressed with the great labors which Brother Pratt had accomplished. He had died leaving his family destitute. (*Id.*, p. 275.)

Elder Grant gives an interesting insight into his priorities in his January 1, 1891 diary entry. Looking back on the preceding year, the year the Manifesto had been adopted, he records what was most important to him. First, it is a financial matter, secondarily is the harmony between members of the Twelve. He does not mention the Manifesto. The entry reads:

> The most important event financially of the year has been the organization of the State Bank of Utah . . . Above all things I have been thankful for the wonderful meetings that have been held by the Apostles wherein they have become more united in heart and spirit than they have ever been before since I became a member of the Quorum. (*Id.*, p. 126.)

In a meeting of the First Presidency and Twelve on April 1, 1892, Elder Grant reflected on his preoccupation with business to the exclusion of seeking spiritual experiences. He is quoted by Apostle Abraham Cannon as saying:

I would like to be relieved of financial matters if it were possible and in accord with the minds of my brethren, and go upon a mission so that I can get those great spiritual blessings of which the brethren speak but which I have never enjoyed. I find that dissensions are growing to some extent among my brethren engaged with me in business, and this I do not want.[312]

His "business" which resulted in "dissensions" involved his dealings with Bullion Beck Mining Company, Utah Sugar Company, State Bank of Utah, Grant Bros. Livery Company, and other interests that continually occupied his time. There were those who believed he showed more interest in his businesses than his calling as an Apostle. But he also said he "regretted deeply that financial matters had occupied nearly [all] of his time." (*Heber J. Grant Diaries*, p. 152.) Even his closest associates did not always understand his motivation. He viewed the business ventures he devoted so much energy to as both necessary, and a service to his fellow Latter-day Saint.

Apostle Grant's idea that business was appropriate for a church leader did not originate with him. The view was shared by other leaders. In a letter by the First Presidency to Bishop John R. Winder on March 18, 1891, the reasons for business among the leaders are explained: "Those of us who have grown up with this country, and have been so favored of the Lord since we came here in the accumulation of means, owe it to the community that we should do our share in helping to develop home industries." (*Id.*, p. 130.)

---

[312] *The Diaries of Abraham H. Cannon, 1889-1895.* Salt Lake City: Signature Books, 2010, p. 317.

Despite the benefits to the saints in need of employment, and the larger economy, Apostle Grant acknowledged there was a widespread view that he cared more for making money than anything else. His mother informed him of his unfavorable reputation:

> [July 19, 1889] Mother called this morning and we had a long talk. I learned that it was the opinion of a great many of the latterday saints that I was filled with pride and that there was nothing in this [life] that I cared about so much as I did about making money. It was the opinion of some that the Lord should remove me out of my place as I was so worldly minded and so full of pride. I had no respect for the poor among the people. (*Id.*, pp. 97-98.)

Elder Grant's diary is a valuable window into his heart and life. Recording criticism from his own mother proves that record is an authentic and candid source. He is not trying to hide himself in its pages.

He was wounded by the accusation. In the privacy of his journal he explained his real motivation:

> I regret that any of the saints should have any such an opinion of [me] as I do not have the feelings that are charged to my account. I have made many thousands of dollars since I was married but I have invested largely in businesses that have not paid, and the reasons for the investments was that I desired to aid in establishing enterprises that I considered would be in the interests of the people. If I know my own heart I think as much of a poor man as one with wealth and more too if he is a better man. I detest those that think well of people on account of their wealth . . . (*Id.*, p. 98.)

The criticism forced him to explain himself. He went about busily attending to the challenges of the time, and did not concern himself with being understood or appreciated. He presumed others knew why he was fervently engaged in commerce. They did not. John Nuttall, the Secretary to the First Presidency made this observation about Elder Grant: "[F]inancial matters have more weight with ...Heber J. Grant than the things of the Kingdom."[313] Only when he was reacting to accusations did he offer an explanation for attending to so much business as an Apostle.

His business acumen and candor often resulted in a 'tin-ear' for others. He records how he hurt some feelings by his insensitivity. But he would justify himself. Business was, after all, business. Charity was secondary, an effect of his successful business endeavors. It could never assume the foreground. That would be unbusiness-like. Here is an account he wrote justifying his refusal to come to the aid of a brother in the faith for purely economic reasons:

> [December 26, 1890; in New York City] I had a long chat with Brother John W. Young[314] today. He said that he felt hurt at my remark last night that I would not care to loan him money from the funds of the State Bank. I told him that I could not take back what I had said, that while I considered him an honest man at the same time that I felt that he was constantly undertaking more than his means would justify and therefore I had not that confidence in the

---

[313] *In the President's Office: The Diaries of L. John Nuttall, 1879-1892.* Edited by Jedediah Rogers. Salt Lake City: Signature Books, 2007, p. 268.

[314] John W. Young was a counselor to the Quorum of the Twelve who asked to have his service end in October 1891 because of his inability to meet his financial obligations.

success of his undertakings that I wished I had, or which
would inspire me enough so that I would loan him means
from a bank where I was really holding the funds in trust
for others. (*Id.*, p. 125.)

In considering the record of his life, it is apparent he was a
towering businessman, and interested in finding enterprises he
thought would help indirectly members of his faith. He freely
admitted how little he understood of the things of God. He may
have been a visionary businessman, but he confessed he was never
a visionary religious man. His sermons were reminders of virtue,
calls to pay tithing, observe the Word of Wisdom, live chaste lives,
and avoid debts. He dispensed practical advice.

Heber J. Grant was not alone in this world view. Throughout this
period the meetings of the First Presidency and Twelve Apostles
were business meetings. The meetings started with prayer and then
included temple based prayer circles, but the meetings then turned
to practical discussions about political issues, business ventures,
investment opportunities, tithing collections, and development of
the community. The First Presidency and Twelve met to discuss
practical problems. The agendas focused upon solving issues for
the mini-nation of Mormons scattered by colonization from
Canada to Mexico. Brigham Young's colonization and pioneer era
businesses were the leadership's inheritance. They managed these
assets as prudent businessmen. The problems were practical and
required practical solutions. No heavenly choirs or angelic visitors
were needed in the meetings. Often keeping bitter political
opponents at bay was all the leaders could face in those troubled
times. In an exclamation that paints the picture of the times with
some clarity, President George Cannon was moved to make a
business prophecy:

Prest. Cannon said that he felt that as sure as the Lord lives that if we would be united and take up the building of a R.R. that the way would be opened and it would be a grand success. He felt to make this promise in the name of the Lord Jesus Christ & Pres. Woodruff said amen when he had finished his remarks. (*Id.*, p. 171.)

So prophecy was not altogether absent from these meetings. But it almost always concerned the hope for business success by the leaders' various enterprises. At the time, the prophecy concerned a church involved venture that would eventually result in a minority ownership of the San Pedro, Los Angeles & Salt Lake City Railroad, incorporated in 1901. It was later acquired by Union Pacific.[315] The church failed to gain control, but was able to acquire a block of stock in the Union Pacific. The First Presidency and Twelve meetings discussing this venture lasted for years and illustrated how business risks occupied a great amount of church leadership's energy and time. It was not, however, a "grand success."

In 1921, President Grant recorded another incident in his life confirming again his fear that spiritual experiences were likely to result in harm or mischief. He records an incident that happened while investigating post-Manifesto plural marriages. He interviewed Bertha Landon, who had been married as a plural wife after the Manifesto in a ceremony performed by Patriarch Israel Barlow. In

---

[315]The railroad was begun in 1871 with construction from Salt Lake City southward. In 1879 the road was extended to Juab by the Utah Southern, which was controlled by Union Pacific. Another Union Pacific subsidiary extended the line to Milford, Utah in 1880. Work extending the line south from Milford was planned to begin by 1889, but financial issues interrupted plans until 1899, when the route was completed to the Utah-Nevada border.

the course of the interview he asked his secretary, Bertha Irvine, to come and take notes, which were then inserted into his journal under the date of March 15, 1921, and state the following:

> President Grant took occasion to show her that even those who had had the greatest manifestations had been led away when they failed to listen to the counsel of the servants of the Lord placed at the head of the Church; mentioned Oliver Cowdery having seen John the Baptist, Peter, James and John, and even those who had seen the Savior himself, also had fallen away from the Church. He also told of John W. Taylor seeing the Savior when away in the mountains, ...How Bro. Taylor followed after Moses Thatcher instead of listening to President George Q. Cannon, who had the right to counsel and guide him, and though he was warned by the leading brethren and by dreams and otherwise, yet he followed his own course, which took him out of the church. President Grant told Sister Langton [sic] that one living prophet was worth twenty dead ones... (*Id.*, p. 317.)

His reference to John W. Taylor in a conversation involving plural marriage was appropriate. Elder Taylor was expelled from the Twelve and excommunicated from the church over the issue of plural marriage. Taylor maintained his belief in earlier revelations, and thought the Manifesto could not change responsibilities imposed by God. Therefore, Elder Taylor's personal, visionary encounters with the Lord were, in President Grant's view, proof such things were unproductive. They either led to rebellion against church government, or were of no benefit in preventing it. Either way, a visit with the Lord was inferior to fidelity to church leaders. President Grant found the choice between the two easy. He believed church policies[316] should have priority over personal visions or visitations by the Lord.

His reference to Oliver Cowdery, however, is really not applicable. Although it is true he fell away from the church, he died in fellowship, having been rebaptized by Orson Hyde on November 12, 1848. Despite the fact that he was personally alienated from Joseph Smith during the years of his disaffection, he never lost faith in the restoration of the Gospel. "In his ten years outside the Church, Cowdery never succumbed to the considerable pressure to deny his Book of Mormon testimony. Indeed, letters to his LDS relatives show that he was hurt at the Church's rejection but remained a deep believer."[317] For President Grant, however, church status mattered most. Possession of a testimony without church membership was still nothing more to him than apostasy. Therefore, to President Grant's thinking, Oliver Cowdery's years away while having a testimony condemned him all the more.

In a conversation on February 23, 1926 with Bishop Hooper, who was despondent over his daughter running away to marry a man of whom he disapproved, President Grant recorded he gave the following advice:

> ..many of the apostles of the Church could not control their sons and daughters and even the Lord himself had a son that did not make a very good record, judging from the scriptures we have. Told him of the temptations that came

---

[316]"Today the issue is viewed as "modern revelation" controlling over earlier revelation. In the case of Elder Taylor, however, his direct participation in the events behind the scenes led him to regard the Manifesto as less inspired by revelation and more inspired by practical decision-making and political compromise.

[317]*Encyclopedia of Mormonism*, p. 339.

to me to resign because I had never seen the Savior and
that I was unfit to be an apostle etc. (*Id.*, p. 334.)

Near the end of his life, after twenty four years as church
president, he again revisited the topic of spiritual manifestations.
Once again he expressed his distrust of any such things:

[October 4, 1942] I have never prayed to see the Savior, I
know of men— Apostles— who have seen the Savior more
than once. I have prayed to the Lord for the inspiration of
His Spirit to guide me, and I have told him that I have seen
so many men fall because of some great manifestation to
them, they felt their importance, their greatness." (*The
Diaries of Heber J. Grant, 1880-1945, Abridged.* Salt Lake City:
Privately Published, 2010, p. 468.)

For President Heber J. Grant, there was no question of his
fidelity to the church. He accepted its premise and believed it was
God's handiwork. He trusted Joseph Smith was indeed a Prophet
called by God. He believed those who preceded him in the office
of the president were equally entitled to his respect. Six men before
him were presidents. He felt honored by the office, and conformed
to the patterns handed to him from that tradition.

Spiritual manifestations were effectively eliminated from the
church president's office in the third phase, as demonstrated by
President Grant's diary. Nonetheless, he did believe God played a
role which remained central to the church's decision making. God
was presumed to be the overruling power behind the church's
progress. Though He did not appear, speak or send angels, God
was not absent.[318]

---

[318]This is the same view advocated and explained by Elder Boyd K.
Packer in his talk *The Mantle is Far, Far Greater Than the Intellect.* 5th Annual
CES Religious Educator's Symposium. BYU Studies. 22 August, 1981,

Despite his fear and distrust of spiritual manifestations, President Grant trusted the Lord to guide him in church and business responsibilities. He viewed any success achieved in practical business as God's handiwork. For example, the start-up sugar industry was greeted with healthy skepticism by church-member critics. Elder Grant wanted it to succeed to vindicate faith in the First Presidency. He wrote:

> [December 22, 1894] I think there is no one thing that can happen which will strengthen the faith of the people in the wisdom of the advice given by the First Presidency so much as to have this Factory a success, seeing that so many of the people have said that they were sure it would be a failure. (*Heber J. Grant Diaries*, p. 189.)

When a conflict existed between principles he believed and previous church presidents under whom he served, he always submitted to the president, and subdued his own preferences. Ending plural marriage was a personal trial for him. But he submitted. In contrast, there were Apostles who did not submit and whose membership in the church was lost.

Apostles Matthias F. Cowley and John W. Taylor continued to perform plural marriages after being told to stop. When they did so after the Manifesto, it was tolerated. But when they continued after President Joseph F. Smith ended the practice entirely in 1904, it was another matter. Senate hearings to seat Reed Smoot in the US Senate were underway. The clandestine continuation of plural

---

which included the statement we should be able to "see in every hour and in every moment of the existence of the Church, from its beginning until now, the overruling, almighty hand of Him who sent His Only Begotten Son to the world to become a sacrifice for the sin of the world." (Quoting Joseph F. Smith from CR Apr. 1904, p. 2.)

marriages threatened to expose the church as dishonest with the Federal Government. In 1905 President Smith proposed to drop Elder Cowley and Elder Taylor from the Twelve and excommunicate them from the church. In a letter to Joseph F. Smith on January 5, 1906, Heber Grant wrote the following: "What they have done I have done or intended to do, and in so doing I would have done what I thought had the approval of my brethren." (*Id.*, p. 285.) It grieved him to see these peers lost to his Quorum. His plea did not alter the outcome and both were dropped from the Twelve.

Elder Grant saw John W. Taylor the next year and recorded his reaction at seeing his former fellow-Apostle:

> [January 27, 1907] ...When I saw Brother John W [sic] Taylor come in meeting to-day, I could not keep back the tears as I saw him sit down in the audience, and remembered that when I left upon my mission, that he was in full fellowship as a member of the council of the Twelve Apostles. Brother Taylor had supper with us at my cousin's.[319] (*Id.,*. p. 285.)

Tears for his former associate, whom he called "brother," shows loyalty and greatness of his soul. The fact he would attend dinner with this disgraced former Apostle and regard him as "Brother Taylor" is kind and endearing. Principle led Elder Taylor into conflict with the church. Principle led Elder Grant to accept Elder Taylor's expulsion. Friendship and loyalty brought them together for dinner.

Although he accepted the church's abandonment of the practice, in a conversation with Guy C. Wilson about a course for seminary

---

[319]The identity of the cousin is not mentioned, but is likely Anthony Ivins who is frequently identified in the diary as his cousin.

students, President Grant defended teaching plural marriage. He said he wanted the chapter on plural marriage rewritten and made even stronger, pointing out that eight of the Quorum of the Twelve then serving were products of plural marriages. Despite his personal views, he summed up the on-again, off-again commandment to practice plural marriage: "It is a fine thing for the people to get it into their heads that when the Lord tells you to do something and then tells you to quit doing it, he should be obeyed in both cases." (*Id.*, p. 349.)

If the voice and manifestation of the Lord fades from the scene in the third phase of Mormonism, the idea the Lord remains responsible for the church does not. In the first two phases, a prophet, seer and revelator was expected to have visionary manifestations. By the third, such expectations had given way to a more practical approach. Religious qualifications were not as necessary as business management skills and financial acumen. President Lorenzo Snow said in a meeting of the Apostles on January 4, 1889: "The Lord does not always select religious men to do His work, but he selects men of strong will and determination." (*Id.*, p. 243.)

There was an Apostle's meeting in 1890, the beginning of the third phase of Mormonism, in which President George Q. Cannon recorded an ambition he hoped would one day be realized. The minutes are interesting for two reasons. First, the manner in which the First Presidency and Twelve conduct business. Second, the recorded desire to get deference in business matters from the saints. John Beck was a Latter-day Saint, but ignored the First Presidency's wishes in conducting his business. The account states:

> [*October 16, 1890; Thursday*] At 2 p.m. I went to my Council meeting at the Gardo House. There were present

Presidents Woodruff, Cannon and Smith,[320] H[eber] J. Grant and myself. Our room being cold we did not dress in our robes,[321] but had prayers,[322] Bro. Grant being mouth. The subject of the sugar company was then presented. [sic] John Beck,[323] and his satellites have subscribed the majority of the stock with a view to controlling the entire business. He named a directory[324] which is objectionable to many stock-holders, and to which the Presidency are opposed. He says that unless he can have this amount of stock he will not take any, and he hopes by this means to force the company into submission to his views, because it will be difficult go get subscribers to all the stock. The Presidency, however, feel that the issue is now between their influence and the money of Beck and others, and the former do not feel to yield. Bro. Grant and I agreed to stand by their action in this matter, and will do our utmost to get the Sugar Co. stock distributed widely among the people, so

---

[320]These three were the First Presidency at the time, Wilford Woodruff, George Q. Cannon, and Joseph F. Smith.

[321]These were the temple robes, which they would customarily wear in prayer as their meetings began.

[322]The word "prayers" is plural because there were generally both an opening prayer, followed by a prayer circle using the order of prayer comparable to what would occur in a temple ceremony.

[323]John Beck was an independently minded Latter-day Saint who, although a member of the church, often disagreed with church leaders about business matters. He discovered the rich Bullion Beck silver deposit outside Eureka, Utah, which the Bullion Beck Mining Company would develop. Church leaders and the church itself would invest in that mining company, and management decisions involving the Bullion Beck Mining Company were frequently the subject of First Presidency and Twelve Apostles meetings.

[324] Referring to the board of directors for the new business.

that they will give the industry the support it will need. I have personally very grave doubts about the success of the enterprise from a financial standpoint, but am determined to do all I can for its success. Pres. Woodruff said he desired all of the First Presidency and Twelve to subscribe some stock even though it was but little. Father[325] expressed his desire to see the day when the influence and counsel of the Presidency and Twelve shall be sought and felt in financial as well as spiritual affairs. *(Candid Insights of Mormon Apostle: The Diaries of Abraham H. Cannon, 1889-1895.* Edited by Edward L. Lyman. Salt Lake City: Signature Books, 2010, p. 152-153.)

By the end of the third phase this ambition to gain enough influence to affect the saints' business affairs had been accomplished. The president was presumed to have the right to speak on all matters, and the advice he gives on any matter should always be followed. As that idea took, the stage was set for the fourth phase to begin. The pivot between the two happened with the ascendency of David O. McKay, as the ninth church president. His presidency would take full advantage of a cult of personality surrounding the church president. He would become the first living man regularly referred to as a "living prophet" in church publications.

[April 9, 1951] This morning in a solemn assembly session, President David O. McKay was sustained as president of the Church. Elder Stephen L. Richards was sustained as his first and President J. Reuben Clark, Jr. as his second counselor.

---

325 This is referring to Abraham Cannon's father, George Q. Cannon of the First Presidency.

I remember that President Clark said to me on one occasion, "My boy, you always keep your eye on the president of the Church, and if he ever asks you to do anything which is wrong and you do it because of your loyalty to him, the Lord will bless you for it. But you need have no fear; the Lord will never permit his mouthpiece to lead the Church astray. He will take him first. (Appendix 2. *The Diaries of Marion G. Romney, 1941-1961, Abridged*, found in *The Diaries of J. Reuben Clark, Jr., 1933-1961, Abridged*. Salt Lake City: Privately Published, 2010, p. 298.)

In the first phase, an actual ascension to God's presence was the aspiration of every follower of Christ. By the third phase, fearless, unquestioning submission to the church's president replaced the ascent to God. Between these, the alteration of Mormonism was dramatic. The fourth phase included an intensification of business management principles, marketing techniques, and associated success in growth, wealth, and numbers. The fourth phase, where Mormonism is today, is poised to become a world religion now malleable enough to accept changes which contradict, disregard, or denounce principles that governed the faith in previous eras. This was only possible because of events in the third phase. The fourth iteration of Mormonism has proceeded on the bedrock principle that the church's president does not, indeed cannot, err. If he were to do so, God is required to intervene and take him. Therefore, in this final phase it has become possible for Mormon adherents to continue claim to an unbroken heritage descending from the original Prophet, Joseph Smith. Now even jarring contradictions of the original faith are accepted. Any change is presumed to come about as part of God's will because God has not intervened to stop the changes. The operating assumption requires God to literally start killing church presidents before they can be said to have erred.

Presidents are allowed to adopt any new idea no matter how foreign the idea may be to the faith. Rank and file members are assured that so long as they continue to follow in lock-step "the Lord will bless [them] for it."

The one crucial component of all the phases, however, is the concept of priesthood keys. The infallibility of the president is only possible because the church president, like the Catholic Pope, is believed to have keys to bind on earth and in heaven. President J. Reuben Clark saw these claims as essentially identical: "I said that the President of the Church was the representative of Christ on the earth, that he had in fact the position which the Pope tried to assume."[326]

When it is believed a man can bind heaven, then it is believed that salvation is available by and through that man. Therefore, loyalty to him can be rewarded with eternal prosperity, and disloyalty is all the more fearful because he can eternally withhold, as well. Even the scriptural caution about "control, or dominion or compulsion upon the souls of the children of men"[327] is arguably circumvented by such authority thought to be held by a church president. Abuse of his priestly authority is only evident if the Lord kills a church president. Absent that, the fourth phase Mormon president will not, indeed cannot, err or lead astray, and there are

---

[326] *The Diaries of J. Reuben Clark, 1933-1961, Abridged.* Salt Lake City: Privately Published, 2010 entry of November 13, 1959, p. 254.

[327] D&C 121: 37: "That [the priesthood] may be conferred upon us, it is true; but when we undertake to cover our sins, or to gratify our pride, our vain ambition, or to exercise control or dominion or compulsion upon the souls of the children of men, in any degree of unrighteousness, behold, the heavens withdraw themselves; the Spirit of the Lord is grieved; and when it is withdrawn, Amen to the priesthood or the authority of that man."

none who can molest his authority. He reigns over all, as the spokesman of God. To challenge him is to challenge the vicar of God. This marked the coming of the Mormon Pontiff and the modern fourth phase of Mormonism. Other elements were added, but the cult of personality was a necessity. It enabled the other changes to take place without resistance from rank and file Mormons.

Chapter 10

THE TEMPLE AT NAUVOO

The pace of revelations received by Joseph Smith slowed in Nauvoo. There was only one significant revelation, and it warned the saints that they would be rejected by the Lord if they did not complete the Nauvoo Temple in the time provided.[328] Between the revelation in January 1841 and May 5,

---

[328]The following sections of the Doctrine & Covenants came from the Nauvoo era: Sections 124, 125, 126, 127, 129, 130, 131, 132 and 135. Of these, only Sections 124, 125 and 126 were Nauvoo revelations. Section 132 was received years earlier, and written down in Nauvoo. Sections 127 and 128 were letters Joseph wrote. Sections 129, 130, and 131 were comments Joseph made while teaching. Section 135 was written by John Taylor announcing the killings of Joseph and Hyrum. Section 124 commands the temple to be built and warns of rejection if it is not completed in the "sufficient time" which had been "appointed" by the Lord to complete the work. (V. 32-33.) There is no specific end given to that "sufficient time" but it is clear from the revelation it involved haste, because the materials were to be called for by sending "swift messengers." (V. 26.) The other two Nauvoo revelations concerned a city on the opposite side of the Mississippi River to be named Zarahemla (4 verses), and informing Brigham Young in 1841 he needn't leave his family as in times passed (3 verses). Only Section 124 stands as the

1842, work on the temple proceeded slowly. There were many other pressing Nauvoo matters requiring attention, capital, and effort.

By May 5, 1842, Joseph Smith decided to begin providing a temple endowment ceremony over his red brick store. It is interesting to contrast the actions taken by Joseph with the words of the revelation commanding the temple be built. The revelation stated:

> For there is not a place found on earth that he may come to and restore again that which was lost unto you, or which he hath taken away, even the fulness of the priesthood. ...For this ordinance belongeth to my house, and cannot be acceptable to me, only in the days of your poverty, wherein ye are not able to build a house unto me. (D&C 124: 28, 30.)

Taken at face value, the decision Joseph made to introduce the endowment on May 5, 1842 could not have conferred the fullness of the priesthood, which had by then been "taken away" from the saints. It needed to be "restore[ed] again," and for that to occur the Nauvoo Temple was a required pre-condition.

Nevertheless, Joseph instituted a form of temple endowment in May, 1842. Those rites became the pattern that Brigham Young and the Twelve would use for ceremonies they would administer, beginning in November, 1845, in the attic of the incomplete Nauvoo Temple. Neither Joseph's red brick store, nor the still incomplete temple satisfied the requirements of Section 124 to permit the fullness of the priesthood to be restored. The saints were told if they followed the instructions given them in the

---

Nauvoo era revelation, and it warns the church of pending rejection if they did not proceed with haste to complete the Nauvoo Temple.

revelation through Joseph they would be blessed, receive the fullness of the priesthood, and not be exiled again. The spot would become holy, and therefore protected by the Lord against their enemies. But if the work was not done, the saints would be cursed, suffer the Lord's wrath, and lose their appointed place.

> And verily I say unto you, let this house be built unto my name, that I may reveal mine ordinances therein unto my people; For I deign to reveal unto my church things which have been kept hid from before the foundation of the world, things that pertain to the dispensation of the fulness of times. And I will show unto my servant Joseph all things pertaining to this house, and the priesthood thereof, and the place whereon it shall be built. And ye shall build it on the place where you have contemplated building it, for that is the spot which I have chosen for you to build it. If ye labor with all your might, I will consecrate that spot that it shall be made holy. And if my people will hearken unto my voice, and unto the voice of my servants whom I have appointed to lead my people, behold, verily I say unto you, they shall not be moved out of their place. But if they will not hearken to my voice, nor unto the voice of these men whom I have appointed, they shall not be blest, because they pollute mine holy grounds, and mine holy ordinances, and charters, and my holy words which I give unto them. And it shall come to pass that if you build a house unto my name, and do not do the things that I say, I will not perform the oath which I make unto you, neither fulfil the promises which ye expect at my hands, saith the Lord. For instead of blessings, ye, by your own works, bring cursings, wrath, indignation, and judgments upon your own heads, by your follies, and by all your abominations, which you practise before me, saith the Lord. (D&C 124: 40-48.)

The language of this revelation offers revelations about hidden things which go back to before the foundation of the world. It offers additional information about priesthood and its fullness. But it requires the Nauvoo Temple as the sole place where this was to occur.

The Nauvoo Temple was never available for Joseph to pass along anything to anyone. It was incomplete at his death, and so he introduced a form of endowment in his red brick store.

Why, if the fullness could only be restored in the Nauvoo Temple, would Joseph begin to perform additional rites in his red brick store in May, 1842?

Why, if the fullness of the priesthood could only be bestowed in the temple, would Brigham Young later assert he got it from Joseph Smith outside the Nauvoo Temple?[329]

Why, if the saints were driven from Nauvoo by mobs, never allowed to complete and use the temple before being exiled, does the church claim they successfully accomplished all required of them, and avoided "cursings, wrath, indignation and judgments" from God for their failure?

What evidence is there the Nauvoo saints met the Lord's condition that "if my people will hearken unto my voice, and unto the voice of my servants whom I have appointed to lead my people, behold, verily I say unto you, they shall not be moved out of their place?" Does the fact the saints were expelled from Nauvoo without being able to use a completed temple, shed any light on the saints' success? Since they were "moved out of their

---

[329] As we saw earlier, Brigham Young initially based his claim to have all the keys upon his ordination to the Apostleship. That ordination did not involve the ceremonies in the red brick store. It happened in Kirtland in February, 1835 rather than in Nauvoo, and did not involve Joseph in that ordination.

place" in Nauvoo, did they meet the Lord's requirement? If so, then why were they moved?

Were they rejected? Were they cursed? Did they experience the Lord's indignation? His judgments?

Why were they not moved out of their place instead of driven from the land?

Does the fact the Nauvoo Temple was burned by an arsonist on November 10, 1848 as the saints finally abandoned the city,[330] shed any light on the saints' compliance with what the Lord required of them?

The burned Nauvoo Temple was further destroyed by a tornado on May 27, 1850,[331] making it a dangerous edifice. As a precaution, the city tore what remained of the building down. The destruction of the Nauvoo Temple was so complete, there was not one stone left upon another which was not thrown down.[332] What does that suggest about the Lord's promise: "If ye labor with all your might, I will consecrate that spot that it shall be made holy." Was it consecrated by Him? Made holy by Him? Protected by Him?

These are interesting questions to ponder. The answers suggest perhaps a different narrative about the saints' conduct in Nauvoo, and all their subsequent trials, than the one presented by the church. It also raises the question of why Joseph Smith introduced a form of endowment in his red brick store in May, 1842. And

---

[330]Roberts. B.H. *The Rise and Fall of Nauvoo*. Salt Lake City: Deseret News Publisher, 1900. [reproduction of first edition printed in June, 2002, commemorating the rebuilding of the Nauvoo Temple] p. 369.

[331]*Id.*

[332]See Luke 21: 5-6.

what underlying purpose was served by laying out rites to be instituted in a temple Joseph would never live to see complete.

The traditional narrative claims what the saints did, and how Joseph then proceeded was sufficient to restore the fullness of the priesthood in the red brick store. But this narrative contradicts the revelation. The revelation states the fullness could only have returned in the Nauvoo Temple, which did not happen. It also ignores the displacement from Nauvoo, when the Lord promised He would "consecrate that spot that it shall be made holy." If the saints had done what He required, He promised they "shall not be moved out of their place." The traditional narrative ignores the failure of the Nauvoo Temple to become consecrated by the Lord's appearance there. It ignores that the saints were moved out of their place forcibly by uncontrolled mob violence. The traditional narrative also fails to interpret subsequent events against the language of the revelation which warns there would come "cursings, wrath and indignation" against the saints. Therefore, the expulsion, westward migration into the wilderness, hardships, turmoil, and distresses are not viewed as God's chastening hand. Instead these terrible ordeals are merely further evidence of the nobility of the people of Nauvoo. If the traditional narrative is wrong, what purpose was served by Joseph instituting the rites in 1842 outside the temple?

In the original form of endowment Joseph instituted, the ceremony initiated one couple at a time. The persons being initiated were part of the ceremony, as performers in the ritual. The man became the ceremonial player Adam, and the woman became the ceremonial player Eve. There was no audience. Only those participating in the ceremony were there. Brigham Young would later alter the form to allow for a bigger number of endowments to take place in a compressed time. He changed it to become, in effect, a vicarious endowment for the living, where patrons watched others play the roles of Adam and Eve. The presentation would be interrupted intermittently, and the audience would covenant at the appropriate time as if they were Adam and Eve.

In the endowment presented by Joseph, the role of Adam, and the role of Eve was part of the initiation for each person endowed. In the endowment altered by Brigham Young the patrons were told the roles of Adam and Eve were simply figurative, and that each person attending should consider themselves respectively as if Adam and Eve.[333]

In Joseph's initiation and endowment, each man and woman was taken on a personal journey from creation, to fall, to redemption, and back to the Father's presence. The message of the endowment was the personal journey each person took away from and then back again to God. It was a journey all were expected to take for themselves.

Earlier we discussed what Joseph Smith restored, and saw Joseph was a modern, living example proving the promise given in James 1: 5. His life was a testament to the principle of continuing revelation. He taught this was the right of everyone. The time was to shortly come when every person, all flesh, was entitled to dream dreams and see visions.[334] It was "not yet fulfilled, but shortly

---

[333]This took the form of an instruction in the ceremony until 1990. When the changes were made the statement that the presentation was "simply figurative so far as the man and the woman are concerned" and that "as you sit here you should consider yourselves as if Adam and Eve" were dropped. Also at that time the role of the "Minister" of false religion was likewise dropped.

[334]See JS-H 1: 41, quoting Joel 2: 28.

would be," according to the angel who visited Joseph. (JS-H 1: 41.) This message rings through all Joseph restored, taught, revealed and said.

If Joseph knew the season given to the saints by the Lord was drawing to a close, and the opportunity would not exist to restore the fullness of the priesthood which had been lost, then he needed to nevertheless institute the means by which the angel's prophecies could be fulfilled. His ministry was designed to establish a new dispensation of the Gospel of Jesus Christ. Although those to whom he ministered may have been unwilling to receive what was offered, there was nevertheless an obligation imposed upon Joseph to teach correct principles, and leave the means for the dispensation to succeed even in the face of short term failure in Nauvoo.

How did Joseph receive the fullness? He obtained it in the only way it can be obtained by any man - from heaven itself. Therefore, if Joseph was going to be taken before the Nauvoo Temple was completed, he needed to leave something to allow the Dispensation of Fullness of Times to survive. The scriptures alone were not enough. There needed to be forms, covenant-making patterns, and ritualized knowledge of mysteries to survive the ignorance, apathy, and spiritual darkness of Nauvoo. The Book of Mormon was a powerful tool, but there needed to be another restored witness to the path back as well. In the endowment ceremony, Joseph delivered that second witness, and an inspired invitation to each person to return to God's presence. He left something that was unlikely to become so corrupt as to lose its ability to instruct about higher knowledge. Men may alter it because of ignorance or because the institution would remove and reject some of its truths. They may decide to discard portions of it from embarrassment or corruption, but the ritualized form was likely to survive in a satisfactory enough manner long enough to permit some to see through the ritual to the underlying invitation itself. These future saints may see the temple rites as merely a form, and not as the substance. What is symbolized in form becomes an invitation to return to God's presence in fact. For such sheep who "hear His voice" Joseph's ritual retains power to inspire the upward reach toward God.

Prophetic messages can be suppressed, censored or discarded. They can be ignored or condemned. Ceremonies are more durable. Particularly when ceremonies are not well explained or completely understood. They acquire a mythical meaning, even if these mistaken assumptions are also false or foolish. They can become the objects of veneration without any real understanding. Superstitions attach to ceremonies. The form becomes an end in itself. Rituals can be empty, hollow, and fail to have any power. But as long as the ceremony remains, even if corrupted, as it was in the hands of the hierarchy in the Dispensation of Moses; and even if it is edited or incomplete, the ceremony retains the power to convey ideas. When, at last, there comes along a penitent soul who is prepared to receive the ideas, the truth of those ideas can still take hold. Whenever someone is ready to see the power in what is left of the ceremony, new power can come from heaven to another generation. When the darkness of prevailing institutional error is ignored, light from heaven itself can emerge through the ceremony.

In the dispensation that followed the death of Moses, there were ceremonies, rites, festivals, and rules of conduct which preserved a message of redemption through sacrifice of unblemished and innocent animals. The message was lost on many of those who performed them. The rites of the law of Moses acquired foolish meanings, and were surrounded with superstition. Many who ignorantly performed the sacrifices presumed the rites themselves had a cleansing effect upon them, making the participants better than other people. They prized their special relationship with God, which they believed the ceremonies celebrated. Since gentiles could only enter an outer court, and Israelites could enter the inner courts, they knew they were closer to God by reason of the physical separation in the Lord's House. They were "holy" and others were unclean. Not only that, but others were unable to become clean because they lacked the ceremonial capacity to rid themselves of sin. They could not enter in; they were not chosen.

These rites were performed daily from the time of Moses until the coming of Jesus Christ. The ceremonies were not intended, however, to rid the Israelites of sin, make them holy, or set them apart as better than other nations. They were intended to bear testimony of the Son of God. It was the Son of God who was typified in the various rites. It was always the Son of God who was intended to be the "lamb which taketh away the sin of the world."[335]

Despite this embedded ceremonial message, the Jews not only failed to recognize Christ, they rejected Him. Isaiah saw the underlying message of the rites. Isaiah saw in the rites the underlying promise of a sacrifice to be given for all mankind. He realized there was to be one sent who would bear our griefs and carry our sorrows. Such a soul would be stricken, smitten, afflicted, and sacrificed. Yet, He would be without sin, without blemish. He would be cut off from the land of the living, and numbered with

---

[335]John 1: 29.

the transgressors. But having made His soul a sacrifice for sins, He would have power to justify many.

Realizing this pattern, and humbling himself to know more, Isaiah sought to see what this coming sacrifice would involve. He was not content with the rites, but wanted to know the author of the rites. He sought the face of God.

Isaiah found Him. And in finding Him, he also found the full meaning of the rites which had been handed down from Moses. As a witness of the Lord, and a prophet possessing a testimony of Christ, he could then proclaim the real meaning of the rituals:

> Surely he hath borne our griefs, and carried our sorrows: yet we did esteem him stricken, smitten of God, and afflicted. But he was wounded for our transgressions, he was bruised for our iniquities: the chastisement of our peace was upon him; and with his stripes we are healed. All we like sheep have gone astray; we have turned every one to his own way; and the Lord hath laid on him the iniquity of us all. He was oppressed, and he was afflicted, yet he opened not his mouth: he is brought as a lamb to the slaughter, and as a sheep before her shearers is dumb, so he openeth not his mouth. He was taken from prison and from judgment: and who shall declare his generation? for he was cut off out of the land of the living: for the transgression of my people was he stricken. And he made his grave with the wicked, and with the rich in his death; because he had done no violence, neither was any deceit in his mouth. Yet it pleased the Lord to bruise him; he hath put him to grief: when thou shalt make his soul an offering for sin, he shall see his seed, he shall prolong his days, and the pleasure of the Lord shall prosper in his hand. He shall see of the travail of his soul, and shall be satisfied: by his knowledge shall my righteous servant justify many; for he shall bear their iniquities. (Isa. 53: 4-11.)

Joseph Smith's ceremony above the red brick store were always intended to become part of the rites belonging to the restoration of the Gospel. They were intended for the saints' temple. They were an inspired message for the Latter-day Saints. It was to become their inspired inheritance, an imbedded message of how each person can find redemption from the fall.[336] They are a constant reminder to all with eyes to see that we are not left in a fallen, lone, and dreary world without hope of returning to God's embrace. It promises when God embraces you there will be infinite blessings given for both time and eternity.

In the ceremony as originally performed, the man Adam and the woman Eve were promised they would receive, from time to time, true messengers. For so long as the false minister remained as a part of the ceremony, it was clear to those who participated that there were no mortal sources who could claim they were "true messengers." Mortal men were universally depicted as false ministers in the ceremony Joseph restored. The only source of true messengers was God or angels sent by Him. The true messengers He sent came directly from God and delivered only His instruction. They were depicted as angels. Even so any angel claiming to have such a message was not to be accepted until they were first tested to determine they bore correct signs of truth and light.[337] We have scriptures that warn us Satan can transform himself to seem as an angel of light.[338] The full meaning of that warning has been lost by almost everyone. False messengers always imitate the true ones,

---

[336]Redemption from the fall happens whenever a mortal regains God's presence. See, e.g., Ether 3: 13.

[337]D&C 129: 4-8.

[338]2 Cor. 11: 14.

claiming to be what they are not. They seek, of course, to deceive the very elect if it is possible.[339]

The temple ceremony confirmed angels were intended as God's authorized means to minister to men, women and children, just as the Book of Mormon teaches.[340] The temple tells us to look for true messengers sent by Him, bearing signs and tokens, having hidden knowledge, who will inform us in the way of truth and light. As originally portrayed, these angelic ministers would become the exclusive conduit through which the Lord would give us guidance and instruction.

The Book of Mormon is, as my prior books have shown, the premiere text of scripture for illustrating the fullness of the Gospel of Jesus Christ. It is a veritable manual for returning to God's presence. Almost all of its major contributors were redeemed from the fall, entered Christ's presence, and wrote their records to help others to find the way to salvation.

Angels are sent to declare the conditions of repentance to those who seek redemption. Then when men repent, they are brought to the presence of the Son. It is only through Christ, not men, that we obtain forgiveness of sin, and the promise of eternal glory. As

---

[339] As Christ put it: "And except those days should be shortened, there should no flesh be saved: but for the elect's sake those days shall be shortened. Then if any man shall say unto you, Lo, here is Christ, or there; believe it not. For there shall arise false Christs, and false prophets, and shall shew great signs and wonders; insomuch that, if it were possible, they shall deceive the very elect. Behold, I have told you before. Wherefore if they shall say unto you, Behold, he is in the desert; go not forth: behold, he is in the secret chambers; believe it not. For as the lightning cometh out of the east, and shineth even unto the west; so shall also the coming of the Son of man be. For wheresoever the carcase is, there will the eagles be gathered together." (Matt. 24: 22-28.)

[340] See, e.g., Alma 32: 23.

explained in the Book of Mormon, "he should not come to redeem them in their sins, but to redeem them from their sins. And he hath power given unto him from the Father to redeem them from their sins because of repentance; therefore he hath sent his angels to declare the tidings of the conditions of repentance, which bringeth unto the power of the Redeemer, unto the salvation of their souls." (Hel. 5: 10-11.) An angel delivered the Book of Mormon to Joseph. That same angel showed three witnesses the physical plates from which the book was translated, while the voice of God declared the translation was correct.[341] Therefore, The Book of Mormon is, in its entirety, the primary message sent by an angel for mankind in our day. Our casual treatment of that book is one of the reasons we collectively do not have more angelic ministers visiting us.[342] When you have studied the words of the angels (the Book of Mormon) enough to learn its precepts, and prove to God you are ready to receive more, then the heavens can and will give you more.

Joseph's message repeatedly invited us to return to God's presence, and gain our own promise of eternal life. Joseph was not interested in being a "boss" of others. He taught others how to govern themselves, and expected them to follow through to gain what he obtained. Joseph's plea to all of us was to make our calling and election sure. In other words, all of us were to return to God's presence, obtain promises and covenants from Him, and gain the hope of eternal life– just as all others who have a hope in Christ have done before us.

Speaking of our individual return to God, Joseph said:

---

[341] See Testimony of the Three Witnesses, in the front of the Book of Mormon.

[342] See D&C 84: 54-57.

When the Lord has thoroughly proved him, and finds that the man is determined to serve Him at all hazards, then the man will find his calling and his election made sure, then it will be his privilege to receive the other Comforter, which the Lord hath promised the Saints, as is recorded in the testimony of St. John, in the 14th chapter, from the 12th to the 27th verses. (*TPJS*, p. 150.)

In expounding on the Second General Epistle of Peter to the New Testament church, Joseph said:

Another point, after having all these qualifications, he lays this injunction upon the people "to make your calling and election sure." He is emphatic upon this subject-after adding all this virtue, knowledge, etc., "Make your calling and election sure." What is the secret-the starting point? "According as His divine power hath given unto us all things that pertain unto life and godliness." How did he obtain all things? Through the knowledge of Him who hath called him. There could not anything be given, pertaining to life and godliness, without knowledge. (*TPJS*, p. 305.)

Our covenants are meaningless unless they are ratified by heaven. All our oaths, covenants, even our expectations for the next life, must be sealed by the Holy Spirit of Promise, or the voice of God, or we have nothing.[343] As Joseph put it:

We have no claim in our eternal compact, in relation to eternal things, unless our actions and contracts and all things tend to this. But after all this, you have got to make your calling and election sure. If this injunction would lie largely on those to whom it was spoken, how much more those of the present generation! (*TPJS*, p. 306.)

---

[343] See D&C 132: 7.

He elaborated:

> 1st key: Knowledge is the power of salvation. 2nd key:
> Make your calling and election sure. 3rd key: It is one thing
> to be on the mount and hear the excellent voice, etc., and
> another to hear the voice declare to you, You have a part
> and lot in that kingdom. (May 21, 1843.) (*TPJS*, p. 306.)

To Joseph, this was the gospel. He warned that when men
attempt to teach otherwise they should be cursed, not followed:

> Oh! I beseech you to go forward, go forward and make
> your calling and your election sure; and if any man preach
> any other Gospel than that which I have preached, he shall
> be cursed; and some of you who now hear me shall see it,
> and know that I testify the truth concerning them. (*TPJS*,
> p. 366.)

This saving event is between the individual and God. But it is
available to all. All are invited to come to Him, see His face, and
receive redemption from the fall. "Verily, thus saith the Lord: It
shall come to pass that every soul who forsaketh his sins and
cometh unto me, and calleth on my name, and obeyeth my voice,
and keepeth my commandments, shall see my face and know that
I am[.]" (D&C 93: 1.)

When Moses came into God's presence, was redeemed from the
fall, and obtained His promise of eternal life,[344] he became the
Lord's temple. When we read the Lord's admonition to Moses to
"[put] the shoes from off thy feet, for the place whereon thou

---

[344]The Lord declared to Moses, "behold, thou art my son" while they
were together on the Mount. (Moses 1: 4.)

standest is holy ground,"[345] we tend to put the emphasis on "the place." We should instead put the emphasis on "thou." That is, no matter where Moses stood, having been redeemed from the fall, he always stood on holy ground.

The true temple of God is therefore the redeemed individual. A revelation to Joseph explained:

> For man is spirit. The elements are eternal, and spirit and element, inseparably connected, receive a fulness of joy; And when separated, man cannot receive a fulness of joy. The elements are the tabernacle of God; yea, man is the tabernacle of God, even temples; and whatsoever temple is defiled, God shall destroy that temple. (D&C 93: 33-35.)

The Apostle Paul put it more simply: "Know ye not that ye are the temple of God, and that the Spirit of God dwelleth in you?" (1 Cor. 3: 16.) Joseph's work in restoring temple worship was not intended as an end. It was merely a ceremonial message to point the way for man to return to God's presence and receive redemption. Men are supposed to become the Temple of God.

It is a corruption of Joseph's original teaching to think of the temple rites as an end in themselves. They were never intended to be so. They were introduced to explain, to show the way, to prepare the mind of man to comprehend God's ways. The culture in which the restoration of the Gospel came was more secular, less faithful and far more corrupt than the ideal. It was important for God's purposes that the temple rites were given to help bridge the gap between secular life and God's ways. It was a great gift from the Lord to provide a ceremonial path. It was a blessing to ask the saints to build a sacred building, set apart from the world, where

---

[345]Exo. 3: 5.

rites could be practiced inside a holy place. Everything about the temple was intended to inform man how to cleanse themselves from this fallen world and regain God's companionship. Everything, from how patrons were to dress, the symbols on the building which point to the heavens, the oaths, covenants, penalties, and ritualized learning, all of it to the final ceremonial encounter with God through the veil, was intended as a blueprint to gain redemption.

Just as in former days, however, it has again become possible to misread the temple and turn it into an object of cultic veneration, a source of pride devoid of saving power. The temple at Jerusalem did the Jews little good in recognizing Him to whom the rites pointed. There were few, if any, of Christ's followers who recognized in the hostile cries to "crucify him! Crucify him!"[346] that His death was to become the real Passover sacrifice. The Passover ceremonies then underway were merely a symbol; His death was the real thing. In an irony for the ages, those who were responsible for having Him killed wanted His body taken down so as not to profane the high holy day coming at nightfall.[347] They did this without any appreciation of how necessary it was for Him to die for them on that very day. His own followers did not grasp it either. He was required to suffer, and to do it at the very moment when He came. The high holy day on which He died pointed to Him.

On the day of His resurrection, He spent hours walking with two disciples, and relating why these things happened: "Then he said unto them, O fools, and slow of heart to believe all that the

---

[346]Luke 23: 21.

[347]John 19: 31.

prophets have spoken: Ought not Christ to have suffered these things, and to enter into his glory? And beginning at Moses and all the prophets, he expounded unto them in all the scriptures the things concerning himself." (Luke 24: 25-27.)

The temple rites of His day were of little use to most men. Even His disciples were unable to understand them. The rituals and feasts also did them no good. Instead, these religious symbols were viewed as something independently important, not a type of Him. Even among those who received Him, they did not appreciate the underlying testimony of Him embedded in "Moses and all the prophets" until He expounded it to them.

Joseph's temple rites were similarly intended as a shadow, a type, an invitation to redemption. In the first phase the rites were looked upon as a sacred mystery that empowered those who received them to be saved. They were sacred knowledge which made those who obtained initiation think themselves saved before God. When Joseph stood as the officiator, possessing the power to seal in heaven and on earth, given him by the voice of God, perhaps those expectations were then justified.

With Joseph's passing, the question of how much authority the ordinances retained was less certain. It is clear the rites held full power to point the way back to God. Even now, the rites, symbols and information as a testimony of how any soul may be redeemed remain full of power. When Brigham Young changed the ceremony making the roles of Adam or Eve players rather than the participants, converting to a vicarious endowment for the living, it still retained the power to inform, instruct and point the way. There have been many changes in the temple ceremony since Joseph. These include, but are not limited to, the elimination of penalties, the removal of the false minister, altered forms of covenant making, discarded symbols, automated film presentations, introduction of theatrical elements such as special visual effects and a dramatic musical score, and merely symbolic washing rather than washing specific areas of the body. Still, the temple rites nevertheless proclaim each soul may return to God's presence and gain eternal life. Whatever changes have happened to the rites, and whatever superstitions have attached to the latter-day temple ceremonies, the temples remain valuable as a witness of the restored Gospel of Jesus Christ. A reflective visit to the temple can give a prepared disciple more information about the Lord and His ways than perhaps the same amount of time spent with the scriptures. The temple uses sight, sound, movement, touch, clothing, water, oil, and covenants to tell a story. It exposes patrons to another culture, where all things testify of God's glory.

If the temple is viewed as an end, its purpose fails. When it is viewed as the blueprint for finding God in this lone and dreary world, it empowers.

The first phase of Mormonism ended without a temple where they could conduct a temple ceremony. Joseph did what he could in the red brick store. But he never had the benefit of a temple structure in which to work out details. He told Brigham Young it was not right, and would need further work to finish it. Here is what Brigham Young claimed Joseph told him:

> "Brother Brigham this is not arranged right, but we have done the best we could under the circumstances in which we are placed, and I wish you to take this mater [sic] in hand and organize and systematize all these ceremonies with the signs, tokens, penalties and key words." I did so and each time I got something more; so that when we went through the Temple at Nauvoo, I understood and knew

how to place them there. We had our ceremony pretty correct.[348]

If this statement from Brigham Young is accurate (and we have no basis to think otherwise), then Joseph Smith never expected to be around when the Nauvoo Temple was completed. He knew in 1842 as he began temple rites in his red store that he would be taken before he would have a temple to use. Since he would be gone before the Nauvoo Temple was finished, he realized he would not have a chance to finish work on temple rites, but that would be left to another.

The only significant revelation received at Nauvoo began with these words: "Verily, thus saith the Lord unto you, my servant Joseph Smith, I am well pleased with your offering and acknowledgments[.]" (D&C 124: 1.) Joseph's "offering" was his life. He offered it to get more time for the saints. He "acknowledged" the saints were difficult and unwilling, but asked for another season to teach them in the hope they might receive the fullness of the priesthood from God. He acknowledged that if he failed to get them to do so within that season, he would surrender his life.

By May, 1842 Joseph could see the temple would never be completed in the time allowed. He introduced rites that would later be used by the saints. But the terms of his bargain were not satisfied, his life was forfeited, and the conditions laid out by the Lord were not kept. Therefore, in the first phase of Mormonism

---

[348] Nutall, L. John. *Diary*, Feb. 7, 1877. L. Tom Perry Special collections, Harold B. Lee Library, Brigham Young University, Provo, Utah. DIARY STARTS IN 1879

Joseph anticipated the Nauvoo failure. He knew the saints would fail to gain a holy spot from which they would not be moved.[349]

As the second phase of Mormonism began, the attic of the unfinished Nauvoo Temple was prepared and used to repeat the temple ceremonies for the Nauvoo saints. These temple rites for the larger Nauvoo population took place between November 1845 and February 1846. When the church leadership abandoned Nauvoo in February 18, 1846, the rites were no longer performed in Nauvoo.

The second phase of Mormonism instituted a somewhat different, standardized form of temple rites. Ultimately, before Brigham Young's death, these rites would be reduced to writing. In the early part of third phase Mormonism, Joseph F. Smith authorized and began making changes to the endowment ceremony.[350] Changes were made occasionally thereafter, until the fourth phase. The changes made in the fourth phase have been significantly more frequent and more sweeping in scope than anything done in all prior phases. If this represents a trend, then the trend is toward greater changes to be made more frequently.

Despite all this, the basic power of the temple rite to communicate the need for individual redemption from the fall still remains. In that respect, the rites Joseph introduced remain a powerful witness, along with the Book of Mormon, of how the Gospel of Jesus Christ provides mankind the opportunity to know

---

[349] D&C 124: 44-45.

[350] An attempt to gather evidence of changes has been made in Devery S. Anderson's new book. Anderson, Devery S. *The Development of LDS Temple Worship: 1846-2000*. Salt Lake City: Signature Books, 2011.

God. This knowledge is not abstract or basic belief, it is meeting the God of creation while still mortal.[351]

Like any ritual, however, it can be misunderstood. Instead of understanding it as an invitation to repent and receive the heavenly gift, it can be twisted to constitute the heavenly gift itself. When it becomes a substitute for actually receiving the heavenly gift offered by the Lord, it can make those who participate think they are better than others who cannot. This potential abuse allows those who are misled to display the same foolishness we see in the Old Testament, the New Testament, and the Book of Mormon. Nephi prophesied this would happen among the latter-day gentiles. The result of this error is always the passing of the heavenly gift from among mankind. Until the dormant power is reignited again by His sheep, who hear His voice in the rites and ordinances. Then the light is rekindled in the still smoldering invitation restored through Joseph Smith.

---

[351] For a discussion of the teachings given in the restored Gospel on this topic, see Snuffer, Denver C., Jr. *The Second Comforter: Conversing With the Lord Through the Veil.* Salt Lake City: Mill Creek Press, 2006.

Chapter 11

THE PRIESTHOOD WAS TAKEN FROM ISRAEL

A revelation given on September 22, 1832 explained the significance of higher priesthood, and the plight of ancient Israel when they lost Moses, who held that priesthood:

> And this greater priesthood administereth the gospel and holdeth the key of the mysteries of the kingdom, even the key of the knowledge of God. Therefore, in the ordinances thereof, the power of godliness is manifest. And without the ordinances thereof, and the authority of the priesthood, the power of godliness is not manifest unto men in the flesh; For without this no man can see the face of God, even the Father, and live. Now this Moses plainly taught to the children of Israel in the wilderness, and sought diligently to sanctify his people that they might behold the face of God; But they hardened their hearts and could not endure his presence; therefore, the Lord in his wrath, for his anger was kindled against them, swore that they should not enter into his rest while in the wilderness, which rest is

the fulness of his glory. Therefore, he took Moses out of their midst, and the Holy Priesthood also; And the lesser priesthood continued, which priesthood holdeth the key of the ministering of angels and the preparatory gospel; Which gospel is the gospel of repentance and of baptism, and the remission of sins, and the law of carnal commandments, which the Lord in his wrath caused to continue with the house of Aaron among the children of Israel until John, whom God raised up, being filled with the Holy Ghost from his mother's womb. (D&C 84: 19-27.)

The greater priesthood had privileges that were required to establish Zion. With it, men were able to see the face of God. Without it, they were barred from God's presence. There is an inescapable connection between higher priesthood and entering God's presence. And God's presence is required for Zion. It might be said God's presence *is* Zion. He must be able to dwell with the residents for the residents to claim Zion has returned. This was the reason Joseph tried to restore the "fullness of the priesthood."[352] Redemption from the fall requires the saints to return to God,[353] and they could not return without the power to do so. That power is contained in the fullness of the priesthood.

While Moses was with ancient Israel, God was also with them. Moses saw God, and spoke face to face with Him.[354] Therefore, Moses was regarded as a "god" to Israel.[355] This was not because Moses was more than a man, but because he was able to speak with

---

[352]D&C 124: 28.

[353]Ether 3: 13.

[354]See, e.g., Moses 1: 2, 31; Exo. 33: 11; Deu. 34: 10.

[355]Exo. 7: 1.

(and for) God. Since he spoke with God, he was told to deliver His messages.[356] Moses did not use his position to deliver his own learning, good advice, inspirational stories, or any kind of independent message. He fabricated nothing. He brought the message delivered to him by God. When he did, it was clear the message was the Lord's.

Moses attempted to prepare Israel to have the same access to God he had. It was not his ambition to monopolize such access; he wanted all men know God for themselves.[357] He wanted this, but Israel refused.[358] They rebelled and declined the offer. Because of this, they were unable to receive the priesthood God wanted to give them.

When Moses was taken, Israel still retained a limited form of priesthood, but it did not permit them to see the face of God. They had access to angels, but not God.   Even so, their priesthood was still enough. Angels can teach men everything needed for repentance.[359] Angels can confer keys, power, authority, rights, dominions, and priesthood. It was through the ministry of angels Joseph Smith learned all he needed to establish a new dispensation

---

[356]See, e.g., Exo. 3: 14-15.

[357]Num. 11: 29.

[358]"And all the people saw the thunderings, and the lightnings, and the noise of the trumpet, and the mountain smoking: and when the people saw it, they removed, and stood afar off. And they said unto Moses, Speak thou with us, and we will hear: but let not God speak with us, lest we die. And Moses said unto the people, Fear not: for God is come to prove you, and that his fear may be before your faces, that ye sin not. And the people stood afar off, and Moses drew near unto the thick darkness where God was." (Exo. 20: 18-21.)

[359]Hel. 5: 11.

of the Gospel.[360] Therefore, possession of the lesser priesthood is enough, if it is actually used to receive angels. It can lead to the higher priesthood. It was not institutionally available to the ancient Israelites once Moses was taken, but it was still possible to receive.

Although the priesthood in general was limited, there were still those who received a fullness during the Dispensation of Moses. Joseph explained:

> Answer to the question, Was the Priesthood of Melchizedek taken away when Moses died? All Priesthood is Melchizedek, but there are different portions or degrees of it. That portion which brought Moses to speak with God face to face was taken away; but that which brought the ministry of angels remained. All the prophets had the Melchizedek Priesthood and were ordained by God himself. (*TPJS*, p. 180.)

This means despite a general limitation, there were those who obtained higher priesthood. They obtained it from contact with "God himself." When they came into contact with "God himself," they needed and obtained the same priesthood which permitted "Moses to speak with God face to face." For those who sought this higher priesthood, the refusal by their peers to receive what God offered had no effect. They received everything God offers to Zion. They received it individually, from God. It did not come from the priests who conducted temple rites, collected tithes,

---

[360]Joseph saw and heard "[T]he voice of Michael, the archangel; the voice of Gabriel, and of Raphael, and of divers angels, from Michael or Adam down to the present time, all declaring their dispensation, their rights, their keys, their honors, their majesty and glory, and the power of their priesthood; giving line upon line, precept upon precept; here a little, and there a little; giving us consolation by holding forth that which is to come, confirming our hope!" (D&C 128: 21.)

exercised authority, held offices, or presided over Israel. Those priests couldn't give it to them. God could and did.

Throughout the Dispensation of Moses, there were two traditions that operated independent of one another. The one was official and priestly. The other was unofficial and prophetic. The priestly tradition held recognized office, and could be easily identified. The other was "ordained by God himself," and those who possessed it had His word to them as their only credential. They oftentimes "were tortured, not accepting deliverance; that they might obtain a better resurrection: And others had trial of cruel mockings and scourgings, yea, moreover of bonds and imprisonment: They were stoned, they were sawn asunder, were tempted, were slain with the sword: they wandered about in sheepskins and goatskins; being destitute, afflicted, tormented; (Of whom the world was not worthy:) they wandered in deserts, and in mountains, and in dens and caves of the earth. (Heb. 11: 35-38.) They were not merely regarded as unofficial. They were persecuted by both the leaders and followers of the official religion. They suffered for their testimony of the truth.[361] In this estate things are arranged so that in every dispensation the truth taught in purity must come from unheralded, questioned and reviled sources. Therefore, those who obtained this higher priesthood during the Dispensation of Moses were denounced, rejected and almost always came from outside the recognized hierarchy. There was only one exception (Samuel).

---

[361] Joseph elaborated on the value of this suffering: "God having provided some better things for them through their sufferings, for without sufferings they could not be made perfect." (JST-Heb. 11: 40.)

We touched briefly upon Joseph Smith's priesthood earlier. Joseph entered God's presence while a young boy.[362] He could not have done so and lived, unless he obtained this higher priesthood, as the previous revelation explains. We have no account of Joseph's ordination to any form of priesthood before May 15, 1829.[363] Therefore, we are left to conclude Joseph Smith came bearing priesthood authority from before the foundation of the world.[364] Although the scriptures repeatedly refer to this form of priesthood as "without father or mother,"[365] and reckoning from the "foundation of the world,"[366] there are few explanations of what this means. One comes from Alma:

> And thus being called by this holy calling, and ordained unto the high priesthood of the holy order of God, to teach his commandments unto the children of men, that they also might enter into his rest-- This high priesthood being after the order of his Son, which order was from the foundation of the world; or in other words, being without beginning of days or end of years, being prepared from eternity to all eternity, according to his foreknowledge of all things-- Now they were ordained after this manner--being called with a holy calling, and ordained with a holy ordinance, and taking upon them the high

---

[362]JS-H 1: 16-20.

[363]*Id.*, v. 72.

[364]See Alma 13: 2-5.

[365]See, e.g., Heb. 7: 3.

[366]See, e.g., Alma 13: 3, 5. Joseph states he was "ordained from before the foundation of the world." (D&C 127: 2.) Christ refers to prophets whose destiny to be slain for His testimony reckons from "the foundation of the world." (Luke 11: 50.)

priesthood of the holy order, which calling, and ordinance, and high priesthood, is without beginning or end-- Thus they become high priests forever, after the order of the Son, the Only Begotten of the Father, who is without beginning of days or end of years, who is full of grace, equity, and truth. And thus it is. Amen. (Alma 13: 6-9.)

This form of priesthood is "without beginning of days or end of years" because it does not originate in "time" or in mortality.[367] It is "without father and mother" because it does not come from a mortal to another mortal, but from heaven itself. The "order" is something that "was from the foundation of the world" or, in other words, reckons from before mortal life. If it is "from eternity to all eternity," then it may be said to be 'from the pre-earth life, through mortality, and into the eternal afterlife' of those holding this form of holy order. We know there are varying degrees of priesthood.[368] The degree these teachings speak of is not Aaronic or Levitical. Aaronic Priesthood ordination in mortality is normal.[369] But this is a higher degree, which holds extraordinary authority, including the power to be in the presence of God. It involves authority which rarely appears among men, and an associated body of doctrine that is rarely understood.

---

[367] "[A]ll is as one day with God, and time only is measured unto men." (Alma 40: 8.)

[368] "Answer to the question, Was the Priesthood of Melchizedek taken away when Moses died? All Priesthood is Melchizedek, but there are different portions or degrees of it. That portion which brought Moses to speak with God face to face was taken away; but that which brought the ministry of angels remained. All the prophets had the Melchizedek Priesthood and were ordained by God himself." (*TPJS*, p. 180.)

[369] See, e.g., Lev. 16: 32.

Joseph explained how this higher priesthood is conferred upon a man. It comes from God's own voice declaring it to the man. That is, the man came to mortality holding the authority, and God's voice is required to activate it for him while he is mortal. God declares from heaven to the man that he holds this power and authority. It was by the voice of God that Melchizedek received or had the authority delivered to him:

> Now Melchizedek was a man of faith, who wrought righteousness; and when a child he feared God, and stopped the mouths of lions, and quenched the violence of fire. And thus, having been approved of God, he was ordained an high priest after the order of the covenant which God made with Enoch, It being after the order of the son of God; which order came, not by man, nor the will of man; neither by father nor mother; neither by beginning of days nor end of years; but of God; And it was delivered unto men by the calling of his own voice, according to his own will, unto as many as believed on his name. (JST-Gen. 14: 26-29.)

Several concepts in this scripture are notable. First, the man for whom Melchizedek priesthood is named was a man of faith. Second, beyond faith, he was determined to work righteousness; or in other words, his conduct conformed to the truths he understood. As a result, there was no gap between what he understood God wanted of him and what he did. He lived his life in obedience to God. Third, the priesthood he obtained came "by [God's] own voice" and according to "[God's] own will." It pleased the Lord to honor the man with His voice confirming to him God's approval. In the church we think of priesthood coming only

from the laying on of hands by those who are in authority.[370]
Clearly there is authority that can be passed from man to man this
way, as evidenced by the Aaronic Priesthood. Also The Church of
Jesus Christ of Latter-day Saints is a house of order, and there is no
recognized authority apart from the official roster kept by the
church and sustained by the members.

But in the case of the man Melchizedek, the priesthood power
that came to him was conferred by God's voice. It was a separate
order of higher priesthood involving a man who knows God. That
order is only granted by God's own voice. It makes the holder
"ordained an high priest after the order of the covenant which God
made with Enoch, It being after the order of the son of God;
which order came, not by man, nor the will of man; neither by
father nor mother; neither by beginning of days nor end of years."
For this priestly power, God must be directly involved. His servant
must be called by Him, and not receive it from another man; nor
be indebted to any living mortal. Such an High Priest cannot
reckon his right to hold priesthood from another man, or his
earthly parents. The 'line of authority' consists of only one: God.
Only by this connection can the holders of this priesthood feel the
necessary assurance to do what God requires of them. Without it,
they would falter when they were "tortured, not accepting
deliverance; that they might obtain a better resurrection: And
others had trial of cruel mockings and scourgings, yea, moreover
of bonds and imprisonment: They were stoned, they were sawn
asunder, were tempted, were slain with the sword: they wandered
about in sheepskins and goatskins; being destitute, afflicted,

---

[370] 5th Article of Faith: "We believe that a man must be called of God, by
prophecy, and by the laying on of hands by those who are in authority,
to preach the Gospel and administer in the ordinances thereof."

tormented." Those who only pretend to have God's power are fearful, and they envy true messengers like the Old Testament prophets. The reaction to them was based upon this fear and jealousy. The true prophets, however, were secure in knowing God gave them the power to deliver their message. Therefore, the rejection, criticism, violence, and hatred did not stop them from delivering their messages.

When this priesthood appears on the earth, it has certain prerogatives. Those prerogatives are directly related to the covenant between God and Enoch. The terms of this covenant make it possible to establish Zion using the priesthood; even if the only resident is the prophet. So long as he has the Lord's presence he has Zion. In Enoch's time, the covenant originally related to Zion. But the covenant extended to all subsequent times when other instances of "Zion" would occur.[371] Without it, Zion cannot be formed:

> For God having sworn unto Enoch and unto his seed with an oath by himself; that every one being ordained after this order and calling should have power, by faith, to break mountains, to divide the seas, to dry up waters, to turn them out of their course; To put at defiance the armies of nations, to divide the earth, to break every band, to stand

---

[371] Enoch saw the redemption of last days, and therefore wanted the covenant he obtained, for this priesthood would be needed again in the last days: "And it came to pass that Enoch saw the day of the coming of the Son of Man, in the last days, to dwell on the earth in righteousness for the space of a thousand years; But before that day he saw great tribulations among the wicked; and he also saw the sea, that it was troubled, and men's hearts failing them, looking forth with fear for the judgments of the Almighty God, which should come upon the wicked. And the Lord showed Enoch all things, even unto the end of the world; and he saw the day of the righteous, the hour of their redemption, and received a fulness of joy;" (Moses 7: 65-67).

in the presence of God; to do all things according to his will, according to his command, subdue principalities and powers; and this by the will of the Son of God which was from before the foundation of the world. (JST-Gen. 14: 30-31.)

You can identify those who have held this priesthood by those who displayed the power. For example, Moses divided the seas (Exo. 14: 21), Enoch turned waters out of their course (Moses 7: 13), Nephi broke the bands binding him in the desert (1 Ne. 7: 16-18.), Elisha held at defiance the armies of Syria (2 Kings 6: 14-23), and Joseph Smith stood in the presence of God, and received of His fullness (D&C 76: 20). There are many other examples. From these few, however, we can see the power to establish Zion does not mean Zion returns. Moses could have established it, but the people were unwilling. Nephi could, but there was too much wickedness and division among his people. Elisha lived among the rebellious, and he was rejected by Israelite kings and priests, therefore Zion could not be brought. Joseph could have established it, but the saints of his day were too quarrelsome and disobedient. They provoked the Lord's judgments upon them repeatedly, because of disobedience. As John Taylor put it a year after Joseph's death:

> The reason why we do not live in peace is because we are not prepared for it. We are tempted and tried, driven, mobbed, and robbed; apostates are in our midst, which causes trouble and vexation of spirit, and it is all to keep down our pride and learn us to honor the God of Jacob in all things and make us appear what we really are. The gospel turns us inside out and makes manifest every good and every evil way. ...It is necessary that we should be tried and kicked, and cuffed, and twisted round, that we may learn obedience by the things we suffer. ...I am glad to see

people in trouble when I know that it is for their salvation. ...I pray that I may ...act all the time with reference to eternity. ...Persecution is for our good, and if we have hard things to endure let us round up our shoulders and bear them in the name of the Lord, and not murmur.

–From an Address by John Taylor, July 6, 1845.[372]

Zion cannot exist except when people live according to the principles which control such a community. In the economy of heaven, those who could have established Zion were sent to minister from time to time. The authority to establish Zion appears far more frequently than does an actual community of peace. John Taylor's explanation about the saints' continual struggles is the reason Zion is not (and still cannot be) established in the dispensation founded through Joseph Smith. The prophecies foretell of another time when a remnant of the Book of Mormon people will establish Zion.[373] A few gentiles will assist. But the work will be that of the remnant themselves.

---

[372]Leonard, Glen. *Nauvoo: A Place of Peace, A People of Promise.* Salt Lake City: Deseret Book, 2002, p. 268.

[373]Christ prophesied He would destroy the gentiles, preserving only a few faithful who will occupy the limited role of "assisting" in building the city in which He will come to dwell: "And I will execute vengeance and fury upon them, even as upon the heathen, such as they have not heard. But if they will repent and hearken unto my words, and harden not their hearts, I will establish my church among them, and they shall come in unto the covenant and be numbered among this the remnant of Jacob, unto whom I have given this land for their inheritance; And they shall assist my people, the remnant of Jacob, and also as many of the house of Israel as shall come, that they may build a city, which shall be called the New Jerusalem. And then shall they assist my people that they may be gathered in, who are scattered upon all the face of the land, in unto the New Jerusalem. And then shall the power of heaven come down among them; and I also will be in the midst." (3 Ne. 21: 21-25.)

When the Lord allows this power to be used, it is never by "the will of man." The power is released only "according to His will." It will always be the case that when the power of God is used, it is with God's direct command or permission. It is never by the choice of the servant. Servants who are unwilling to follow God's will cannot ever be trusted with the power.

Moses did not go about parting seas for show, or to satisfy curiosity. He was able to command the sea when the Lord willed it.[374] When he commanded according to the Lord's will, the sea parted. When Enoch turned the waters out of their course, he did so to protect the holy city, and with God's approval and direction. When Nephi broke the bands, it was after first asking God to permit it. Elisha did what the Lord wanted, for it was the Lord who sent the hosts of heaven to protect him. And Joseph was invited to the Father's presence, after asking to know the answer to an inspired question about the afterlife. This authority is held only by the meek, and is only exercised meekly.[375]

The purpose of this power is to permit those who are faithful to establish the city of God, or Zion. Without it, Zion cannot return to the earth. As in the past, this power must return for the final scenes to occur in the Dispensation of Fullness of Times. To understand what is required, we need to look at an account of a past city of peace established through, and protected by this power:

> And men having this faith, coming up unto this order of God, were translated and taken up into heaven. And now, Melchizedek was a priest of this order; therefore he obtained peace in Salem, and was called the Prince of

---

[374]Exo. 14: 15-16.

[375]For a discussion about this see my earlier book *Beloved Enos*, where this doctrine is explained.

peace. And his people wrought righteousness, and obtained heaven, and sought for the city of Enoch which God had before taken, separating it from the earth, having reserved it unto the latter days, or the end of the world; And hath said, and sworn with an oath, that the heavens and the earth should come together; and the sons of God should be tried so as by fire. And this Melchizedek, having thus established righteousness, was called the king of heaven by his people, or, in other words, the King of peace. (JST-Gen. 14: 32-36.)

The City of Enoch was protected by this power.[376] Melchizedek established a city with the same power, and it became a City of Peace, a place of righteousness, a part of heaven. Because of this, it followed the same order as the earlier city of Enoch which was taken to heaven. Melchizedek's city of peace was also worthy to be taken to heaven. People protected by the power are people who deserve heaven's protection. They establish an environment where angels and Christ can dwell. They are holy, their city is holy, and nature itself will protect such people.

Joseph Smith foresaw the establishment of another city in the last days that would also function under this same order. In that future city there would be a great power hovering over it that will hold at defiance the armies of nations. It will be a place where God's power will protect the citizens from all harm. The wicked will say it is "too terrible" a place for them to confront, and they will leave it in peace. As a prophecy describes it:

> And it shall come to pass among the wicked, that every man that will not take his sword against his neighbor must needs flee unto Zion for safety. And there shall be

---

[376]Moses 7: 13.

gathered unto it out of every nation under heaven; and it shall be the only people that shall not be at war one with another. And it shall be said among the wicked: Let us not go up to battle against Zion, for the inhabitants of Zion are terrible; wherefore we cannot stand. And it shall come to pass that the righteous shall be gathered out from among all nations, and shall come to Zion, singing with songs of everlasting joy. (D&C 45: 68-71.)

Another prophecy of Joseph's confirms the Lord will dwell in this city of peace. Those who have power to occupy this city, therefore, must be worthy of the Second Comforter; for He will dwell there:

And the Lord, even the Savior, shall stand in the midst of his people, and shall reign over all flesh. And they who are in the north countries shall come in remembrance before the Lord; and their prophets shall hear his voice, and shall no longer stay themselves; and they shall smite the rocks, and the ice shall flow down at their presence. And an highway shall be cast up in the midst of the great deep. Their enemies shall become a prey unto them, And in the barren deserts there shall come forth pools of living water; and the parched ground shall no longer be a thirsty land. And they shall bring forth their rich treasures unto the children of Ephraim, my servants. And the boundaries of the everlasting hills shall tremble at their presence. And there shall they fall down and be crowned with glory, even in Zion, by the hands of the servants of the Lord, even the children of Ephraim. And they shall be filled with songs of everlasting joy. (D&C 133: 25-33.)

It was for this purpose Joseph worked to deliver the fullness of the priesthood to the saints. He wanted to obtain the heavenly city, and establish it while he was here holding the keys. If the saints had done what was asked of them, Joseph had the necessary priesthood. With him, the saints could have avoided being moved out of their city in Nauvoo.[377] But, as we have seen, the saints did not build the Nauvoo Temple while Joseph was alive. John Taylor explained the saints were just not prepared for it. Therefore, they lost their city, had their temple burned, torn to the ground so not one stone was left atop the other, and the saints were driven into the wilderness where calamity after calamity befell them.

The saints still claim we fulfilled everything required by the revelation in January, 1841 (Section 124). The proud descendants of Nauvoo, who have always retained control of the church's top leadership positions, claim to hold all the keys ever given to Joseph Smith. They teach that they can bind on earth and in heaven. They are the 'new Popes' having the authority the Catholic Pope claims to possess, as J. Reuben Clark remarked.[378] According to their account of the historical narrative, all is well in their Zion. They intend to build Zion some day, when they get around to it. In the meantime, they continually curtail the scope of the restored faith, reducing the topics authorized to be taught in Sunday School, Priesthood, and Relief Society. Working to move farther and farther from what will be required for Zion. Their plan seems at odds with the end they seek.

Therefore, the question arises as to how similar the current situation of the Latter-day Saints is to ancient Israel when Moses was taken from their midst. We deny the analogy fits us, claiming

---

[377] See D&C 124: 44-45.

[378] "I said that the President of the Church was the representative of Christ on the earth, that he had in fact the position which the Pope tried to assume." (*The Diaries of J. Reuben Clark, 1933-1961, Abridged.* Salt Lake City: Privately Published, 2010, entry of November 13, 1959, p. 254.)

we have done a much better job with our opportunity than ancient Israel did with theirs. We believe our ordinances superior to theirs, our authority greater, and our privileges guaranteed by covenant and election. There is a statement attributed to Joseph Smith, often repeated, assuring us the work he established would never be thrown down or given to another people.[379] If the statement was accurately reported, the statement may not mean what we have come to claim. Moses was removed, and his priesthood with him, but Israel remained nonetheless "chosen." They were not "thrown down," nor was the Lord's work done by another people. They remained the Lord's people in a limited, condemned state. The church's preferred interpretation presumes the statement is accurate, and means we suffer from no such failing. But our interpretation contradicts the Lord's prophecy about the inevitable rejection of the fullness by the gentiles,[380] as well as many other passages of the Book of Mormon.[381]

Each person should answer the question for themselves about how the Latter-day Saints' current standing before the Lord seems

---

[379]The comment was given by Dimick B. Huntington in 1878, thirty-five years after it was supposed to have been said by Joseph. The words he attributed to Joseph were: "I have set up the Kingdom, no more to be thrown down forever nor never to be given to another people." (*Joseph Smith's Quorum of the Anointed: 1842-1845*. Editors Devery S. Anderson and Gary James Bergera. Salt Lake City: Signature Books, 2005, p. 4; quoting Undated Statement of Dimick B. Huntington made previously on December, 1878, in Mary Brown Firmage Papers, L. Tom Perry Special Collections, Harold B. Lee Library, Brigham Young University, Provo, Utah.)

[380]3 Nephi 16: 10.

[381]I've discussed this subject on my blog, and in the book reprinting the blog discussion: *Removing the Condemnation*. I would refer the reader to that material for treatment of that topic.

to them. Even if you give the most optimistic assessment of the restoration and current condition of the church, it can do nothing for the individual Latter-day Saint. We must all find salvation for ourselves. Each person must get their own covenant, their own promise of election directly from God, or find themself departing this life uncertain of their eternal state. When the promise of salvation is given by the Lord directly to an individual, he can know for certain his standing. It appears from the explanations given in scripture that we must choose between relying on the arm of flesh and promises given by men, and the word of God spoken directly to us.[382]

Returning to ancient Israel, there was one moment when the Lord arranged things so another who held keys, power, and authority stood at the head His people. At a time when the word of the Lord was rare, and there was no open vision experienced by Israel,[383] God's own voice called to Samuel. His voice called Samuel three times before Eli realized and told Samuel it was God who called him.[384] Samuel was called by God, then taken to His presence, and He spoke with the boy as He had done earlier with Moses.

The family of Eli had filled the Lord's House with corruption, extortion, and sexual perversion. Because of that, the Lord determined to do a thing which would make the ears of all who heard it tingle. Eli and his house were to be killed, every heir, and the office taken from them and given to Samuel:

---

[382]See, e.g., 2 Ne. 28: 31-32

[383]1 Sam. 3: 1.

[384]*Id.*, vs. 4-8.

And the Lord said to Samuel, Behold, I will do a thing in Israel, at which both the ears of every one that heareth it shall tingle. In that day I will perform against Eli all things which I have spoken concerning his house: when I begin, I will also make an end. For I have told him that I will judge his house for ever for the iniquity which he knoweth; because his sons made themselves vile, and he restrained them not. And therefore I have sworn unto the house of Eli, that the iniquity of Eli's house shall not be purged with sacrifice nor offering for ever. And Samuel lay until the morning, and opened the doors of the house of the Lord. And Samuel feared to shew Eli the vision. Then Eli called Samuel, and said, Samuel, my son. And he answered, Here am I. And he said, What is the thing that the Lord hath said unto thee? I pray thee hide it not from me: God do so to thee, and more also, if thou hide any thing from me of all the things that he said unto thee. And Samuel told him every whit, and hid nothing from him. And he said, It is the Lord: let him do what seemeth him good. (1 Sam. 3: 11-18.)

Samuel was called by God. Although he was not of the chosen family, he received the prophecy. Through him, God condemned the family of Eli, foretelling their destruction. They had gone beyond the power of offering a sacrifice to prevent God's judgment.

From the time the Lord appeared to Samuel, the words of His chosen prophet were all fulfilled. The Lord let none of them "fall to the ground" or, in other words, not be fulfilled.[385] From this we can know Samuel held the higher priesthood, possessed sealing power, and was a priest forever after the Order of the Son of God.

---

[385] 1 Sam. 3: 19.

The end of Eli's house came in a single day. His sons, Hophni and Phinehas were killed by the Philistines, who also took the Ark of the Covenant captive. At the news, Eli fell backwards, fracturing his skull and dying. Phinehas' pregnant wife heard of her husband and father-in-law's death, and she died that same day in childbirth.[386] Thus ended the house of Eli.

God's judgments established Samuel as the new, presiding priest and prophet. When this happened, once again there was a man among the Israelites who could provide what Moses had earlier offered. For a second time, the Lord arranged for the redemption of His people and the possibility of bringing Zion. However, Israel was not interested. They wanted a king like other nations, and demanded Samuel give them one. The sub-dispensation established through Samuel would end with Israel remaining as it was before he came. Israel rejected the prophet, preferring instead for the Lord to:

> [M]ake us a king to judge us like all the nations. But the thing displeased Samuel, when they said, Give us a king to judge us. And Samuel prayed unto the Lord. And the Lord said unto Samuel, Hearken unto the voice of the people in all that they say unto thee: for they have not rejected thee, but they have rejected me, that I should not reign over them. According to all the works which they have done since the day that I brought them up out of Egypt even unto this day, wherewith they have forsaken me, and served other gods, so do they also unto thee. Now therefore hearken unto their voice[.] (1 Sam. 8: 5-9.)

From the time of Samuel, Israel would have kings to preside over them. Still, from time to time, the Lord would also send prophets

---

[386]1 Sam. 4: 10-22.

to cry repentance to them. But their history was thereafter dominated by kings, and their religion dominated by a priestly class more interested in political influence, and gathering wealth than in teaching righteousness.

Throughout the Dispensation of Moses, there were continual sacrifices in the temple. After Moses' departure, first the Tabernacle was used as the place for sacrifice. Then Solomon built a permanent location in Jerusalem. It was destroyed, then rebuilt. Before the New Testament record opened, Herod rebuilt and expanded the temple, improving its size and elaborating on its style. It was the center of worship at the time of Christ. But it was presided over by a corrupt priestly class who conspired to kill Him. Despite this, Christ called the Temple of Herod His "father's house."[387] Christ visited, taught, and performed miracles there. For Him it was a respected place of worship, despite the flaws which may have existed in both its limited ceremonies and those who presided over it.

Real saints always appreciate anything the Lord condescends to give them. They are never ungrateful, impatient, or demanding. They qualify by patience and obedience to receive more. Then they petition in humility and gratitude to receive it. Having done as they were asked, they wait on the Lord to send it to them. They trust in His promises. They qualify to receive what He offers. The general failure of ancient (or modern) Israel has no effect upon them.

If we find ourselves in a circumstance where our privileges are less than we hoped they would be, then it is not the Lord's doing. We cannot fault Him for what men have failed to respect and retain.

---

[387]See John 2: 16.

If after Joseph was taken, the saints mirrored the condition of ancient Israel when Moses was taken, there is still hope. Ancient Israel still had both Aaronic/Levitical priesthood and the associated right to have the ministry of angels. Angels in turn can give everything else which may be lacking. Therefore, the absence of the authority of the fullness does not prevent the remaining authority from leading to eternal life.

There have been questions raised about the church's practice of ordaining or conferring priesthood. The issue involves whether priesthood should be conferred before ordaining a man to an office, or if ordaining to an office alone is enough. The question assumes there is a great difference between the use of one term or another, and it also relies on a technical requirement being critical to transfer priestly authority. In the church, there was a time when practices shifted for conducting priesthood ordinations. As we saw earlier, the church has independently identified offices which exist whether there is priesthood present or not.[388] In the view of Heber J. Grant, this distinction did not exist. He sent a letter in 1919 explaining the practice and affirming that, in the view of the First Presidency, there was nothing important in the process:

CONFERRING THE PRIESTHOOD

To prevent disputes over this subject that may arise over the procedure presented on page 169, we draw attention to the fact that until recently, from the days of the Prophet Joseph Smith, ordinations to the Priesthood

---

[388]See the earlier discussion about Section 20 of the D&C, where the church's offices are identified and include the office of "member" among others. As a result of the language of Section 20, there are offices of apostle, elder, priest, teacher, deacon, and member which exist in the church, in addition to those offices also existing as part of the priesthood.

were directly to the office therein for which the recipient was chosen and appointed, in form substantially as follows:

As to the Melchizedek Priesthood-"By authority (or in the authority) of the Holy Priesthood and by the laying on of hands, I (or we) ordain you an Elder, (or Seventy, or High Priest, or Patriarch, or Apostle, as the case may be), in the Church of Jesus Christ of Latter-day Saints, and confer upon you all the rights, powers, keys and authority pertaining to this office and calling in the Holy Melchizedek Priesthood, in the name of the Lord Jesus Christ, Amen."

As to the Lesser Priesthood-"By (or in) the authority of the Holy Priesthood I (or we) lay my (or our) hands upon your head and ordain you a Deacon (or other office in the Lesser Priesthood) in the Church of Jesus Christ of Latter-day Saints, and confer upon you all the rights, powers and authority pertaining to this office and calling in the Aaronic Priesthood on the name of the Lord Jesus Christ, Amen."

In reference to the form of procedure mentioned on page 169, and that set forth in this addendum as adopted by the leading authorities of the Church from the beginning, our beloved and departed President, Joseph F. Smith, when questioned concerning them, decided, as of record, "It is a distinction without a difference," and "either will do." Persons, therefore, who have been ordained in either way hold the right to officiate in all the duties of their respective offices in the Priesthood.

HEBER J. GRANT,
ANTHON H. LUND,
CHARLES W. PENROSE,

First Presidency.[389]

During President Grant's tenure, ordinations could be made to office without conferring priesthood, it being the view that ordination to office was enough. The issue had been controversial for two decades before President Grant decided the matter. Apostle Rudger Clawson wanted it resolved in 1902, when he brought it up for discussion among the First Presidency and Twelve.[390]

President McKay changed the practice to confer priesthood first, then ordain to an office. The changes raise a question of whether, during the practices of that time period, a man was ordained to an office in the church without having priesthood conferred upon him; or instead if although ordained to an office without conferring the priesthood he nevertheless was granted priesthood. It was a matter of controversy before being settled. Most Mormons today are unaware the controversy ever existed. Now the view is generally entertained in the church that what happened in whatever form it happened was sufficient. It was a "distinction without a difference" and "either will do." As Joseph Fielding Smith would

---

[389]Clark, James. *Messages of the First Presidency, 6 Vols.* Salt Lake City: Bookcraft, 1965-1975, Vol. 5, p. 121.

[390]"Apostle Clawson called attention to the fact that there is a lack of uniformity in the church in ordaining men to the priesthood; for example, some of the brethren in ordaining a man to be a high priest would first confer upon him the Melchizedek Priesthood and then ordain him a high priest, while others would follow the usual procedure, i.e., ordain him a high priest conferring upon him all the keys, powers, and blessings pertaining to that calling in the Melchizedek Priesthood." (*A Ministry of Meetings: The Apostolic Diaries of Rudger Clawson.* Edited by Stan Larson. Salt Lake City: Signature Books, 1993, p. 427.)

later explain, we now make distinctions which were not understood in earlier times:

> In his account the Prophet declared that the angel ordained him and Oliver Cowdery. The proper word would have been conferred the Priesthood. In the early days of the Church the term "ordain" was used in the sense of conferring or setting apart. The distinction which we make today between conferring, setting apart and ordaining, had not been clearly drawn. The Angel John, however, used the proper expression. Joseph Smith and Oliver Cowdery, as the record shows, were not ordained to any office, but the Priesthood was conferred upon them. All of the offices of the Priesthood come out of, and are appendages to, the Priesthood. (See D. and C. 107:5.) Priesthood has existed independently of the Church at times, but the offices pertain to the Church organization and are conferred by the sanction of the Church. This is also true of the bestowal of the Melchizedek Priesthood. Under the hands of Peter, James and John, Joseph Smith and Oliver Cowdery had conferred upon them the Melchizedek Priesthood and all of the offices come out of this Priesthood after the organization of the Church. The first office held in this dispensation was that of Elder. Joseph Smith was ordained by Oliver Cowdery to be the first Elder of the Church, and Oliver Cowdery was ordained to be the second Elder of the Church, on the 6th day of April, 1830. Following this ordination, as the Church increased in membership deacons, teachers, and priests were ordained, also other elders. On the third day of June, 1832, the first high priests were ordained. Among this number was Joseph Smith the Prophet.[391]

---

[391] Smith, Joseph Fielding. *Church History and Modern Revelation*, 4 Vols. Salt Lake City: Deseret Book, 1946, vol. 1, pp. 56 - 57

All of this is based upon the presumption the church offices identified in Section 20 are necessarily priesthood offices. Today we do not recognize any longer that church offices began as something separate from the priesthood. Church office and priesthood are, however, two different things. The church can call and ordain officers, sustain and uphold them, and they can have the right to preside because of our common consent. All of that does not necessarily require any priesthood by such office holders. Earlier we discussed David Whitmer's argument that priesthood for church officials was a later view, and not the original view of the Mormons. For our phase four Mormonism, church offices and priesthood have become regarded as being identical. That, however, is not necessarily true.

The argument about language used to ordain or confer priesthood has been made primarily by dissenting groups who urge the conclusion that the church has lost its priestly power. Their arguments are meaningless for two reasons: First, as will later be covered in some detail, the church remains the Lord's, just as ancient Israel was the Lord's, despite removing Moses and the higher priesthood. It has always had, and continues to have, the right to continue to preach, teach, exhort, expound, baptize, administer the sacrament, and perform other preparatory ordinances. It has the right to elect officers to preside through common consent, and when they are sustained in their offices they have the right to receive and provide direction to the church and its members. Apart from the common consent of the members of the church, no one has any right to govern in the church of Jesus Christ. The dissenters therefore, have no right or basis to claim superior authority over those who have been sustained to preside through common consent. This would be true even if the presiding authority did not have any priesthood.

Second, as the scriptures have taught us, the form of priesthood which is after the Order of the Son of God comes to a man in only one manner: "And it was delivered unto men by the calling of his own voice, according to his own will, unto as many as believed on his name. (JST-Gen. 14: 29.) For all such holders of higher priesthood the Lord Himself makes the call. It was never possible to institutionalize such authority in any dispensation of the Gospel. It comes directly from the Lord, and only to such persons as qualify to enter His presence, hold at defiance the armies of nations, break every band, command waters to dry up, and so on. This authority can be here without Zion, but it is absolutely required for Zion to return. Therefore, arguments by dissenters over who has the right to be recognized, to control, command or direct others, is merely an exercise in pride and ambition without any real meaning. It is foolish for any person to entertain the ambition to lead others. Those claiming authority to preside who have not been first sustained by common consent of the church are never properly authorized.[392] Nor can someone go about building a branch of the Lord's church without the authorization to do so coming from the church's presiding authorities.[393] Every saint is commanded to teach the doctrine of the kingdom to one another,[394] but that does not give anyone the right to establish a splinter group, lead others away, or gratify their ambition to lead by

---

[392]D&C 20: 65.

[393]D&C 42: 11.

[394]D&C 88: 77.

claiming they have the right to preside. We should remain a united body of believers, even if our beliefs differ among ourselves about some issues. Even if we mourn changes or alterations to the faith, we should remain united, and trust the Lord will correct matters when enough of the saints are willing to accept the sacrifice necessary for His intervention.

If someone knows truth, then let them preach, teach, exhort, expound, and instruct others so we can come to the unity of faith. It is the obligation of everyone, from the highest office of Apostle to the lowest office of member, to labor for a unity of faith.[395] Let those who are sustained in office preside, and let anyone who believes they have some true principle to explain proceed to explain it. An authentic message of truth does not require an office to make it legitimate. Truth stands independent of its advocate. Those who dissent away from the church only do themselves harm. They would be better advised to remain among the saints, and preach such truths as they understand, to correct and be corrected by others who share belief in Christ and in His latter-day restoration of the Gospel. A gentle word of reproof for others is enough. Contention will never win hearts. Breaking away and forming another splinter group has been tried by prideful and foolish men from before Joseph's death until now. Even when they had a valid complaint, their splinter either failed or is in the process of failing now. It is clear to me the Lord wants the church to remain intact. It may be under condemnation, and have provoked His judgments and wrath, but it is still His. He will remember it. Being rebuked by those He sends from time to time, who are true messengers with an authentic message, is evidence the Lord still

---

[395]Eph. 4: 11-16.

loves and watches over us.[396] It is unlikely a true messenger will attempt to assert any right to control, preside or exercise dominion in the church. Stating the truth is enough.

As a church we retain the power of common consent. Whatever foolish choices we make can be corrected by our own choice to do better. There is no limit on how quickly we can change things by our common voice. It only requires the saints to be persuaded to make a change for such a change to then be made binding for the church. This is why the saints have always been responsible for moving from phase to phase. Without consent, leaders can do nothing.

Eventually the saints will receive the result merited by their choices. When fully ripe, judgments will diminish our numbers. Those who are more wicked are slain, and those who will accept truth are spared.[397] This is always the Lord's way. The Lord's hand is stretched out still, inviting all who are willing to accept the truth a chance to do so. The "more wicked part" will always be targeted first, so those who will repent are stirred up to do so. But the invitation is to all Latter-day Saints, not just to some splinter group, filled with pride, thinking themselves too good to remain associated with others. Remember, neither Christ nor His New

---

[396]See, e.g., Rev. 3: 19.

[397]Those who were spared in the great Book of Mormon destruction were described: "And it was the more righteous part of the people who were saved, and it was they who received the prophets and stoned them not; and it was they who had not shed the blood of the saints, who were spared-- And they were spared and were not sunk and buried up in the earth; and they were not drowned in the depths of the sea; and they were not burned by fire, neither were they fallen upon and crushed to death; and they were not carried away in the whirlwind; neither were they overpowered by the vapor of smoke and of darkness." (3 Ne. 10: 12-13.)

Testament church disconnected from the Jews. Throughout the history in Acts, the Lord's disciples continued to meet in synagogues[398] and to worship in the temple at Jerusalem.[399] It was after the apostasy of the New Testament church before Christianity became something other than an affiliated subset of Judaism. For us, however, the coming sifting will be done by the Lord, not by us dividing ourselves into splinters.[400] Of course, the church can judge and reject true believers. If it elects to do so, and to thereby cause a separation, the responsibility for that will lie with the church leaders. Leaders have already been warned about persecuting the saints, as this will result in them forfeiting whatever priesthood remains with them.[401] But the Lord's saints have no right to voluntarily divide themselves from the church, even if you believe it has been condemned, rejected and cursed for departing from His instructions.

---

[398]See, e.g., Acts 13: 14-15; 14: 1; 17: 1-4; 17: 10-11; 18: 4; 18: 19; 19: 8 (where Paul spent 3 months teaching in the same synagogue).

[399]See, e.g., Acts 2: 46; 3: 1-8; 5: 19-21 (where "the angel of the Lord" commanded them to teach in the temple); 21: 26.

[400]D&C 112: 25.

[401]"That they may be conferred upon us, it is true; but when we undertake to cover our sins, or to gratify our pride, our vain ambition, or to exercise control or dominion or compulsion upon the souls of the children of men, in any degree of unrighteousness, behold, the heavens withdraw themselves; the Spirit of the Lord is grieved; and when it is withdrawn, Amen to the priesthood or the authority of that man. Behold, ere he is aware, he is left unto himself, to kick against the pricks, to persecute the saints, and to fight against God." (D&C 121: 37-38.)

w/o compulsion

Chapter 12

PROPHECY VS. THE TRADITIONAL NARRATIVE

We pointed out earlier the article[402] of LDS Assistant Church Historian Davis Bitton titled, "*I Don't Have A Testimony of The History of The Church.*"[403] He acknowledges "no one ever said that the history of the church was the history of perfect people."[404] It does not take long for any fair minded person to reach the conclusion the history of The Church of Jesus Christ of Latter-day Saints has been lived by flawed people. In that respect, all history is alike. Only one person came here and lived without sin, and His contemporaries condemned and killed Him. In part, because they believed they were killing a wicked man.

This book suggests a different view of the people and events than the traditional church explanation. Reasons I reject the

---

[402]It was first delivered as a talk, then published as an article in FARMS Review.

[403]Found at FARMS Review, Vol. 16, 2 (2004) beginning at p. 337.

[404]*Id.*, p. 344.

traditional account will be addressed in this chapter. I have studied, and once believed the traditional accounts. I still find them uplifting. I used to hope they were true in every respect. But by careful examination of the events, and rethinking them as a whole, they leave gaps, and leap to conclusions which seem unjustified. Most of the faithful accounts begin with the conclusion. These authors accept a proposition as a matter of faith, then reason backward from their faith to interpret events. This approach never guarantees the truth. It develops an argument to support an outcome.

On the topic of priesthood authority, the Roman Catholic Church and The Church of Jesus Christ of Latter-day Saints advance mutually incompatible propositions. If the Catholics have retained priesthood, there was no reason to restore it. If the Mormons had it restored to them, then it needed to return because the Catholics lost it. Catholic claims to priesthood are rejected by Mormons because we understand priesthood authority is not immutable, and it can be lost. If priesthood cannot be lost, then the Catholic claims are justified. If Mormon claims are correct, it is necessary for priesthood authority to recognize it can be lost by apostasy from the truth.

The great Catholic debate over this issue involved what came to be known as the Donatist Heresy. It was a "heresy" because Donatists lost the argument. The argument involved whether or not a wicked bishop or priest removed his priesthood authority. The winning side in that dispute decided priestly authority was not dependent on the officiator's worthiness (or outright wickedness). Priesthood authority was indelible, and endured beyond sin.

If this proposition is correct, then Catholics could not have forfeited priesthood. Wickedness, error, and foolishness would never be a reason to remove their authority. Once conferred, only death would remove the power to perform ordinances from a bishop or priest. Mormons reject this notion.

For Mormons, Joseph Smith answered this question about losing priesthood power before it ever arose. In an 1839 revelation dealing with priesthood power and authority, it was established:

> Behold, there are many called, but few are chosen. And why are they not chosen? Because their hearts are set so much upon the things of this world, and aspire to the honors of men, that they do not learn this one lesson-- That the rights of the priesthood are inseparably connected with the powers of heaven, and that the powers of heaven cannot be controlled nor handled only upon the principles of righteousness. That they may be conferred upon us, it is true; but when we undertake to cover our sins, or to gratify our pride, our vain ambition, or to exercise control or dominion or compulsion upon the souls of the children of men, in any degree of unrighteousness, behold, the heavens withdraw themselves; the Spirit of the Lord is grieved; and when it is withdrawn, Amen to the priesthood or the authority of that man. (D&C 121: 34-37.)

Priesthood's rights are "inseparably connected with the powers of heaven." There is no such thing as priesthood that functions independent of heaven. If the holder loses his connection to heaven, he loses priesthood. Heaven has nothing to do with the unrighteous.[405] Therefore, it follows that priesthood cannot be controlled or handled unless the person holding it is "righteous." If priesthood is conferred upon a person, their authority ends, and priesthood is forfeited as soon as the person covers their sins rather than repenting of them. When he is prideful, ambitious, and uses

---

[405]Hosea 4: 6.

priesthood to control or compel others to bend to his will, the heavens withdraw from that man. When the heavens withdraw, he has no priesthood. It is withdrawn. "Amen to the priesthood or the authority of that man." He can continue to claim a title, even have an office in the church, but he is devoid of priesthood.

This presents a dilemma for Mormons. How can you know of a priest's worthiness? That is the same dilemma Catholics faced in the fourth and fifth centuries. It is that dilemma that led them to denounce the Donatists as heretics. They decided they would prefer to make claims to authority based on immutability, rather than to defend their actions as having been worthy. For Mormons this argument is not possible. Unless you are willing to ignore the 1839 revelation, and reason backward from the conclusion you intend to justify.

Reasoning backward requires you to begin with the result. On this topic, the conclusion you want is the priesthood has persisted from the time of Joseph Smith until the present. To reach this outcome, you then proceed with whatever assumptions as are required to justify the conclusion. An example of this can be found in a recent article written by a respected LDS scholar, Daniel C. Petersen. His 2006 article responds to Paul Toscano's Sunstone paper titled *Priesthood Concepts in the Book of Mormon.*[406] Brother Petersen writes:

> Unless and until superior priesthood authority withdraws permission to exercise priestly functions, a legitimately ordained holder of the priesthood may continue to perform valid priesthood ordinances –however unrighteous he may personally be, however dead to spiritual promptings, and however unlikely it may be that

---

[406]Sunstone, December 1989, p. 8.

he will ever actually exercise his priesthood. [Ftnt: The ancient Christian church faced this problem in the form of the Donatist schism, which was finally declared heretical in AD 405. The Donatists held that unrighteousness in a bishop or priest invalidated any and all ordinances that he might have performed. However, the Synod of Arles determined in AD 314 that the validity of baptisms and ordinations and the like did not depend upon the worthiness or merit of the officiator. ...Granted, the Christian church at this period was essentially apostate, but Latter-day Saints take basically the same position, and for good reason. If serious sin, as such, invalidated priesthood ordinances, we could never know whose marriage was legal, or who was really a member of the church. Did the man who ordained you to the priesthood have a secret, unrepented sin? Then your ordination is invalid. Your mission was illegitimate, any converts you baptized are actually nonmembers, and you are living in adultery since you should never have been admitted to the temple. Any of your converts who served missions and baptized are similarly fraudulent, and the consequences ripple onward and outward in utterly unforseen ways. How can we ever be sure of anything?][407]

Brother Peterson's reasoning is not only exactly the same as the Catholics, he even cites to the Catholic precedent to justify Mormon claims! If the result is unwanted (loss of priesthood), then you treat the idea as unthinkable, unallowable, never to be admitted. Therefore, the reasoning concludes, the result you want to avoid absolutely CANNOT be true. If it cannot be true, then it is safe to ignore the possibility of the unacceptable result, and

---

[407]Peterson, Daniel C. *Authority in the Book of Mosiah.* Provo: FARMS Review, Vol. 18, 1, 2006, p. 164-165.

connect the dots in a manner which allows you to avoid it. But Mormonism is not Catholicism. And despite how the Synod of Arles decided the question, for the restored Gospel serious sin does in fact invalidate priesthood authority. The power or authority of priesthood is inseparably connected with heaven. If a man is dead to spiritual promptings, he is powerless and has no priesthood. Wicked men do not have and never have had priesthood. Heaven does not allow it. That is what our scriptures say. Our necessity does not change it. Our ambition does not forgive it. Our earnest desire cannot alter it.

The problems Brother Petersen lists are indeed problems. But they cannot be solved merely by bombast and a strongly felt need. The priesthood is not available based upon the will of man or men, but comes from God's will alone. In the case of the highest form of priesthood, it comes directly from God, as we have seen: "It being after the order of the son of God; which order came, not by man, nor the will of man; neither by father nor mother; neither by beginning of days nor end of years; but of God; And it was delivered unto men by the calling of his own voice, according to his own will, unto as many as believed on his name." (JST-Gen. 14: 28-29.)

The problem is not that this is just "too hard" for men. Rather the problem is the unwillingness of men to repent. The conditions for salvation have always been the same.[408] They do not change because men wish them to, find them hard, or do not want to comply. Joseph Smith was really sent to establish Zion, given the

---

[408]"There is a law, irrevocably decreed in heaven before the foundations of this world, upon which all blessings are predicated-- And when we obtain any blessing from God, it is by obedience to that law upon which it is predicated." (D&C 130: 20-21.)

power from heaven to establish it, and could have done so if the saints were willing to rise to the invitation. However, as John Taylor explained: "The reason why we do not live in peace is because we are not prepared for it."[409]

Another part of the Mormon narrative driven by need is the idea added in phase two, and then read back into phase one, concerning Elijah's visit to the Kirtland Temple. The significance of the event recorded in 1836 by Warren Cowdery, which later became Section 110, is completely absent from phase one. It was nearly a decade after Joseph's death before the revelation was printed for the first time. So far as any record exists, Joseph never mentioned it, or taught it. Oliver Cowdery did not record the event. Between 1836 and his death, there is no mention of the event. It was years after Joseph's death before any claim was made that Elijah restored something. Further, as we discussed earlier, Section 110 does not describe Elijah as restoring anything.[410] In the text of Section 110 Elijah merely confirms the restoration was then completed. He stated: "Therefore, the keys of this dispensation are committed into your hands; and by this ye may know that the great and dreadful day of the Lord is near, even at the doors." (D&C 110: 16.)

The traditional view is explained by Glen M. Leonard, former director of the Museum of Church History and Art of The Church of Jesus Christ of Latter-day Saints. He writes about the Kirtland Temple dedication:

---

[409] *Nauvoo: A Place of Peace, A People of Promise, supra*, p. 267.

[410] He confirms the promise in Malachi was fulfilled, that the hearts of the children should turn to the fathers, to avoid a curse at the Lord's coming. (D&C 110: 14-15.) However, no keys, authority or power is transferred. Elijah only notes that the keys had, as of 1836, been fully restored to Joseph and Oliver.

It was during the week of dedication that Joseph Smith and Oliver Cowdery witnessed appearances of Jesus, Moses, Elias and Elijah above the pulpits of the temple and received special priesthood authority from them. These visits, recorded in Doctrine and Covenants 110, had profound influence on the development of Nauvoo's temple theology.[411]

This is reading events in reverse. There is no indication from Joseph or Oliver to justify the notion this event in any way affected subsequent temple rites. Brother Leonard goes on to explain the traditional view:

The essence of these [eternal marriage] teachings was embodied in a revelation that had been unfolding for more than a decade. Components of the revelation were committed to writing on July 12, 1843. The central focus was the principle of eternal marriage. Later published as Doctrine and Covenants 132, the revelation explained that Elijah's key was the same binding power given by Christ to Peter. Among other uses, this authority solemnized marriages with an eternal potential and bound generations together in a perpetual chain of families.[412]

The July 12, 1843 revelation is Section 132. The head note to Section 132 states: "it is evident from the historical records that the doctrines and principles involved in this revelation had been known by the Prophet since 1831."[413] As part of the written

---

[411] *Nauvoo: A Place of Peace, A People of Promise, supra,* p. 257.

[412] *Id.,* p. 264.

[413] I explained earlier my view that this revelation was received most likely during the translation of Jacob, in the Book of Mormon. If I am correct, the revelation was received in 1829.

revelation, Joseph was told "whatsoever you seal on earth shall be sealed in heaven." (D&C 132: 46.) Brother Leonard attributes this language in Section 132 to the Kirtland events in 1836. "Elijah's key was the same binding power given by Christ to Peter," as he puts it. However, Joseph's sealing power came exactly as Melchizedek's - not from Elijah, but by the voice of God. The only way this kind of authority comes to men is by the voice of God.[414] It did not, does not, and cannot come from Elijah. Though Elijah may have a message to deliver confirming the keys are held, it is the voice of God which confers this power on a man.[415] Nor does the earlier revelation (received between 1829 and 1831), written down as Section 132 (in 1843), have language which was informed by Elijah's appearance in 1836. Here is the sequence:

-1st Approximately 1829, Joseph received the revelation concerning plural wives. (D&C 132: 1-44.)

-2nd Beginning in 1831, Joseph obeyed the revelation, at some considerable personal sacrifice. (D&C 132: 50.)

-3rd Sometime following 1831, Joseph's sacrifice was accepted, and the Lord confirmed his calling and election, and granted him the sealing power. (D&C 132: 46-49.)

-4th On December 27, 1832, Joseph used the power given to him by God's voice to seal on earth and in heaven to seal a group of faithful saints to eternal life. (D&C 88: 2-5.) This requires him to be in possession of the power to seal by this date at the latest.

---

[414]"And it was delivered unto men by the calling of his own voice, according to his own will, unto as many as believed on his name." (JST-Gen. 14: 29.)

[415] Joseph probably received it on the occasion mentioned in D&C 128: 21.

-5$^{th.}$ On April 3, 1836, the events recorded in Section 110 involving Elijah happened. (D&C 110.)

Therefore, I do not believe that Elijah's appearance conferred sealing power on Joseph Smith. Instead, I believe it came to Joseph just as it came to Melchizedek, and just as it came to any who received it from the time of Enoch till today. It is delivered by the calling of God's own voice. Elijah confirmed the Dispensation keys were in Joseph's possession as of April, 1836. The words of Section 112 are also an important part of the traditional view of the church. It states:

> For unto you, the Twelve, and those, the First Presidency, who are appointed with you to be your counselors and your leaders, is the power of this priesthood given, for the last days and for the last time, in the which is the dispensation of the fulness of times. Which power you hold, in connection with all those who have received a dispensation at any time from the beginning of the creation; For verily I say unto you, the keys of the dispensation, which ye have received, have come down from the fathers, and last of all, being sent down from heaven unto you. (D&C 112: 30-32.)

It has been argued the words "for the last days and for the last time" mean it will endure despite any failure by the gentile church. The reasoning goes that it will never be lost, and "last of all" will be kept intact. However, this argument may go too far and be mistaken. For example, in Section 76, the revelation uses the same words to speak of the revelation of Jesus Christ. It states: "And now, after the many testimonies which have been given of him, this is the testimony, last of all, which we give of him: That he lives!" (D&C 76: 22.) If the same meaning was attributed to the words "last of all" for Joseph's testimony in Section 76, it would mean no one after 1832 would receive a testimony of Jesus. It would negate the appearance four years later to Oliver and Joseph in the Kirtland Temple, and the testimony in Section 110. It would also negate Joseph F. Smith's vision of the Lord's visit to the world of spirits in Section 138. Therefore, the words "for the last days and for the last time" probably should be read to mean "for our use in the latest delivery of priesthood to mankind." If that is the meaning, it has nothing to add to the subject of whether priesthood power can be forfeited.

There was a claim made by Orson Hyde, after Joseph's death and after the fight over succession in Nauvoo, published in the *Millennial Star*. Brother Francis G. Bishop wanted to be ordained a high priest. He urgently pressed to be ordained, which convinced the saints he wanted something he did not merit. He was an elder, and sent out on a mission as an elder. He could not muster a vote to get him approved to be ordained a high priest. In response he claimed he had been ordained a high priest by "an angel from heaven." This caused a stir, and came to Joseph's attention. Joseph called for Elder Bishop, and when he arrived questioned him about his claims.[416] During the questioning he contradicted himself, became confused, then embarrassed, and finally broke down and, falling on his knees, confessed he had lied and begged to be forgiven. They forgave him. The account picks up at that point and states:

> Brother Joseph observed to Bishop that he knew
> he had lied before he confessed it; that his declarations

---

[416]It is interesting Joseph did not dismiss the claim out of hand when he first heard it. He wanted to interview Elder Bishop before reaching a conclusion. When his story did not stand up to questioning, then Joseph decided the matter.

were not only false in themselves, but they involved a false principle. An angel, said Joseph, may administer the word of the Lord unto men, and bring intelligence to them from heaven upon various subjects; but no true angel from God will ever come to ordain any man, because they have once been sent to establish the priesthood by ordaining me thereunto; and the priesthood being once established on earth, with power to ordain others, no heavenly messenger will ever come to interfere with that power by ordaining any more. He referred to the angel that came to Cornelius and told Cornelius to send for Peter; but if there had been no Peter with keys and power to administer, the angel might have done it himself; but as there was, the angel would not interfere. Saul was directed to go to Ananias for instruction and to be administered to by him; but if there had been no Ananias with power and authority on the earth to administer in the name of Christ, the Lord might have done it himself. You may therefore know, from this time forward, that if any man comes to you professing to be ordained by an angel, he is either a liar or has been imposed upon in consequence of transgression by an angel of the devil, for this priesthood shall never be taken away from this church.

This testimony was delivered in an upper room, in the south-west corner of the White Store and dwelling-house, formerly occupied by Whitney and Gilbert, situate on Kirtland Flats.[417]

This event probably does not altogether solve the question of whether angels will continue to confer authority on men for at least three reasons. First, the office he was claiming (high priest) had been added as a church position by the time this incident occurred.

---

[417]*Millennial Star 8,* (November 20, 1846), p. 139.

Offices in the church were and are controlled by the church's authorities, conferred by common consent, and are not granted in the absence of a vote of a congregation.[418] Second, it is beyond dispute that so long as Joseph Smith was among the saints it would be unnecessary for angels to do what a living prophet who had the fullness could do. Heaven does not generally perform unnecessary work. The inverse is also true. If it is necessary for heaven to perform a work, then it is likely man cannot. Third, in a revelation to Joseph about future events, he was told those who would be sealed up to eternal life before the Lord's return would receive their sealings from the "angels" holding "power" and sent by God. The revelation concerns a group of 144,000 who, in the last days, will be sealed up as referred to in Revelation 7. It explains:

> 11 Q. What are we to understand by sealing the one hundred and forty-four thousand, out of all the tribes of Israel--twelve thousand out of every tribe?
>
> A. We are to understand that those who are sealed are high priests, ordained unto the holy order of God, to administer the everlasting gospel; for they are they who are ordained out of every nation, kindred, tongue, and people, by the angels to whom is given power over the nations of the earth, to bring as many as will come to the church of the Firstborn.

If the authority to perform this sealing was always kept by men, then the sealing would not be performed "by the angels to whom is given power over the nations of the earth, to bring as many as will come to the church of the Firstborn." If the power to do this

---

[418]D&C 20: 65: "No person is to be ordained to any office in this church, where there is a regularly organized branch of the same, without the vote of that church[.]"

remained with the church, then it would follow, the church, and not angels, would be assigned to accomplish the sealing. The church does not have, and never will have, an office called "angel." Angels are sent by God, and come with a message directly from Him.[419]

The traditional narrative also does not account for Book of Mormon prophecies concerning gentile failures in the last days. The church restored through Joseph Smith is referred to throughout the Book of Mormon as the "gentiles." Joseph knew this, and in the Kirtland Temple dedicatory prayer, which came to him as a revelation, explained how the church was regarded by the Lord.[420] Christ prophesied to the Nephites the following:

> And thus commandeth the Father that I should say unto you: At that day when the Gentiles shall sin against my gospel, and shall reject the fulness of my gospel, and shall be lifted up in the pride of their hearts above all nations, and above all the people of the whole earth, and shall be filled with all manner of lyings, and of deceits, and of mischiefs, and all manner of hypocrisy, and murders, and priestcrafts, and whoredoms, and of secret abominations; and if they shall do all those things, and shall reject the fulness of my gospel, behold, saith the Father, I will bring

[handwritten: → in the past? not currently but?]

---

[419] Joseph explained that all "angels" either have or do belong to this earth: "But there are no angels who minister to this earth but those who do belong or have belonged to it." (D&C 130: 5.) Meaning angels are called from those who were or are mortals here. Their status as "angel" comes from the fact they have met with God, gotten both their assignment and authority from Him, and deliver only the message He instructs should be delivered. They are in His service, and the message is confined to what He has told them to do.

[420] See D&C 109: 60: "Now these words, O Lord, we have spoken before thee, concerning the revelations and commandments which thou hast given unto us, who are identified with the Gentiles."

[handwritten: yea this]

the fulness of my gospel from among them. And then will
I remember my covenant which I have made unto my
people, O house of Israel, and I will bring my gospel unto
them. And I will show unto thee, O house of Israel, that
the Gentiles shall not have power over you; but I will
remember my covenant unto you, O house of Israel, and
ye shall come unto the knowledge of the fulness of my
gospel. (3 Ne. 16: 10-12.)

Christ's prophecy does not anticipate gentile success. The gentiles
will reject the fullness offered to them. "At that day when the
Gentiles shall sin against my gospel" does not raise the possibility
of "if" but only "when." According to Christ, the gentiles "shall
reject the fullness of my gospel." Taking these words at their plain
meaning, it leaves no room for gentiles to obtain and perpetuate
the fullness of the priesthood. They will instead reject it when it is
offered them. But, despite having rejected it, gentiles are allowed
to repent, and join the remnant of the Book of Mormon people
and be saved. Christ's prophecy continues with this hopeful
offering to the gentiles:

> But if the Gentiles will repent and return unto me, saith the
> Father, behold they shall be numbered among my people,
> O house of Israel. And I will not suffer my people, who are
> of the house of Israel, to go through among them, and
> tread them down, saith the Father. But if they will not turn
> unto me, and hearken unto my voice, I will suffer them,
> yea, I will suffer my people, O house of Israel, that they
> shall go through among them, and shall tread them down,
> and they shall be as salt that hath lost its savor, which is
> thenceforth good for nothing but to be cast out, and to be
> trodden under foot of my people, O house of Israel. Verily,
> verily, I say unto you, thus hath the Father commanded
> me--that I should give unto this people this land for their
> inheritance. (3 Ne. 16: 13-16.)

Although the gentiles will reject the fullness, and leave the path, they can still "repent and return." You cannot "return" unless you leave first. Therefore, the gentiles must depart. If we have already rejected the fullness and departed from the Lord, as the interpretation of the events in this book suggests, then we need to "repent and return" to the Lord. If we do, then we are promised we will once again "be numbered among [Christ's] people." But the land where Christ spoke when He visited with the Nephites belongs to the Nephite descendants. Therefore, when the Lord fulfills His covenant to the Nephite remnant, the unconverted gentiles will be swept away.

Gentiles who repent will be numbered among His people and receive the same promises. They alone will survive the coming holocaust in which the gentiles will be "cast out, and ...trodden under foot."

Nephi's prophecy about the future gentile history is also speaking directly of the latter-day church.

> Nevertheless, thou beholdest that the Gentiles who have gone forth out of captivity, and have been lifted up by the power of God above all other nations, upon the face of the land which is choice above all other lands, which is the land that the Lord God hath covenanted with thy father that his seed should have for the land of their inheritance; wherefore, thou seest that the Lord God will not suffer that the Gentiles will utterly destroy the mixture of thy seed, which are among thy brethren. Neither will he suffer that the Gentiles shall destroy the seed of thy brethren. Neither will the Lord God suffer that the Gentiles shall forever remain in that awful state of blindness, which thou beholdest they are in, because of the plain and most precious parts of the gospel of the Lamb which have been kept back by that abominable church, whose formation thou hast seen. Wherefore saith the Lamb of God: I will be

merciful unto the Gentiles, unto the visiting of the remnant of the house of Israel in great judgment. And it came to pass that the angel of the Lord spake unto me, saying: Behold, saith the Lamb of God, after I have visited the remnant of the house of Israel--and this remnant of whom I speak is the seed of thy father--wherefore, after I have visited them in judgment, and smitten them by the hand of the Gentiles, and after the Gentiles do stumble exceedingly, because of the most plain and precious parts of the gospel of the Lamb which have been kept back by that abominable church, which is the mother of harlots, saith the Lamb--I will be merciful unto the Gentiles in that day, insomuch that I will bring forth unto them, in mine own power, much of my gospel, which shall be plain and precious, saith the Lamb. (1 Ne. 13: 30-34.)

Just as Nephi foresaw, the European gentiles have obtained possession of this land, and have not utterly destroyed the original inhabitants. The "mixture of [Nephi's] seed" remains among the aboriginal tribes of America. The proud Latter-day Saint gentiles may not acknowledge the importance of these Nephite descendants, but it is this Nephite remnant who are the rightful heirs to this promised land. They will eventually sweep the gentiles away and regain possession. However, the gentiles have had promises given to them while they are in possession.

The gentiles have not remained in an "awful state of blindness" about the Gospel of the Lamb. Through Joseph Smith's ministry, the Book of Mormon has been brought to light. "Much of [Christ's] Gospel" has been given to the gentiles. Significantly, Nephi does not foresee the gentiles obtaining "all" or a fullness, but only "much" of the gospel. We are now still in possession of "much" of Christ's Gospel. We were offered more. The "fullness" that was lost to the gentiles was offered again, they only had to complete the Nauvoo Temple as required.[421] The traditional Mormon view is that Joseph was able, outside the temple, to transfer all keys in his red brick store, and the church received and has kept the fullness. However, Nephi's description of what was to be given the gentiles says only "much" will be returned, not that a "fullness" will be given.

The traditional narrative also requires the language of revelation be not only meaningless, but contradicted. The requirement to build the Nauvoo Temple was because, as the Lord explained it: "For there is not a place found on earth that he may come to and restore again that which was lost unto you, or which he hath taken away, even the fulness of the priesthood." (D&C 124: 28.) If a red brick store is an adequate substitute for a temple, then there must have been plenty of places that could be found for the Lord to come and restore again the fullness.

The distinction between "all" and "much" in Nephi's word choice also suggests the traditional narrative presumes too much. If we failed to obtain the fullness, and have been left with "much" of the Gospel, then what has happened was foreseen and prophesied over two thousand years before the events. The saints' failure to gain the fullness is not a surprise to heaven. It was always foreseen this would be the case.

Nephi also described the post-restoration state of the gentiles. He makes no distinction between the latter-day church restored to the gentiles, and other churches in the last days. The gentiles who will receive "much" of the gospel will regard themselves as "Zion," and proudly claim they are more favored than all others. Nephi prophesies:

---

[421]D&C 124: 25-28, 31-32, 40-48.

Yea, they have all gone out of the way; they have become corrupted. Because of pride, and because of false teachers, and false doctrine, their churches have become corrupted, and their churches are lifted up; because of pride they are puffed up. They rob the poor because of their fine sanctuaries; they rob the poor because of their fine clothing; and they persecute the meek and the poor in heart, because in their pride they are puffed up. They wear stiff necks and high heads; yea, and because of pride, and wickedness, and abominations, and whoredoms, they have all gone astray save it be a few, who are the humble followers of Christ; nevertheless, they are led, that in many instances they do err because they are taught by the precepts of men. (2 Ne. 28: 11-14.)

The churches of the gentiles have "all gone out of the way; they have become corrupted." There is no exception. There isn't a "one true church" which stands out against a background of fallen, false churches. All of them are out of harmony with the Lord. Gentiles have not maintained the gospel in purity and power.

The gentiles will be prideful, taught by false teachers, and learning false doctrine. The result will be pride in themselves, rather than the required fearful repentance and humility. Their "stiff necks" and their "high heads" are because they believe themselves particularly favored by God, and justified in all they do. They think they do not need to repent, because they have God's power. They come to believe, as Brother Petersen explained, it does not matter how wicked or evil a man is who holds priesthood power, the keys of the church will guarantee it cannot be lost. According to Nephi, the result is wickedness, abominations, and whoredoms. As a result, they have "all gone astray" with only the exception of a "few, who are the humble followers of Christ." Nevertheless, these few who are humble and seek to follow Christ rather than men "are led, that in many instances they do err because they are taught by the precepts of men." Nephi targets the leadership and their false teachings. For those who want to follow Christ, they must ignore the "precepts of men" which are offered as the false religion.

It is always a contest between faithfully following Christ on the one hand, and the precepts of men on the other. False religions offer everything but worship of Christ. They will use good ideas, virtues, even true concepts as a distraction to keep followers from coming to Christ. The way to prevent souls from receiving redemption is to distract them. Good people want to do good things. So long as they are kept occupied with hollow virtues and sentimental stories they cannot come to Christ, enter His presence, and gain salvation. The stories urged by false teachers are filling, but not nourishing to the soul. As long as the false precepts of men distract the "humble followers of Christ" from coming to Him, it is enough. Nephi says this will happen.

Nephi foretells of the gentiles' latter-day claim to have "Zion." But what he sees is a false and corrupt Zion. Nephi predicts a false Zion will claim to be the real thing, while not possessing any of Zion's necessary attributes. If any dare to criticize the false Zion and its corrupt teachings, they will be met with anger, even rage. Satan will have power over people because they do not know Christ. As the prophet puts it:

> For behold, at that day shall he rage in the hearts of the children of men, and stir them up to anger against that which is good. And others will he pacify, and lull them away into carnal security, that they will say: All is well in Zion; yea, Zion prospereth, all is well--and thus the devil cheateth their souls, and leadeth them away carefully down to hell. And behold, others he flattereth away, and telleth

them there is no hell; and he saith unto them: I am no
devil, for there is none--and thus he whispereth in their
ears, until he grasps them with his awful chains, from
whence there is no deliverance. Yea, they are grasped with
death, and hell; and death, and hell, and the devil, and all
that have been seized therewith must stand before the
throne of God, and be judged according to their works,
from whence they must go into the place prepared for
them, even a lake of fire and brimstone, which is endless
torment. Therefore, wo be unto him that is at ease in Zion!
Wo be unto him that crieth: All is well! Yea, wo be unto
him that hearkeneth unto the precepts of men, and denieth
the power of God, and the gift of the Holy Ghost! (2 Ne.
28: 20-26.)

The false virtues will be defended as the whole truth, despite the
fact they do not lead men to Christ. Those who claim repentance
is necessary will be accused of looking beyond the mark. They will
be thought of as false messengers, with a false message, trying to
steady the ark. They will be asked by what authority they preach
repentance, because they are not called to lead. However, Nephi
condemned those who "lead" because they "teach by the precepts
of men," and not by the Holy Ghost. Therefore, a call to
repentance cannot come from a leader. It must come from
elsewhere. When it does, the result will be anger, even rage, as
Satan stirs up the hearts of men.

The gentile church will be secure with false teachings that tell
them Zion is intact. Everything is fine. The power to redeem, to
bind on earth and in heaven is with them. Zion is prospering and
enjoys God's favor. There is no need to repent and return to
Christ, because everything is well with the church. But these ideas
are not only false, they come from the devil who "whispereth in
their ears, until he grasps them with death, and hell." The plan to

sell a devalued gospel, lacking the power to save, without any connection to Christ, originated with the adversary. Its result will be to condemn to hell those who believe it. Perhaps sensing their fate, the gentiles will console themselves with the thought that "there is no hell,"instead only varying degrees of glory. In the end all will be saved to some state of glory. Repentance can be postponed. So, also, can study of the Gospel of Jesus Christ. There is no hurry. We have enough to save us, therefore be content. The promise will be made: Follow the broad mainstream of the institution, and all will be given in the Lord's own time as we are prepared to receive more.

But this promise will be followed by giving less and less. All will sense something has been lost. Therefore, it will be necessary for the leaders to proclaim, "All is well!" Without that continual assurance, the hollow, vacuous precepts of men upon which the latter-day gentile Zion will rest, could be detected.

So each week these gentiles will declare to one another "I know the church is true" as a mantra to console them. Yes, "All is well" with this imitation Zion. It does prosper, after the world's meaning of that term. But Nephi warns us in unmistakable sobriety: "wo be unto him that is at ease in Zion! Wo be unto him that crieth: All is well! Yea, wo be unto him that hearkeneth unto the precepts of men, and denieth the power of God, and the gift of the Holy Ghost." If a gentile follower of this false Zion encounters an inspired view of their own awful state, they can awaken and quickly come to realize Nephi is speaking to us. Unfortunately, that is unlikely because anger and rage at the truth will keep them from seeing it.

Libraries of material will be written to defend Zion's health and well being. Only the Book of Mormon, and voices from the sidelines will tell the truth. The precepts of men offer gratifying pride. The call to repentance will be painful, difficult to bear, and unpopular.

At one time in the Temple endowment the player enacting the role of the false minister asked Satan what to do if someone came with a prophetic message. Satan told the minister how to defeat any such claim. He advised, "If any should come claiming revelation or apostleship, then you should ask them to cut off an arm, or some other member of the body, and then restore it again, so that people could know they come with power." Of course, as soon as the minister applied the test, he was informed true messengers do not perform such acts to draw attention to themselves. The role of the false minister is gone from the endowment now. Missing also is the message taught by his example. He represented all mortal teachers. When it comes to truth, only heaven can vouchsafe content. Unless the Spirit witnesses to the truth, or an angel comes bearing unmistakable signs, no teaching should be accepted.

The problem faced by the latter-day gentiles is gaining confirmation of the truth through revelation. They confuse sentiment for the Holy Ghost. They do not understand that "No man can receive the Holy Ghost without receiving revelations. The Holy Ghost is a revelator." (*TPJS*, p. 328.) The effect of the Holy Ghost is not sentimental. Moving someone to tears or thrilling them is a false emotional tool, employed by storytellers, writers, film makers, and composers. The gentiles could avoid errors if they had the Holy Ghost. But they confuse sentiment for the gift. Joseph tried to explain how the Holy Ghost worked:

> There are two Comforters spoken of. One is the Holy
> Ghost, the same as given on the day of Pentecost, and that
> all Saints receive after faith, repentance, and baptism. This
> first Comforter or Holy Ghost has no other effect than

pure intelligence. It is more powerful in expanding the mind, enlightening the understanding, and storing the intellect with present knowledge, of a man who is of the literal seed of Abraham, than one that is a Gentile, though it may not have half as much visible effect upon the body; for as the Holy Ghost falls upon one of the literal seed of Abraham, it is calm and serene; and his whole soul and body are only exercised by the pure spirit of intelligence; while the effect of the Holy Ghost upon a Gentile, is to purge out the old blood, and make him actually of the seed of Abraham. That man that has none of the blood of Abraham (naturally) must have a new creation by the Holy Ghost. In such a case, there may be more of a powerful effect upon the body, and visible to the eye, than upon an Israelite, while the Israelite at first might be far before the Gentile in pure intelligence. (*TPJS*, p. 149.)

The Holy Ghost infuses with pure intelligence. What was once mystifying becomes suddenly clear and comprehensible. What was unknown is suddenly known with clarity and understanding. It enlightens and enlivens. It is not sentimentality. It is not showy, loud or self-promoting. It is a still, small voice which penetrates to the very heart.[422]

Without the Holy Ghost and its accompanying revelations from heaven, the gentiles will be in a state of awful darkness. They will not know revelation when it comes, and reject it when offered to them. They will say they have a body of doctrine and trusted leaders, and they do not need anything more. As Nephi prophesied:

Yea, wo be unto him that saith: We have received, and we need no more! And in fine, wo unto all those who tremble,

---

[422] 1 Kings 19: 12.

and are angry because of the truth of God! For behold, he that is built upon the rock receiveth it with gladness; and he that is built upon a sandy foundation trembleth lest he shall fall. Wo be unto him that shall say: We have received the word of God, and we need no more of the word of God, for we have enough! For behold, thus saith the Lord God: I will give unto the children of men line upon line, precept upon precept, here a little and there a little; and blessed are those who hearken unto my precepts, and lend an ear unto my counsel, for they shall learn wisdom; for unto him that receiveth I will give more; and from them that shall say, We have enough, from them shall be taken away even that which they have. (2 Ne. 28: 27-30.)

These latter-day gentiles will be unenlightened by the Holy Ghost, rejecting the Spirit's condemnation of them, and unwilling to receive anything more from God. When truth is spoken to them, they will be angry because of it. According to Nephi, the great latter-day, gentile error consists in their refusal to receive more of the word of God. They will be content with what they have. But the religion of Christ, the Gospel of Christ, requires continual revelation. Since the Holy Ghost is a revelator, unless there is a constant stream of revelation coming to the latter-day gentiles then they do not have the gift they claim. Their religion is vain. It teaches only the precepts of men.

When they reject revelation, refusing the Holy Ghost, then the course is only downward. They will lose what they have. Those who say they "have enough" will lose what little they want to keep. They, and all the truths they pretend to protect, will be lost. The result will be a state of darkness where the devil can take them captive.

Nephi's prophecy is not without hope. Although He will curse those who take the arm of flesh as their guide, the Lord stands ready to receive all those gentiles who will repent and return to Him:

> Cursed is he that putteth his trust in man, or maketh flesh his arm, or shall hearken unto the precepts of men, save their precepts shall be given by the power of the Holy Ghost. Wo be unto the Gentiles, saith the Lord God of Hosts! For notwithstanding I shall lengthen out mine arm unto them from day to day, they will deny me; nevertheless, I will be merciful unto them, saith the Lord God, if they will repent and come unto me; for mine arm is lengthened out all the day long, saith the Lord God of Hosts. (2 Ne. 28: 31-32.)

If Nephi's warnings are understood to include The Church of Jesus Christ of Latter-day Saints, then the traditional narrative is mistaken. It overstates the accomplishments of the gentiles. It fails to recognize the full extent of our failure and spiritual peril. There are those, of course, who dismiss the idea Nephi is speaking to the saints. They believe his target to be the non-Mormon populations. They presume a book of prophecy, whose author saw our day, and knew who would be reading his warnings, chose to ignore his readers and deliver only a warning message to and about those who will never read his warnings. That view fundamentally changes Nephi's meaning as to make the reader proud. Not only do they not need to repent, but they can also be smug about their own enlightenment. They can look down on the gentiles all around them and entertain the gratifying thought that "all is well" for them.

Although it is not necessary to have a testimony of church history, I choose to believe Nephi is warning me. I think perhaps my own repentance needs to be continual, searching, and sincere. Rather than trust ordinances which may have become invalid, blessings which may have been unauthorized, and messages which may have become tainted, I will seek for Christ and His presence. I want to know my standing before Him, not whether a man has recommended me.

The final night of Joseph's life he had a dream which he related in the morning of the day he would be killed. He said:

Joseph related the following dream which he had last night: I was back in Kirtland, Ohio, and thought I would take a walk out by myself, and view my old farm, which I found grown up with weeds and brambles, and altogether bearing evidence of neglect and want of culture. I went into the barn, which I found without floor or doors, with the weather-boarding off, and was altogether in keeping with the farm.

"While I viewed the desolation around me, and was contemplating how it might be recovered from the curse upon it, there came rushing into the barn a company of furious men, who commenced to pick a quarrel with me.

"The leader of the party ordered me to leave the barn and farm, stating it was none of mine, and that I must give up all hope of ever possessing it.

"I told him the farm was given me by the Church, and although I had not had any use of it for some time back, still I had not sold it, and according to righteous principles it belonged to me or the Church.

"He then grew furious and began to rail upon me, and threaten me, and said it never did belong to me nor to the Church.

"I then told him that I did not think it worth contending about, that I had no desire to live upon it in its present state, and if he thought he had a better right I would not quarrel with him about it but leave; but my assurance that I would not trouble him at present did not seem to satisfy him, as he seemed determined to quarrel with me, and threatened me with the destruction of my body.

"While he was thus engaged, pouring out his bitter words upon me, a rabble rushed in and nearly filled the barn, drew out their knives, and began to quarrel among themselves for the premises, and for a moment forgot me, at which time I took the opportunity to walk out of the barn about up to my ankles in mud.

"When I was a little distance from the barn, I heard them screeching and screaming in a very distressed manner, as it appeared they had engaged in a general fight with their knives. While they were thus engaged, the dream or vision ended." (*TPJS*, pp. 393-394.)

The dream may be about the future of the church. If his "farm" is the church, then its future following Joseph's death would suffer from neglect and be overgrown with "weeds and brambles." It would become a scene of desolation and suffer from a "curse upon it."

Those who will rule over Joseph's farm would become furious and hostile to Joseph. Instead of respecting the farm's owner, they want to dispossess him. When Joseph asserted the farm was his, the leader became enraged and threatening. Joseph reflected on the circumstances and determined he had no interest in the farm in the condition it had devolved. The threat to Joseph abated when the mob occupying it turned on one another and began destroying each other with knives.

If Joseph's final dream is a prophecy about the future state of the church after June, 1844, then it also suggests the traditional narrative is wrong. There is no official interpretation of the dream.

Joseph gave none, as he died later that day. As his final visionary report, however, the interpretation seems to be worth considering.

A great deal more can be said of the traditional narrative. It claims the heavenly gift was passed to Joseph Smith, and in turn, through generations of Nauvoo era family descendants until our own day. There is something quite assuring in the traditional narrative. But it is not without at least the possibility of being wrong. Each of us is supposed to obtain a portion of the heavenly gift for ourselves. Through it we can come to know the truth of all things.[423] It would seem, therefore, we could learn through the Holy Ghost if the traditional narrative is merely a sentimental hope, or based in truth.

The highest form of priesthood power is given by God alone, but there are other degrees of priestly authority which can be handed from man to man. Whether the church continues to hold all keys as it claims or not, we know the church retains some priesthood authority. Even without priesthood, there are church offices which can be filled by common consent. We also know the church remains part of the Lord's plan.

Next we discuss the acceleration of changes in the church through the Correlation process. Through Correlation, change has become an institutionalized feature of phase four.

---

[423] Moroni 10: 5.

Chapter 13

CORRELATION:
CONTROLLING AND CURTAILING

There was a series of dramatic changes made to phase four of Mormonism. These changes reshaped Mormonism into what it is now. It is very unlike any of the earlier phases. The full extent of the new version is generally not appreciated because there is a conscious effort to use vocabulary and images from past phases as if there were no underlying recent changes. It is important for the faithful to think the religion today is the same as in the past. The collection of causes and resulting innovations in the fourth phase are described in this chapter.[424]

One of the forces leading to change was the rapid growth of the church. Growth did not cause the changes, but motivated church leaders to allow the changes. It is unlikely the changes would have taken the form they have if the church had remained confined to the Mormon corridor running through Alberta, Idaho, Utah,

---

[424]The topics and events are limited by dealing with this in a single chapter. Much more could be written about this fourth phase in addition to this brief overview.

Arizona and northern Mexico. On the first of January 1900, The Church of Jesus Christ of Latter-day Saints had approximately 284,000 members confined almost entirely to this corridor. For the first time in 1947, church membership exceeded one million members. David O. McKay became president in 1951. His church administration saw the church grow to two million members by 1963. He died on January 18, 1970, and the following year the church reached the three million member milestones.

Mormonism changed radically during President McKay's tenure. It shifted from a Utah- Mormon corridor organization, to include a large California and western United States membership. Shortly thereafter followed a significant Central and South American presence, then a European presence was added, then the Far East and South Africa. Although it would remain for others to consolidate foreign growth and make it truly global, the pioneering effort to manage international growth happened during his presidency.

There were many adjustments made to cope with the new Mormon landscape. One of them involved how the top leader of the church was viewed. The fourth phase marked the first time the term "Prophet" was openly and consistently applied to a living church leader. Although leaders in the First Presidency, Presiding Patriarch[425] and Quorum of Twelve, were sustained as "prophets, seers and revelators," the church's president was always identified as "President" and never as "Prophet." References to Brigham

---

[425]Church President Spencer W. Kimball made the church Patriarch Eldred G. Smith emeritus (retired) October 6, 1979. Until then he was sustained as one of the church's "prophets, seers and revelators." Since that time no replacement church Patriarch has been called, although Patriarch Smith is still living and, at this writing, 104 years old (born Jan. 9, 1907).

Young for example, were always "Brother Brigham" or "Brother Young" or "President Young" and never "Prophet Young."

By the mid-1950s a change was underway in Mormonism that profoundly affected its political influence. The hierarchy and church publications encouraged an unprecedented adoration of church president David O. McKay. His "a graceful, witty manner, his imposing physical appearance, his deep warmth, all made people see him as THE prophet, to be classed with Joseph Smith and Brigham Young." Extensive television broadcasts of two general conferences annually after 1953 heightened McKay's personal and ceremonial impact on members of the church. By the late-1960s LDS publications and speakers routinely identified McKay as "the Prophet," "our Prophet," and "beloved Prophet." Those terms has previously applied to the martyred prophet, Joseph Smith, while the living LDS president had simply been "the President."

That changing devotional status of the LDS president can be dated precisely through the official *Church News*. Published weekly by the *Deseret News* since 1931, every headline reference of *Church News* to each LDS president referred to him as "President" until 1955. During those twenty-four years no headline referred to the living LDS president as "prophet," and that term was used exclusively to refer to Joseph Smith or to prophets of the Bible and Book of Mormon. In February 1955 the *Church News* published the first headline reference to the living LDS president as the "Prophet."

Concerning such "adulation," a First Presidency secretary acknowledged that McKay liked his "celebrity status," and wanted "to be recognized, lauded, and lionized." However, that was something J. Reuben Clark had declined to give to any of the church presidents he had served as a counselor since the 1930s, and he seemed to

avoid calling anyone "the Prophet" except Joseph Smith.
Rather than adulation, Clark reminded LDS religion
teachers in July 1954 that "even the President of the
Church has not always spoken under the direction of the
Holy Ghost." The only known time Clark referred to
McKay by any other title than "President" was in a letter to
the church president's secretary about "your Chief." Clark's
influence may have been the reason why no other
reference to McKay as "the Prophet" appeared in the
Church News until after the counselor's death.[426]

The transition was slow at first. The next headline that referred
to David O. McKay as "the Prophet" was eight years later,
commemorating his birthday on September 7, 1963. The headline
read: "Portrait of a Prophet at 90." Another headline read:
"Huntsville is the Prophet's birthplace." The headlines used the
term, but the *Church News* continued to refer to him as "President
McKay" until 1965.[427]

In what would become an unfortunate, well-publicized event,
the First Presidency attempted to persuade eleven LDS members
of Congress to vote to retain anti-union legislation by sending a
letter to each of them. Seven members of Congress issued a joint-
answer rebuffing the First Presidency telling them "we cannot yield
to others our responsibilities to our constituency." The press
reported on this event in July-August 1965.[428]

In apparent response to this "loyal opposition"
against the First Presidency's political wishes, the *Church
News* began emphasizing that David O. McKay was "the

---

[426]Quinn, D. Michael. *Mormon Hierarchy: Extensions of Power.* Salt Lake
City: Signature Books, 1997, p. 363.

[427]*Id.*, p. 364.

[428]*Id.*

Prophet." On 11 September 1965 there was an article headline: "Honors For a Prophet," and within a year typical headlines proclaimed: "The Beloved Prophet, Seer, and Revelator, President David O. McKay."[429]

This public rebuff by LDS congressmen demonstrated the limit of the church's president to persuade even members of his own faith to follow him. The church reacted by using an image calculated to gain greater influence over members' reactions to the president. Changing the term used meant greatly changing the degree of control he held.

If the tendency to use the term "the Prophet" began with hesitation, it grew to become unabashed. The frequency with which the term was used for the living office holder would have shocked second and third phase Mormons. But in fourth phase Mormonism, the idea of "the Prophet" has displaced almost everything else in the faith as the central tenet of true religion. In some respects, adoration of "the Prophet" *is* fourth phase Mormonism:

> LDS leaders from the mid-1960s on encouraged popular adoration of whatever man filled the office of church president. In the secular world of politics, this is called "the cult of personality"; sociologists refer to this as "institutionalized awe." ...
>
> Beyond this emphasis on the LDS president, general authorities have recently claimed virtual infallibility for all decisions of the LDS hierarchy, even though a First Presidency counselor affirmed half a century earlier "We are not infallible in our judgment, and we err." By contrast, in November 1994 Apostle M. Russell Ballard instructed 25,000 students at Brigham Young University: "We will not

---

[429] *Id.*, pp. 364-365.

lead you astray. We cannot." He repeated those words to a similar meeting less than two years later. In April 1996 First Presidency counselor James E. Faust told general conference that the LDS president "will never mislead the Saints."

This "de facto infallibility" claimed by current general authorities further reduces the likelihood that faithful Mormons will even privately dissent from the political "counsel" of LDS headquarters.[430]

The resulting cult of personality attaching to the office of the president may have commenced slowly with David O. McKay, but it became a deluge. The frequency of using "the Prophet" has grown with subsequent office holders. The *Church News* now regularly refers to the church president as "the Prophet" in articles mentioning the office holder. The campaign of adoration has become so well entrenched that typical fast and testimony meetings consist of the constant reaffirmation that speakers "know [fill in the current office holder's name] is a living prophet of God."

Unlike fourth phase adoration of the church president, earlier phases were more circumspect in treatment of both the office and its occupant. Heber J. Grant was sustained as church president in a General Conference which had been postponed until June 1919.[431] After he was sustained, and delivered his inaugural talk as president, some of the comments made concerning his ascendency to the office were altogether modest in comparison to later

---

[430]*Id.*, pp. 368-369.

[431]Conference was postponed from April to June because of widespread influenza. It was considered dangerous to assemble until the sickness abated somewhat.

adoration. This came from First Presidency counselor Anthon H. Lund, who spoke first after President Grant:

> President Grant has spoken to us this morning. He has told us what he intends to do, and I know he will carry it out, because he has always kept the pledges he has made; so I do not think that now, as president of the Church, he will go back upon such conduct. The Lord will bless him. There is a great work for him to do, to which the Lord has called him, and God will give him wisdom and strength to accomplish it and enable him to carry the great responsibility that the office imposes upon him.

These circumspect comments about the new president from phase three contrast sharply with what is now said. "He has always kept the pledges he has made" is, at best, a modest endorsement of a man who has been newly sustained as a "prophet, seer and revelator."

Elder B. H. Roberts of the Seventy used the word "prophet" in his comments, and said the following:

> We stand at the point where one presidency leaves us, and another is inaugurated. I think it is fitting that we should not only have our minds drawn out towards the man who is taking on new responsibilities, viz., President Heber J. Grant, but that we should also remember in loving kindness the faithful labors of him who, so short a time ago, was the President, ...I congratulate the Church upon the noble men who have become God's representatives as the presidency of his Church in this dispensation. We this day inaugurate the seventh president of the Church of Jesus Christ of Latter-day Saints; they represent a line of men who for simplicity of life and character, for greatness of soul, for bigness of faith, for fidelity to the trust which God and the Church imposed in them, stand unparalleled in the religious history of the world. Thank God, not only

for a prophet, but for all our prophets, the presidents of the Church, in the name of Jesus Christ. Amen.

Elder J. Golden Kimball of the Seventy gave brief comments. He did not say anything directly about President Grant, but spoke indirectly of the human frailty of all the leaders of the church:

I have always honored and respected and sustained President Joseph F. Smith, and I am glad of it. But I discovered, in the time that I have labored in the Church, that he was human just like the rest of us. I want to learn the lesson, Cursed be the men who trust in man. You want to learn that lesson, if you are to be tested and meet difficulties, and you will not stumble and lose the faith. I place my trust in God, the eternal Father, and it is my business to get a clear and true conception of God, and of Jesus Christ, and to realize that these men whom we have sustained are servants of the people: they are servants of God, and we sustain them, and we uphold them. If there were no people, there would be no need of a Church, so that we all say-at least I do-God save the people. God bless you. Amen.

Elder Rulon S. Wells of the Seventy said nothing about President Grant. Elder Joseph W. McMurrin of the Seventy said the following: "We were instructed by President Heber J. Grant, when we were appointed to come to this meeting, to devote our time and the remarks that we made to the memory of President Joseph F. Smith." Elder Charles H. Hart and Elder Levi Edgar Young, both of the Seventy did not mention President Grant at all.

President Seymour B. Young of the Seventy said the following:

President Heber J. Grant has now been sustained by the congregations of the Saints, and by the special quorums of the priesthood, and I beseech for him that love, reverence, and sustaining power that he so well deserves and has so well merited through his life of devotion and faithful labors all the days of his life. For I have known him since the days of Nauvoo, and I say that I have never known better and truer men, than President Joseph F. Smith and President Heber J. Grant. We are all glad today that so noble a man has been chosen by the people and sanctioned by the voice of our heavenly Father to be the President of the Church of Jesus Christ of Latter-day Saints. May the Lord add his blessings to you fathers and mothers, boys and girls, friends and strangers, who are here attending our general conference, I pray in the name of Jesus Christ. Amen.

First Presidency counselor Charles W. Penrose said the following about the newly sustained President Grant:

I am thankful in my soul today that I am privileged to be here and take part in the installation of President Heber J. Grant as prophet, seer and revelator, and President of the Church of Jesus Christ of Latter-day Saints, his authority extending through all the world. And with all my heart I joined with the brethren this morning in lifting up my right hand in token to the heavens that I accepted these men in their several callings as servants of the Most High, holding the authority of the holy priesthood, which is after the order of the Son of God.

He went on to add: "I believe that the prophet Joseph will be near to Heber J. Grant when necessary-Joseph F. Smith, I mean."

Elder George Albert Smith of the Twelve said, "So it is a power of strength that has been reared today to our beloved president, Heber J. Grant, and his counselors, as we voted for them in this solemn assembly."

Fellow Apostle Orson F. Whitney said:

So it was with Brigham Young, with John Taylor, with Wilford Woodruff, with Lorenzo Snow, with Joseph F.

Smith; and so it is with Heber J. Grant, our beloved President of today. He has great gifts, a big heart, a kind soul, and because God is with him he will do a great and glorious work. But without God, neither he nor any other man could accomplish anything worth while.[432]

These quotes from the first general conference at which President Grant presided contrast with the comments now made at the ascension of a new president. In the fourth phase, the adoration of the office holder is emphasized immediately upon his ascent to the position. Following President Gordon B. Hinckley's death on January 27, in the April 2008 General Conference, the theme was repeated by speakers throughout the conference that Thomas S. Monson not only ascended to the office of church president, but also affirmed his stature as "the Prophet" to the church.

President Dieter Uchtdorf stated: "President Monson is the prophet of God for our days; I honor him and pledge my heart, might, mind, and strength to this great work. ...I bear witness of Jesus Christ, our Savior, who is the head of this Church. President Monson is the prophet of God today."

President Henry Eyring stated: "I have seen the same miracle in the service of President Monson as he received the call to preside as the prophet and President of the Church and to exercise all the keys of the priesthood in the earth. ...I testify that Thomas S. Monson is His living prophet."

Apostle Dallin Oaks said: "I know that we are led today by a prophet, President Thomas S. Monson, who holds the keys to

---

[432] All quotes are taken from the June, 1919 *Conference Report*.

authorize priesthood holders to perform the ordinances prescribed for our progress..."

Apostle Quentin Cook said: "We have had the great privilege this morning in a solemn assembly to sustain President Thomas S. Monson as our prophet, seer, and revelator[.]" He goes on to give the most enthusiastic claims. He taught the words of President Monson are as important as any scripture, and comprise God's own words.

Apostle D. Todd Christofferson stated: "I declare my testimony of the calling of President Thomas S. Monson as the prophet and President of the Church of Jesus Christ in this time and pledge my loyalty to him and his counselors in their sacred roles."

Apostle Joseph Wirthlin said: "I have known President Monson for a long time. He is a mighty man of Israel who was foreordained to preside over this Church. ...President Thomas S. Monson is the Lord's anointed and guides His Church today. I so testify in the name of Jesus Christ, amen."

Ronald Rasband of the Seventy stated: "President Thomas S. Monson is the Lord's prophet on earth."[433]

These various testimonies given immediately upon ascent to the office reinforce the institutional stature of any person holding the office of church president. *Church News* headlines had affirmed his status as "the Prophet" since he assumed the office of president on February 3, 2008. It was only 16 days after he became president when his daughter, Ann Dibb, spoke to the students at BYU-Idaho, and delivered a devotional address titled *My Father is a Prophet.* That kind of adoration and praise is one of the chief fourth phase innovations. But to those who live in this era it seems

---

[433] All quotes taken from the May, 2008 *Ensign.*

normal, even necessary. The idea of the church being led by someone who is not "the Prophet" would now be troubling, and disorienting to Mormons in the fourth phase. Therefore, a constant reaffirmation of institutional awe, of adoration, and cult of personality is now a regular feature of modern Mormonism.

Institutional adoration of the office holder among Mormons is akin to Catholic veneration of the Pope. As shown earlier, J. Reuben Clark regarded the authority claimed by the Popes to be, in fact, possessed by the LDS church presidents. This adoration of the office holder is one of the indispensable new hallmarks. Only Joseph Smith, during the first phase, had similar public regard while still living. Therefore, this cult of personality in the fourth phase could be regarded as an attempt to return to the first phase veneration. There is, of course, a difference between fourth phase office holders and Joseph Smith. Joseph's revelations, translations, scriptures, teachings, ordinances, the testimony of angels to him, his claims to have seen God the Father and Jesus Christ, and receiving authority, power and keys from angels distinguish him from all subsequent office holders.

This emphasis that the president of the church is a living prophet in the fourth phase is made *for* the office holder, but not *by* the office holder. None of those who have held the office have ever directly claimed to be a prophet. Rather, others testify they are prophets, and they remain silent on the point.[434] In contrast Joseph directly claimed to be a prophet.[435]

The fourth phase claim of similar status to Joseph Smith is based on the idea of having perpetuated a line of authority founded by Joseph. It is claimed that the heavenly gift given to Joseph has been passed along through an unbroken line of succession. This authority in the fourth phase comes derivatively, not directly. In contrast, Joseph's was direct from heaven. The current claim is that because they got it from others, who got it from Joseph Smith, who got it from angels, they are entitled to the adoration of

---

[434]There have been direct questions asked to church presidents about their status as a "prophet." For example, during the Reed Smoot Hearings before the US Senate, President Joseph F. Smith was asked: "Are you prophet, seer, and revelator?" His answer was: "I am so sustained and upheld by my people." When questioning turned directly to the topic of revelations, President Smith was asked: "You have revelations, have you not?" He responded: "I have never pretended to nor do I profess to have received revelations. I have never said I had a revelation except so far as God has shown to me that so-called Mormonism is God's divine truth; that is all." *The Mormon Church on Trial: Transcripts of the Reed Smoot Hearings.* Edited by Michael H. Paulos. Salt Lake City: Signature Books, 2008, pp. 20, 33. When President Hinckley was asked a similar question by a news reporter, his answer was to the same effect, that is, he is sustained as a prophet by his church.

[435]Joseph's revelations included many first-person quotes of the Lord ("thus saith the Lord"). See, e.g., D&C 21: 7, 12; 36: 1; 38: 1; 44: 1, among many others. But he would extend the definition of prophet to apply to any person who had a testimony: "Salvation cannot come without revelation; it is in vain for anyone to minister without it. No man is a minister of Jesus Christ without being a Prophet. No man can be a minister of Jesus Christ except he has the testimony of Jesus; and this is the spirit of prophecy. Whenever salvation has been administered, it has been by testimony. Men of the present time testify of heaven and hell, and have never seen either; and I will say that no man knows these things without this." (*TPJS*, p. 160.)

followers. It is this practice of adoration, or cult of personality, that makes other fourth phase changes possible. Without it, the other innovations could not have been as easily made.

When church growth became explosive in numbers and diverse in location, controlling the result of that growth became the greatest challenge facing the church. Mormonism had to choose between widely different practices and teachings from one location to another, or seeking to gain uniformity across national boundaries, diverse languages and cultures. The ambition to gain control over this diversity began in earnest in 1961. It started as an attempt to unify the materials used for teaching.

President McKay wrote a letter addressing the issue of coordinating teaching materials between various church divisions. The church had five separate divisions, each of which had autonomy in preparing lesson manuals. The five divisions were priesthood quorums, relief society, Sunday school, mutual improvement society, and primary. Each of these created their own lessons, had their own fund-raising, and controlled their own budgets. They acted independently. Although the president of the church, or a stake president, or a bishop might call people to fill these various priesthood or auxiliary organizations at each level, once they were organized they acted independently.

President McKay's original intent was not to consolidate these five divisions, but to coordinate what was being taught. He hoped to see the same manual used for all divisions. The coordination of shared teaching materials was called "Correlation." Originally the First Presidency did not believe it would be appropriate for Correlation to subordinate these divisions to the priesthood leadership.

The Correlation process was headed by Elder Harold B. Lee. Unlike the First Presidency, Elder Lee held ambitions for Correlation that would revolutionize the church's entire structure. He wanted to subordinate everything to central, priesthood dominion. The First Presidency was alarmed at his intent. Private meetings recorded that Elder Lee's plans were viewed as inappropriate, in conflict with scripture, and that they included the same kind of excess which caused the original Christian apostasy. In May 1962 President McKay said to his secretary: "We cannot run the Church as we would run a business."[436] On September 18, 1962, a meeting of the First Presidency about Elder Lee's ambitions for Correlation is recorded by President McKay in his diary:

> At the conclusion of the discussion, President Moyle said: "Do you think this correlation which has to do with primarily the class work in the various organizations, should transfer any of the responsibilities that are now placed in the Presidency to the Twelve, for genealogical work, as an example?
>
> I said that the correlation work affects primarily the duplication of courses of study, and that it should not affect the organization of the Church.
>
> President Brown said that the Prophet [Joseph Smith] had a wonderful sense of propriety and of revelation when he said that it is the nature and disposition of almost all men when they get a little authority as they suppose to extend it, and to reach out for more and more.
>
> I quoted: "Hence, many are called and few are chosen. Why are they not chosen? Because they have not learned this one lesson, etc."

---

[436]Prince, Gregory and Wright, Robert. *David O. McKay and the Rise of Modern Mormonism.* Salt Lake City: University of Utah Press, 2005, p. 150.

President Moyle added, "That no power or influence can or ought to be maintained."

And I quoted, "Only upon the principle of righteousness."

I then said that these matters of correlation of our work are for all three of the First Presidency to decide; that when we are united, we can take the next steps and until we are united, we do not take any step.[437]

The concern that was discussed arises from the scripture they referenced, D&C 121: 34-46. Verse 41 states, "No power or influence can or ought to be maintained by virtue of the priesthood[.]" President Moyle referred to it, and President McKay finished the verse: "only by persuasion, by long-suffering, by gentleness and meekness, and by love unfeigned[.]" In other words, the First Presidency was concerned that they and other priesthood holders had no right to impose control over other organizations. They could "persuade" using "gentleness and meekness" to get others to cooperate, but they had no right to direct or dictate. They viewed themselves as holding only limited authority which required them to persuade in order to accomplish anything. But "no power or influence" could be claimed just because of "priesthood." Such a course of conduct would end their priestly authority; or in the words of the revelation: "amen to the priesthood of that man."

After thinking about the matter overnight, the next morning the First Presidency met again. They concluded Elder Lee was not only exceeding his direction, but his ambitions could lead to outright apostasy of the church:

This correlation work is applicable to course of study of priesthood and auxiliaries to avoid duplication. *That is the*

---

[437]*Id.*, p. 151.

purpose of the correlation work. That is the heart of it, and further than that as it affects the organization of the Church, we will have to decide and tell them so. That is where we stand on that. ...It is easy to understand how the Apostasy took place in the early days.

President Brown added, "Take the heads away, and you are done."

President Moyle said, "Leave this alone, and you get something contrary to the Church. That is the way the Roman branch of the Church took precedence. As big as we are now, the amount of assistance and instruction and supervision that we can give is essential to maintain the integrity of the Church and the efficiency of our work."

I said we are holding that whole proposition up, that it is going farther than the correlating of studies. It is going to the point of suggesting a change in the organization of the Church. That is the vital point now.

President Moyle said, "This program was suggested in 1948, it is in the files." I said that I did not remember it.

President Moyle said that it was presented at great length to the Presidency and the Twelve; and I said, "Yes, but we didn't accept it." President Moyle replied, "No, we did not."

I said, "This latest suggestion is striking at the very heart of it. They wanted to see me, but I told them we shall have to take it under further consideration, and that is where it is standing."[438]

The next week, out of concern that Elder Lee was overstepping things in this effort at Correlation, President McKay said it was to

---

[438] *Id.*, pp. 151-152, italics in original.

be limited to "courses of study; *that there will be no change in Church Government, and that now is a good time to get that clearly defined.*"[439]

However correlation did not stop with the church courses of study, despite the concerns held by the First Presidency. Elder Lee wanted to push Correlation into the very structure of church government. He wanted the priesthood to exercise control and dominion over the church. He wanted all power and influence in the church to be in the priesthood, ultimately in the office of the President. He accomplished it. Ironically, he did so while claiming the mandate for making the changes originated with President McKay as "the Prophet," and the change to church government was "inspired" and a "revelation." The church's president, who thought the process would lead to apostasy, is given credit for accomplishing the very change he opposed.

Today the independence of priesthood quorums and church auxiliaries has completely been overcome. None of these have a separate budget, nor do they have any capacity for separate fund-raising, nor can any of them act apart from the direct administrative involvement of the presiding priesthood leader. Bishops in wards, stake presidents in stakes, area presidents, and other general authorities— ultimately the church's president - control everything. A relief society president, for example, cannot conduct any activity without approval of her presiding priesthood authority. Now the scripture on how priesthood is to be used has been inverted: "all power and influence is maintained by virtue of the priesthood; and it is no longer necessary to use persuasion, pure knowledge or refrain from compulsion."[440] A person is thought to

---

[439] *Id.*, p. 152, italics in original.

[440] In contrast, see D&C 121: 37, 41-42.

be an apostate if they fail to submit to domination by church authorities in all matters of faith and practice. The church has been thoroughly correlated, resulting in consolidation of power which is intended to forever prevent insubordinate conduct or thought.

Correlation parlays the cult of personality into this greater control over church members. The claim is now made that all the church's demands originate from "the Prophet." His involvement has become the fulcrum to move members to conform to any new church ambition. In practice, "the Prophet" need not even know about the demands of the church on the members. It is enough for "the Prophet" to preside over the process. Once the process produces a result, the result is attributed to him. Since the new reorganization of the church through Correlation makes the presiding authority responsible for everything happening in the church, the attribution seems plausible.

Correlation has relied on committees to accomplish the tedious tasks of overall restructuring. Therefore, another change in phase four is the nature of the involvement of the First Presidency and Twelve in daily church affairs. At the same time Correlation was altering church governance, outside consultants advised the highest level of church leadership to remove themselves from involvement with direct management. "The services of elite consulting firms (Cresap, McCormack, and Paget of New York, and Safeway Stores, Inc. of Oakland) were secured. At their suggestion the Quorum of Apostles and other General Authorities were advised to concern themselves less with day-to-day matters so they could manage the overall operation of the Church."[441] The highest levels of church

---

[441] Smith, Daymon M. *The Last Shall be First and the First shall be Last: Discourse and Mormon History. A Dissertation in Anthropology.* Presented to the Faculties at the University of Pennsylvania, 2007, p. 442.

leadership have now assumed essentially a board of directors' role. They have been turned into senior management policy makers, instead of directly managing and implementing policies.

At the very moment when Correlation reaches into every aspect of the church to consolidate control, those who are sustained as "prophets, seers and revelators" have become only indirectly involved with day-to-day operations. They set overall policy. Other subordinates borrow from the leader's credibility, relying on the cult of personality to legitimize their actions, overcome resistance, and to control responses. At the bottom level of the church, members are now subjected to coercion to accept and conform to anything which comes from the Correlated church. Every action, manual, policy, product, program, or announcement has been Correlated. As a result, anything and everything can be said to proceed from "the Prophet" who is presumed to preside over and approve everything. To reject or challenge anything provided through Correlation is to show disloyalty to "the Prophet." It is all designed to make members think they are on a collision course with God if they resist the changing program. In an irony almost lost on church members, these changes convey the notion God is busily involved with church decision-making. Otherwise, there would not be so many changes underway.

Correlation has been in place for more than forty years now, and therefore, almost all living active Latter-day Saints know no other form of Mormonism. The largest portion of current church members are "Correlated" and cannot see outside this viewpoint. Some however, sense the church has changed in a fundamental way, but have a hard time articulating why they have this impression.

Correlation, as an approach to Mormon teachings, has radically redefined the faith. It is anti-historical for two reasons. First, history has become separated from words. Context has been lost, or, more correctly, it has been deliberately discarded. Second, by using focus groups and opinion polling, the latest thinking is given priority.

Those who write Correlation manuals sift through statements made by past church leaders, including Joseph Smith, and gather their words into topical discussions. There are seventy-two topics Correlation allows to now be taught. Some of the topics that have been excluded from study include, "Eternalism" and "The Patriarchal Order."[442] Although Joseph Smith's final Nauvoo era teachings focused on "calling and election," that topic is also excluded from Correlation. So is "the Second Comforter." By limiting topics, Correlation has steered the faith away from what was once regarded as its most important doctrines. The result is that the new Christian religion restored through Joseph Smith has changed from its once innovative and expansive doctrine of the first phase. Now it has more in common with mainstream Protestantism. Approved topics Mormons are allowed to teach include, "Home and Family," "Faith," "Obedience," "the Millennium," "Agency," "Sacrament," and "Atonement." By limiting the discussion, Correlated Mormons hear the same messages repeated often, and therefore presume they know all they need to know.[443]

---

[442] *Id.*, p. 464.

[443] A newly called Apostle gave a talk in October, 2008 Semi-annual General Conference titled, "*You Know Enough.*" The talk included the following reassurance: "While there are many experiences like the one we are having today, full of spiritual power and confirmation, there are also

By disconnecting history from past conduct, the inquisitorial "Home Missionaries" used by Brigham Young to further his Reformation of Mormonism has been converted seamlessly to appear like the "Home Teaching" program of modern Mormonism. Brigham's attempts to find apostates and intimidate them is gone. As is his threatening theology of "blood atonement" slaying for apostasy. No longer remembered are the catechism questions posed by the Home Missionaries to coerce orthodoxy among church members. Indeed the entire background out of which the Home Missionary program arose is gone. By destroying the history, Correlation allows Home Missionaries and Home Teaching to become an example of continuity. Correlated Mormonism makes Mormons think there has been a benign continuation from one radically different era into another. History is gone. Only words are left, and they seem to discuss the same things. Therefore, in fourth phase Mormonism the Correlation department has adopted a new form of Mormonism which renders all previous forms unknown, and undetectable to church members who take their information exclusively through church approved materials. This unintentionally creates a crisis of faith for those Correlated Mormons who discover church history from outside sources. As soon as the contradictions are discovered, they begin

---

days when we feel inadequate and unprepared, when doubt and confusion enter our spirits, when we have difficulty finding our spiritual footing. Part of our victory as disciples of Christ is what we do when these feelings come. Nearly 40 years ago as I contemplated the challenge of a mission, I felt very inadequate and unprepared. I remember praying, 'Heavenly Father, how can I serve a mission when I know so little.' I believed in the Church, but I felt my spiritual knowledge was very limited. As I prayed, the feeling came: 'You don't know everything, but you know enough!'" (Anderson, Neil L. *You Know Enough*. Ensign CR, November 2008.)

to think the church has not been honest with them. They have a deep sense of betrayal. Church opponents work to exploit this Correlated ignorance of history, with increasing success. Even full time missionaries are now targeted by anti-Mormon critics who know these young people lack a realistic understanding of the church's past. The most recent statistics show approximately 50% of returned LDS missionaries fall into inactivity within two years of returning from their mission.[444] Part of the problem arises from the disorienting effects of Correlation teaching materials and censorship of material used to teach within the church.

All of this is deliberate anti-historical revisionism. To succeed it is required for history to be removed.

The second anti-historical Correlation technique arises from using social science to drive decision making by church leadership. When a problem needs solving, or anything new is considered, sophisticated social science tools are used to test ideas before they are adopted. The church is among the earliest adopters of cutting edges statistical tools.[445] Significant numbers of Church Office

---

[444]I've been trying to locate a citeable source for this statistic. This was discussed in a Mission-wide meeting I attended as a High Council representative of my stake, but I have been unable to find anything other than my notes of that meeting to confirm this statistic.

[445]Richard Bitner Wirthlin, close adviser to President Ronald Reagan, pollster for Presidents Richard Nixon and Gerald Ford, German Chancellor Helmut Kohl, British Prime Minister Margaret Thatcher, developed sophisticated polling techniques. He was an economics professor at BYU, and a General Authority from 1996 to 2001. He was known as the father of modern polling. He pioneered techniques in voter-precinct targeting, computer-assisted telephone interviews, "values" research, "people-meter" groups and Internet-based surveys. (See Koepp, Paul. *Richard Bitner Wirthlin, LDS General Authority and Pollster for Ronald Reagan, dies at 80.* Deseret News, March 17, 2011. He was the son of LDS Presiding Bishop Joseph L. Wirthlin and brother of LDS

Building employees are engaged in conducting opinion polls and focus groups. These employees and the tools they use cost millions of dollars annually.

The social science tools, however, are only as valid as shifting opinions. Scripture suggests such opinion-based ideas are unstable and unreliable. Reuben's patriarchal blessing, recorded in Genesis, includes the warning: "Unstable as water, thou shalt not excel[.]" (Gen. 49: 4.) His instability, like water, is also analogous to shifting opinions of larger groups. John saw a great whore, who sat upon many waters, and she had a name written on her forehead: "Mystery, Babylon the Great, the Mother of Harlots and Abominations on the Earth."[446] Concerning this great whore seated on the waters, the angel informed John: "The waters which thou sawest, where the whore sitteth, are peoples, and multitudes, and nations, and tongues." (Rev. 17: 15.) Like water, opinions are constantly changing. They are unstable and unreliable. For this reason, only the most current polling data matters, because its value is lost as soon as opinions change.

In this respect the social sciences are not only anti-historic, they are also the opposite of leadership. They tell you what has or is happening now. They do not tell you what should happen. And, since they are based upon merely transitory opinions, they cannot be said to be true or false, they just happen, shift, change and alter. They are more like sand than a rock, and Correlation's social

---

Apostle Joseph B. Wirthlin.

[446]Rev. 17: 5.

science infrastructure is built in large measure upon this unstable footing.[447]

Daymon M. Smith's PhD in anthropology qualified him to work within the Correlation infrastructure of the church. He wrote a fictionalized account of his experience while employed there. It is apparent from his story that the Correlation employees are aware of their self interests. They can (and have) utilized opinion polling driven by job security and not science. Instead of using the results to provide meaningful information regarding what works and what does not work, they use it to justify their products. They have also discovered the utility of "personas" or imaginary people.[448] Personas are fictional people who can be used to influence unstable opinions through social media, on-line comments to news articles, and even bogus testimonials posted on the church's website. Correlation has learned to shape opinions by using fictional people to say and do what Correlation would like them to say and do. This, then actually influences real people into thinking and saying the same sorts of things. In this way opinions can be influenced, turning well-written fiction from a nonexistent persona into the actual opinion of a living person. LDS "members" are invented as personas belonging to fictional wards, possessing addresses, backgrounds, sex, age, ethnicity and employment. The more details the better. If a picture is needed, it can be generated through

---

[447]See Matt. 7: 24-27.

[448]His fictional account is Smith, Daymon M. *The Book of Mammon*. Self-published, 2010. I have met with him to discuss his book. I told him I thought the book was somewhat inaccessible to the average reader because it is fiction and has an anthropological orientation, he has rejected the idea of changing it to make it more palatable to the average reader. It contains both a technical anthropological vocabulary and occasional obscenities-- which could be viewed as redundant.

photographic software. There is no way to know how many of the "lds.org" testimonials are personas and how many are real. Nor is it now possible to know if personas were used to 'prime the well' and, after inspiring enough imitations, were removed. Only the employees directly involved in managing the personas could tell you that. However, job security and confidentiality agreements will prevent that information from being available for many years.[449]

Major political parties regularly use the persona technique to influence public opinion. Personas are used to respond to political discussion groups or react to articles on the web. This creates "astro-turf," or fiction designed to appear as grass-roots opinion. Correlation employs this same approach. Both techniques come from a common science, having a common purpose, and will result in common implementation. The result of correlating the church has gone far beyond anything which could have been imagined by President McKay. Ironically, even though he opposed it, and thought it would lead to apostasy by the church, he continues to be given "credit" for Correlation in the official narrative.

While President McKay did not want Correlation to go beyond coordinating lesson manuals between independent church organizations (while leaving them otherwise independent), today the phase four church consists entirely of Correlation. General Conference and other talks are reviewed and approved, lesson manuals are generated, ideas are tested, staffing is scrutinized, doctrine is excluded or approved, history is discarded, and even on-line discussions are fabricated by the process and infrastructure which began as the "Correlation" of lesson manuals. When opinion

---

[449]Those church employees I've discussed this with are unwilling to be quoted because of confidentiality agreements restricting such disclosures.

polling determined temple-attending, active Latter-day Saints were troubled by some aspects of temple ceremonies, then the question was whether changing the ceremony would generate any negative reaction.[450] Therefore, the survey included the question of whether those polled, consisting of at least one-time temple worshiping saints, accepted the idea the president of the church was a prophet leading the only true church: "Do you believe the president of The Church of Jesus Christ of Latter-day Saints is a prophet of God? Do you believe The Church of Jesus Christ of Latter-day Saints is the only true church on the earth?" (Questions 70-a and 70-b.) The answers led Correlation to report to church leaders that the church's president could make changes to the endowment without resistance, and some of the changes would actually be welcomed. With that knowledge, in 1990 the church proceeded to make more substantial changes to the temple rites than had been made since the time of Joseph Smith and Brigham Young. For a few months after the changes, there was an announcement reminding the patrons of the president's (and First Presidency and Council of the Twelve's) status as "prophets, seers and revelators" implying they had both the right, and God's authority to make changes to the temple ordinances.

With this powerful new kind of Correlated Mormonism in place, the church can be as nimble as changing opinions require. The church's views, teachings, practices, structure, and even word

---

[450]The survey involved approximately 3,400 church members in the United States and Canada. Questions included inquiries about the endowment: "Did you feel spiritually uplifted by the experience? And, "were you confused by what happened?" (Question 28.) "Briefly describe how you felt after receiving your endowment." (Question 29.) "Have you ever fallen asleep during sessions?" (Question 39-b.) "Do you have any doubts about specific LDS doctrines and teachings?" (Question 77-g.)

phrasing can be as focused as needed to persuade members that the church remains an unbroken continuation of what God restored through Joseph Smith. It is chameleon-like in the ability to read opinion, respond to it with plausible arguments, and seem to be whatever is needed for success. It has harnessed the vocabulary to keep traditional believers on board, while using that vocabulary to construct a new iteration unlike anything in the first three phases.

In summary, the current iteration of Mormonism has taken a series of steps which have led to the modern face of Mormonism. Growth at the beginning of the fourth phase was unlike anything before. This led to rethinking how to manage a much larger organization. Business consultants recommended, and the church accepted the idea its top leadership should discontinue their direct day-to-day involvement in church management. Adoration or a cult of personality for the church president was adopted as a powerful tool to get compliance from Mormons. Then Correlation extended adoration to include literally every program or policy of the church. It made it possible for the institution to claim anything and everything done has been Correlated, and therefore has the sanction of "the Prophet." To question anything is to come into conflict with God's living mouthpiece. Or, to put the proposition more directly, resistance is rebellion against God. The goal of Correlating the teaching was conflated with controlling and limiting what is taught. By using opinion polls and focus groups to determine what aspects of Mormonism caused negative reactions, the faith's teachings could be redirected, edited and curtailed to make larger public acceptance more likely. With these components in place, fourth phase Mormonism has now separated its history from the faith, and dramatically curtailed the body of doctrine allowed to remain part of the religion. Although it claims it is nothing different from first phase Mormonism, it bears little resemblance.

Chapter 14

GENTILES SHALL REJECT THE
FULLNESS OF THE GOSPEL

*W*hen the events of our Dispensation are examined in this new light, there is reason to rethink the traditional narrative. If we conclude the history of the church is something other than an unmitigated string of successes, as the proud descendants of Nauvoo have claimed, some of the suffering and troubles following Joseph Smith's death take on new meaning. The troubles are not the world striking unfairly at a beleaguered group of highly favored people, over whom God has given continual care. Instead, they are reminders of the price paid for ingratitude in rejecting what was offered and unaccepted.[451]

The saints are understandably reluctant to reach the conclusion they failed in Nauvoo and were rejected. However, Joseph Smith's restored scriptures, revelations, prophecies, and teachings all contain statements which urge that conclusion. We turn to those

---

[451]"For what doth it profit a man if a gift is bestowed upon him, and he receive not the gift? Behold, he rejoices not in that which is given unto him, neither rejoices in him who is the giver of the gift." (D&C 88: 33.)

statements in this chapter. Not all of them are gathered here, but enough to show if there has been a failure by Mormonism to accept and preserve what was offered, that is consistent with what Joseph Smith revealed, prophesied and taught.

In 1832 the church was told it was under condemnation because of how little regard had been given to the Book of Mormon and other revelations. The church was then riddled with "unbelief." In the Book of Mormon, the word "unbelief" is almost always used to describe the act of rejecting truth, and then "dwindling in unbelief" because of the refusal to retain or respect the truth.[452] When the revelation describing Latter-day Saints concludes there is "unbelief" among the saints, the word needs to be understood. It suggests the process of "dwindling" had then begun. The 1832 revelation included the following:

> And your minds in times past have been darkened because of unbelief, and because you have treated lightly the things you have received-- Which vanity and unbelief have brought the whole church under condemnation. And this condemnation resteth upon the children of Zion, even all. And they shall remain under this condemnation until they repent and remember the new covenant, even the Book of Mormon and the former commandments which I have given them, not only to say, but to do according to that which I have written-- (D&C 84: 54-57.)

The condemnation of the church by the Lord has never been removed. President Ezra Taft Benson reiterated the condemnation in fourth phase of Mormonism:

---

[452]See, e.g., 1 Ne. 12: 22-23; 13: 35; 2 Ne. 1: 10; Alma 45: 10, among other places.

As I participated in the Mexico City Temple dedication, I received the distinct impression that God is not pleased with our neglect of the Book of Mormon. The object of studying the Book of Mormon is to learn from the experiences of those who have gone before us that blessings come by keeping the commandments of God and that tragedy is the result of disobedience. By learning from the lessons of the past, mistakes need not be repeated in our own lives. You will gain a firm and unshakable testimony of Jesus Christ and the absolute knowledge that the origin of the Book of Mormon, as described by Joseph Smith, is true. Reading and pondering the Book of Mormon and other scriptures brings spiritual-mindedness.

...

The Lord declares that the whole Church and all the children of Zion are under condemnation because of the way we have treated the Book of Mormon. This condemnation has not been lifted, nor will it be until we repent. (See D&C 84: 51-81.) (Benson, Ezra Taft. *The Teachings of Ezra Taft Benson*. Salt Lake City: Bookcraft, 1988, p.51 and 64, emphasis added.)

We have grown accustomed and comfortable living with this condemnation. Elder Oaks reiterated the church remains under this condemnation. I've written a chapter in *Eighteen Verses* on our collective neglect of the Book of Mormon.[453] I explain how very little this condemnation has motivated us to change the way we treat the new covenant we've been offered.

At least the 1832 condemnation has been recognized and discussed by church leaders and the saints. There is another, more

---

[453]See the chapter titled *Trial of Faith*, pp. 1-20, in Snuffer, Denver C., Jr. *Eighteen Verses*. Salt Lake City: Mill Creek Press, 2007.

ominous warning that has been ignored by them. That more serious warning came through a Nauvoo revelation nine years later.

The words of the only significant Nauvoo-era revelation from the Lord threatened to reject the church. The traditional Mormon account dismisses the idea the church was rejected. It only makes sense to consider the possibility we failed to repent and meet the required condition. Here is the 1841 revelation language threatening rejection:

> But I command you, all ye my saints, to build a house unto me; and I grant unto you a sufficient time to build a house unto me; and during this time your baptisms shall be acceptable unto me. But behold, at the end of this appointment your baptisms for your dead shall not be acceptable unto me; and if you do not these things at the end of the appointment ye shall be rejected as a church, with your dead, saith the Lord your God. (D&C 124: 31-32.)

We know the house was not finished while Joseph was alive. Nor was it completed while the Twelve were still in Nauvoo. There was never any endowment performed in the completed Nauvoo Temple. Those endowments, and sealings performed by Joseph Smith in Nauvoo were done in the upper room of his red brick store. Those done by Brigham Young were performed in the attic of an incomplete Nauvoo Temple. When the Twelve abandoned Nauvoo in February, the temple was neither completed nor dedicated. It would be months before that happened. When it was finally completed and dedicated, there were no ordinances performed there. The same revelation which threatens to reject the church explains the fullness of the priesthood had been lost, as to the church. It commands the church to proceed, "with all your precious things of the earth; and build a house to my name, for the

Most High to dwell therein. For there is not a place found on earth
that he may come to and restore again that which was lost unto
you, or which he hath taken away, even the fulness of the
priesthood." (D&C 124: 27-28.) The "fullness"– if it was
transferred by Joseph Smith to other church leaders while in
Nauvoo as we claim– was never done in the Nauvoo Temple. Yet
the Nauvoo Temple was the only acceptable place where the Lord
could "come to and restore again that which was lost unto you...
even the fulness of the priesthood." According to George Q.
Cannon, the Nauvoo Temple was never completed, period.[454]

Although the church overlooks even the possibility of failure in
Nauvoo, the language of the revelation, and the subsequent events
should at least raise the possibility we were condemned, and then
rejected as a church. However unpleasant that conclusion may
seem, we should want to know if that is what happened.

The revelation offers to make the proposed temple holy: "If ye
labor with all your might, I will consecrate that spot that it shall be
made holy. And if my people will hearken unto my voice, and unto
the voice of my servants whom I have appointed to lead my
people, behold, verily I say unto you, they shall not be moved out
of their place." (D&C 124: 44-45.) A holy place is visited by angels.
Because He was to come personally to "restore again that which
was lost," the Lord's presence was promised. There is no record of
angelic visitors to the Nauvoo Temple. The Lord did not come to

---

[454]"And so also the completion of the temple at Nauvoo brought many
blessings; that is, so far as it was completed, for the enemies of God's
kingdom did not permit us to complete it entirely; but so far as it was
completed God accepted the labor of the hands of his servants and
people, and great and precious blessings were bestowed upon the Church
of Jesus Christ of Latter-day Saints for the faithfulness and diligence of
its members in rearing that house." (JD 14: 124.)

visit there. Instead, the temple was utterly destroyed, not one stone left atop another. It seems plausible, therefore, the Lord did not make "that spot... holy" by His power. Also, clearly the saints were "moved out of their place." This at least raises the unthinkable possibility the church has been rejected, with our dead.

The revelation continues with an ominous explanation of what would happen if the church failed to measure up to the Lord's request and was rejected:

> And it shall come to pass that if you build a house unto my name, and do not do the things that I say, I will not perform the oath which I make unto you, neither fulfil the promises which ye expect at my hands, saith the Lord. For instead of blessings, ye, by your own works, bring cursings, wrath, indignation, and judgments upon your own heads, by your follies, and by all your abominations, which you practise before me, saith the Lord. (D&C 124: 47-48.)

The events that followed this revelation have been interpreted through the eyes of those who could not accept the idea of rejection. The proud refugees from Nauvoo and their descendants have always claimed they succeeded in doing all that was required. The revelation explains how to identify our failure. We meet the description of rejection. We know for certain: 1) The spot was not consecrated by the Lord, or made holy by His or the angels' presence. At least there is no record of it having occurred. 2) The church was moved out of the spot. 3) The temple was utterly destroyed. 4) The migration westward was more than difficult and harrowing. Not only the trek westward, but the arrival was marked by suffering, hunger, cold, privation and many deaths along the way. It at least suggests the possibility of "cursings, wrath, indignation, and judgments" on our heads. These events were avoidable. Enduring them may mean we were rejected, then cursed because of our collective failure to do what the Lord asked.

If this is the case, then it raises two important questions. First, was this in keeping with a prophetic plan for this dispensation? We are considering that question in this chapter. Second, what does that mean for the church? Is it still important? Does it retain a role? If so, what is the role? That will be dealt with in the next chapter.

As to the prophecies restored through Joseph Smith, the Book of Mormon predicts the gentiles will be offered the fullness of the Gospel, and reject it. Then, after gentile rejection, the remnant of the Book of Mormon people will be given the fullness. The rejection by the gentile church is a condition to precede the remnant receiving the fullness. Therefore, if the Book of Mormon is true, we should expect to find the gentiles rejecting the fullness.

Earlier we referred to Christ's prophecy in 3 Nephi 16: 10-12:

> And thus commandeth the Father that I should say unto you: At that day when the Gentiles shall sin against my gospel, and shall reject the fulness of my gospel, and shall be lifted up in the pride of their hearts above all nations, and above all the people of the whole earth, and shall be filled with all manner of lyings, and of deceits, and of mischiefs, and all manner of hypocrisy, and murders, and priestcrafts, and whoredoms, and of secret abominations; and if they shall do all those things, and shall reject the fulness of my gospel, behold, saith the Father, I will bring the fulness of my gospel from among them. And then will I remember my covenant which I have made unto my people, O house of Israel, and I will bring my gospel unto them. And I will show unto thee, O house of Israel, that the Gentiles shall not have power over you; but I will remember my covenant unto you, O house of Israel, and ye shall come unto the knowledge of the fulness of my gospel.

As we have looked at the various phases of Mormonism some of the events suggest the gentile latter-day church has already done these things. Each of us should answer for ourselves whether or not there has been lying, deceit, mischief, hypocrisy, murder, priestcraft, whoredoms and abominations among the saints in the church's history. Each of us can decide for ourselves if we see any such things underway. If it has not occurred yet, then the rejection of the fullness by the church will be future. Either way, Christ's prophecy foretells it "shall" occur. It is not a question of "if" but only "when." Christ's prophecy provides a framework wherein to consider our history and to govern our conduct.

The first argument used to ignore the Lord's prophecy is to distinguish between "gentiles," who will reject the gospel, and members of The Church of Jesus Christ of Latter-day Saints, who claim they have accepted it. This premise avoids the issue by entirely excluding the church from the warning. So, the question of whom the "gentiles" are, in the language of the Book of Mormon, must be answered. If the "gentiles" spoken of by the Lord are non-Latter-day Saints, then there is nothing to concern church members.

If "gentiles" refer only to non-Latter-day Saints, then the book warns only non-readers of their impending doom. For those who will receive it as scripture, there is nothing to warn about. Under this assumption, those people who were foreseen by Nephi, Mormon and Moroni and who are addressed in the book's prophecies will never be warned. In fact, all believing readers can take some measure of confidence in knowing everybody around them is condemned, while they can be lifted up in their pride because they are special, even chosen. If that seems like the intent of the prophets of the Book of Mormon perhaps you should read the book again. The idea lacks common sense. The book attacks pride. It does not encourage it.

However, it is not necessary to use common sense alone. Joseph Smith answered the question directly with the Kirtland Temple dedicatory prayer, which he received by revelation. The prayer identifies the church as gentile when it states: "Now these words, O Lord, we have spoken before thee, concerning the revelations and commandments which thou hast given unto *us, who are identified with the Gentiles.*" (D&C 109: 60, emphasis added.)

Nephi also identified those who would be led to the Americas. These people are the original Mormon converts. According to Nephi, these are all gentiles. (1 Ne. 13.) It was the gentiles who occupy the Americas and displace the remnant of Nephi's people. (1 Ne. 13: 14-15.) For the gentiles, the Lord promised He would have compassion: "Neither will the Lord God suffer that the Gentiles shall forever remain in that awful state of blindness, which thou beholdest they are in, because of the plain and most precious parts of the gospel of the Lamb which have been kept back by that abominable church, whose formation thou hast seen." (1 Ne. 13: 32.) It will be to the gentiles the Lord promised: "I will be merciful unto the Gentiles in that day, insomuch that I will bring forth unto them, in mine own power, much of my gospel, which shall be plain and precious, saith the Lamb." (1 Ne. 13: 34.) It was to the gentiles the Book of Mormon was delivered through Joseph Smith. The European migrants who acquired possession of North America are "gentiles." (1 Ne. 13: 35.)

As the title page of the Book of Mormon explains, this book was "to come forth in due time by way of the Gentile." It came through Joseph Smith. However much Joseph may be associated with authentic Israelite blood in church teachings, he is identified as a "gentile" by the Book of Mormon. So are those who receive the Book of Mormon— the Latter-day Saints. Therefore, the conclusion is inescapable that the church is identified in prophecy as gentiles. The very book containing Christ's direful prophecy about the gentile rejection of the fullness tells us the identity of the group. The Book of Mormon is a voice of warning to the people who have had it published to them: the Latter-day Saints, or, to use Book of Mormon terminology, the "gentiles." Us.

If the Latter-day Saints are the gentiles, then each of us should decide whether there is any reason to conclude we have already rejected the fullness. As the prophecy details, the rejection was because we are "filled with all manner of lyings, and of deceits, and of mischiefs, and all manner of hypocrisy, and murders, and priestcrafts, and whoredoms, and of secret abominations." If we accept the traditional narrative of our history, we haven't lied, deceived, been hypocrites, caused or condoned murders, engaged in priestcrafts, or been involved with secret abominations. We are noble. We are good people. We believe we are not involved with secret abominations.[455] We think we have preserved the heavenly gift once bestowed upon Joseph Smith.

But Christ's words are emphatic: "*When* the Gentiles *shall* reject the fulness..." Our rejection is inevitable, and if the gentiles are the Latter-day Saints, the conclusion is inescapable. Either we have, or we will reject the fullness. It is either in our past, or in our future. For Christ's words to be fulfilled,[456] the gentiles "shall" reject the fullness at some point.

There is another prophecy given by Christ (restored by Joseph Smith in JST-Matt. 21: 51-56) which likewise foretells of the latter-day gentile rejection of truth, and our ultimate destruction. Christ told a parable about the vineyard entrusted to husbandmen who abuse the servants sent to them by the owner of the vineyard. Ultimately, they kill the owner's son. Christ clarified the parable to His disciples. He told them about both the Jews and the latter-day gentile failures and destruction:

> Verily, I say unto you, I am the stone, and those wicked ones [Jews] reject me. I am the head of the corner. These

---

[455] The July 19, 1990 *Memorandum* written by Bishop Glen L. Pace, then Second Counselor in the Presiding Bishopric of the church, addressed to the Strengthening Church Members Committee addressed Satanic ritualistic child abuse occurring among Latter-day Saints. Although it was impossible to determine the extent of the abuse, his report confirms it exists. This kind of child abuse had as its goal to cause dissociative disorder in victims. After interviewing sixty Latter-day Saint victims located in Utah, Idaho, California, Mexico and elsewhere, he concluded this form of perversion existed among church members. He concluded: "Satan is here with his secret combinations in all of the ugliness that existed in previous dispensations." (P. 12.) The credibility of victims is diminished by the dissociative disorder forced on them, and as a result there are few prosecutions even possible. However, Bishop Pace's report does not question the existence of this insidious evil among the saints.

[456] Christ has declared all His words will be fulfilled. See, D&C 1: 38.

Jews shall fall upon me, and shall be broken. And the kingdom of God shall be taken from them, and shall be given to a nation bringing forth the fruits thereof; (meaning the Gentiles.) Wherefore, on whomsoever this stone shall fall, it shall grind him to powder. And when the Lord therefore of the vineyard cometh, he will destroy those miserable, wicked men, and will let again his vineyard unto other husbandmen, even in the last days, who shall render him the fruits in their seasons. And then understood they the parable which he spake unto them, that the Gentiles should be destroyed also, when the Lord should descend out of heaven to reign in his vineyard, which is the earth and the inhabitants thereof.

While the gentiles would accept His Gospel, ultimately they will be "destroyed also" just as the Jews would be. All this because they rejected the full truth offered them. Both groups have occupied the vineyard. Both have been sent messengers, including the Son. Since each in turn rejected the truth offered them, the result will necessarily be their destruction at His return.

When reading the interpretation of this parable, we are reminded of the goal of the restored Gospel. The purpose of the Gospel is to prepare a group who could endure His presence. The "whole earth" is going to be smitten at His return, except only those who have had the "hearts of the children" turn to them as "fathers."[457] The original meaning   (in phase one Mormonism) meant connecting living souls to Abraham, Isaac and Jacob through

---

[457] D&C 2: 1-3: "Behold, I will reveal unto you the Priesthood, by the hand of Elijah the prophet, before the coming of the great and dreadful day of the Lord. And he shall plant in the hearts of the children the promises made to the fathers, and the hearts of the children shall turn to their fathers. If it were not so, the whole earth would be utterly wasted at his coming."

binding priesthood power, and a living covenant between God and man. Those souls who entered into that kind of covenant would be able to stand in the presence of God. Because they could endure His glory, they would not be "cursed" at His return. They were adopted as children to those "fathers" who now sit upon thrones.[458] By phase four, we are no longer adopted, but perform ordinances to seal together families along genealogical lines. Whether or not a person connects to Joseph Smith, then in turn to Abraham, Isaac and Jacob, is no longer included in either our ordinances or teachings. Joseph emphasized and taught this doctrine. We have discarded it. In its place the church has a practice originating through Wilford Woodruff.

The progression from condemnation, to rejection, and finally to cursing is a downward descent only possible because the gentiles either have, or will turn from the fullness. Because they were offered a three-fold blessing, the condemnation, rejection and cursing are also three-fold. Joseph tried to warn us of the seriousness of what we were offered, and in turn the seriousness of how we ought to regard it: "I want you to know that God, in the last days, while certain individuals are proclaiming his name, is not trifling with you or me."[459] He lamented the failure of those around him to accept what was offered. "[A]ny person who is exalted to the highest mansion has to abide a celestial law, and the whole law too. But there has been a great difficulty in getting anything into the heads of this generation. It has been like splitting hemlock knots with a corn-dodger [cornbread] for a wedge, and a pumpkin

---

[458]D&C 132: 7.

[459]*TPJS*, p. 347.

for a beetle [hammer]. Even the saints are slow to understand."[460]
When we make our individual assessment of how well we received
the fullness from Joseph Smith, his comment is not encouraging.
It rather appears he was frustrated at our failure to understand
what we were rejecting.

Christ is not the only one in the Book of Mormon who spoke of
the gentile rejection. Moroni spoke directly to the gentile audience
who would read the Book of Mormon. Moroni prophesied to us:

> Behold, I speak unto you as if ye were present, and yet ye
> are not. But behold, Jesus Christ hath shown you unto me,
> and I know your doing. And I know that ye do walk in the
> pride of your hearts; and there are none save a few only
> who do not lift themselves up in the pride of their hearts,
> unto the wearing of very fine apparel, unto envying, and
> strifes, and malice, and persecutions, and all manner of
> iniquities; and your churches, yea, even every one, have
> become polluted because of the pride of your hearts.
> (Mormon 8: 35-36.)

Since Moroni saw us, knew of our deeds, and addresses his warning
to those of us who read his record, it necessarily follows he had
Latter-day Saint gentiles in mind. His warning could not be more
clear. He tells us our churches, "even every one" of them "have
become polluted." He did not allow for any exception. There is
simply no church belonging to us gentiles that has not become
"polluted" because of our "iniquities." If Moroni's words are taken
at face value, he is telling us we have filled every church, including
ours, with iniquities.

---

[460] *Id.*, p. 331.

He elaborates: We love money instead of people.[461] We have secret abominations among us.[462] He asks us: "O ye pollutions, ye hypocrites, ye teachers, who sell yourselves for that which will canker, why have ye polluted the holy church of God?" (Mormon 8: 40.) Since he saw our day, it is unlikely he would call any denomination other than the Latter-day Saints the "holy church of God." It makes no sense for him to refer to Catholics or Lutherans as the "holy church of God." It strains credulity to read this warning as a caution to those who do not accept the Book of Mormon as scripture. At the plainest of meanings, Moroni prophesies we have polluted the holy church of God.

Although much more can be said, this is enough to show a gentile rejection of the fullness is consistent with Book of Mormon prophecies. Joseph Smith also spoke against the church's iniquity. He said:

> We have thieves among us, adulterers, liars, hypocrites. If God should speak from heaven, he would command you not to steal, not to commit adultery, not to covet, nor deceive, but be faithful over a few things. As far as we degenerate from God, we descend to the devil and lose knowledge, and without knowledge we cannot be saved, and while our hearts are filled with evil, and we are studying evil, there is no room in our hearts for good, or studying good. Is not God good? Then you be good; if He is faithful, then you be faithful. Add to your faith virtue, to virtue knowledge, and seek for every good thing.
>
> The Church must be cleansed, and I proclaim against all iniquity. A man is saved no faster than he gets knowledge, for if he does not get knowledge, he will be

---

[461]Mormon 8: 37, 39.

[462]*Id.*, v. 40.

brought into captivity by some evil power in the other world, as evil spirits will have more knowledge, and consequently more power than many men who are on the earth. Hence it needs revelation to assist us, and give us knowledge of the things of God. (*TPJS*, p. 217.)

If Joseph declared there were "adulterers, liars, hypocrites" among the saints in his day, then the Lord's warning that the gentiles would be filled with "lyings, and of deceits, and of mischiefs, and all manner of hypocrisy, and murders, and priestcrafts, and whoredoms, and of secret abominations" (see 3 Ne. 16: 10-12) may have already happened.

Joseph's dream the night before his surrender to the Illinois authorities who would kill him has already been mentioned.[463] If

---

[463]"I was back in Kirtland, Ohio, and thought I would take a walk out by myself, and view my old farm, which I found grown up with weeds and brambles, and altogether bearing evidence of neglect and want of culture. I went into the barn, which I found without floor or doors, with the weather-boarding off, and was altogether in keeping with the farm.

"While I viewed the desolation around me, and was contemplating how it might be recovered from the curse upon it, there came rushing into the barn a company of furious men, who commenced to pick a quarrel with me.

"The leader of the party ordered me to leave the barn and farm, stating it was none of mine, and that I must give up all hope of ever possessing it.

"I told him the farm was given me by the Church, and although I had not had any use of it for some time back, still I had not sold it, and according to righteous principles it belonged to me or the Church.

"He then grew furious and began to rail upon me, and threaten me, and said it never did belong to me nor to the Church.

"I then told him that I did not think it worth contending about, that I had no desire to live upon it in its present state, and if he thought he had a better right I would not quarrel with him about it but leave; but my assurance that I would not trouble him at present did not seem to satisfy him, as he seemed determined to quarrel with me, and threatened me with the destruction of my body.

Joseph's "farm" is the church, then it has become "overgrown with weeds" and dominated by a company of "furious men."

Since we needn't have a testimony of church history, it is really left for each of us to decide for ourselves whether the prophesied gentile rejection has already happened, or remains in our future. Either way, the Book of Mormon assures us that we gentiles will reject the fullness. Although we are loath to conclude we have departed from the faith restored through Joseph Smith, Yale University Professor Harold Bloom gave his conclusion in 1990:

> It has become somewhat of a commonplace to observe that modern Mormonism tends to reduce itself to another Protestant sect, another Christian heresy, while the religion of Joseph Smith, Brigham Young, Parley and Orson Pratt and other leading early Mormons was a far more radical swerve away from Protestant tradition.[464]

Professor Bloom's 1990 observation is not unlike the view of Elder Orson Pratt, expressed 107 years earlier, in 1873. Elder Pratt was an eye witness to the church's history in phase one and two. He was among the church's first Apostles. He stated:

> There must be a reformation, there will be a reformation among this people, for God will not cast off this kingdom

---

"While he was thus engaged, pouring out his bitter words upon me, a rabble rushed in and nearly filled the barn, drew out their knives, and began to quarrel among themselves for the premises, and for a moment forgot me, at which time I took the opportunity to walk out of the barn about up to my ankles in mud.

"When I was a little distance from the barn, I heard them screeching and screaming in a very distressed manner, as it appeared they had engaged in a general fight with their knives. While they were thus engaged, the dream or vision ended." (*TPJS*, p. 393-394.)

[464]The Annual David P. Gardner Lecture, Kingsbury Hall, University of Utah, November 15, 1990.

and this people, but he will plead with the strong ones of
Zion, he will plead with this people, he will plead with
those in high places, he will plead with the Priesthood of
this Church, until Zion shall become clean before him. I do
not know but that it would be an utter impossibility to
commence and carry out some principles pertaining to
Zion right in the midst of this people. They have strayed so
far that to get a people who would conform to heavenly
laws it may be needful to lead some from the midst of this
people and commence anew somewhere in the regions
round about in these mountains.[465]

There are scriptures, revelations, teachings, statements, and dreams
that suggest the gentile rejection would not only happen, but
happened coincident with Joseph Smith's death. The narrative
which refuses this idea is perhaps reassuring. But being reassured
by a lie does little good. The truth of the answer is left for each of
us to decide.

President McKay and his First Presidency were concerned about
concentrating power into the hands of priesthood leadership. To
dominate the church by a powerful central hierarchy would be to
desecrate it, invite ambition and control into the holy church of
God. It is hard for fourth phase Mormons to imagine a church
where the standing high councils of established stakes possess
presiding authority equal to the First Presidency and Quorum of
Twelve. But that is what the revelation states.[466] It is difficult for us
to imagine a Quorum of Twelve and Seventy whose authority

---

[465] *JD*, 15: 360 - 361.

[466] D&C 107: 36: "The standing high councils, at the stakes of Zion, form
a quorum equal in authority in the affairs of the church, in all their
decisions, to the quorum of the presidency, or to the traveling high
council."

exists only outside organized stakes. Within stakes the members' common consent is controlling. It is hard to imagine a church where the Twelve and Seventy are assigned exclusively to build up the church in the mission field, among the unconverted.[467] It is hard to think that in contrast, where there is an organized stake, the standing high council and stake presidency preside as an authority equal to the Twelve and Seventy.[468] It is difficult for us to imagine a church where local leaders are selected and elected to office by local congregations, rather than chosen by General Authorities. The "congregationalist" form of Mormonism was never allowed to develop after Brigham Young gained control. He intended and succeeded in having all others subordinate to his central command.

Joseph's description of the restoration included a blueprint that was never followed. If followed, it would result in men and women becoming "kings and queens, priests and priestesses" with the ability to establish their own kingdoms. Joseph would preside as suzerain, others as vassals. But the "kings" would be responsible for going out into the world and establishing their own kingdoms. When they converted, taught, ordained and endowed still other

---

[467] *Id.*, 33-35: "The Twelve are a Traveling Presiding High Council, to officiate in the name of the Lord, under the direction of the Presidency of the Church, agreeable to the institution of heaven; to build up the church, and regulate all the affairs of the same in all nations, first unto the Gentiles and secondly unto the Jews. The Seventy are to act in the name of the Lord, under the direction of the Twelve or the traveling high council, in building up the church and regulating all the affairs of the same in all nations, first unto the Gentiles and then to the Jews; The Twelve being sent out, holding the keys, to open the door by the proclamation of the gospel of Jesus Christ, and first unto the Gentiles and then unto the Jews."

[468] *Id.*, v. 36, *supra*.

"kings" the "kingdom of God" would roll forth and fill the earth.[469] All these various "kings" would be subject to Joseph as the head "king" or vassal. The whole to be delivered to Christ, at His return.[470] They would reign as benevolent priestly leaders, teaching

---

[469]"President J Smith arose and said it is impossible to continue the subject that I spoke upon yesterday in Consequence of the weekness of my lungs. Yet I have a proclamation to make to the Elders you know the Lord has led the Church untill the present time I have now a great proclamation for the Elders to teach the Church hereafter which is in relation to Zion, The whole of North and South America is Zion, the mountain of the Lords House is in the Centre of North & South America, when the House is done, Baptism font erectd and finished & the worthy are washed, anointed, endowed & ordained Kings & priests, which must be done in this life, when the place is prepared you must go through all the ordinances of the house of the Lord so that you who have any dead friends must go through all the ordinances for them the same as for yourselves; then the Elders are to go through all America & build up Churches untill all Zion is built up, but not to commence to do this untill the Temple is built up here and the Elders endowed then go forth & accomplish the work & build up stakes in all North and South America, Their will be some place ordained for the redeeming of the dead I think this place will be the one, so their will be gathering fast enough here. President Smith lungs failed him and he appointed Elder G. J. Adams to occupy the time during the foornoon He however remarked that his proclamation just made was the greatest ever made as all could not come here; but it was necessary that enough should come to build up the temple & get an endowment so that the work could spread abroad." (*WJS*, p. 364, footnotes omitted.) This talk was given on April 8, 1844. He would be dead two months later, without the temple completed in which this work to create "Kings & priests" was planned.

[470]"Daniel in his seventh chapter speaks of the Ancient of Days; he means the oldest man, our Father Adam, Michael, he will call his children together and hold a council with them to prepare them for the coming of the Son of Man. He (Adam) is the father of the human family, and presides over the spirits of all men, and all that have had the keys must stand before him in this grand council. This may take place before some of us leave this stage of action. The Son of Man stands before him, and there is given him glory and dominion. Adam delivers up his stewardship

righteousness and, being endowed with power from heaven, bless the lives of those who converted and accepted the Gospel. It was through this process they would learn to be "gods."[471]

When the Lord returns, according to Joseph's original plan, it would be to reign as the King of kings. Indeed, Christ will come with a name written upon Him which identifies the purpose for which the restoration was intended: "And he hath on his vesture and on his thigh a name written, KING OF KINGS, AND LORD OF LORDS." (Rev. 19: 16. See also Rev. 17: 14 and 1 Tim. 6: 15.)

Joseph's plan was explained by Orson Hyde in an article written in the Millennial Star two and a half years following Joseph's death. The article included a diagram of the future Celestial family of God, which has its beginning in ordinances restored in a new Dispensation. The article had the following description:

> ...The eternal Father sits at the head, crowned King of kings and Lord of lords. Wherever the other lines meet, there sits a king and a priest unto God, bearing rule, authority, and dominion under the Father. He is one with the Father, because his kingdom is joined to his Father's and becomes part of it.   The most eminent and distinguished prophets who have laid down their lives for their testimony (Jesus among the rest), will be crowned at the head of the largest kingdoms under the Father, and will be one with Christ as Christ is one with his Father; for their kingdoms are all joined together, and such as do the

---

to Christ, that which was delivered to him as holding the keys of the universe, but retains his standing as head of the human family." (*TPJS*, p. 157.)

[471] "You have got to learn how to be a god yourself in order to save yourself-to be priests & kings as all Gods has done-by going from a small degree to another-from exaltation to ex-till they are able to sit in glory as with those who sit enthroned." (*WJS*, p. 357, footnotes omitted.)

will of the Father, the same are his mothers, sisters, and brothers. He that has been faithful over a few things, will be made ruler over many things; he that has been faithful over ten talents, shall have dominion over ten cities, and he that has been faithful over five talents, shall have dominion over five cities, and to every man will be given a kingdom and a dominion, according to his merit, powers, and abilities to govern and control. It will be seen by the above diagram that there are kingdoms of all sizes, an infinite variety to suit all grades of merit and ability. The chosen vessels unto God are the kings and priests that are placed at the head of these kingdoms. These have received their washings and anointings in the temple of God on this earth; they have been chosen, ordained, and anointed kings and priests, to reign as such in the resurrection of the just. Such as have not received the fulness of the priesthood, (for the fulness of the priesthood includes the authority of both king and priest) and have not been anointed and ordained in the temple of the Most High, may obtain salvation in the celestial kingdom, but not a celestial crown. Many are called to enjoy a celestial glory, yet few are chosen to wear a celestial crown, or rather, to be rulers in the celestial kingdom. (*WJS*, pp. 298-299, quoting from Orson Hyde, *A Diagram of the Kingdom of God*," Millennial Star 9 [15 January 1847]: 23-24.)

During the first phase, Joseph had an integrated vision of how mankind was to be prepared for the Second Coming. It involved conveying the "fullness of the priesthood" to faithful saints. They would thereby become "kings and queens, priests and priestesses" sealed to Joseph, and through him to the "fathers." These "fathers" would hold the same "priesthood" and be the seed of Abraham.[472]

---

[472]Joseph was translating the Book of Abraham during the final months of his life. As a result he taught doctrines which he was recovering from

Like Abraham, they would be entitled to stand at the head of a branch of the heavenly family. To occupy that position they would need to be royal. These eternal family positions are always royal.[473]

The plan Joseph hoped to bring back in a fullness required angels to constantly attend to the development of the anticipated kingdom. Heaven could not abandon it. Joseph said seeking the presence of the Lord as a presiding King was always the object of the Gospel in every age where it is present.[474] If angels are no

---

this ancient source. Among them were the ideas covered by these verses, spoken to Abraham: "My name is Jehovah, and I know the end from the beginning; therefore my hand shall be over thee. And I will make of thee a great nation, and I will bless thee above measure, and make thy name great among all nations, and thou shalt be a blessing unto thy seed after thee, that in their hands they shall bear this ministry and Priesthood unto all nations; And I will bless them through thy name; for as many as receive this Gospel shall be called after thy name, and shall be accounted thy seed, and shall rise up and bless thee, as their father; And I will bless them that bless thee, and curse them that curse thee; and in thee (that is, in thy Priesthood) and in thy seed (that is, thy Priesthood), for I give unto thee a promise that this right shall continue in thee, and in thy seed after thee (that is to say, the literal seed, or the seed of the body) shall all the families of the earth be blessed, even with the blessings of the Gospel, which are the blessings of salvation, even of life eternal." (Abr. 2: 8-11.)

[473] 1 Pet. 2: 9: "But ye are a chosen generation, a royal priesthood, an holy nation, a peculiar people; that ye should shew forth the praises of him who hath called you out of darkness into his marvellous light[.]"

[474] "I saw Adam in the valley of Ah-dam-ondi-Ahman -he called together his children & blessed them with a Patriarchal blessing. The Lord appeared in their midst, & he (Adam) blessed them all, & foretold what should befall them to the latest generation-See D.C. Sec III 28, 29 par-This is why Abraham blessed his posterity: He wanted to bring them into the presence of God. They looked for a city, &c. -Moses sought to bring the children of Israel into the presence of God, through the power of the Pristhood, but he could not. In the first ages of the world they tried to establish the same thing-& there were Elias's raised up who tried

longer working with mankind, then we may have seen the passing of the heavenly gift from the earth at the death of Joseph Smith. If that is so, angels will need to return for us to regain what was rejected by the gentiles.

Many of the most lofty ideas taught by Joseph Smith are no longer included in the Correlated topics for study in fourth phase Mormonism. Though they were once central to Mormonism, they are no longer included in approved teaching materials. In Professor Harold Bloom's words, the Correlated church resembles "another Protestant sect, another Christian heresy." Though biting, they are accurate.

Assuming the saints failed and the church was rejected, what then? We turn next to the questions asked earlier. What does this new narrative mean for the church? Is the church still important? Does it retain an important role?

---

to restore these very glories but did not obtain them. But (Enoch did for himself & those that were with Him, but not for the world. J.T.) they prophesied of a day when this Glory would be revealed.-Paul spoke of the Dispensation of the fulness of times, when God would gather together all things in one &c &. Those men to whom these Keys have been given will have to be there. (I.E. when Adam shall again assemble his children of the Priesthood, & Christ be in their midst) the Ancient of Days come &c &c J.T.) And they without us cannot not be made perfect. These men are in heaven, but their children are on Earth. Their bowels yearn over us. God sends down men for this reason, Mat. 13. 41. & the Son of man shall send forth his Angels &c-All these authoritative characters will come down & join hand in hand in bringing about this work-" (*WJS*, p. 9-10, footnotes omitted.)

Chapter 15

A CHURCH OF DESTINY

For purposes of this chapter, I am going to assume the church never obtained the fullness offered by the Lord in Nauvoo. Even if our history reflects the passing of the heavenly gift at Joseph Smith's death, there is still every reason to believe the Lord remains involved in the destiny of The Church of Jesus Christ of Latter-day Saints. The continuing relevance of the church will be discussed in this chapter.

There is no scriptural precedent where Zion was established as a result of generations of incremental work. It has only been established when a legal administrator is sent with authority directly from heaven, with a commandment from God to establish it. Enoch did not lay a foundation upon which others gradually built over generations. Nor did Melchizedek. They came with power, held a fullness, and through teaching the truth to people willing to live it, established Zion. Both times the Lord came and dwelt with them.

In the Nephite example, it was the Lord who established a people of peace. His community then dwelt in harmony for generations. The Lord left translated ministers among them.[475]

Whenever Zion has been, or will be built, it is under the Lord's direct command. It requires a presiding prophet called by God as His agent to found the city. We have no way of knowing how often the Lord has offered to "gather[ed] [us], as a hen gather[eth] her chickens under her wings"[476] into Zion. Almost always, mankind has refused to be gathered. Ingratitude, pride and worldliness have interfered. Whenever one is sent who could teach enough truth to establish Zion, there has been an offer from the Lord to "gather us, as a hen gathers her chicks under her wings." The offer has been extended by the Lord apparently so often He could only lament: "how often might I have gathered you!" If the full history were known, we would no doubt be shocked at the frequency of His invitation and the persistence of mankind's indifference.

When a servant sent from Him is rejected, there is always an amount of time that must pass before another servant is sent. Those in the generation who reject an offer must all die before the next opportunity will be extended. This is why Joseph lamented the failure to complete the Nauvoo Temple, and the temporary opportunity that existed with him: "And I would to God that this temple was now done, that we might go into it, and go to work and improve our time, and make use of the seals while they are on

---

[475]For a description of the power of their ministry see 3 Ne. 28: 4-23.

[476]See D&C 43: 24 as to the "nations of the earth;" see also Matt. 23: 37; Luke 13: 24.

earth." (*TPJS*, p. 330.) He knew the "seals" would soon depart. Joseph died and Zion had not been brought again.

We have moved further away from Zion since the time Joseph Smith was Prophet. The Lord will extend the offer again, but until He sends someone who can teach what is necessary in order to establish Zion, we will continue to lose light, discard, truth, forget what is expected, and dwindle in unbelief. Until we remember the Book of Mormon and renew ourselves by accepting what was once offered through that "covenant," our minds will remain darkened.[477] In the revelation telling the church it was condemned, the Lord explains the condemnation will result in a season of trouble for the church, which will last until we "bring forth fruit meet for their Father's kingdom; otherwise there remaineth a scourge and judgment to be poured out upon the children of Zion. For shall the children of the kingdom pollute my holy land? Verily, I say unto you, Nay." (D&C 84: 58-59.) We need to awaken to our awful situation.[478] We must face the wretchedness of our circumstances. If we recognize we are now enduring a "scourge and judgment" which has been "poured out upon the children of Zion" we can conclude two things: First, we have not brought forth the kind of "fruit" which will meet the Lord's high expectations for us. Therefore, we must repent and end our rebellion. Second, though we are out of the way, condemned, rejected and even cursed, the Lord still refers to us as "the children of Zion" and "children of the kingdom." He intends for some remnant of the saints, some fraction from among us, to rally around His next offer to "gather us as chickens under a hen's

---

[477]D&C 84: 54-57.

[478]See, e.g., 2 Ne. 1: 13; Ether 8: 24.

wings." When He sends that invitation it will be to all His "children" including the whole church. It is apparent, however, only a few will understand it has arrived and repent of their sins. Zion cannot be polluted by "children of the kingdom" who will not "bring forth fruit meet for their Father's kingdom." That fruit is grounded in repentance from sins. The first step in the return is to heed the warning to repent and turn back to God. The saints will be given the invitation first. If they refuse, the invitation will then be extended to others, including the remnant of the Nephites.

Once the church was established by the Lord's direct hand, it became His work. He will watch over it. He has never said His condemnation, rejection and cursings upon us cannot be remedied. Nor has He said He would fail to work with those few gentiles who will repent, and remember Him. The scriptures give us a blueprint of the way the Lord deals with those whom He has chosen, but who forsake Him.

After the Lord delivered Israel from Egyptian captivity, they rebelled. They were unwilling to do all He asked of them. But He did not cut them off, ignore them or leave them in silence. He sent messengers to minister to them. As Moses led them in the wilderness they began to rebel, and the Lord considered destroying them. They were spared as a result of Moses pleading before the Lord on their behalf:

> [Y]e rebelled against the commandment of the Lord your God, and ye believed him not, nor hearkened to his voice. Ye have been rebellious against the Lord from the day that I knew you. Thus I fell down before the Lord forty days and forty nights, as I fell down at the first; because the Lord had said he would destroy you. I prayed therefore unto the Lord, and said, O Lord God, destroy not thy people and thine inheritance, which thou hast redeemed

through thy greatness, which thou hast brought forth out
of Egypt with a mighty hand. Remember thy servants,
Abraham, Isaac, and Jacob; look not unto the stubbornness
of this people, nor to their wickedness, nor to their sin:
Lest the land whence thou broughtest us out say, Because
the Lord was not able to bring them into the land which he
promised them, and because he hated them, he hath
brought them out to slay them in the wilderness. Yet they
are thy people and thine inheritance, which thou
broughtest out by thy mighty power and by thy stretched
out arm. (Deu. 9: 23-29.)

The rebellious, ancient, Israelites did not stop being the Lord's
people because of their rebellion. They remained His. Although He
threatened to destroy them, His servant Moses interceded on their
behalf. The Lord was willing to bear with them for His servant's
sake. In our day we can see the same thing, if we are willing to
open our eyes to it. In the very revelation the Latter-day Saints are
warned they are going to be rejected, the Lord acknowledged
Joseph's intercession. "Verily, thus saith the Lord unto you, my
servant Joseph Smith, I am well pleased with your offering and
acknowledgments, which you have made; for unto this end have I
raised you up, that I might show forth my wisdom through the
weak things of the earth." (D&C 124: 1.) Joseph Smith offered his
life to purchase the saints more time. He acknowledged our
shortcomings and failures, and his failure to get repentance from
us. He thought he could do more if he were given more time. The
Lord accepted Joseph's offer, gave more time, but ultimately we
failed to accomplish what was required. Joseph's life was forfeited,
but Joseph's blood was not shed in vain. We remain the Lord's
people and have inherited a covenant which still provides power to

any who will repent. Until we repent, however, the condemnation, rejection and cursing remain in effect.

Despite their rebellion, the ancient Israelites were never abandoned by the Lord. Instead, their privileges were curtailed and the higher priesthood removed. A modern revelation explains the way the Lord dealt with those who were unwilling to receive the greater blessings offered to them:

> And this greater priesthood administereth the gospel and holdeth the key of the mysteries of the kingdom, even the key of the knowledge of God. Therefore, in the ordinances thereof, the power of godliness is manifest. And without the ordinances thereof, and the authority of the priesthood, the power of godliness is not manifest unto men in the flesh; For without this no man can see the face of God, even the Father, and live. Now this Moses plainly taught to the children of Israel in the wilderness, and sought diligently to sanctify his people that they might behold the face of God; But they hardened their hearts and could not endure his presence; therefore, the Lord in his wrath, for his anger was kindled against them, swore that they should not enter into his rest while in the wilderness, which rest is the fulness of his glory. Therefore, he took Moses out of their midst, and the Holy Priesthood also; And the lesser priesthood continued, which priesthood holdeth the key of the ministering of angels and the preparatory gospel; Which gospel is the gospel of repentance and of baptism, and the remission of sins, and the law of carnal commandments, which the Lord in his wrath caused to continue with the house of Aaron among the children of Israel until John, whom God raised up, being filled with the Holy Ghost from his mother's womb. (D&C 84: 19-27.)

Though they were unfit for greater things, they were worthy to be baptized and receive a lesser law to help them repent if they were willing to do so. The Dispensation of Moses was a dispensation marked throughout by Israelite apostasy, together with the loss of higher priesthood authority. Nevertheless, they were given ordinances to perform designed to help them remember the Lord, and what they could have obtained had they been faithful. These ordinances were repeated for over a thousand years. It would not be until John the Baptist that the Dispensation of Moses would close and a new dispensation open.

During this long wait, however, there were messengers sent from time to time to warn the rebellious Israelites, and to call them to repentance. As to the messengers sent by the Lord, Joseph Smith explained that like Moses, they all held higher priesthood. Their power and authority came directly from the Lord, not from a priestly hierarchy which perpetuated authority:

> Answer to the question, Was the Priesthood of Melchizedek taken away when Moses died? All Priesthood is Melchizedek, but there are different portions or degrees of it. That portion which brought Moses to speak with God face to face was taken away; but that which brought the ministry of angels remained. All the prophets had the Melchizedek Priesthood and were ordained by God himself. (*TPJS*, p. 180.)

Although the higher priesthood was taken when Moses departed, the Lord still sent messengers with the kind of priesthood that allowed a man "to speak with God face to face." We see this in testimonies left by Isaiah,[479] Daniel,[480] Samuel,[481] Jeremiah,[482] and Ezekiel.[483] All these (and many more) came with the same Holy Priesthood as Moses, and actually stood before the Lord. Therefore, Israel's apostasy could not prevent some men from repenting of their sins, seeking for the Lord and finding Him.[484]

When prophets conversed with the Lord face to face during the Dispensation of Moses, they were commissioned to deliver a message. The message was always a call to repent and return to the Lord. Isaiah warned Israel against their false worship, intermarriage with others not of their faith, idolatry and pride. (See Isa. 2: 6-22.) Their sexual practices were like Sodom's and they had no shame. (Isa. 3: 9.) Israel was like wild grapes, unworthy to be harvested. (Isa. 5: 4.) Though the Lord sent them words which could save them, they would not understand– as a result they would be destroyed. (Isa. 6: 9-11.) Although God could still hear, and had power to deliver, their iniquities separated them from God, and He hid His face from them. (Isa. 59: 1-2.) The fact Isaiah was sent to Israel is evidence their failure did not separate them from the Lord's love. He sent Isaiah as His messenger because He remained committed to them, even if they were not committed to Him.[485]

---

[479] Isaiah 6: 1-11.

[480] Dan. 10: 5-21.

[481] 1 Sam. 3: 4-10, 19, 21.

[482] Jer. 31: 3.

[483] Eze. 1: 24-28; 10: 4-7.

[484] See 2 Chron. 15: 4.

[485] Isa. 49: 15.

Jeremiah told Israel they had forsaken the Lord. (Jer. 2: 17.) Their own bad choices would be their punishment as they went from error to error. (Jer. 2: 19.) Israel was intended to be a vine that brought forth fruit which could be laid up. Instead, she became a harlot seeking after false gods. (Jer. 2: 20-21.) Although called to be the Lord's house, they were a den of robbers. (Jer. 7: 10-11.) The Lord still called to Israel by His own voice, but it was Israel who refused to hear. (Jer. 7: 13.) Their land was filled with adultery which hardened them from being able to hear His voice; while those who claimed to be prophets were profane and wicked. (Jer. 23: 10-11.) They listened to the false prophets. When the Lord sent true prophets to warn them to repent, none would listen. (Jer. 35: 15.) Israel was apostate. But the fact God sent Jeremiah to them shows how great the Lord's commitment remains to His people, to His covenant. Sin alone does not separate them from His watchful care.

Ezekiel began his message by telling Israel they were a rebellious nation, children of apostate fathers. (Eze. 2: 2-3.) He was required to warn them, leaving to them to decide if they would hear or reject his words. (Eze. 3: 10-11.) If he did not warn them he would be responsible for their blood, but if he did warn them, and they rejected his message then he would not be responsible for their blood. (Eze. 3: 16-19.) Their apostasy would result in them being destroyed by desolation, waste and the sword. (Eze. 6: 1-7.) A remnant would be preserved who will know the Lord's judgments were provoked by their wickedness. (Eze. 6: 8-10.) Ezekiel saw the private abominations of the leaders, whose carefully guarded wickedness in dark chambers were not hidden from the Lord or His servant. (Eze. 8: 9-12.) Even in the Lord's temple they practiced wickedness. (Eze. 8: 15-17.) The Lord will deal with them in His fury. (Eze. 8: 18.) Israel failed to preserve the faith delivered to them, instead copying the false religions which surrounded them. (Eze. 11: 12.) He declared the "prophets of Israel," who taught only from their own wisdom, and had seen nothing from the Lord, were false. (Eze. 13: 1-3.) These false teachers were compared to the predatory and sly foxes in the desert, where nothing is fruitful and nothing but desolation can be found. (Eze. 13: 3.) False prophets claim they speak for the Lord, but He has not spoken to them. (Eze. 13: 6-8.) God intends to deal with the false prophets, and as a result all will know that He is the Lord. (Eze. 13: 9.) Those false prophets who cry "peace" when there is no peace will be overthrown and a great, violent storm will overtake them. (Eze. 13: 10-14.) They had become a wild vine, not bringing fruit worthy to preserve, and therefore, were to be burned. (Eze. 15: 6-8.) The false prophets who led them were only interested in feeding themselves, getting praise and amassing power. They were not interested in teaching righteousness. (Eze. 22: 25-26.) They claimed to speak for the Lord when the Lord had never spoken to them. (Eze. 22: 28.) They used the Lord's name to oppress people. (Eze. 22: 28-29.) But the destruction which would come upon them would leave them astonished, even drunk with desolation that was to come. (Eze. 23: 32-34.) All this was because they had forgotten the Lord, and had become distracted by their lewd and apostate practices. (Eze. 23: 35.) Such a message could only come to an apostate and corrupt people. Yet God did not ignore them, instead He sent Ezekiel as a prophet to warn them again.

Many more examples could be used, but these make the point. False prophets benefit from their claims. True ones are never popular, and always preach repentance. Joseph Smith said this:

The world always mistook false prophets for true ones, and those that were sent of God, they considered to be false prophets, and hence they killed, stoned, punished and imprisoned the true prophets, and these had to hide themselves "in deserts and dens, and caves of the earth," and though the most honorable men of the earth, they banished them from their society as vagabonds, whilst they cherished, honored and supported knaves, vagabonds, hypocrites, impostors, and the basest of men. (*TPJS*, p. 206.)

Joseph used the exact right words. It is always "the world" which rejects the true prophets. Because any time a true prophet is sent, all who reject him become part of "the world." Those who are of "the world" fail to receive the messengers God sends, preferring the false ones that men admire. The result of their false religion is damnation alongside the liars, adulterers and whoremongers.[486]

If we change the narrative of this dispensation and admit we have already experienced our own apostasy, we see instantly that

---

[486]"And the glory of the telestial is one, even as the glory of the stars is one; for as one star differs from another star in glory, even so differs one from another in glory in the telestial world; For these are they who are of Paul, and of Apollos, and of Cephas. These are they who say they are some of one and some of another--some of Christ and some of John, and some of Moses, and some of Elias, and some of Esaias, and some of Isaiah, and some of Enoch; **But received not the gospel, neither the testimony of Jesus, neither the prophets, neither the everlasting covenant.** Last of all, these all are they who will not be gathered with the saints, to be caught up unto the church of the Firstborn, and received into the cloud. These are they who are liars, and sorcerers, and adulterers, and whoremongers, and whosoever loves and makes a lie. These are they who suffer the wrath of God on earth. These are they who suffer the vengeance of eternal fire. These are they who are cast down to hell and suffer the wrath of Almighty God, until the fulness of times, when Christ shall have subdued all enemies under his feet, and shall have perfected his work[.]" (D&C 76: 98-106, emphasis added.)

we are now reliving the same pattern as anciently. We are, in fact, like ancient Israel after Moses was taken. The fullness of the heavenly gift was offered through Joseph. The early saints of this dispensation were unwilling to accept it. "Apostasy" means a deliberate, intentional, or willful rejection or refusal to accept what God offers to man. It is a rebellion. When we limit what we will permit God to reveal, setting boundaries to His teachings, we rebel. But that rebellion limits only ourselves.

> The great thing for us to know is to comprehend what God did institute before the foundation of the world. Who knows it? It is the constitutional disposition of mankind to set up stakes and set bounds to the works and ways of the Almighty. ...I say to all those who are disposed to set up stakes for the Almighty, You will come short of the glory of God. (*TPJS*, pp. 320, 321.)

If we set bounds to what we would accept in Nauvoo, then we have come short of the glory which we might have obtained. We lost the opportunity for a holy spot and an inheritance from where we would not be moved. The result was condemnation, then rejection, and finally cursing as we witnessed the passing of the heavenly gift from among us. Our condition is anticipated, and the means to recover from it are explained in the Book of Mormon. That book has far more to say on this topic than we have ever taught. The gentile condemnation, rejection and cursing was foreseen. But it was always intended to be temporary, at least for some small fragment of the gentiles. Christ explains what will unfold after the rejection of the fullness by the gentiles:

> I will bring the fulness of my gospel from among them. And then will I remember my covenant which I have made unto my people, O house of Israel, and I will bring my gospel unto them. And I will show unto thee, O house of

Israel, that the Gentiles shall not have power over you; but
I will remember my covenant unto you, O house of Israel,
and ye shall come unto the knowledge of the fulness of my
gospel. But if the Gentiles will repent and return unto me,
saith the Father, behold they shall be numbered among my
people, O house of Israel. And I will not suffer my people,
who are of the house of Israel, to go through among them,
and tread them down, saith the Father. But if they will not
turn unto me, and hearken unto my voice, I will suffer
them, yea, I will suffer my people, O house of Israel, that
they shall go through among them, and shall tread them
down, and they shall be as salt that hath lost its savor,
which is thenceforth good for nothing but to be cast out,
and to be trodden under foot of my people, O house of
Israel. (3 Ne. 16: 10-15.)

To be numbered among those who will bring again Zion, the
gentiles must "repent and return unto [the Lord]." Although only
a few are predicted to be willing to repent and bring forth fruit, any
who do will be added to the triumphant covenant people.

Mormon included in his record of Christ's visit to the Nephites
Christ's plea to the latter-day gentiles to repent. These are Christ's
words directed to us:

For thus it behooveth the Father that it should come forth
from the Gentiles, that he may show forth his power unto
the Gentiles, for this cause that the Gentiles, if they will
not harden their hearts, that they may repent and come
unto me and be baptized in my name and know of the true
points of my doctrine, that they may be numbered among
my people, O house of Israel; And when these things come
to pass that thy seed shall begin to know these things--it
shall be a sign unto them, that they may know that the
work of the Father hath already commenced unto the

fulfilling of the covenant which he hath made unto the people who are of the house of Israel. (3 Ne. 21: 6-7.)

We were given the Book of Mormon to make available to us the Lord's true points of doctrine. His true doctrine connects us with the Lord's power. He can bring back to life lost and forgotten people. Their prophets, unknown for nearly two thousand years, will speak from the dust again. We should be stirred into repentance because of such a wonder. To understand the true points of Christ's doctrine necessarily comes before being "numbered among [His] people." To lose His true doctrine is more than to dwindle in unbelief. Losing the true points of His doctrine separates us from Him. "A man is saved no faster than he gets knowledge." (*TPJS*, p. 217.)[487] The gentiles are involved only to fulfill the promised pattern. The Jews are first, then the gentiles [New Testament]; thereafter the gentiles are first and then the Jews [restoration through Joseph Smith]. The first to be last again, the last to be first again. Therefore, gentiles needed to be involved to fulfill the promised pattern.

The offer to give the gentiles the fullness is a sign the covenant the Father made with the house of Israel is about to be fulfilled. The sign has been given. Now we await that generation in which the Lord will again offer to gather us. The only way that offer can be accepted is by repenting, coming unto Him, being baptized in His name, and knowing the true points of His doctrine.

Later in the Book of Mormon text, the Lord explains what gentiles must stop doing to repent and be forgiven:

---

[487]The kind of knowledge that will save is discussed in the next chapter.

Hearken, O ye Gentiles, and hear the words of Jesus Christ, the Son of the living God, which he hath commanded me that I should speak concerning you, for, behold he commandeth me that I should write, saying: Turn, all ye Gentiles, from your wicked ways; and repent of your evil doings, of your lyings and deceivings, and of your whoredoms, and of your secret abominations, and your idolatries, and of your murders, and your priestcrafts, and your envyings, and your strifes, and from all your wickedness and abominations, and come unto me, and be baptized in my name, that ye may receive a remission of your sins, and be filled with the Holy Ghost, that ye may be numbered with my people who are of the house of Israel. (3 Ne. 30: 1-2.)

Our wickedness and evil come from "lyings and deceivings." We prefer the lie that tells us we need no repentance to the truth that we must repent or perish. We deceive ourselves into believing we are Zion. The truth is we are far from it, and getting farther away every day. Our whoredoms are twofold. We both worship a false image rather than the living God, and we are also sexually impure. Our secret abominations are the conspiracies that run among us to manipulate, get gain, use religion to promote a cause, obtain commercial advantage, and wield political influence. We idolize men, rather than Christ. We claim to hold keys that would allow men filled with sin to forgive sins on earth and in heaven, to grant eternal life, or to bar from the kingdom of God. Using that false and useless claim, we slay the souls of men, thereby committing murder.[488] We are riddled with priestcrafts. Men seek the praise of

---

[488]See Alma 36: 14: "Yea, and I had murdered many of his children, or rather led them away unto destruction; yea, and in fine so great had been my iniquities, that the very thought of coming into the presence of my

others rather than to bring again Zion. We envy those who fill leadership positions because we want the power granted through priestly office and position. Because we lack the Spirit as a guide, and rather than learning by gaining light through obedience, we engage in strife with one another to settle points of doctrine. Any voice crying repentance is labeled a dissenter, and their words are condemned and attacked. They are thought to be "of the devil." By stirring up strife we succeed in making people fear truth. We close our minds, become deaf and blind.[489] Christ's words should take precedent over the smooth things we hear from the philosophies of men, but they do not. We have again mirrored the ancient pattern Isaiah warned about:

> That this is a rebellious people, lying children, children that will not hear the law of the Lord: Which say to the seers, See not; and to the prophets, Prophesy not unto us right things, speak unto us smooth things, prophesy deceits: Get you out of the way, turn aside out of the path, cause the Holy One of Israel to cease from before us. (Isa. 30: 9-11.)

Although we remain part of the Lord's latter-day agenda, we are not going to be collectively saved. Only those few who will repent and return to Him will be numbered among His people. For the rest, they will follow false guides down to destruction.

Christ warned in modern revelation that His final judgments will begin upon The Church of Jesus Christ of Latter-day Saints. From those who claim to be "His house," He will show the world that righteousness is the single standard required of man. Conceit and

---

God did rack my soul with inexpressible horror."

[489] 2 Ne. 9: 31-32: "And wo unto the deaf that will not hear; for they shall perish. Wo unto the blind that will not see; for they shall perish also."

deceit are no substitute for knowing the true points of His doctrine, and the true points of His doctrine can only be learned from Him. Our minds continue to be dark recesses. We are not filled with light. We say we understand, and will be judged on our claims.

> Verily, verily, I say unto you, darkness covereth the earth, and gross darkness the minds of the people, and all flesh has become corrupt before my face. Behold, vengeance cometh speedily upon the inhabitants of the earth, a day of wrath, a day of burning, a day of desolation, of weeping, of mourning, and of lamentation; and as a whirlwind it shall come upon all the face of the earth, saith the Lord. And upon my house shall it begin, and from my house shall it go forth, saith the Lord; First among those among you, saith the Lord, who have professed to know my name and have not known me, and have blasphemed against me in the midst of my house, saith the Lord. (D&C 112: 23-26.)

In other words, when the Lord begins the final day of purging and refining, it will fall first upon the Latter-day Saints. The burning of that day will cut them off entirely, both ancestor and descendant, for they will have failed to have turned their hearts to the fathers.[490] The refining process will burn up those who are unprepared, and cleanse and purify the few who are penitent and humble.[491]

Once again, however, the prophecy of our destruction proceeds from (and reiterates) the relevance of the church to God's activities in the last days. He identifies the Latter-day Saints as His

---

[490]See Mal. 4: 1-6.

[491]*Id.*, 3: 1-3.

"house."[492] Therefore, even if we are condemned, rejected and cursed, we continue to be included in His plans. Just as He continued to care and send authorized messengers from time to time to warn ancient Israel and declare repentance to them, we should expect such messages to be sent to us. Their message from Him, just as anciently, will necessarily be a plea for us to repent.

Just like ancient Israel, after Moses' departure, we have been instructed in how to perform mandatory ordinances. We know if we follow these ordinances we please the Lord and draw closer to Him. Even among people who have strayed, both anciently and today, if we follow Him we can still find Him. His voice continues to call out to us.

Here is a modern revelation about how we are to be saved:

That as many as would believe and be baptized in his holy name, and endure in faith to the end, should be saved-- Not only those who believed after he came in the meridian of time, in the flesh, but all those from the beginning, even as many as were before he came, who believed in the words of the holy prophets, who spake as they were inspired by the gift of the Holy Ghost, who truly testified of him in all things, should have eternal life, As well as those who should come after, who should believe in the gifts and callings of God by the Holy Ghost, which beareth record of the Father and of the Son; Which Father, Son, and Holy Ghost are one God, infinite and eternal, without end. Amen. And we know that all men must repent and believe on the name of Jesus Christ, and worship the Father in his name, and endure in faith on his name to the end, or they cannot be saved in the kingdom of God. And we know that justification through the grace of our Lord

---

[492]See, e.g., D&C 88: 34; 94: 1; 101: 55; 103: 22, 30, 34; 105: 16, 27; 132: 18, among others.

and Savior Jesus Christ is just and true; And we know also, that sanctification through the grace of our Lord and Savior Jesus Christ is just and true, to all those who love and serve God with all their mights, minds, and strength. But there is a possibility that man may fall from grace and depart from the living God; Therefore let the church take heed and pray always, lest they fall into temptation; Yea, and even let those who are sanctified take heed also. (D&C 20: 25-34.)

Whether others receive Him or not, any of us can believe on Him. Any of us can repent and be baptized. Any of us can endure in faith to the end. Any of us can be saved. The Holy Ghost comes to any soul who repents and seeks for God. It does not matter whether there is an officiator with authority from God on the earth or not. "A man may receive the Holy Ghost, and it may descend upon him and not tarry with him." (D&C 130: 23.) This verse is taken from a talk given on April 2, 1843 at Ramus, Illinois by Joseph Smith. The full account of this statement reads: "The Holy Ghost is a personage, and a person cannot have the personage of the H. G. in his heart. A man receive the gifts of the H. G., and the H. G. may descend upon a man but not to tarry with him." (*WJS*, p. 170, taken from William Clayton's Diary.)

It would be good to have an authorized minister to perform the ordinance, but the language of Section 20 is not contingent upon authority. Rather, it is the faith of one receiving baptism which determines the ordinance's validity. The church offices described in Section 20 are not dependent on priesthood authority. Nor is authority given to the church dependent upon a man. The direction to organize the church is all that was required. After that, the presiding authorities derive their right to preside from the common consent of church members.[493] Even in the first phase, when the founding prophet was in direct communication with the Lord, the church body still retained the final control through common consent: "And all things shall be done by common consent in the church, by much prayer and faith, for all things you shall receive by faith. Amen." (D&C 26: 2.) The First Presidency of the church has no authority to function unless they are upheld by the church's confidence, prayers and sustaining vote for them. As soon as it is withdrawn, they are no longer empowered to act: "Of the Melchizedek Priesthood, three Presiding High Priests, chosen by the body, appointed and ordained to that office, and upheld by the confidence, faith, and prayer of the church, form a quorum of the Presidency of the Church." (D&C 107: 22.) If a man is called to any office, even in the Quorum of Twelve, and he does not receive a sustaining vote, he may be called but he is not chosen and therefore cannot serve.[494] The church was divinely established and

---

[493]D&C 28: 13.

[494]"The offices of Patriarch and Assistant-President were held by Hyrum Smith until the martyrdom. The office of Patriarch was then offered to William Smith, the only surviving brother of the Prophet, and President Brigham Young declared it was his *by right*. William Smith confirmed the saying of the Lord, 'many are called, but few are chosen,' for he failed to magnify this calling, turned against his brethren, and was excommunicated. *He was never sustained by the vote of the people, and therefore never did legally act*; *he was called, but was not chosen*." (Smith, Joseph Fielding. *Doctrines of Salvation.* Edited by Bruce R. McConkie. Salt Lake City: Bookcraft, 1956, Vol. 3, p.168, emphasis added.) Even Harold B. Lee, whose preference for central control led to the Church Correlation Program discussed earlier, confirmed the necessity of common consent for any officer in the church: "No officer is to preside over a branch or a stake until he is sustained by a vote of that body over which he is to preside. They may reject, but they do not nominate and they do not release." (Lee, Harold B. *Teachings of Harold B.*

holds a prophetic destiny. But the church is responsible for what happens to it because it must consent to the leaders and their actions. We cannot shirk that responsibility.

If the new view of history is more correct than the narrative offered by the proud descendants of Nauvoo, the church still has a Divine commission. By analogy, we, like ancient Israel, are performing sacred and authorized ceremonies. But we are not in full fellowship with God. Even so, we have the obligation to continually perform His ordinances. Although Moses and the Holy Priesthood was taken, there remained a lesser priesthood holding heaven's authorization.[495] This lesser priesthood consisted of only outward commandments and performances, and was not contingent upon the holder's worthiness.

After all the condemnation spoken against Israel by Isaiah, Jeremiah, Ezekiel, Daniel, Hosea, Amos, and others, when Christ came to the fallen and apostate Jews, He did not question their right to perform outward priesthood ordinances. Indeed, He sent

---

Lee. Edited by Clyde J. Williams. Salt Lake City: Deseret Book, 1996, p. 550.) James Talmage explained: "In line with the principle of common consent, which characterizes the Church administration in general, officers of the auxiliary institutions, while nominated by or with the approval of the administrative officers of the Priesthood, are sustained in their places by the vote of the members in the local or general units within which they are appointed to serve." (Talmage, James E. *The Articles of Faith.* Salt Lake City: Deseret Book, 1984, p. 194.)

[495] D&C 84: 25-27: "Therefore, he took Moses out of their midst, and the Holy Priesthood also; And the lesser priesthood continued, which priesthood holdeth the key of the ministering of angels and the preparatory gospel; Which gospel is the gospel of repentance and of baptism, and the remission of sins, and the law of carnal commandments, which the Lord in his wrath caused to continue with the house of Aaron among the children of Israel until John, whom God raised up, being filled with the Holy Ghost from his mother's womb."

those He healed to offer the required sacrifices under the law.[496] The Church of Jesus Christ of Latter-day Saints cannot be worse today than the ancient Israelites, and is therefore, still authorized to baptize for remission of sins. If the loss of Joseph Smith caused the loss of the fullness of the priesthood in the same way the removal of Moses did anciently, then like ancient Israel, the church continues to have the "lesser priesthood continued, which priesthood holdeth the key of the ministering of angels and the preparatory gospel; Which gospel is the gospel of repentance and of baptism, and the remission of sins, and the law of carnal commandments[.]" (D&C 84: 26-27.)

Baptism continues to be essential to salvation for any soul.[497] The church has the right to baptize. The church has also been given the correct covenant language for baptism.[498] Since the language of the baptismal covenant was given by revelation, it has been approved by the Lord. Using the language for the ceremony authorizes the covenant to be performed.

The church has also received by revelation the correct covenant language to perform the sacrament of the Lord's Supper for both

---

[496] See Luke 17: 12-14: "And as he entered into a certain village, there met him ten men that were lepers, which stood afar off: And they lifted up their voices, and said, Jesus, Master, have mercy on us. And when he saw [them], he said unto them, Go shew yourselves unto the priests. And it came to pass, that, as they went, they were cleansed." There is more to this story, discussed in *Come, Let Us Adore Him*.

[497] 2 Ne. 31: 5.

[498] D&C 20: 73.

the bread[499] and wine.[500] More than just authorized to practice the Lord's Supper, the church has been commanded to do so.[501] This sacrament is also entrusted to the church and necessary to perform.[502] Tithing is also commanded of the Lord's Saints.[503] The church is authorized to receive tithes.[504]

Christ lived at a time when the presiding authorities were corrupt and wicked. They conspired to kill Him. He knew this was their intent, but He still showed respect to their offices. Even as He condemned their evil, He taught obedience to them.[505] It is not the responsibility of church members to judge church authorities. The Lord will judge all and render just recompense to every person. He knows there are abominations among us. He has told of our deceivers and hypocrites. He declared in 1831:

> Behold, I, the Lord, have looked upon you, and have seen abominations in the church that profess my name. But blessed are they who are faithful and endure, whether in life or in death, for they shall inherit eternal life. But wo unto them that are deceivers and hypocrites, for, thus saith

---

[499]D&C 20: 77; Moroni 4: 3.

[500]D&C 20: 79; Moroni 5: 2.

[501]See D&C 20: 46, 58, 68; 27: 2; 46: 4-5; 62: 4, among other places.

[502]3 Ne. 20: 8.

[503]D&C 64: 23.

[504]D&C 85: 3.

[505]"Then spake Jesus to the multitude, and to his disciples, Saying, The scribes and the Pharisees sit in Moses' seat: All therefore whatsoever they bid you observe, that observe and do; but do not ye after their works: for they say, and do not." (Matt. 23: 1-3.)

the Lord, I will bring them to judgment. Behold, verily I say unto you, there are hypocrites among you, who have deceived some, which has given the adversary power; but behold such shall be reclaimed; But the hypocrites shall be detected and shall be cut off, either in life or in death, even as I will; and wo unto them who are cut off from my church, for the same are overcome of the world. (D&C 50: 4-8.)

Today the Lord understands our true condition. We cannot hide what we are from Him. He may be patient, nevertheless He will take judgment into His hands when it is required: "Leave judgment alone with me, for it is mine and I will repay. Peace be with you; my blessings continue with you." (D&C 82: 23.)

Even if the church has been condemned, rejected and cursed, it is still part of His plan. Through it we receive authorized ordinances. We pay our tithes and offerings to the church. And we serve one another within the church. Baptism is important; as is our opportunity and duty to fellowship one another after baptism. Alma explained this beside the waters of Mormon:

[A]s ye are desirous to come into the fold of God, and to be called his people, and are willing to bear one another's burdens, that they may be light; Yea, and are willing to mourn with those that mourn; yea, and comfort those that stand in need of comfort, and to stand as witnesses of God at all times and in all things, and in all places that ye may be in, even until death, that ye may be redeemed of God, and be numbered with those of the first resurrection, that ye may have eternal life-- Now I say unto you, if this be the desire of your hearts, what have you against being baptized in the name of the Lord, as a witness before him that ye have entered into a covenant with him, that ye will serve him and keep his commandments, that he may pour out his Spirit more abundantly upon you? (Mosiah 18: 8-10.)

The church is filled with weak, errant and flawed individuals. But that was forseen. The Lord's house (the church) is the place where His judgments will first begin. We may be astonished at the fierce anger to be poured out,[506] but if the pure in heart have repented they will be spared. Everyone who fails to repent and produce good fruit will be destroyed by His anger. Membership in the church is no protection. However, membership in the church is where preparation and repentance begin.

In the next chapter we will look at what it means to repent and produce fruit which justifies the Lord in saving us at the coming harvest.

---

[506]See, e.g., D&C 29: 17-20: "And it shall come to pass, because of the wickedness of the world, that I will take vengeance upon the wicked, for they will not repent; for the cup of mine indignation is full; for behold, my blood shall not cleanse them if they hear me not. Wherefore, I the Lord God will send forth flies upon the face of the earth, which shall take hold of the inhabitants thereof, and shall eat their flesh, and shall cause maggots to come in upon them; And their tongues shall be stayed that they shall not utter against me; and their flesh shall fall from off their bones, and their eyes from their sockets; And it shall come to pass that the beasts of the forest and the fowls of the air shall devour them up."

Chapter 16

FINDING HOPE

I have defined the word "hope" in an earlier book, *Eighteen Verses*. The definition clarifies it means something more substantial than desire, wish or longing. It is a concrete expectation based on promises given from heaven. Discussing D&C 128: 20-21:[507]

---

[507] "And again, what do we hear? Glad tidings from Cumorah! Moroni, an angel from heaven, declaring the fulfilment of the prophets--the book to be revealed. A voice of the Lord in the wilderness of Fayette, Seneca county, declaring the three witnesses to bear record of the book! The voice of Michael on the banks of the Susquehanna, detecting the devil when he appeared as an angel of light! The voice of Peter, James, and John in the wilderness between Harmony, Susquehanna county, and Colesville, Broome county, on the Susquehanna river, declaring themselves as possessing the keys of the kingdom, and of the dispensation of the fulness of times! And again, the voice of God in the chamber of old Father Whitmer, in Fayette, Seneca county, and at sundry times, and in divers places through all the travels and tribulations of this Church of Jesus Christ of Latter-day Saints! And the voice of Michael, the archangel; the voice of Gabriel, and of Raphael, and of divers angels, from Michael or Adam down to the present time, all declaring their dispensation, their rights, their keys, their honors, their majesty and glory,

This, then, is the context in which "hope" is used in this verse. It is a lively expectation, based upon the witness from heaven, promising a thing shall surely be. It is because of a person's confidence in God's promise to them they enjoy this kind of "hope." Joseph wrote of "hope" because he has had so many witnesses to him from beyond the veil that his faith was unshakable in the expectation of all the promises to be realized.[508]

I use the word "hope" in this chapter the same way. Foundational to "hope" is knowledge from heaven. Heaven's promise comes first from ministering angels, then directly from the Lord. Between the time of the promise and the fulfillment of the promise the term "hope" applies. The one possessing "hope" knows he has a promise from God. Until the promise is realized, he remains certain because of the promise from heaven he received; which is called "hope" by the prophets.

Nephi's brother Jacob tied his "hope" to the "many revelations and spirit of prophecy" which gave him "hope." His "hope" was so powerful a force he could "command mountains" in the name of Jesus and be obeyed.[509] He was not

---

and the power of their priesthood; giving line upon line, precept upon precept; here a little, and there a little; giving us consolation by holding forth that which is to come, confirming our hope!"

[508] Snuffer, Denver C., Jr. *Eighteen Verses*. Salt Lake City: Mill Creek Press, 2007, p. 66.

[509] Jacob 4: 6: "Wherefore, we search the prophets, and we have many revelations and the spirit of prophecy; and having all these witnesses we obtain a hope, and our faith becometh unshaken, insomuch that we truly can command in the name of Jesus and the very trees obey us, or the mountains, or the waves of the sea."

speaking of a wish or longing. He is describing a powerful connection to heaven.

In the afterlife, between the crucifixion and resurrection of the Lord, there were those who met Him in the world of the spirits of the deceased. Those who were able to gather into His light and converse with Him did not include all of the dead. It required the ability to endure His presence. The audience who met Him had acquired glory in mortality, and therefore, could endure His glory while in the spirit world.[510] Those who had not acquired glory by obedience while mortal, dwelt in darkness in the afterlife, and were unable to enter into the glory of His countenance.[511]

Those who had the required glory to endure His presence in the world of deceased spirits had acquired the necessary "hope" while they were mortal. Before they died, they were living with promises from heaven that they were heirs entitled to a glorious resurrection. Here is how they are described: "All these had departed the mortal life, firm in the hope of a glorious resurrection, through the grace of God the Father and his Only Begotten Son, Jesus Christ." (D&C 138: 14.)

They had knowledge of Jesus Christ. They had a testimony from Jesus. Their "knowledge" came from entering into His

---

[510]The revelation describes them in these words: "Their countenances shone, and the radiance from the presence of the Lord rested upon them, and they sang praises unto his holy name." (D&C 138: 24.)

[511]"But unto the wicked he did not go, and among the ungodly and the unrepentant who had defiled themselves while in the flesh, his voice was not raised; Neither did the rebellious who rejected the testimonies and the warnings of the ancient prophets behold his presence, nor look upon his face. Where these were, darkness reigned, but among the righteous there was peace[.]" (D&C 138: 20-22.)

presence while still in the flesh. Moroni, who also possessed this knowledge of Christ,[512] describes it using the Brother of Jared:

> And now, as I, Moroni, said I could not make a full account of these things which are written, therefore it sufficeth me to say that Jesus showed himself unto this man in the spirit, even after the manner and in the likeness of the same body even as he showed himself unto the Nephites. And he ministered unto him even as he ministered unto the Nephites; and all this, that this man might know that he was God, because of the many great works which the Lord had showed unto him. And because of the knowledge of this man he could not be kept from beholding within the veil; and he saw the finger of Jesus, which, when he saw, he fell with fear; for he knew that it was the finger of the Lord; and he had faith no longer, for he knew, nothing doubting. Wherefore, having this perfect knowledge of God, he could not be kept from within the veil; therefore he saw Jesus; and he did minister unto him. (Ether 3: 17-20.)

The Lord bestows upon those who love Him and purify themselves before Him "knowledge" of Him. This knowledge is glory, it is intelligence.[513] If it is received here it equips the recipient to endure His presence in a world of glory.[514] Every

---

[512]Moroni gives some explanation of the extent of his knowledge in Mormon, chapter 8.

[513]"The glory of God is intelligence, or, in other words, light and truth." (D&C 93: 36.)

[514]"But great and marvelous are the works of the Lord, and the mysteries of his kingdom which he showed unto us, which surpass all understanding in glory, and in might, and in dominion; Which he commanded us we should not write while we were yet in the Spirit, and are not lawful for man to utter; Neither is man capable to make them

one of us are invited to receive it. Every soul gains this knowledge in the same way, based on the same conditions.[515]

During the first phase of Mormonism, Joseph Smith taught this information and encouraged all mankind to go forward and have their calling and election made sure. The entire world was invited by Joseph Smith to seek their calling and election:

> We have no claim in our eternal compact, in relation to eternal things, unless our actions and contracts and all things tend to this. But after all this, you have got to make you calling and election sure. If this injunction would lie largely on those to whom it was spoken, how much more those of the present generation! (*TPJS*, p. 306.)

This sacred knowledge that your calling is sure comes from heaven. When it is given, the recipient has an anchor to their soul. They have hope. Their hope cannot be dimmed by any earthly trial or difficulty. It secures for them a perfect brightness of hope which can never fade.

---

known, for they are only to be seen and understood by the power of the Holy Spirit, which God bestows on those who love him, and purify themselves before him; To whom he grants this privilege of seeing and knowing for themselves; That through the power and manifestation of the Spirit, while in the flesh, they may be able to bear his presence in the world of glory." (D&C 76: 114-118.)

[515]"Verily, thus saith the Lord: It shall come to pass that every soul who forsaketh his sins and cometh unto me, and calleth on my name, and obeyeth my voice, and keepeth my commandments, shall see my face and know that I am; And that I am the true light that lighteth every man that cometh into the world; And that I am in the Father, and the Father in me, and the Father and I are one–" (D&C 93: 1-3) "There is a law, irrevocably decreed in heaven before the foundations of this world, upon which all blessings are predicated--And when we obtain any blessing from God, it is by obedience to that law upon which it is predicated." (D&C 130: 20-21.)

Joseph taught that every Latter-day Saint needed to acquire knowledge of God for themselves, and not to rely on others for saving knowledge. If they did not have this knowledge they could not gain eternal life.[516] Unless they possess this knowledge, they will grow weary in their minds and will be unable to endure in hope until the end.[517] Those who do not gain this hope by a promise directly from heaven have only a vain religion. It cannot save them. They will never be able to lay hold on eternal life.[518]

---

[516]"An actual knowledge to any person, that the course of life which he pursues is according to the will of God, is essentially necessary to enable him to have that confidence in God without which no person can obtain eternal life. It was this that enabled the ancient saints to endure all their afflictions and persecutions, and to take joyfully the spoiling of their goods, knowing (not believing merely) that they had a more enduring substance. (Heb. 10:34.)" (*Lectures*, 6: 2.)

[517]"Such was, and always will be, the situation of the saints of God, that unless they have an actual knowledge that the course they are pursuing is according to the will of God they will grow weary in their minds, and faint; for such has been, and always will be, the opposition in the hearts of unbelievers and those that know not God against the pure and unadulterated religion of heaven (the only thing which insures eternal life), that they will persecute to the uttermost all that worship God according to his revelations, receive the truth in the love of it, and submit themselves to be guided and directed by his will; and drive them to such extremities that nothing short of an actual knowledge of their being the favorites of heaven, and of their having embraced the order of things which God has established for the redemption of man, will enable them to exercise that confidence in him, necessary for them to overcome the world, and obtain that crown of glory which is laid up for them that fear God." (*Lectures* 6: 4.)

[518]"It is in vain for persons to fancy to themselves that they are heirs with those, or can be heirs with them, who have offered their all in sacrifice, and by this means obtained faith in God and favor with him so as to obtain eternal life, unless they, in like manner, offer unto him the same sacrifice, and through that offering obtain the knowledge that they are accepted of him." (*Lectures* 6: 8.)

This knowledge is required for eternal life. So, also is the "testimony of Jesus." Only those who have a testimony spoken to them by Jesus that they are heirs of salvation will be able to endure the glory of the Celestial Kingdom. As Joseph explained it:

> Now for the secret and grand key. Though they might hear the voice of God and know that Jesus was the Son of God, this would be no evidence that their election and calling was made sure, that they had part with Christ, and were joint heirs with Him. They then would want that more sure word of prophecy, that they were sealed in the heavens and had the promise of eternal life in the kingdom of God. Then, having this promise sealed unto them, it was an anchor to the soul, sure and steadfast. Though the thunders might roll and lightnings flash, and earthquakes bellow, and war gather thick around, yet this hope and knowledge would support the soul in every hour of trial, trouble and tribulation. Then knowledge through our Lord and Savior Jesus Christ is the grand key that unlocks the glories and mysteries of the kingdom of heaven. (*TPJS*, p. 298.)

The testimony to them from Jesus, promising them eternal life, is the more sure word of prophecy. Christ provides it. It is in this sense that the "testimony of Jesus" is used in scripture. It is not something one possesses, speaks or bears to another. It is something Christ delivers by His own voice to them. Christ testifies; hence the phrase "the testimony of Jesus." All those who seek His glory will need to acquire His testimony to them that they are saved. They must acquire His Word. When Joseph and Sidney were shown the Celestial Kingdom, they saw those who obtained

this glory. They were sealed by the Holy Spirit of promise.[519] Those
who fall short of this, and do not receive this witness from Christ
in mortality but receive it afterwards, will be heirs of the Terrestrial
Kingdom.[520] These good but deluded souls trusted in men, rather
than in Christ. As a result they fall short of the glory necessary to
enter God's presence. They do not die firm in the hope of a
glorious resurrection, because Christ has not promised it to them.

In the first phase, this kind of hope was offered to all. Joseph
spoke of it frequently. His revelations confirm it was a vital part of
the restored faith. All followers of Christ's Gospel were expected
to obtain hope from Him. It would come from the Holy Spirit of

---

[519]"And again we bear record--for we saw and heard, and this is the
testimony of the gospel of Christ concerning them who shall come forth
in the resurrection of the just-- They are they who received the testimony
of Jesus, and believed on his name and were baptized after the manner
of his burial, being buried in the water in his name, and this according to
the commandment which he has given-- That by keeping the
commandments they might be washed and cleansed from all their sins,
and receive the Holy Spirit by the laying on of the hands of him who is
ordained and sealed unto this power; And who overcome by faith, and
are sealed by the Holy Spirit of promise, which the Father sheds forth
upon all those who are just and true." (D&C 76: 50-53.)

[520]"And again, we saw the terrestrial world, and behold and lo, these are
they who are of the terrestrial, whose glory differs from that of the
church of the Firstborn who have received the fulness of the Father,
even as that of the moon differs from the sun in the firmament. Behold,
these are they who died without law; And also they who are the spirits of
men kept in prison, whom the Son visited, and preached the gospel unto
them, that they might be judged according to men in the flesh; Who
received not the testimony of Jesus in the flesh, but afterwards received
it. These are they who are honorable men of the earth, who were blinded
by the craftiness of men." (D&C 76: 71-75.)

promise sealing a person up to eternal life by revelation from God.[521]

By the fourth phase of Mormonism, a church controlled ceremony known as the Second Endowment or Second Anointing replaced the first phase aspiration to receive an audience with Christ. There are many records that testify of the church's practice of giving Second Anointings to individuals who occupy church leadership,[522] or who provide evidence of extraordinary loyalty to church leaders.[523] The criteria requiring loyalty to church leaders, even to the point of surrendering life to protect and defend them, contrasts somewhat with Joseph Smith's first phase teachings about devotion and sacrifice to Christ. The second anointing ceremony originated with Joseph Smith in the first phase. However, Joseph (and revelations received through him) explained the need for all promises to be sealed by heaven. One of Joseph's foundational principles of priesthood power or authority was the necessity for

---

[521]See D&C 76: 23; 132: 18-19.

[522]For a discussion about the church's practice in the fourth phase, see Anderson, Devery S. *The Development of LDS Temple Worship: 1846-2000.* Salt Lake City: Signature Books, 2011, Buerger, David John. *The Mysteries of Godliness.* San Francisco: Smith Research Associates, 1994.

[523]"Recommends for the second anointing should only be given to men and women who have lived together as husband and wife, and who through long years of faithfulness are still found to be worthy before the Lord and their brethren. They should be men of good report, men whose faith has never been shaken, whose integrity to the Lord and his servants has been beyond question, men who have been valiant for the truth, men who have either defended the servants of the Lord or would do so at all hazards should circumstances require it at their hands." (Buerger, David John. *The Mysteries of Godliness.* San Francisco: Smith Research Associates, 1994, citing Joseph F. Smith and Anthon Lund's letter of October 23, 1911 to Stake President William C. Partridge, p. 120.)

a connection to heaven. Without heaven being involved, there was, and is, no priesthood power or authority.[524] The idea that heaven remains involved in fourth phase practice is still given lip service. But it is no longer expected for the heavens to open, nor for the Lord to be involved in fourth phase second anointing rites. I have searched for an example of a fourth phase, second anointing account that includes any instance of the Lord appearing, or any angelic ratification to confirm the ordinance, and have been unable to find one. The latest book to discuss second anointing practices has details of many of the dates and persons involved, but lacks any example of heavenly ratification or involvement.

In the fourth phase of Mormonism, the ceremony is performed by a church leader or leaders, and involves washing feet, sealing up to eternal life by the authority held by the living president of the church– handed down to him from Joseph Smith through a line of successors– and is done inside the temple holy of holies.[525] The ceremony is claimed to make the calling and election sure to the recipients.

After the ceremony is concluded, the need for any subsequent audience with Christ has been removed, at least in the mind of the

---

[524]See, e.g., D&C 121: 36.

[525]George Q. Cannon described the practice of Brigham Young, which still continues to be followed: "When he sealed a man up to eternal life, he bestowed upon him the blessings pertaining to eternity, and to the Godhead, or when he delegated others to do it in his stead, God in the eternal world recorded the act; the blessings that were sealed upon that man or that woman, they were sealed to be binding in this life, and in that life which is to come; they became part of the records of eternity, and would be fulfilled to the very letter upon the heads of those upon whom they were pronounced, provided they were faithful before God, and fulfilled their part of the covenant." (JD 24: 274.)

recipient. In the journals of those who have received this ceremony, there is no record of any person continuing thereafter to press forward and receive an audience with the Lord.

Joseph Smith explained having one's calling and election is to gain "an anchor to the soul." When a man knows he is the Lord's, there is no apprehension about his standing before the Lord, the life he has lived, or what defines his greatest life's worth. These people possess a knowledge from Christ, which removes all doubt, as in the case of the Brother of Jared. Joseph Smith's teaching mirrored the explanation given by Moroni:

> And because of the knowledge of this man he could not be kept from beholding within the veil; and he saw the finger of Jesus, which, when he saw, he fell with fear; for he knew that it was the finger of the Lord; and he had faith no longer, for he knew, nothing doubting. Wherefore, having this perfect knowledge of God, he could not be kept from within the veil; therefore he saw Jesus; and he did minister unto him. (Ether 3: 19-20.)

When this knowledge from Christ is obtained, and the Lord has directly ministered to a man, the person does not thereafter have doubts. They no longer have faith. They possess knowledge.

The church's second anointing ceremony does not seem to have the same effect. In the example of J. Reuben Clark, Jr., a member of the First Presidency, he received his second anointing from other church leaders. Initially, he was recommended for this blessing in a letter sent by an Apostle to church President Grant in 1942. Recommending the ordinance for Elder Clark, the letter said, in relevant part:

> Dear President Grant:
>
> If the following named brethren, General Authorities of the Church, and their wives have received

their Second blessings, the Salt Lake Temple Records do not disclose the fact. I therefore conclude that they have not except possibly Pres[ident] Hart who may have received his blessings in the Logan Temple: J. Reuben Clark Jr., ...

I understand that it is in order for a member of the Council of Twelve to recommend worthy members to the President of the Church to receive their Second blessings. Accordingly, I recommend that these brethren and their wives be invited to receive their blessings. –George F. Richards diary, Apr. 19, 1934[526]

Eight months later, in a meeting between the First Presidency, Quorum of Twelve and Patriarch, the matter was taken up and approved. The second anointing of J. Reuben Clark, Jr. was to be performed by Apostle George F. Richards, as directed by President Grant:

I attended regular Thu[rsday] meetings. At 10:00 A.M. meeting of the [First] Presidency, the Twelve and the Patriarch held in the Temple, the matter of allowing the administration of second blessings was considered. I brought up the subject at our last Quarterly meeting of the Twelve held in the Temple Sept. 29th last. I made quite an extended talk on the subject at that time at the conclusion of which it was decided by vote to present the question to the Council of First Presidency, the Twelve and the Patriarch. ...I had a chance to explain, and it was decided that the four members of the Council, viz. J. Reuben Clark Jr., ... should be privileged to receive theirs and others whom the members of this council may recommend and the Council sustain. Pres. [Heber J.] Grant appointed me to

---

[526] Anderson, Devery S. *The Development of LDS Temple Worship: 1846-2000.* Salt Lake City: Signature Books, 2011, pp. 237-238.

administer these blessings. ...–George F. Richards diary, Dec. 10, 1942.[527]

Therefore, the second anointing was given to President Clark. He had the church's ceremony promising eternal life.

Many years later, after having served in the highest councils of the church, including First Counselor in the First Presidency, President Clark was in declining health and had stopped attending his meetings. Elder Marion G. Romney would visit President Clark at his home. Elder Romney kept a diary of his visits with President Clark and recorded the following entry concerning President Clark's thoughts about his greatest accomplishment in life:

> [November 9, 1960] ...Speaking of a possible biography, he didn't express much expectation that anything would be done. He said that it had been his observation that when the funeral cortege returned from the cemetery, that usually ended that chapter. Referring to things he had done during his life which might be worthy of note was the memorandum he had written while in the State Department on the Monroe Doctrine, and also the memorandum dealing with claims against foreign governments (this one he especially mentioned). He seemed to feel that his Monroe Doctrine was his masterpiece, stating some attention had been given to re-writing the meaning of the Monroe Doctrine by others in the State Department following his time, but that it had not been done.[528]

---

[527] *Id.*, pp. 270-271.

[528] Appendix 2, *The Diaries of Marion G. Romney, 1941-1961, Abridged*, beginning on p. 282 in *The Diaries of J. Reuben Clark, 1933-1961, Abridged.* Salt Lake City: Privately Published, 2010, p. 338.

Since this was a private meeting between a member of the First Presidency and an Apostle, recorded in a private diary not then anticipated for public use, there was no reason for President Clark to be anything other than candid. The second anointing was mentioned in the diary. Therefore there was no reason to exclude anything from this discussion on the topic. It is interesting that at the end of his life he thought what was most noteworthy was his work with the State Department, rather than his church service. The power, effect, or "anchor to the soul" of the church ceremony which is said to have made his calling and election sure was not mentioned, though both of these men were familiar with its purported meaning and effect.

A month later, Elder Romney recorded this about President Clark: "[December 15, 1960] ...He was morose, tender, and discouraged."[529]

Another month later Elder Romney recorded these remarks from President Clark:

> [January 20, 1961] ... He said he thought he was about through, that he did not dread the going, but that he'd like to have a blessing because he wants peace in his mind. He said he knew he had not lived a perfect life, but that he was not conscious of ever having done any great sin. This statement he repeated several times while we were with him.[530]

This request to have a blessing to relieve his mind about his imperfect life contrasts somewhat with Joseph's teaching:

---

[529] *Id.*

[530] *Id.*, p. 339.

They then would want that more sure word of prophecy, that they were sealed in the heavens and had the promise of eternal life in the kingdom of God. Then, having this promise sealed unto them, it was an anchor to the soul, sure and steadfast. Though the thunders might roll and lightnings flash, and earthquakes bellow, and war gather thick around, yet this hope and knowledge would support the soul in every hour of trial, trouble and tribulation. (*TPJS*, p. 298.)

Later still, Elder Romney records this entry about President Clark: "[August 7, 1961] ...He was very depressed. I had a private conversation with him for half an hour and, at his request, gave him a blessing."[531]

Joseph Smith approached death with less apprehension. John Taylor, who was with him till the end, wrote this about Joseph's view of his coming slaughter:

When Joseph went to Carthage to deliver himself up to the pretended requirements of the law, two or three days previous to his assassination, he said: "I am going like a lamb to the slaughter; but I am calm as a summer's morning; I have a conscience void of offense towards God, and towards all men. I SHALL DIE INNOCENT, AND IT SHALL YET BE SAID OF ME--HE WAS MURDERED IN COLD BLOOD." (D&C 135: 4, emphasis in original.)

Others went to their deaths willingly, and without apprehension of their standing before the Lord. Stephen testified before the Jewish high council about Christ. As he finished his testimony of Christ and against them, they reviled him, gnashed their teeth upon

---

[531]*Id.*, p. 341.

him, stoned and killed him. But he went to his death confident in the glory which was his:

> When they heard these things, they were cut to the heart, and they gnashed on him with their teeth. But he, being full of the Holy Ghost, looked up stedfastly into heaven, and saw the glory of God, and Jesus standing on the right hand of God, And said, Behold, I see the heavens opened, and the Son of man standing on the right hand of God. Then they cried out with a loud voice, and stopped their ears, and ran upon him with one accord, And cast him out of the city, and stoned him: and the witnesses laid down their clothes at a young man's feet, whose name was Saul. And they stoned Stephen, calling upon God, and saying, Lord Jesus, receive my spirit. And he kneeled down, and cried with a loud voice, Lord, lay not this sin to their charge. And when he had said this, he fell asleep. (Acts 7: 54-60.)

The scriptures tell us all those who have this hope in them do not taste death. The bitterness of death is swallowed up in the joy of Christ. "And it shall come to pass that those that die in me shall not taste of death, for it shall be sweet unto them; And they that die not in me, wo unto them, for their death is bitter." (D&C 42: 46-47.) This is what Joseph meant by having an "anchor to the soul" through the hope of a glorious resurrection in Christ.

Joseph begged us to not forget this doctrine. He cursed any who would teach different than this:

> Oh! I beseech you to go forward, go forward and make your calling and your election sure; and if any man preach any other Gospel than that which I have preached, he shall be cursed;[532] and some of you who now hear me shall see

---

[532] Earlier in the same sermon Joseph commented: "False prophets always arise to oppose the true prophets and they will prophesy so very near the truth that they will deceive almost the very chosen ones." (*TPJS*, p. 365.)

it, and know that I testify the truth concerning them. (*TPJS*, p. 366.)

From Joseph's perspective, abandonment of this kind of teaching would invoke cursing, rather than blessings. When Correlation published the 2007 Priesthood and Relief Society manual, *Teachings of the Presidents of the Church: Joseph Smith*, this quote was omitted.[533] This was a first phase teaching, but has become inapplicable to fourth phase Mormonism. Correlation has eliminated the topic of "calling and election" from permitted subjects in church teaching materials. Those who have done this, in Joseph's words, "shall be cursed."

Earlier we asked, "What did Joseph Smith Restore?" The answer at that time focused on first phase Mormonism. In it, his example and teachings all focused on the opening of heaven. Not just for him, but for any soul who would ask of God, as James instructed.[534] The Book of Mormon does not ask any one to trust in it, but to ask God about it and trust God.[535] Joseph's restored religion was based on people obtaining knowledge from God for themselves. It pronounces cursing on those who rely on men, and do not use revelation to get knowledge from God for themselves.

His sermon implies any deliberate abandonment of this teaching is tantamount to becoming a "false prophet" resulting in a curse upon such a man, or men.

[533] I searched the text to find it and could not. Thinking I may have made a mistake, I visited the church's website (www.lds.org) and did an on-line search for this quote in the electronic version. The automated search did not find this quote.

[534] See James 1: 5, JS-H 1: 13.

[535] Moroni 10: 4-5.

It warns us against thinking Christ has finished His work and given His power unto men.[536] It denounces those who believe small errors will not matter because God will be content to administer mild punishment before exalting them.[537] It denounces those who are proud, and warns that all of us have gone astray, even the humble followers of Christ, because we are led astray by the incorrect precepts of men.[538] It tells those of us who claim we are "Zion" that we should never be at ease, thinking we prosper and therefore, it is well for us.[539] It demands we listen only to God, and never to men who will advance their own precepts.[540] It tells us that we should never stop receiving revelation to guide us, because when we stop receiving our own revelation we will be damned.[541] It includes this warning:

---

[536] See 2 Ne. 28: 5.

[537] See 2 Ne. 28: 7-9.

[538] "Yea, they have all gone out of the way; they have become corrupted. Because of pride, and because of false teachers, and false doctrine, their churches have become corrupted, and their churches are lifted up; because of pride they are puffed up. They rob the poor because of their fine sanctuaries; they rob the poor because of their fine clothing; and they persecute the meek and the poor in heart, because in their pride they are puffed up. They wear stiff necks and high heads; yea, and because of pride, and wickedness, and abominations, and whoredoms, they have all gone astray save it be a few, who are the humble followers of Christ; nevertheless, they are led, that in many instances they do err because they are taught by the precepts of men." (2 Ne. 28: 11-14.)

[539] See 2 Ne. 28: 21, 24-25.

[540] See 2 Ne. 28: 26, 28-30.

[541] See 2 Ne. 28: 26-29.

Cursed is he that putteth his trust in man, or maketh flesh his arm, or shall hearken unto the precepts of men, save their precepts shall be given by the power of the Holy Ghost. Wo be unto the Gentiles, saith the Lord God of Hosts! For notwithstanding I shall lengthen out mine arm unto them from day to day, they will deny me[.]" (2 Ne. 28: 31-32.)

These first phase teachings still exist in the Book of Mormon. Fourth phase Mormonism still accepts that volume of scripture. However, the current view applies those words to people outside the church. They mean someone other than us. The people fourth phase Mormonism believes to be in peril of damnation are non-Mormons who fail to accept the church, refuse to be baptized, won't accept the Book of Mormon, and reject our ordinances. But, as we have seen, warning the non-audience makes no sense. These warnings address the Latter-day Saints.

First phase Mormonism sought to revolutionize the individual, taught individual salvation, required individual revelation, and claimed the heavens were again open to all. Joseph taught: "I advise all to go on to perfection, and search deeper and deeper into the mysteries of Godliness." (*TPJS*, p. 364.) Fourth phase Mormonism encourages devotion to the institution, offers institutional salvation,[542] claims God has entrusted the power to

---

[542]"[The] President is the mouthpiece of God, the revelator, the translator, the seer, and the Prophet of God to the whole Church. It is he who holds the keys of this Holy Priesthood-the keys which unlock the doors of the Temples of God and of the ordinances of His house for the salvation of the living and the redemption of the dead. It is he who holds the sealing power, by which man may bind on earth and it shall be bound in heaven, and by which men duly authorized and appointed of him who holds the keys may loose on earth and it will be loosed in heaven. This is the order of the Holy Priesthood." (*Teachings of the Presidents of the*

save or damn to man because keys to the heavenly gift are currently in possession of the church,[543] and the church is Zion.[544] Searching into "mysteries" is discouraged and, according to church manuals, unnecessary.[545]

The contrast between the first and fourth phases can be explained in part because of growth. Joseph Smith presided over a church that grew from a handful to approximately 25,000. The saints were all encouraged to gather to a central location and be instructed directly by a very accessible Prophet Joseph. In contrast, fourth phase Mormonism numbers in the millions, is spread across the globe, speaking diverse languages and living in divergent cultures. "Because of the multicultural base of the Church and its rapid growth, gospel teachers are asked to teach a wide array of

---

Church: Joseph F. Smith. Salt Lake City: Intellectual Reserve Inc., 1998, p. 141.)

[543]"The priesthood of God holds the keys of salvation." (*Teachings of the Presidents of the Church: Harold B. Lee*. Salt Lake City: Intellectual Reserve, Inc., 2000, p. 89.)

[544]"Who should attend sacrament meetings? The commandment was addressed through the Prophet to those 'whose feet stand upon the land of Zion,' the membership of his church [see D&C 59:3, 9]. The requirement is not confined to adults but includes young and old alike." (*Teachings of Presidents of the Church: Spencer W. Kimball*. Salt Lake City: Intellectual Reserve Inc., 2006, p. 172.)

[545]This statement appears in the *New Testament Gospel Doctrine Teacher's Manual*, p.170: "Elder Joseph B. Wirthlin counseled: 'God has revealed everything necessary for our salvation. We should teach and dwell on the things that have been revealed and avoid delving into so-called mysteries. My counsel to teachers in the Church, whether they instruct in wards and stakes, Church institutions of higher learning, institutes of religion, seminaries, or even as parents in their homes, is to base their teachings on the scriptures and the words of latter-day prophets' (in Conference Report, Oct. 1994, 101; or Ensign, Nov. 1994, 77)."

members with radically different backgrounds, needs, and levels of understanding and spiritual preparation. This continues to be a major challenge to the Church."[546] In Joseph Smith's time, his approach to leading was far more simple: "I teach them correct principles and they govern themselves."[547]

Not all the differences are attributed to these contrasts. Growth may have motivated the changes, but deliberate choices have been made along the way. In phase four, the church management system compels change. This is because much of the decision-making adapts church programs and language to reflect social statistical trends in both church members and target convert populations.

Ultimately, the church has an institutional life separate from its individual members. The church has always been an earthly institution. It will always be an earthly institution. Individuals, in one way or another, will continue forever.[548] Therefore, salvation is always an individual challenge. Now we turn to the real purpose for the Gospel's restoration. How do we obtain salvation.

---

[546] *Encyclopedia of Mormonism,* p. 1443.

[547] Quoted by John Taylor, in *Millennial Star* 13 [15 November 1851]: p. 339.

[548] "I am dwelling on the immortality of the spirit of man. Is it logical to say that the intelligence of spirits is immortal, and yet that it had a beginning? The intelligence of spirits had no beginning, neither will it have an end. That is good logic. That which has a beginning may have an end. There never was a time when there were not spirits; for they are co-equal [co-eternal] with our Father in heaven." (*TPJS*, p. 353.) Joseph Smith used the word "co-equal" and Joseph Fielding Smith as editor inserted the bracketed word "co-eternal" because he understood it was in that sense Joseph used the word "co-equal."

Chapter 17

INDIVIDUAL SALVATION

*f*ourth phase Mormonism not only institutionalizes change, it cannot resist changing. Focus groups and polling data, the primary management tools used by the church, leave it unable to resist change as a result of the shifting public preferences.

The Internet has reduced attention spans and brought us a world full of sound-bite answers. Deep introspection and careful analysis are becoming the limited provence of a few academics. Mormonism in its original form mandated careful, solemn and ponderous thought from its believers.[549] Today such thought is not required, and in many instances not well tolerated. Correlation has not created this new kind of superficial mind set, but it takes advantage of it. Instead of insisting the saints delve deeply into their faith, Correlation has accepted, and now propound a

---

[549] "[T]he things of God are of deep import; and time, and experience, and careful and ponderous and solemn thoughts can only find them out." (*TPJS*, p. 137.)

superficial approach to Mormonism. The four-year cycle of Sunday school/relief society/priesthood manuals attempts to survey the four standard works (Old Testament, New Testament, Book of Mormon and Doctrine and Covenants/Church History) by devoting a year to each volume of scripture. The rate at which these volumes of scripture are covered provides only a broad survey of the material. Those who trust the church is doing exactly what Christ wants it to do conclude these hasty trips through the scriptures are the inspired approach. We have the impression that God wants us to know a little, perhaps very little, about doctrine. We believe He wants us to feel good, and be assured we are the special, loved, elect followers. In other words, we are chosen people. Such an approach fails to offer a careful analysis of Joseph's teachings. It avoids unpleasant information about the history of the church, and conceals all the direful warnings about how the Latter-day Saint church was predicted to fail, and in all likelihood has failed to secure the fullness of the priesthood.

No matter which phase of Mormonism is considered, two things remain constant. First, salvation as explained by the doctrines of the Gospel has always been individual, and never collective. Second, the foundational principals of the religion claim that any individual can approach God on the same terms any other saved soul. This has been true from the time of Adam, and includes all those in scripture who have been similarly saved. Early in this book we asked what Joseph Smith restored. At bedrock he restored the idea God still cares about each soul, and will reveal Himself to anyone. The great benefit of living after Joseph Smith is his vast doctrinal legacy implemented through well defined ordinances. Now, in addition to James 1: 5, which tells us to ask God, who is no respecter of persons, we also have the Book of Mormon, the

Doctrine & Covenants, the Pearl of Great Price, and volumes of Joseph's teachings, diaries, and history where it is repeatedly reconfirmed that God will reveal Himself to mankind. If the heavens opened to Joseph Smith with only the Old and New Testament to guide him, certainly we can do the same. We have far more available to guide us. A chorus of prophetic voices have been added to James'. They all join together to encourage us to find our way back to God's presence.

As Christ's mortal ministry drew to a close, He promised it would not be the end. In one of His final sermons, He adopted the image of the "vine" used by Isaiah, Ezekiel and Jeremiah. These earlier prophets condemned Israel for failing to bear fruit. His teaching explained how living "fruit" could return:

> I am the true vine, and my Father is the husbandman. Every branch in me that beareth not fruit he taketh away: and every branch that beareth fruit, he purgeth it, that it may bring forth more fruit. Now ye are clean through the word which I have spoken unto you. Abide in me, and I in you. As the branch cannot bear fruit of itself, except it abide in the vine; no more can ye, except ye abide in me. I am the vine, ye are the branches: He that abideth in me, and I in him, the same bringeth forth much fruit: for without me ye can do nothing. If a man abide not in me, he is cast forth as a branch, and is withered; and men gather them, and cast them into the fire, and they are burned. If ye abide in me, and my words abide in you, ye shall ask what ye will, and it shall be done unto you. Herein is my Father glorified, that ye bear much fruit; so shall ye be my disciples. (John 15: 1-8.)

Fruit comes only from Him. Not from the outward observance of physical ordinances. Not from a claim to be "chosen" by God. Not from having scriptures written by authentic messengers sent by

God. Nor from claims to righteous conduct. Although you may be among the chosen, you still must study scripture, and display righteous conduct. These are the result of connecting to the Living Vine. Signs of your faith in Him are not your own independent good conduct or mere imitation. As soon as we connect to Him as the "true vine" His grace, power and light begins to animate you from within. You begin to "live" in Him. Apart from Him, all of us are merely "withered branches," which will be "cast into the fire."

Even if we belong to a church He claims as His, and have received all its ordinances, we are nothing apart from Him. Ancient Israel was His, but they were condemned for failing to bear fruit. Those He came to visit in mortality were His. But only a few accepted Him, allowed Him to minister to them, and received the light of His countenance,[550] thereby becoming part of the true vine. This concept applied not only to the generation He lived in as a mortal, but it is how any man in any age must follow Him. Joseph's

---

[550]The Psalmist petitioned for the Lord's deliverance in these words: "We have heard with our ears, O God, our fathers have told us, what work thou didst in their days, in the times of old. How thou didst drive out the heathen with thy hand, and plantedst them; how thou didst afflict the people, and cast them out. For they got not the land in possession by their own sword, neither did their own arm save them: but thy right hand, and thine arm, and the light of thy countenance, because thou hadst a favour unto them. Thou art my King, O God: command deliverances for Jacob." (Psm. 44: 1-4.) The prayer offered by Zechariah in the Temple just prior to Gabriel's appearance petitioned: "Bless us, O our Father, all of us as one, with the light of Thy countenance. For in the light of Thy countenance has Thou, Jehovah, our God, given us the law of life, and loving mercy, and righteousness, and blessing, and compassion, and life, and peace." (Edersheim, Alfred. *The Temple: Its Ministry and Services*. Massachusetts: Hendrickson Publishers, 1994, p. 129.)

restored religion reaffirms Christ is the vine, and we must live in Him and He in us.

Christ commanded us to "abide" in Him, promising He in turn will abide in us. This is something more and different from the gift of the Holy Ghost. The Lord promised He intends to personally be involved in our lives. He is not a distant personality we learn about from scripture or testimony from others. He will directly, immediately abide **in** us. He said any branch claiming salvation cannot bear fruit of itself. According to Joseph, the only way for fruit to appear is for you to abide in the vine. You must let Him take up His abode with you.[551] He will come to you, as He has promised.[552]

In the first phase of Mormonism, Joseph Smith taught everyone should expect Christ's personal ministry. He insisted that everything he received was available to even the least of the Latter-day Saints. Joseph said we all should welcome the Second

---

[551] See John 14: 23: "Jesus answered and said unto him, If a man love me, he will keep my words: and my Father will love him, and we will come unto him, and make our abode with him." This promise was made in contemplation of Christ's coming death. The promise compels the conclusion that He always intended a post-resurrection ministry to His followers.

[552] See, e.g., Rev. 3: 20-22: "Behold, I stand at the door, and knock: if any man hear my voice, and open the door, I will come in to him, and will sup with him, and he with me. To him that overcometh will I grant to sit with me in my throne, even as I also overcame, and am set down with my Father in his throne. He that hath an ear, let him hear what the Spirit saith unto the churches." Read again the words of the sacrament prayer, D&C 20: 77, 79. It is a petition for "His spirit"– i.e., Christ's– to be with you. Not the Holy Ghost, which you should have previously received.

Comforter, or the personal ministry of Jesus Christ in our lives.[553] This personal appearance of Christ to His followers was an intended part of the Gospel in first phase Mormonism.

Joseph explained the appearance of Christ was promised in the Gospel of John:

> The other Comforter spoken of is a subject of great interest, and perhaps understood by few of this generation. After a person has faith in Christ, repents of his sins, and is baptized for the remission of his sins and receives the Holy Ghost, (by the laying on of hands), which is the first Comforter, then let him continue to humble himself before God, hungering and thirsting after righteousness, and living by every word of God, and the Lord will soon say unto him, Son, thou shalt be exalted.

> When the Lord has thoroughly proved him, and finds that the man is determined to serve Him at all hazards, then the man will find his calling and his election made sure, then it will be his privilege to receive the other Comforter, which the Lord hath promised the Saints, as is recorded in the testimony of St. John, in the 14th chapter, from the 12th to the 27th verses. (*TPJS*, p. 150.)

The verses Joseph mentions are in the New Testament where we find the promises from Christ that he would visit His followers

---

[553]See *TPJS*, p. 149: " This principle ought (in its proper place) to be taught, for God hath not revealed anything to Joseph, but what He will make known unto the Twelve, and even the least Saint may know all things as fast as he is able to bear them, for the day must come when no man need say to his neighbor, Know ye the Lord; for all shall know Him (who remain) from the least to the greatest. How is this to be done? It is to be done by this sealing power, and the other Comforter spoken of, which will be manifest by revelation."

after His death. Christ, and the Father would visit them.[554] John 14: 23: "Jesus answered and said unto him, If a man love me, he will keep my words: and my Father will love him, and we will come unto him, and make our abode with him." Joseph explained: "John 14: 23--The appearing of the Father and the Son, in that verse, is a personal appearance; and the idea that the Father and the Son dwell in a man's heart is an old sectarian notion, and is false." (D&C 130: 3.)

Christ explained we cannot produce fruit except we abide in Him. He is the vine from which any branch must take nourishment or it will die. But, if we do abide in Him, He will abide in us. That connection is so vital, Christ reduced all our other efforts to nothing: "for without me ye can do nothing." The most remarkable thing about Joseph Smith's teachings is his confident assertion that this is possible for anyone and available to everyone. The religion he established claimed this was not only available, but essential to salvation.

The Lord does still personally appear to mankind. I am a witness to that fact. He first appeared to me February 13, 2003. I have written a book about the topic titled *The Second Comforter: Conversing With the Lord Through the Veil*. That book does not contain any details about the Lord's ministry to me, but affirms it took place.

---

[554]"I will not leave you comfortless: I will come to you. Yet a little while, and the world seeth me no more; but ye see me: because I live, ye shall live also. At that day ye shall know that I am in my Father, and ye in me, and I in you. He that hath my commandments, and keepeth them, he it is that loveth me: and he that loveth me shall be loved of my Father, and I will love him, and will manifest myself to him. Judas saith unto him, not Iscariot, Lord, how is it that thou wilt manifest thyself unto us, and not unto the world? Jesus answered and said unto him, If a man love me, he will keep my words: and my Father will love him, and we will come unto him, and make our abode with him." (John 14: 18-23.)

For anyone who reads this book I soberly declare: I know He lives. I have seen and spoken with Him. The body of quotes used in *The Second Comforter* to establish the doctrine come almost exclusively from the teachings in the first phase of Mormonism. I declare those teachings are true. The Lord can, and does still minister and save souls in the same way and on the same terms as He did with Adam, Enoch, Noah, Moses, Isaiah, Elijah, Elisha, Ezekiel, Jeremiah, Lehi, Nephi, Alma, Malachi, John the Baptist, Peter, James, John, Mormon, Moroni, Joseph Smith and others. I have added only a brief punctuation to their testimonies, inserting a comma in place of the period some believe exists. The story of Christ's ministry continues still. It continues for you. You were intended to find Him during mortality. You were intended to be redeemed, mount up on wings of faith,[555] and walk back to His presence.[556] The Church of Jesus Christ of Latter-day Saints is more than a great aid in this process. It is a restored blueprint to accomplish it. Even if part of the blueprint has been removed, and unnecessary additions are now scribbled on them, the plan still remains in the church.

I converted to Mormonism in its fourth phase. The radical changes described in this book had already taken place. Despite

---

[555] Isa. 40: 31: "But they that wait upon the Lord shall renew their strength; they shall mount up with wings as eagles; they shall run, and not be weary; and they shall walk, and not faint."

[556] Brigham Young explained: "Let me give you the definition in brief. Your *endowment* is, to receive all those ordinances in the House of the Lord, which are necessary for you, after you have departed this life, to enable you to walk back to the presence of the Father, passing the angels who stand as sentinels, being enabled to give them the key words, the signs and tokens, pertaining to the Holy Priesthood, and gain your eternal exaltation in spite of earth and hell." (*JD*, 2: 31.)

that, all of the first phase's teachings still exist, and I found them. Whether the church has kept them in their fullness, altered them in significant part, or abandoned important portions of them, by your study and faith[557] you can still find the first phase teachings, implement them, and receive first phase blessings. God restored a great body of scripture. He clarified ordinances and gave instructions for new ordinances. He established a church that was commanded to perform those ordinances. We are not to ignore, reject, or forsake it. Any earthly institution will be riddled with human failings. That is to be expected. Even with its imperfections, the church remains important.

We are commanded to be baptized in a specific way, with specific language used as part of the ordinance.[558] The church provides that ordinance. After baptism, each person is commanded to receive an ordinance of laying on hands for the Holy Ghost.[559] The church provides that ordinance.

---

[557] D&C 88: 118: "And as all have not faith, seek ye diligently and teach one another words of wisdom; yea, seek ye out of the best books words of wisdom; seek learning, even by study and also by faith."

[558] D&C 20: 72-74: "Baptism is to be administered in the following manner unto all those who repent-- The person who is called of God and has authority from Jesus Christ to baptize, shall go down into the water with the person who has presented himself or herself for baptism, and shall say, calling him or her by name: Having been commissioned of Jesus Christ, I baptize you in the name of the Father, and of the Son, and of the Holy Ghost. Amen. Then shall he immerse him or her in the water, and come forth again out of the water."

[559] D&C 20: 41-43: "And to confirm those who are baptized into the church, by the laying on of hands for the baptism of fire and the Holy Ghost, according to the scriptures; And to teach, expound, exhort, baptize, and watch over the church; And to confirm the church by the laying on of the hands, and the giving of the Holy Ghost[.]"

If Joseph died before the fullness was restored, we are no worse off than ancient Israel. After Moses was taken, outward ordinances could still be performed. Ancient Israel lost the "holy priesthood," but still kept authority to administer ordinances, including baptism, and to have angels minister to them.[560] If our circumstances are analogous, the church still has authority. It still offers some proper ordinances. We should draw close to the church, receive all it has to offer, and be blessed because of it. Because we have far more information, revelations, and scripture to guide us, we are far better off than ancient Israel. Our potential to understand more and get closer to God is much greater.

We are commanded to pay tithes.[561] The church is authorized to receive them. We are commanded to bear with one another, serve one another and give relief to those suffering under burdens so the Lord can pour out His Spirit upon us.[562] Withdrawing from

---

[560] D&C 84: 24-27: "But they hardened their hearts and could not endure his presence; therefore, the Lord in his wrath, for his anger was kindled against them, swore that they should not enter into his rest while in the wilderness, which rest is the fulness of his glory. Therefore, he took Moses out of their midst, and the Holy Priesthood also; And the lesser priesthood continued, which priesthood holdeth the key of the ministering of angels and the preparatory gospel; Which gospel is the gospel of repentance and of baptism, and the remission of sins, and the law of carnal commandments, which the Lord in his wrath caused to continue with the house of Aaron among the children of Israel until John, whom God raised up, being filled with the Holy Ghost from his mother's womb."

[561] See, e.g., D&C 64: 23: "Behold, now it is called today until the coming of the Son of Man, and verily it is a day of sacrifice, and a day for the tithing of my people; for he that is tithed shall not be burned at his coming."

[562] See Mosiah 18: 7-10: "And he did teach them, and did preach unto them repentance, and redemption, and faith on the Lord. And it came to

fellowship in the church interferes with redemption. Voluntarily leaving it is almose always wrong.[563]

Our current temple ordinances are conditional. They do not take effect until we have proven ourselves faithful. Then, if we are faithful, the time will come when we will be called up, chosen and anointed to become kings and priests, queens and priestesses, whereas now we are only ordained to become such. The realization of these blessings has always depended upon our faithfulness. You can remain true and faithful, even if all others do not. You can keep your covenants. God always recognizes those who serve and seek Him. It will be Him who confirms the final ordination. It will be Him who will anoint you as king and queen, priest and priestess. He employs no servant there.

---

pass that he said unto them: Behold, here are the waters of Mormon (for thus were they called) and now, as ye are desirous to come into the fold of God, and to be called his people, and are willing to bear one another's burdens, that they may be light; Yea, and are willing to mourn with those that mourn; yea, and comfort those that stand in need of comfort, and to stand as witnesses of God at all times and in all things, and in all places that ye may be in, even until death, that ye may be redeemed of God, and be numbered with those of the first resurrection, that ye may have eternal life-- Now I say unto you, if this be the desire of your hearts, what have you against being baptized in the name of the Lord, as a witness before him that ye have entered into a covenant with him, that ye will serve him and keep his commandments, that he may pour out his Spirit more abundantly upon you?"

[563]Even those who, like Lehi and his family, are led away into the wilderness do not depart until they are first rejected by the people. Until rejected, the prophets stayed, taught, ministered and served. Many died because they were not told to leave. This was the case with Isaiah, Christ, Stephen and James. The servants get rejected, but they almost always do not reject. They remain and serve.

Suppose the case Daniel Peterson made is wrong. He argues, in complete opposition to scripture,[564] that Latter-day Saints cannot lose priesthood authority even if we are wicked. Remember his statement quoted earlier:

> Unless and until superior priesthood authority withdraws permission to exercise priestly functions, a legitimately ordained holder of the priesthood may continue to perform valid priesthood ordinances —however unrighteous he may personally be, however dead to spiritual promptings, and however unlikely it may be that he will ever actually exercise his priesthood. [Ftnt: The ancient Christian church faced this problem in the form of the Donatist schism, which was finally declared heretical in AD 405. The Donatists held that unrighteousness in a bishop or priest invalidated any and all ordinances that he might have performed. However, the Synod of Arles determined in AD 314 that the validity of baptisms and ordinations and the like did not depend upon the worthiness or merit of the officiator. ...Granted, the Christian church at this period was essentially apostate, but Latter-day Saints take basically the same position, and for good reason. If serious sin, as such, invalidated priesthood ordinances, we could never know whose marriage was legal, or who was really a member of the church. Did the

---

[564]See D&C 121: 36-38: "That the rights of the priesthood are inseparably connected with the powers of heaven, and that the powers of heaven cannot be controlled nor handled only upon the principles of righteousness. That they may be conferred upon us, it is true; but when we undertake to cover our sins, or to gratify our pride, our vain ambition, or to exercise control or dominion or compulsion upon the souls of the children of men, in any degree of unrighteousness, behold, the heavens withdraw themselves; the Spirit of the Lord is grieved; and when it is withdrawn, Amen to the priesthood or the authority of that man. Behold, ere he is aware, he is left unto himself, to kick against the pricks, to persecute the saints, and to fight against God."

man who ordained you to the priesthood have a secret, unrepented sin? Then your ordination is invalid. Your mission was illegitimate, any converts you baptized are actually nonmembers, and you are living in adultery since you should never have been admitted to the temple. Any of your converts who served missions and baptized are similarly fraudulent, and the consequences ripple onward and outward in utterly unforseen ways. How can we ever be sure of anything?][565]

Suppose that we retain only lesser authority, limited to administering outward ordinances but without higher, spiritual matters entrusted to us. If this is the case, we are still in a better condition than was Joseph Smith. He lived at a time when there was no authority to minister even the lesser, outward ordinances. Despite this, he found God. If the church has some– or any– authority at all, then we have so much the advantage over Joseph when he began. It also stands to reason if we have some– or any – authority, then we should respect it, and gain whatever we can from its rites. It is foolish to refuse to accept what has been preserved and is still offered, or to withdraw because of human failing.[566] Worse than foolish, it is ungrateful.

Suppose a man is given the gift of the Holy Ghost by the laying on of hands, but the person performing the ordinance lacks faith, is unworthy, or is without priesthood authority. Despite this, any person may still be visited by the Holy Ghost, whether they have

---

[565]Peterson, Daniel C. *Authority in the Book of Mosiah*. Provo: FARMS Review, Vol. 18, 1, 2006, p. 164-165.

[566]D&C 88: 33: "For what doth it profit a man if a gift is bestowed upon him, and he receive not the gift? Behold, he rejoices not in that which is given unto him, neither rejoices in him who is the giver of the gift."

"the gift" or not. This is because, in Joseph's revelations, an ordinance is not necessary for the Holy Ghost to visit you: "A man may receive the Holy Ghost, and it may descend upon him and not tarry with him." (D&C 130: 23.) Joseph gave a further explanation:

> There is a difference between the Holy Ghost and the gift of the Holy Ghost. Cornelius received the Holy Ghost before he was baptized, which was the convincing power of God unto him of the truth of the Gospel, but he could not receive the gift of the Holy Ghost until after he was baptized. Had he not taken this sign or ordinance upon him, the Holy Ghost which convinced him of the truth of God, would have left him. Until he obeyed these ordinances and received the gift of the Holy Ghost, by the laying on of hands, according to the order of God, he could not have healed the sick or commanded an evil spirit to come out of a man, and it obey him; for the spirits might say unto him, as they did to the sons of Sceva: "Paul we know and Jesus we know, but who are ye?" It mattereth not whether we live long or short on the earth after we come to a knowledge of these principles and obey them unto the end. I know that all men will be damned if they do not come in the way which He hath opened, and this is the way marked out by the word of the Lord. (*TPJS*, p. 199.)

If the Holy Ghost can visit Cornelius before baptism, how much more may it visit with us after we have received a proper baptism? If we will receive light, it will grow within us.[567] Church leaders often teach that the Holy Ghost is a temporary gift, withdrawing as soon as you sin. That describes the temporary, occasional

---

[567]D&C 50: 24: "That which is of God is light; and he that receiveth light, and continueth in God, receiveth more light; and that light groweth brighter and brighter until the perfect day."

visiting of the Holy Ghost which can happen to anyone, even without an authoritative ordinance. Before I joined the church I prayed, received an answer through the Holy Ghost, and was converted. Like Cornelius, I needed no ordinance for God to answer me. This happens all the time, all over the world, as missionaries instruct the new investigator. Every returned missionary knows unbaptized people ask and receive answers through the power of Holy Ghost. People of other faiths who seek inspiration can, and do similarly, receive a visit from the Holy Ghost.

If the Holy Ghost will visit you even without an authoritative ordinance, then the responsibility to live so as to invite the Spirit is all you need to have that same companionship the ordinance could confer. There are two routes. One is through humility, sincerity, a willingness to repent, and asking God. The other is through an authoritative ordinance from one holding power.[568] Both of them put a person in contact with the Holy Ghost. The absence of an authoritative ordinance cannot prevent you from receiving the Holy Ghost.

---

[568]See, e.g., Acts 8: 14-20: "Now when the apostles which were at Jerusalem heard that Samaria had received the word of God, they sent unto them Peter and John: Who, when they were come down, prayed for them, that they might receive the Holy Ghost: (For as yet he was fallen upon none of them: only they were baptized in the name of the Lord Jesus.) Then laid they [their] hands on them, and they received the Holy Ghost. And when Simon saw that through laying on of the apostles' hands the Holy Ghost was given, he offered them money, Saying, Give me also this power, that on whomsoever I lay hands, he may receive the Holy Ghost. But Peter said unto him, Thy money perish with thee, because thou hast thought that the gift of God may be purchased with money."

The conditional temple rites administered through the church are likewise intended to be ratified by the Holy Spirit of promise.[569] Suppose we cannot find an officiator in the church who has been "anointed and appointed unto this power," who can seal by the Holy Spirit of Promise, through the power God has entrusted to the man.[570] That still does not impair your ability to receive all the things which the temple rites offer directly from heaven. You still can offer a broken heart and contrite spirit.[571] Everything is still available if you approach God to receive it. We still have, at a minimum, priesthood which includes the ministry of angels.[572] The angels have the same authority as Joseph received. Joseph received his authority from the angels.[573] The Lord revealed to Joseph that the latter-day sealing of the chosen will be done by angels, not men.[574] If angels are to continue sealing the chosen, then any lack

---

[569] D&C 132: 18: "And again, verily I say unto you, if a man marry a wife, and make a covenant with her for time and for all eternity, if that covenant is not by me or by my word, which is my law, and is not sealed by the Holy Spirit of promise, through him whom I have anointed and appointed unto this power, then it is not valid neither of force when they are out of the world, because they are not joined by me, saith the Lord, neither by my word; when they are out of the world it cannot be received there, because the angels and the gods are appointed there, by whom they cannot pass; they cannot, therefore, inherit my glory; for my house is a house of order, saith the Lord God."

[570] See D&C 132: 7, 18, 19.

[571] See D&C 59: 7-8.

[572] See, e.g., the authority remaining after Moses' removal, D&C 84: 24-27.

[573] See, e.g., D&C 128: 19-21.

[574] D&C 77: 11: "Q. What are we to understand by sealing the one hundred and forty-four thousand, out of all the tribes of Israel--twelve thousand out of every tribe? A. We are to understand that those who are

of authority among men is irrelevant. It was always planned for John, the Three Nephites, and other "holy men that ye know not of"[575] to be involved in sealing the saved in the last days. I have written three chapters on this subject in *Beloved Enos*.[576] The members of the church which was restored through Joseph have never been and will never be abandoned. Although we have collectively rebelled and been condemned, rejected and cursed, we are not abandoned. But that alone gives us nothing. Individually, we occupy the same standing before the Lord as any other person has from the beginning of time. Our only advantage is that because of the restoration through Joseph Smith, and the church organization he established, we have some additional information to guide us. The church prints scriptures, practices ordinances and offers blessings grounded in Joseph's ministry.

The church was always expected to be afflicted. Even in the earliest part of our dispensation, Joseph foresaw we would pass through great difficulties before we would see Zion again.[577] He

---

sealed are high priests, ordained unto the holy order of God, to administer the everlasting gospel; for they are they who are ordained out of every nation, kindred, tongue, and people, by the angels to whom is given power over the nations of the earth, to bring as many as will come to the church of the Firstborn."

[575]D&C 49: 8: "Wherefore, I will that all men shall repent, for all are under sin, except those which I have reserved unto myself, holy men that ye know not of."

[576]See the discussion in Chapters 10-12, The Sealing Power: Part 1: Those Holding the Power; The Sealing Power: Part 2: Receiving Authority Part of Calling and Elections; and The Sealing Power: Part 3: The Kind of Person Who Receives, pp. 128-167.

[577]"I have always expected that Zion would suffer some affliction, from what I could learn from the commandments which have been given. But

knew he would be taken before Zion would return. He also knew it would be a great while between his departure from the saints, and when they would reach their destiny.[578] Joseph was a messenger, sent to declare salvation. But salvation comes only in and through Jesus Christ. Christ defined eternal life:

> These words spake Jesus, and lifted up his eyes to heaven, and said, Father, the hour is come; glorify thy Son, that thy Son also may glorify thee: As thou hast given him power over all flesh, that he should give eternal life to as many as thou hast given him. And this is life eternal, that they might know thee the only true God, and Jesus Christ, whom thou hast sent. (John 17: 1-3.)

Knowing God is Christ's definition of eternal life and salvation. Joseph Smith clarified this does not mean to learn something about

---

I would remind you of a certain clause in one which says, that after much tribulation cometh the blessing. By this, and also others, and also one received of late, I know that Zion, in the due time of the Lord, will be redeemed; but how many will be the days of her purification, tribulation, and affliction, the Lord has kept hid from my eyes; and when I inquire concerning this subject, the voice of the Lord is: Be still, and know that I am God; all those who suffer for my name shall reign with me, and he that layeth down his life for my sake shall find it again." (*TPJS*, p. 34.)

[578]Joseph said to the Relief Society: " As he had this opportunity, he was going to instruct the ladies of this Society, and point out the way for them to conduct themselves, that they might act according to the will of God; that he did not know that he should have many opportunities of teaching them, as they were going to be left to themselves; they would not long have him to instruct them; that the Church would not have his instructions long, and the world would not be troubled with him a great while, and would not have his teachings [in person]." (*TPJS*, p. 225.) The words "in person" were inserted by Joseph Fielding Smith, to clarify what he understood Joseph meant.

Him. Rather, it is to meet Him. It is to have Him minister to you, face to face, as one man speaks to another.[579] Joseph elaborated:

> Here, then, is eternal life-to know the only wise and true God; and you have got to learn how to be Gods yourselves, and to be kings and priests to God, the same as all Gods have done before you, namely, by going from one small degree to another, and from a small capacity to a great one; from grace to grace, from exaltation to exaltation, until you attain to the resurrection of the dead, and are able to dwell in everlasting burnings, and to sit in glory, as do those who sit enthroned in everlasting power. And I want you to know that God, in the last days, while certain individuals are proclaiming his name, is not trifling with you or me. (*TPJS*, pp. 346-347.)

We are expected to learn of Him through revelation. Ultimately, the final revelation comes when He reveals Himself:

> When we begin to learn this way, we begin to learn the only true God, and what kind of a being we have got to worship. Having a knowledge of God, we begin to know how to approach him, and how to ask so as to receive an

---

[579] See Abraham's statement: "Now, after the Lord had withdrawn from speaking to me, and withdrawn his face from me, I said in my heart: Thy servant has sought thee earnestly; now I have found thee[.]" (Abr. 2: 12.) See also Moroni's declaration: "And now I, Moroni, bid farewell unto the Gentiles, yea, and also unto my brethren whom I love, until we shall meet before the judgment-seat of Christ, where all men shall know that my garments are not spotted with your blood. And then shall ye know that I have seen Jesus, and that he hath talked with me face to face, and that he told me in plain humility, even as a man telleth another in mine own language, concerning these things; And only a few have I written, because of my weakness in writing. And now, I would commend you to seek this Jesus of whom the prophets and apostles have written, that the grace of God the Father, and also the Lord Jesus Christ, and the Holy Ghost, which beareth record of them, may be and abide in you forever. Amen." (Ether 12: 38-41.)

answer. When we understand the character of God, and know how to come to him, he begins to unfold the heavens to us, and to tell us all about it. When we are ready to come to him, he is ready to come to us." (*TPJS*, pp. 349-350.)

He is as willing to come to us today as He was willing to come to Joseph. When we are ready for Him, He is waiting. Jesus invited all to come: "Come unto me, all ye that labour and are heavy laden, and I will give you rest." (Matt. 11: 28.) What is the "rest" which He offers? It is to become part of the "living vine" and to have Him take up His abode with you.[580]

The Brother of Jared was "redeemed from the fall" by entering into the Lord's presence. "And when he had said these words, behold, the Lord showed himself unto him, and said: Because thou knowest these things ye are redeemed from the fall; therefore ye are brought back into my presence; therefore I show myself unto you." (Ether 3: 13.) Knowing God is not optional. It is required for salvation. If you do not know Him you do not have eternal life. "If any man does not know God, and inquires what kind of a being he is,— if he will search diligently his own heart— if the declaration of Jesus and the apostles be true, he will realize that he has not eternal life; for there can be eternal life on no other principle." (*TPJS*, p. 344.) True messengers who want you saved will always teach you this principle. This is the first principle of Christ's Gospel, and is how salvation comes to any of us.

---

[580]See also Alma 16: 17: "That they might not be hardened against the word, that they might not be unbelieving, and go on to destruction, but that they might receive the word with joy, and as a branch be grafted into the true vine, that they might enter into the rest of the Lord their God."

It is the first principle of the Gospel to know for a certainty the Character of God, and to know that we may converse with him as one man converses with another, and that he was once a man like us; yea, that God himself, the Father of us all, dwelt on an earth, the same as Jesus Christ himself did; and I will show it from the Bible. [Italics in the original] (*TPJS*, pp. 345-346.)

The temple ordinances portray a walk back to God's presence. Although the ceremonies are presented in symbols, they testify of, and invite the actual return to Him. The washings, intended to cleanse us, are more than a physical ordinance. They testify to us about necessary individual purity and spiritual cleanliness. Anointing with olive oil symbolizes the Holy Spirit. Through the Holy Spirit we are sanctified. It is holy, and when we receive it we become holy through our association with it. When we are clothed with a garment, it symbolizes the sacrifice of Christ, laying down His body to cover our sins with His atonement. These are powerful symbols of how intimately our individual redemption is connected to Him.

The endowment instructs us about creation, and our own journey through mortal life. We must consider ourselves as if we are respectively, Adam and Eve. When we do, we find an explanation of our mortal condition. It tells us we came from God's presence, and now live in a fallen world. To regain God's presence we need to obey, make sacrifices, follow Christ's Gospel, observe the law of chastity, and consecrate our lives to Him. As we do, we will receive sacred knowledge from His messengers. Such messengers are sent by Him. Men will try and mislead us with false teachings that mingle the philosophies of men with scripture. But if we remain true and faithful to whatever light we receive from Him, He will always send more. Messengers will come from the presence of

God, bringing His message. They will not offer themselves for worship, adoration, or respect. They will warn you against the adoration of men and false teachings, because the Lord alone can save. Those who substitute worship of men for worship of the Lord will be condemned, thrust down to hell, and suffer torment. Such teachers are only liars, sorcerers and adulterers:

> For these are they who are of Paul, and of Apollos, and of Cephas. These are they who say they are some of one and some of another--some of Christ and some of John, and some of Moses, and some of Elias, and some of Esaias, and some of Isaiah, and some of Enoch; But received not the gospel, neither the testimony of Jesus, neither the prophets, neither the everlasting covenant. Last of all, these all are they who will not be gathered with the saints, to be caught up unto the church of the Firstborn, and received into the cloud. These are they who are liars, and sorcerers, and adulterers, and whoremongers, and whosoever loves and makes a lie. These are they who suffer the wrath of God on earth. These are they who suffer the vengeance of eternal fire. (D&C 76: 99-105.)

If the church has been condemned, rejected and cursed, it may be a blessing for you. If a new narrative acknowledging this, allows us to avoid inappropriate adoration of men, it may save your soul. The purpose of true messengers has always been to direct worship to Christ. True messengers labor to have you come to know Christ. They want all to be redeemed from the fall.

The purpose of the temple is to guide you back to Him. It is not the real thing, but only a symbol pointing to the real thing. It is not enough to read what has been written in scripture or taught by true messengers. You must get an experience for yourself so you also know God. The real thing is found when the veil parts and you gaze into heaven.

Could we read and comprehend all that has been written
from the days of Adam, on the relation of man to God and
angels in a future state, we should know very little about it.
Reading the experience of others, or the revelation given to
them, can never give *us* a comprehensive view of our
condition and true relation to God. Knowledge of these
things can only be obtained by experience through the
ordinances of God set forth for that purpose. Could you
gaze into heaven five minutes, you would know more than
you would by reading all that ever was written on the
subject. (*TPJS*, p. 324.)

Whatever the church as an institution has retained or lost, you
have lost nothing. The fullness of the Gospel is still available to any
of us. But it is obtained the same way Joseph Smith obtained it, not
through an institution. You are as equipped to receive it as any soul
who went before. First phase Mormonism still exists. As long as
you follow the same Gospel restored in the first phase, you can still
live first phase Mormonism. Even the required priestly authority is
still available through the veil.[581]

---

[581] See *TPJS*, p. 322- 323: "There are three grand orders of priesthood
referred to here.

1st. The King of Shiloam (Salem) had power and authority over that of
Abraham, holding the key and the power of endless life. Angels desire to
look into it, but they have set up too many stakes. God cursed the
children of Israel because they would not receive the last law from
Moses.

"The sacrifice required of Abraham in the offering up of Isaac,
shows that if a man would attain to the keys of the kingdom of an
endless life; he must sacrifice all things. When God offers a blessing or
knowledge to a man, and he refuses to receive it, he will be damned. The
Israelites prayed that God would speak to Moses and not to them; in
consequence of which he cursed them with a carnal law.

"What was the power of Melchizedek? 'Twas not the Priesthood
of Aaron which administers in outward ordinances, and the offering of
sacrifices. Those holding the fulness of the Melchizedek Priesthood are

There needs to be a balance. On the one hand, a healthy skepticism regarding the church's success is useful. Some skepticism is required to prevent worshiping mere men. But to go beyond that, and altogether reject the church is too far. It has a role still, and a prophetic future. The Lord still works through the church. His latest great revelation to mankind established the

---

kings and priests of the Most High God, holding the keys of power and blessings. In fact, that Priesthood is a perfect law of theocracy, and stands as God to give laws to the people, administering endless lives to the sons and daughters of Adam.

"Abraham says to Melchizedek, I believe all that thou hast taught me concerning the priesthood and the coming of the Son of Man; so Melchizedek ordained Abraham and sent him away. Abraham rejoiced, saying, Now I have a priesthood.

"Salvation could not come to the world without the mediation of Jesus Christ.

"How shall God come to the rescue of this generation? He will send Elijah the prophet. The law revealed to Moses in Horeb never was revealed to the children of Israel as a nation. Elijah shall reveal the covenants to seal the hearts of the fathers to the children, and the children to the fathers.

"The anointing and sealing is to be called, elected and made sure.

"'Without father, without mother, without descent, having neither beginning of days nor end of life, but made like unto the Son of God, abideth a priest continually.' The Melchizedek Priesthood holds the right from the eternal God, and not by descent from father and mother; and that priesthood is as eternal as God Himself, having neither beginning of days nor end of life.

"The 2nd Priesthood is Patriarchal authority. Go to and finish the temple, and God will fill it with power, and you will then receive more knowledge concerning this priesthood.

"The 3rd is what is called the Levitical Priesthood, consisting of priests to administer in outward ordinances, made without an oath; but the Priesthood of Melchizedek is by an oath and covenant.

"The Holy Ghost is God's messenger to administer in all those priesthoods.

"Jesus Christ is the heir of this Kingdom-the Only Begotten of the Father according to the flesh, and holds the keys over all this world."

church. The many revelations through Joseph Smith are preserved and published by the church. Flawed though it may be, it is still vital. Redemption can be found only through accepting what it offers. God still loves His people; even through their ingratitude and rejection of what He offered.

The church continues to practice the original baptism and first ordinances in exactly the manner originally restored. The Holy Ghost will visit with anyone who sincerely asks, with real intent.[582] The sacrament has substituted water for wine. The sacrament prayers found in Moroni and D&C 20 still say "wine."[583] Aside from this change, the sacrament prayers are exactly as restored. The temple rites have undergone many deletions. Despite the changes, however, the overall message of returning to God's presence through obedience, sacrifice, following the Gospel, being chaste and consecrating your life has been retained. Those responsible for deleting portions of the ceremonies are always accountable to the

---

[582]This promise, made by Moroni, is given to everyone who reads the Book of Mormon; whether they have received an ordinance yet or not: "And when ye shall receive these things, I would exhort you that ye would ask God, the Eternal Father, in the name of Christ, if these things are not true; and if ye shall ask with a sincere heart, with real intent, having faith in Christ, he will manifest the truth of it unto you, by the power of the Holy Ghost. And by the power of the Holy Ghost ye may know the truth of all things." (Mor. 10: 4-5.) If you do not have the Holy Ghost revealing truth to you, it is because you have not asked in the name of Christ with a sincere heart and real intent while having faith in Christ. It is not because you lack an ordinance.

[583]Moroni 5: 2; D&C 20: 79.

Lord.[584] But faithful seekers will not be injured by someone else's failure or success. We are individually accountable.

You alone determine what you receive. Therefore you alone are accountable for what you choose to receive.

---

[584] Isaiah prophesied ordinances would be changed, resulting in a final curse upon the earth, burning and few being left: "The earth also is defiled under the inhabitants thereof; because they have transgressed the laws, changed the ordinance, broken the everlasting covenant. Therefore hath the curse devoured the earth, and they that dwell therein are desolate: therefore the inhabitants of the earth are burned, and few men left." (Isa. 24: 5-6.)

Chapter 18

WRAPPING UP

Joseph Smith was restoring something different than what we have today. He was working back through prior dispensations to the beginning of time. The final objective was the most ancient (or the original) form of religion. It was intended for us to have available again the faith first given to Adam, when there was only one, unified priesthood. The beginning was the end. From Adam to Enoch there were men who met with God face to face. Adam knew God first in the Garden,[585] then through angels who ministered to him,[586] then in a meeting with the Lord at Adam-ondi-Ahman.[587] When the Lord appeared to Adam three years previous to his death, He appeared to seven others who held The Holy Priesthood: Seth, Enos, Cainan,

---

[585]See, e.g., Moses 3: 15-4: 31.

[586]Moses 5: 6-8.

[587]D&C 107: 53-55.

Mahalaleel, Jared, Enoch, and Methuselah.[588] Enoch, one of those, also later walked with God.[589] He gathered people into a city, taught them truth, and his people also walked with God,[590] who came to dwell with them.[591] The restoration through Joseph Smith was intended to walk things back to the beginning and the return of Zion. It was never meant to stop with a New Testament church.

Joseph only laid a foundation. He did not complete reconstruction of that most ancient religion. It is evident from his teachings there was more coming, and that his vision was never completed. His vision reached back to the first age, when The Holy Priesthood in its original form existed with the animal sacrifices Joseph said would return.

> Thus we behold the keys of this Priesthood consisted in obtaining the voice of Jehovah that He talked with him [Noah] in a familiar and friendly manner, that He continued to him the keys, the covenants, the power and the glory, with which He blessed Adam at the beginning; and the offering of sacrifice, which also shall be continued at the last time; for all the ordinances and duties that ever have been required by the Priesthood, under the directions and commandments of the Almighty in any of the dispensations, shall all be had in the last dispensation, therefore all things had under the authority of the Priesthood at any former period, shall be had again, bringing to pass the restoration spoken of by the mouth of

---

[588] *Id.*, v. 53.

[589] *Id.*, v. 49.

[590] Moses 7: 69.

[591] *Id.*, v. 16.

all the Holy Prophets; then shall the sons of Levi offer an acceptable offering to the Lord. "And he shall sit as a refiner and purifier of silver; and he shall purify the sons of Levi, and purge them as gold and silver, that they may offer unto the Lord." (See Malachi 3:3.)

It will be necessary here to make a few observations on the doctrine set forth in the above quotation, and it is generally supposed that sacrifice was entirely done away when the Great Sacrifice [i.e.,] the sacrifice of the Lord Jesus was offered up, and that there will be no necessity for the ordinance of sacrifice in future; but those who assert this are certainly not acquainted with the duties, privileges and authority of the Priesthood, or with the Prophets.

The offering of sacrifice has ever been connected and forms a part of the duties of the Priesthood. It began with the Priesthood, and will be continued until after the coming of Christ, from generation to generation. We frequently have mention made of the offering of sacrifice by the servants of the Most High in ancient days, prior to the law of Moses; which ordinances will be continued when the Priesthood is restored with all its authority, power and blessings.

Elijah was the last Prophet that held the keys of the Priesthood, and who will, before the last dispensation, restore the authority and deliver the keys of the Priesthood, in order that all the ordinances may be attended to in righteousness. It is true that the Savior had authority and power to bestow this blessing; but the sons of Levi were too prejudiced. "And I will send Elijah the Prophet before the great and terrible day of the Lord," etc., etc. Why send Elijah? Because he holds the keys of the authority to administer in all the ordinances of the Priesthood; and without the authority is given, the ordinances could not be administered in righteousness.

It is a very prevalent opinion that the sacrifices which were offered were entirely consumed. This was not the case; if you read Leviticus 2:2-3, you will observe that the priests took a part as a memorial and offered it up before the Lord, while the remainder was kept for the maintenance of the priests; so that the offerings and sacrifices are not all consumed upon the altar-but the blood is sprinkled, and the fat and certain other portions are consumed.

These sacrifices, as well as every ordinance belonging to the Priesthood, will, when the Temple of the Lord shall be built, and the sons of Levi be purified, be fully restored and attended to in all their powers, ramifications, and blessings. This ever did and ever will exist when the powers of the Melchizedek Priesthood are sufficiently manifest; else how can the restitution of all things spoken of by the Holy Prophets be brought to pass. It is not to be understood that the law of Moses will be established again with all its rites and variety of ceremonies; this has never been spoken of by the prophets; but those things which existed prior to Moses' day, namely, sacrifice, will be continued.

It may be asked by some, what necessity for sacrifice, since the Great Sacrifice was offered? In answer to which, if repentance, baptism, and faith existed prior to the days of Christ, what necessity for them since that time? The Priesthood has descended in a regular line from father to son, through their succeeding generations. (*TPJS*, pp. 171-173.)

From this statement, it is clear Joseph's "restoration of all things" was never finished. We have not seen a return of the original "Holy Priesthood with all its rites," including as its most important key, "obtaining the voice of Jehovah" to direct in all things. When it returns, we will practice "those things which existed prior to

Moses' day, namely, sacrifice," as given to Adam in the beginning. The original form of priesthood at the time of Moses, before it was separated into two divisions (Melchizedek and Aaronic or Levitical), has always been destined to return: "Now this same Priesthood, which was in the beginning, shall be in the end of the world also." (Moses 6: 7.) It includes ordinances not here yet. Joseph had the same kind of priesthood, as he explained above: "the keys of this Priesthood consisted in obtaining the voice of Jehovah that He talked with him." A holder of this priesthood can know all things. When Joseph received it he was told: "For I have conferred upon you the keys and power of the priesthood, wherein I restore all things, and make known unto you all things in due time." (D&C 132: 45.) We examined how the ability to receive an answer from God is the greatest purpose of fullness of the priesthood. And we looked at Brigham Young's statements confirming he would ask God and not get an answer. Brigham never realized his desire to see the Lord. He explained what he did in the absence of revelation:"If I do not know the will of my Father, and what He requires of me in a certain transaction, if I ask Him to give me wisdom concerning any requirement in life, or in regard to my own course, or that of my friends, my family, my children, or those that I preside over, and get no answer from Him, and then do the very best that my judgment will teach me, He is bound to own and honor that transaction, and He will do so to all intents and purposes."[592] Brigham Young substituted another standard. The fullness of the priesthood "consisted in obtaining the voice of Jehovah." But Brigham confessed he could not get that voice and never had an audience with the Lord. He claimed to have

---

[592] *JD* 3: 205.

keys which should have allowed him access to God, but when the access was denied he substituted his own judgment, and claimed God was "bound to own and honor" Brigham's will. That, however, is not the fullness of the priesthood. It is one man's supposition when left with no alternative.

This idea of Brigham Young's has been employed by church leaders since his administration. When a decision is made by a leading church council, the supposition is that God is "bound to own and honor" the decision. Another church president, Lorenzo Snow, gave his explanation of how leaders ought to proceed: "Said that the Lord does not always reveal his will concerning matters of importance— sometimes he does. HE expects us to act and work according to our best wisdom and judgment; he wants to see what we will do."[593]

Any alternative to that is as unthinkable to Mormons just as God's departure from guiding Catholicism in the great ecumenical councils is unthinkable to Catholics. The greatest difference today between Mormonism and Catholicism does not derive from either's ability to open heaven by possession of keys. The important difference is that Mormonism still practices the first ordinances using authorized words, and has also added a great body of revelation affirming that man can still return to God's presence. The temple rites, although dwindling through unbelief, still contain the invitation to converse with the Lord through the veil. Both the Mormon and Catholic hierarchies claim they have keys to bind heaven, and thereby save souls. However Christ's standard requires men to connect with Him, as the living vine, not to men in an organized hierarchy.

---

[593] *A Ministry of Meetings: The Apostolic Diaries of Rudger Clawson.* Edited by Stan Larson . Salt Lake City: Signature Books, 1993, p. 235.

Andrew Ehat grappled with the dispute over succession after
Joseph's death. He presumed the right outcome was obtained, and
proceeded in his Master's Thesis with that assumption. However,
despite that approach, he conceded the claims of the church that
relied on Joseph's last charge to the Twelve are after the fact
interpolations. It was only after Joseph's death that a charge he
gave was used to claim that the Twelve obtained all the keys from
Joseph. Joseph gave a talk on March 26, 1844 in which he
remarked that he was no longer required to carry the burden of
bearing "this kingdom." Speaking to the Council of Fifty (which
included the Twelve), Joseph said, "in the name of the Lord Jesus
Christ I now place it upon my brethren of this council."[594] This
statement in this meeting has become one of the cornerstones of
the foundation to the church's claims to have preserved all the
keys. However, given the meaning Joseph had at the time, his use
of "this kingdom" may not have been referring to the church at all.
Joseph distinguished between "the church" and "the kingdom."
When referring to "the kingdom," he had the Council of Fifty in
mind. Further, the council in which Joseph made the comment was
the Council of Fifty, not the Twelve. Although some of the
Twelve, including Brigham Young, belonged to that council, the
charge did not seem to anyone at the time to clarify who would
succeed Joseph Smith in leading the church. Ehat's conclusion was
that as a result of the charge "the Twelve Apostles inferred their
right to leadership of both the 'Church' and the 'Kingdom of God'

---

[594]Ehat, Andrew. *Joseph Smith's Introduction of Temple Ordinances and the 1844
Mormon Succession Crisis, supra*, p. 163; citing Johnson, Benjamin F., *A
Life's Sketch*, Church Archives

when three months later the Prophet was dead."[595] It was *inferred*, because at the time of the statement, no one understood it to have such meaning. "[A]ny consideration of the application of this 'Last Charge' as the key to the succession question must take into account that it was a deduction on the part of the Twelve Apostles that they had the right to lead."[596] The deduction grew out of necessity. No one wanted the church to die. None of the Twelve wanted to surrender control to Sidney Rigdon, whose unstable behavior[597] grew even more alarming during the succession crisis. Despite this, Rigdon was a powerful influence who changed the course of Mormonism.

Sidney Rigdon came from the Campbellite movement. Alexander Campbell sought to reestablish the New Testament church by founding what he called "the Church of Christ." While this is a topic outside of what is addressed in this book, the result of Rigdon's influence altered the original trajectory of the restoration, because he persuaded Joseph to bend the direction of the restoration toward a New Testament church. This was not the original objective. But it became a useful point along the way. At the time of Joseph's death, a New Testament religion had been married to older practices, making a uniquely ancient Hebraic form of Christianity. However, as seen above, the restoration was

---

[595] Ehat, Andrew. *Joseph Smith's Introduction of Temple Ordinances and the 1844 Mormon Succession Crisis, supra*, p. 162.

[596] *Id.*, p. 166.

[597] Sidney suffered several debilitating head injuries, and may have been afflicted with bi-polar disorder. Throughout his adult life he evidenced dramatic shifts in mood and behavior, which suggests this form of mental disorder. It became particularly evident during the succession controversy.

intended to walk back to the earliest age of man and bring a return of Enoch's City of Zion. A careful examination of the revelations to Joseph show the church he was originally restoring was modeled after the Book of Mormon, not the New Testament. The organizational layout found in D&C 20 takes the baptism form, sacrament prayers, offices and doctrines from the Book of Mormon. It was never intended to end in a New Testament form of church. The Book of Mormon bridged a period from 600 b.c. to 400 a.d. It linked together ancient Israel and Christianity. And the church was a mere tool to reach back further, to the very beginning or Patriarchal Dispensations of the earth. But, again, we are on a topic outside the scope of this book.

The church has not kept intact what Joseph was able to restore. The changes from phase to phase have altered Mormonism so that the present form is a different religion than the first phase. The only things shared by the first phase and the fourth phase are a common vocabulary, and the increasingly less believable claim it is the same. As it has grown away from its origin, it has also moved closer to existing Christian religions.

We saw that the first transition was as a result of Joseph's death. When he departed, there was no ability to resist change. Further, the trauma of his death led Mormons to necessarily accept change as inevitable. Subsequent changes, however, have been voluntary.

One lost teaching stands above all others in importance. It is so important that the world will be cursed, utterly wasted, at the return of Christ if it was lost. Joseph first learned about this on September 22, 1823 when Moroni stated: "Behold, I will reveal unto you the Priesthood, by the hand of Elijah the prophet, before the coming of the great and dreadful day of the Lord. He also quoted the next verse differently: And he shall plant in the hearts of the children the promises made to the fathers, and the hearts of the children shall turn to their fathers. If it were not so, the whole earth would be utterly wasted at his coming." (JS-H 1: 38-39.) This same language is quoted in D&C Section 2.[598] It is such an important warning that Christ quoted the same prophecy to the Nephites, and required them to add it to their scripture.[599] It is a prophecy every volume of scripture (Old Testament, New Testament, Doctrine & Covenants, Book of Mormon, Pearl of Great Price) includes.

Joseph's original instruction on the prophecy connected the living faithful to the "fathers" Abraham, Isaac and Jacob. The connection was through Priesthood, not genealogy, as discussed earlier in this book. Joseph was connected by his priesthood, becoming the "father" of all who would live after to him. Families

---

[598]"Behold, I will reveal unto you the Priesthood, by the hand of Elijah the prophet, before the coming of the great and dreadful day of the Lord. And he shall plant in the hearts of the children the promises made to the fathers, and the hearts of the children shall turn to their fathers. If it were not so, the whole earth would be utterly wasted at his coming." (D&C 2: 1-3.)

[599]His instruction included: "For behold, the day cometh that shall burn as an oven; and all the proud, yea, and all that do wickedly, shall be stubble; and the day that cometh shall burn them up, saith the Lord of Hosts, that it shall leave them neither root nor branch. But unto you that fear my name, shall the Son of Righteousness arise with healing in his wings; and ye shall go forth and grow up as calves in the stall. And ye shall tread down the wicked; for they shall be ashes under the soles of your feet in the day that I shall do this, saith the Lord of Hosts. Remember ye the law of Moses, my servant, which I commanded unto him in Horeb for all Israel, with the statutes and judgments. Behold, I will send you Elijah the prophet before the coming of the great and dreadful day of the Lord; And he shall turn the heart of the fathers to the children, and the heart of the children to their fathers, lest I come and smite the earth with a curse." (3 Ne. 25: 1-6.)

would be organized under Joseph, as the father of the righteous in
this dispensation. Accordingly, men were sealed to Joseph Smith
as their father, and they as his sons. This was referred to as
"adoption" because the family organization was priestly, according
to the law of God, not biological. As soon as Joseph died, the
doctrine began to erode, ultimately being replaced by the substitute
practice of sealing genealogical lines together. In between the
original adoptive sealing to Joseph Smith, and the current practice
of tracking genealogical/biological lines, there was an intermediate
step when families were tracked back as far as research permitted,
then the line was sealed to Joseph Smith.[600] That practice is now
forgotten, and certainly no longer practiced. The growing
uncertainty, redefinition and abandonment of the practice of
"adoption" is traced by Jonathan Stapley in an article which
appears in *The Journal of Mormon History*.[601] His article demonstrates
how quickly the topic became confused. He writes:

> The period after Taylor's death in July 1887 appears to
> have been one of continued confusion regarding the law of
> adoption. Two months later in September 1887, John M.
> Whitaker, John Taylor's son-in-law, wrote: 'I went back to
> the office where I found [Apostle] Brother Lorenzo Snow

---

[600] *Diary of Abraham Cannon*, pp. 488-489, quoting President Wilford
Woodruff: "I was sealed to my father, and then had him sealed to the
Prophet Joseph. Erastus Snow was sealed to his father though the latter
was not baptized after having heard the Gospel. He was, however, kind
to the Prophet, and was a Saint in everything except baptism. The Lord
has told me that it is right for children to be sealed to their parents, and
they to their parents, just as far back as we can possibly obtain the
records, and then have the last obtainable member sealed to the Prophet
Joseph Smith, who stands at the head of this dispensation."

[601] Stapley, Jonathan. *Adoptive Sealing Ritual in Mormonism, The Journal of
Mormon History*, forthcoming edition, pp. 53-117.

and [First Council of the Seventy member] Jacob Gates. They conversed a long time. He finally entered into a deep subject on "The Law of Adoption." Brother Gates said he didn't believe in it as did also Brother Snow. He[?] referenced back to the time that Brigham Young was in Kirtland[;] he had a person asked him about it and he said "I know nothing about it." President Taylor on one different occasion had a letter written to him for the following reason: it was [two undecipherable words] of Prophet J Smith or rather Sister Eliza R. Snow Smith (Brother Gates didn't know which)[;] a bout [sic] 70 persons were adopted into President J Smith's [family;] Sister Snow Smith said "she didn't understand the law" but had no objections to them being sealed to her husband. And this led Brother Gates to write to President Taylor asking him if he knew anything about it. He never answered the letter. But on another occasion Brother Gates saw him and asked him plainly. President Taylor said he knew nothing about it. And also just lately when asked by Brother Snow, President Wilford Woodruff knew nothing about it. ["]It hadn't been revealed to him." I know this at this time to say [or show] a prevailing feeling among the Twelve that they don't understand it. George [undecipherable] Cannon also said he didn't understand it.[602]

Stapley's article observes "the idea of linking to Joseph Smith was eventually dismissed or forgotten."[603] He cites to the deliberate decision in 1922 to remove reference to Woodruff's instruction to

---

[602]*Id.*, at pp. 101-102, citing to *John M. Whitaker, Diary*, Book No. 4, September 16, 1887, to September 20, 1888, November 16, 1887, MS 0002, Marriott Special Collection; transcription from Pitman shorthand by LaJean Purcell Carruth.

[603]*Id.*, pp. 113-114.

seal genealogical lines to Joseph Smith.[604] Today fourth phase Mormons know nothing about the practice, nor the earlier doctrine of adoption.

The oddity of this modern innovation becomes most apparent when the original reason for adoption is remembered. It was intended to avoid "the whole earth being utterly wasted" at the Lord's return. (JS-H 1: 39.) That is, the Second Coming of Christ will destroy the wicked on "the great and dreadful day." (*Id.*, v. 38.) "For behold, the day cometh that shall burn as an oven, and all the proud, yea, and all that do wickedly shall burn as stubble; for they that come shall burn them, saith the Lord of Hosts, that it shall leave them neither root nor branch."[605] (*Id.*, v. 37.) Joseph taught that the connection which would allow living men and women to endure the day of burning was intimately connected with a priestly tie between the living children and the coming "fathers" who will return in consuming glory.[606] Joseph recognized that unless the living who greet them are recognized as "children" through adoption as a component of their priesthood, they will burn as stubble. It goes back to Abraham, whose posterity would include any and all who received the same Gospel and priesthood given Abraham. (Abr. 2: 9.) Everyone who received the Gospel after his day would be "accounted [his] seed, and shall rise up and bless

---

[604] *Id.*, at p. 114, citing the *Utah Genealogical and Historical Magazine* edition of October 1922.

[605] The terms "root" and "branch" are family terms. Meaning the posterity of such people will be cut off, destroyed or unable to continue family lines.

[606] The Lord will come in glory to dispense judgment on the world. It will be His glory, reflected also in those who accompany Him, which is the consuming fire to purge the earth.

[him], as their father." (Abr. 2: 10.) It will be through Abraham's "seed (that is [his] Priesthood)" the world would be preserved. (Abr. 2: 11.) Only in this manner would the families of the earth be preserved. (*Id.*)

Therefore, when knowledge about adoption was lost, so was the chance to avoid destruction on the coming day when those who return will burn them up. On that day only those whose "hearts are turned to the fathers," and who are regarded as their children, and held in remembrance by the "fathers," will be able to endure glory that would otherwise "burn them as stubble, leaving neither root nor branch."

Brigham Young confessed he did not understand the doctrine. Inexplicably, he taught these matters would be attended to and sorted out during the Millennium. He knew it needed to be done, didn't know how to do it, and concluded that when Joseph returned through the resurrection it would all be sorted out:

> After Joseph comes to us in his resurrected body He will more fully instruct us concerning the Baptism for the dead and the sealing ordinances. He will say be baptized for this man and that man and that man be sealed to that man and such a man to such a man, and connect the Priesthood together.
>
> I tell you their will not be much of this done until Joseph comes. He is our spiritual Father. Our hearts are already turned to him and his to us. This [is] the order of the Holy Priesthood and we shall continue to administer in the ordinances of the kingdom of God here on earth.[607]

The obvious defect in this approach is the pre-Millennial return of Christ, and the returning "fathers" to a body who has not prepared

---

[607] *Complete Discourses of Brigham Young*, Vol. 2, p. 1034.

for their return in advance. The preparation must precede the return. In other words, if they are unprepared, or not recognized as descendants of Abraham, Isaac and Jacob through sealing to the "fathers" through Joseph Smith, they will be burned. The Gospel was returned primarily to prepare a people for the return. To say the preparation will happen sometime after the return, during the Millennium, suggests the coming day which will 'burn them up' is inconsequential, or can be ignored with impunity.

In fourth phase Mormonism, Joseph's "adoption" theology has been converted into something altogether different. It is biological and genealogical, not priestly and dispensational. The church now markets itself as an institution that will "strengthen families." It does not inform its members, or prospective converts that the day will come they will be burned up unless they have connected to Abraham, Isaac and Jacob through Joseph Smith as the Dispensation head, in a necessary priestly ordinance. This teaching is one example that shows just how distant fourth phase Mormonism is from Joseph's original vision.

When Joseph's confidential revelation on plural wives became public in the second phase of Mormonism, the reaction of the American people was hostile. Political pressure, including loss of voting rights, laws prohibiting Mormons from acting as jurors, and the confiscation of church property combined to force Mormons to abandon plural marriage. Under the circumstances, the abandonment was inevitable. So the Mormons accepted the surrender of the practice, leading to a third phase of the religion. These first three phases were marked by sudden changes in the religion, they were nevertheless understandable developments to believers. However, fourth phase of Mormonism has come about as a result of deliberate management choices from inside the faith.

The new correlated version of the religion marketed today by the church is something distinct from all prior phases. Correlation has now institutionalized change. The pace of change to the religion in phase four is accelerating. In this new era of correlation, all adult active members forty years old or older cannot help but notice how their faith is assuming a new form. Polls and focus groups are used by managers within the church to make decisions. These include how to market the faith to non-believers, and how to adapt objectionable vestiges to make them more palatable to critics. The marketing of the religion through these techniques is increasingly less effective. A recent Salt Lake Tribune article observes how Mormon leaders are moving so quickly on some issues it leaves members feeling betrayed and, for the first time find themselves "opposing their religion" on issues.[608]

The leaders of fourth phase Mormonism are pursuing a course similar to the Deuteronomists of the Old Testament. Both are responsible for making dramatic changes, discarding earlier understanding ,and forming a fundamentally different religion in order to accomplish what is viewed as an improvement to the religion. The earlier prophetic religion of the Old Testament was brought to a close by the Deuteronomists, and a priestly, controlled religion substituted thereafter. In the Old Testament faith, the heavens had been opened and the canon of scripture grew. The priests closed the canon, then altered it to eliminate what they thought were objectionable ideas, centering worship in the cultic practices of the Temple at Jerusalem. In a similar way, fourth phase Mormonism has substituted ceremonial rites, symbolizing ascent to God's presence through the veil, for any expectation of an actual

---

[608]Fletcher, Peggy Stack. *Some LDS Conservatives Now at Odds With Their Church*. Salt Lake Tribune April 28, 2011.

journey into God's presence. Terms and practices have been changed. Joseph Smith taught the possibility of God speaking to man, confirming from heaven the calling and election of the faithful individual, and the continuing ministry of Christ as the Second Comforter. These topics are not included in the Correlated curriculum of fourth phase manuals. They are not spoken of in General Conference. They have been replaced by a centrally, controlled ceremony performed in temples, access to which is controlled by rules laid down by the hierarchy. Among other requirements, payment of tithes, and acknowledgment of the hierarchy as possessing all keys to salvation are demanded. The questions suggest the priestly authority possessed by the church is able to deliver salvation to the faithful Latter-day Saint.

The church today does not regard direct revelation to a person as a legitimate means of receiving the promise of exaltation through calling and election. Joseph Smith always taught this was not only available, but preferred.[609] The shift has been radical, and not fully understood by rank and file Mormons. Today the most devoted church members view approval from the hierarchy as coequal with approval from God. The greatest desire of faithful members is to rise in the church's ranks, and ultimately receive a second temple ordinance, administered by church leaders, promising exaltation to those who are approved.

In Mormon "testimonies" each Fast Sunday for many years now, fourth phase Mormons praise the church president by reciting a mantra. ("I know President Monson is a prophet of God" and also confirming "I know the church is true.") Seldom does Christ's name get mentioned in Mormon testimonies anymore, other than

---

[609]See *DHC* 3: 380, also *TPJS*, p. 150.

as an appendage to the "testimony" confirming the exalted status of the president of the church, and the truthfulness of the church itself. The church has become a substitute for Christ, and in that sense has become the modern idol of the gentile church, just as Nephi, Christ, Moroni and Joseph Smith predicted.

We have also seen how Correlation has completely transformed the church. Although given credit for Correlation, President David O. McKay opposed it. He feared and opposed the planned Correlation program because he thought it would lead to apostasy by the church. Nevertheless, Harold B. Lee proceeded apace. In an ironic development Harold B. Lee gave credit to President McKay as the person "inspired by God" to implement Correlation. Correlation places every aspect of Mormonism under the control of the central priesthood hierarchy. Today the hierarchy proclaims the value and virtue of Correlation.

History tries to weave together the story of interconnected lives. We live biographies. History attempts to give the story of the cumulative total of the biographies. Unfortunately, all the biographies have not been recorded. When lives end without a biographical record, they are lost to history. Joseph Smith made a conscious effort to preserve his history. Latter-day Saints are a journal-keeping people. We have a great deal more information from which to draw in writing our history than almost any other comparable sized population in the world. Unfortunately, the church has not opened its archives to allow all the records to be seen. As a result, the history of the Latter-day Saints remains incomplete. Our history can be known, but a detailed reconstruction must await the time when the entire record is released to the public.

Even if the entire archive of the church were opened, however, it would still not be enough. We would be better informed than we are now, but there is still a step between biography and history. While people are still alive, and the church has confidential information that could embarrass or injure them, it makes sense to preserve confidences. However, once they and their immediate families are deceased, there is a greater obligation owed to truth than the obligation to preserve confidences.

As I have studied the now-available material while writing this book, I have been struck by the fact many of the diaries used have only recently been published. Many previous Latter-day Saint attempts to write our history have been written with fewer available materials. It is unfortunate. I believe all the journals, diaries, correspondence and records should be public, excepting only cases involving harm to living persons, or their immediate family. Even if the material changes our history or causes us discomfort, it should still be available. As Davis Bitton observed, it is not necessary to have a testimony of the history of the church. We can have faith in Joseph's revelations, and the church restored through him, even if the subsequent history is checkered with more human failing than we would like.

At a 2007 meeting of the Mormon History Association, church representative Rebecca Olpin reported on a survey taken of active Latter-day Saints. The survey results showed "active Latter-day Saints want their church to provide a 'frank and honest' presentation of church history, unvarnished by attempts to sugarcoat the past in order to make it more palatable."[610] The church was prepared to respond to the members' desire, but the managing

---

[610]Moore, Carrie A. *LDS in Survey Call for Unvarnished History.* Deseret News May 27, 2007.

director of family and church history, Steve Olsen, clarified, "there are some restrictions on privacy and intellectual property [as well as on] sacred, private and institutional materials. That's something we just won't budge on, and those things will never be made public."[611]

Eventually the truth will be known. But generations may pass without the benefit of having a more complete record to inform them. For those living while information is hidden, they live and die believing only some of what is true, along with perhaps some of what is untrue. The Church of Jesus Christ of Latter-day Saints will not be destroyed by the truth. Perhaps an infantile and weak mythology will be destroyed, but not the church. It can only benefit from more truth. Faith cannot come from believing in error; that is only unbelief, and that cannot save anyone. The more accurate and complete record we have available, the more accurate the resulting conclusions will be. People of faith should be given every opportunity to know accurately, completely and candidly the way God's hand moves in our day. To deny that information to members reflects institutional insecurity. That is unbecoming in an organization devoted to saving souls.

Witnesses whose lives involved interaction with Joseph Smith, Brigham Young, John Taylor, Wilford Woodruff, the other church fathers, our early events, and church management are critical sources for faithful Latter-day Saints to consider. But the church has adopted a policy deliberately suppressing the journals of church leaders. It began as early as 1904, in an attempt to curtail access by "enemies" to information about how the church operated:

---

[611] *Id.*

Pres. Smith said that he wanted to refer to a matter that had given him much concern —namely, the private journals of the brethren of the council. Many things were written in them which, if they were to fall into the hands of the enemy, might bring trouble upon the church. After the death of the brethren, you cannot tell what may become of their journals, and even now the brethren felt an anxiety in relation to Pres. Geo. Q. Cannon's journal, who made a pretty full account of everything that transpired in the council of the brethren; the same with Abram Cannon and others. Elder Jno. H. Smith said that he was very much concerned about this matter and had been for a long time and felt that some action should be taken in the premises. Pres. Winder said that it was very unsafe and risky for the brethren to write down that which occurred in these meetings. This duty belonged to the clerk of the council and nobody else. Pres. Winder moved that it be the sense and feeling of the council that the brethren should not write in their journals that which took place in the council meetings. Carried by unanimous vote.[612]

In 1904 the "enemies" were political adversaries and newspapers who were opposed to Apostle Reed Smoot being seated as Utah's Senator. Shielding from public view the private discussions was an attempt to clip controversy by hiding what the church did in private. There are currently available diaries that discuss the private meetings, but the policy shows a deliberate effort to keep the information from public view. This may serve the purpose of keeping critics uninformed, but it comes at the price of giving faithful Latter-day Saints no information about issues of legitimate and vital concern to them. If a man cannot be saved in

---

[612] *A Ministry of Meetings: The Apostolic Diaries of Rudger Clawson.* Edited by Stan Larson. Salt Lake City: Signature Books, 1993, p. 777.

ignorance,[613] and if the church is led by inspired councils, as it claims, then faithful members should benefit from access to the records of the church's hierarchy. They would benefit from seeing the claimed inspiration unfold in their council meetings. As long as the participants are deceased, faithful members who sustain the leaders, pay tithing to the church they manage, and trust them as stewards of the Lord's house, have a legitimate claim to access information that will help them understand how the leaders conduct themselves, and the church they manage.

The many meetings covered in the diaries that are available now are noteworthy in the business that was conducted. There is very little religious or doctrinal discussion - ever. Instead, management decisions for various for-profit business interests, land acquisitions, and behind the scenes political maneuvering for the influence of state and federal government dominate the highest level of church leadership meetings. It is no longer necessary to shield from public view the business decisions that were made and implemented decades ago. There is no reason to hide the lobbying, influencing, and paying for political favors which took place within the church more than a half-century ago. It is unnecessary to suppress access to the church management, decision making process from active, faithful members. The policy of concealing decades old, inside information speaks more about the insecurities of those involved than any actual need to preserve confidences for the dead. It is even possible that if every church manager knew their "inside" conduct and comments were destined for public release, it would affect their behavior in a positive way. If that is so, then the change should be made. Managers should know their meetings,

---

[613] "It is impossible for a man to be saved in ignorance." (*TPJS*, p. 301.)

conversations and actions will in time be exposed to full public review. The Lord has such a policy for all of us.[614] The best antiseptic is always sunlight.

Even if everything was available, however, history is another step removed from biography. It attempts to homogenize all the biographies, and tell a larger story of the entire population, amalgamating together all the biographies and other sources. For that step, there are better guides than academic techniques of the trained historian. We have prophecy from the Book of Mormon, and modern revelations to Joseph Smith to give better guidance. They foretell a restoration through the gentiles. But the gentiles would reject the fullness. When they did, the prophecies foretell judgment and rejection of the gentiles by God. The Lord would then offer the fullness to a remnant of Nephi's people. Nevertheless, some few gentiles are going to remain faithful despite the failure of their leaders. These, and other prophecies by Christ concerning gentile deceits, mischiefs, hypocrisy, murders, priestcrafts, whoredoms, and secret abominations must necessarily be part of any attempt to understand Mormon history. History that ignores these prophetic themes coming from, among others, Jesus Christ, are undoubtedly wrong. Even if alternative views are developed using the historian's tools, it will fail to inform us of the truth if the prophecies are ignored. It is just opinion.

We have another source uniquely relevant to Latter-day Saint history. Our history includes God. When history embraces as its primary focus God's interaction with us, the access to available information changes. It includes a direct participant who can still inform us. The men involved may be dead, but God is not. As a

---

[614]D&C 1: 3.

result, the same verse from James[615] that motivated Joseph Smith becomes relevant again to understanding our history. We can "ask God" and get an answer.[616]

The changes to Mormonism discussed in this book have indeed taken place. It may seem odd in a conventional history about a secular topic to suggest the reader ask God if the account should be believed or not. But Mormonism is not secular, and its history less the subject of accumulated biography, and more the subject of God's involvement with mankind. It is therefore, theology as much as history. Mormonism cannot be adequately accounted for unless some attempt is made to grapple with the claim it originated with God. Did God appear and speak to Joseph Smith? If so, then what God said should be considered central to understanding what has happened.

Joseph Smith's history concerns salvation for himself and all of us. If the event did not happen, then his life is interesting, but lacks any universal relevance to man's salvation. Even if the claims made by Joseph Smith are false, the transformation of the religion he founded is important to study. It is a living, contemporary example of how religions are founded, then transform, ultimately seeking accommodation with the world. A study of Mormonism will teach you more about Christianity's first centuries than a study of available documents from the first two centuries after Christ. Today's contemporary Mormon changes are showing, in a living institution, how and why religions change.

The first issue to be answered, however, should always be whether Mormonism has its origin with God or man. If you are

---

[615]James 1: 5.

[616]Moroni 10: 5.

persuaded it originates with God, the next question is how faithfully it has been preserved from Joseph's time through the present. The answer to that involves not merely documented events viewed as history, but also extends to include the prophecy, scriptures, and revelation of the new faith.

Now that we have reached the end of this account of Mormonism, I offer it as the story of how a believer in Mormonism reconciles the problems with the traditional explanation of our history. It is, to the best of my ability to explain it, how Mormonism was originally established, then changed in phases until today it has assumed a form almost completely different from the original. Mormonism in its largest and most successful form is in The Church of Jesus Christ of Latter-day Saints. In its current phase four iteration it is a different religion from phase one. It has been reformed, changed, modified, managed, and adapted to be mass-marketed. Mormonism's transition is unlike any event since the two centuries following the New Testament.

Just like Primitive Christianity of the New Testament evolved into "Historic Christianity," Mormonism has evolved into, and through four distinctly different phases. Each phase can be viewed as a different religion. The challenge in fourth phase Mormonism today is the rapidity of change. The changes now underway are as a result of deliberate planning decisions designed to make the faith more palatable, popular, and marketable, and less cultic and strange. The original aspired to change the world. The current version has been changed by the world. It studies worldly trends, and implements programs designed to take advantage of such studies. Faithful, devoted Latter-day Saints are feeling increasingly alienated from the faith they followed in their youth. This book explains how and why the changes occurred.

There are many details in each phase of Mormonism worth further comment. This book cannot address them all. The more interesting topic to me is the doctrine, prophecies and religion Joseph introduced in his ministry. Although it has been changed, the original was so well established in scriptures written through Joseph, ordinances he introduced , sermons he delivered and rites he revealed, that his original religion can still be found. I'd like to preserve it for future generations.

Many of the greatest events foretold through Joseph Smith's restored scriptures and modern revelation are still future. Our collective rejection of the fullness was foreseen. But The Church of Jesus Christ of Latter-day Saints still remains a people of destiny and the place where God's judgments will first be poured out. It is the institution that publishes the Book of Mormon and other revelations of Joseph Smith. It builds and uses temples, although the rites continue to be redacted. Through it, ordinances are delivered which can point any soul who will look beyond the symbol to find an invitation to know God. I never expect to abandon my membership in or activity with the church. There should be no reason to restore again, "reorganize," or redo the organization of Christ's church. It is here, and it continues to have a Divinely appointed destiny.

The prophecies foretell a time when the Lord will send "one mighty and strong, holding the scepter of power in his hand, clothed with light for a covering, whose mouth shall utter words, eternal words; while his bowels shall be a fountain of truth, to set in order the house of God." (D&C 85: 7.) Since the revelation foretells the "Lord, God will send" him "to set in order the house of God" it compels the conclusion the house of God will necessarily be out of order. It would not be necessary to set it in order if disorder had not set in. Therefore, we should not be surprised or dismayed if some things appear out of order. Fixing it will be the Lord's doing. No volunteer will assume that role. (It is amusing and distressing how many have claimed to be such a "mighty and strong" one over the last century and a half.)

It is still possible to know first phase Mormonism. Although the church has little enthusiasm for first phase Mormons, will excommunicate second phase Mormons, and views third phase Mormons as acceptable, though somewhat out of step, all phases are still practiced today. There should be no breaking apart, abandoning or schism of the church. Through open discussion, free exchange of ideas and inspiration from the Spirit, the saints should still be able to come to a unity of faith.[617] The best way to achieve unity is to have an open discussion. When people who share a common faith ask God for guidance in resolving a dispute, open discussion aids the process. Suppressing ideas weakens faith and causes conflict. To the extent the Correlation process attempts to stifle discussion and ratchet down on free exchange of ideas, fourth phase Mormonism may delay the inevitable. But the hand of God watches over the restoration. Therefore, patience will be rewarded. The Lord's advice in 1833, after the saints failed to establish Zion in Missouri, remains useful today: "let your hearts be comforted concerning Zion; for all flesh is in mine hands; be still and know that I am God." (D&C 101: 16.)

Zion will return. But it will return in accordance with the original, first phase restoration given to Joseph. When Zion does

---

[617]Eph. 4: 11-13.

return, the inhabitants will inherit the fullness which Joseph wanted the saints to accept in Nauvoo. Zion will judge the Mormons:

> For it shall come to pass that the inhabitants of Zion shall judge all things pertaining to Zion. And liars and hypocrites shall be proved by them, and they who are not apostles and prophets shall be known. And even the bishop, who is a judge, and his counselors, if they are not faithful in their stewardships shall be condemned, and others shall be planted in their stead. For, behold, I say unto you that Zion shall flourish, and the glory of the Lord shall be upon her; And she shall be an ensign unto the people, and there shall come unto her out of every nation under heaven. And the day shall come when the nations of the earth shall tremble because of her, and shall fear because of her terrible ones. The Lord hath spoken it. Amen. (D&C 64: 38-43.)

If it is properly understood, Mormon history allows believers to foresee how these scriptures will be fulfilled. It is still a marvelous work and a wonder, just as Isaiah foretold.[618]

THE END

---

[618]See Isaiah 29: 14; see also 2 Ne. 25: 17 and 27: 26.

SELECTED BIBLIOGRAPHY

A Ministry of Meetings: The Apostolic Diaries of Rudger Clawson. Edited by
Stan Larson. Salt Lake City: Signature Books, 1993.

Anderson, Devery S. *The Development of LDS Temple Worship: 1846-2000.*
Salt Lake City: Signature Books, 2011.

Anderson, Neil L. *You Know Enough.* Ensign CR, November 2008.

Backman, Milton V. *Joseph Smith's First Vision.* Bookcraft, Salt Lake City,
1980, 2nd Edition.

Bednar, David. A. *The Spirit of Revelation.* Ensign CR, May 2011.

Benson, Ezra Taft. *The Teachings of Ezra Taft Benson.* Salt Lake City:
Bookcraft, 1988, citing CR October 1960

Bitton, Davis. *I Don't Have A Testimony of The History of The Church.* Provo:
FARMS Review, Vol. 16, 2 , 2004.

Brown Lisle, G. *The Holy Order in Nauvoo.* Copyright by the author:
November 1995.

Buerger, David John. *The Mysteries of Godliness.* San Francisco: Smith
Research Associates, 1994.

Bush, Lester E., Jr. *Mormon's Negro Doctrine: An Historical Overview.*
Dialogue 8: Spring 1973.

Bushman, Richard L. *Joseph Smith's Many Histories,* found in *The Worlds of
Joseph Smith: A Bicentennial Conference at the Library of Congress.*
Edited by John Welch. Provo: BYU, 2006

_____. *Rough Stone Rolling*. New York: Alfred A. Knopf, 2005.

Candid Insights of a Mormon Apostle: The Diaries of Abraham H. Cannon, 1889-1895. Edited by Edward L. Lyman. Salt Lake City: Signature Books, 2010.

Church History and Revelation. Being a Course of Study for the Melchizedek Priesthood Quorums. Salt Lake City: Deseret Book, 1947

Clark, James. *Messages of the First Presidency, 6 Vols*. Salt Lake City: Bookcraft, 1965-1975

Cook, Lyndon W. *A Tentative Inquiry into the Office of Seventy 1835-1845*. Provo: Grandin Book Company, 2010.

_____. *"I Have Sinned Against Heaven, and Am Unworthy of Your Confidence, But I Cannot Live Without a Reconciliation": Thomas B. Marsh Returns To the Church*. BYU Studies, Vol. 20 (1979-1980). Number 4-Summer 1980.

Discourses of Brigham Young. Compiled by John A. Widstoe. Salt Lake City: Deseret Book Company, 1954.

Edersheim, Alfred. *The Temple: Its Ministry and Services*. Massachusetts: Hendrickson Publishers, 1994.

Ehat, Andrew. *Joseph Smith's Introduction of Temple Ordinances and the 1844 Mormon Succession Question*. Master's Thesis BYU, 1981.

Encyclopedia of Mormonism. Edited by Daniel H. Ludlow. New York: Macmillan, 1992

Eyring, Henry B. *The True and Living Church*. Ensign CR, May 2008.

Gentry, Leland H. and Compton, Todd M. *Fire and Sword A History of the Latter-day Saints in Northern Missouri, 1836-1839*. Salt Lake City: Greg Kofford Books, 2011.

Holland, Jeffrey R. *Our Most Distinguishing Feature*. Ensign CR, May 2005

_____. *Prophets in the Land Again*. Ensign CR, November 2006.

In the President's Office: The Diaries of L. John Nuttall, 1879-1892. Edited by Jedediah S. Rogers. Salt Lake City: Signature Books, 2007

Joseph Smith's Quorum of the Anointed: 1842-1845. Edited by Devery S. Anderson and Gary James Bergera. Salt Lake City: Signature Books, 2005

June, 1919 *Conference Report*

Koepp, Paul. *Richard Bitner Wirthlin, LDS General Authority and Pollster for Ronald Reagan, dies at 80.* Deseret News, March 17, 2011,

Lee, Harold B. *Teachings of Harold B. Lee.* Edited by Clyde J. Williams. Salt Lake City: Deseret Book, 1996

Leonard, Glen. *Nauvoo: A Place of Peace, A People of Promise.* Salt Lake City: Deseret Book, 2002

Messenger and Advocate, (October 1835-September 1836). Vol. 2, April 1836 No. 19.

Messenger and Advocate, March 1837, Vol. 3, No. 30, p. 470. *Love of God,* by Warren Cowdery.

Millennial Star 8, (November 20, 1846), p. 139.

Millennial Star 13, (November 15, 1851), p. 339.

Millennial Star 8 [November 20, 1846]

Moore, Carrie A. *LDS in Survey Call for Unvarnished History.* Deseret News May 27, 2007.

Nielsen, Donna B. *Beloved Bridegroom: Finding Christ in Ancient Jewish Marriage and Family Customs.* Salt Lake City: Onyx Press, 1999.

Nutall, L. John. *Diary,* Feb. 7, 1877. L. Tom Perry Special collections, Harold B. Lee Library, Brigham Young University, Provo, Utah.

On the Mormon Frontier: The Diary of Hosea Stout, 1844-1861. Edited by Juanita Brooks. Salt Lake City: University of Utah Press, 1964.

Opening the Heavens: Accounts of Divine Manifestations. Edited by John W. Welch. Salt Lake City: Deseret Book, 2005.

Pace, Glen. L. *Memorandum: Ritualistic Child Abuse.* July 19, 1980. http://www.utlm.org/images.newsletters/no80pacememop1.gif

Packer, Boyd K. *The Mantle is Far, Far Greater Than the Intellect.* 5th Annual CES Religious Educator's Symposium. BYU Studies. 22 August, 1981

_____. *The Power of the Priesthood.* Ensign CR, May 2010.

Peterson, Daniel C. *Authority in the Book of Mosiah.* Provo: FARMS Review, Vol. 18, 1, 2006.

Prince, Gregory and Wright, Robert. *David O. McKay and the Rise of Modern Mormonism.* Salt Lake City: University of Utah Press, 2005.

Quinn, D. Michael. *Early Mormonism and the Magic World View.* Salt Lake City: Signature Books, 1998.

_____. *The Mormon Hierarchy: Extensions of Power.* Salt Lake City: Signature Books, 1997.

_____. *The Mormon Hierarchy: Origins of Power.* Salt Lake City: Signature Books, 1994.

Richards, LeGrand. *A Marvelous Work and a Wonder.* Salt Lake City: Deseret Book, 1976.

Roberts, B.H. *Seventy's Course in Theology*, Vol. 1. Salt Lake City: Deseret Book, 2009.

_____. *The Rise and Fall of Nauvoo*. Salt Lake City: Deseret News Publisher, 1900. [reproduction of first edition printed in June, 2002, commemorating the rebuilding of the Nauvoo Temple.]

Smith, Daymon M. *The Book of Mammon*. Self-published, 2010.

_____. *The Last Shall be First and the First shall be Last: Discourse and Mormon History. A Dissertation in Anthropology*. Presented to the Faculties at the University of Pennsylvania, 2007.

Smith, Joseph Fielding. *Church History and Modern Revelation*. 4 Vols. Salt Lake City: Deseret Book, 1946.

_____. *Doctrines of Salvation*. Edited by Bruce R. McConkie. Salt Lake City: Bookcraft, 1956.

Snuffer, Denver C., Jr. *Beloved Enos*. Salt Lake City: Mill Creek, 2009.

_____. *Eighteen Verses*. Salt Lake City: Mill Creek Press, 2007.

_____. *Ten Parables*. Salt Lake City: Mill Creek, 2008.

_____. *The Second Comforter: Conversing With the Lord Through the Veil*. Salt Lake City: Mill Creek Press, 2006.

_____. *Removing the Condemnation*. Salt Lake City: Mill Creek Press, 2011.

Stack, Peggy Fletcher. *Some LDS Conservatives Now at Odds With Their Church*. Salt Lake Tribune, April 28, 2011.

Stapley, Jonathan. *Adoptive Sealing Ritual in Mormonism, The Journal of Mormon History*, forthcoming edition.

Talmage, James E. *The Articles of Faith*. Salt Lake City: Deseret Book, 1984.

Teachings of the Presidents of the Church: Harold B. Lee. Salt Lake City: Intellectual Reserve, Inc., 2000.

Teachings of Presidents of the Church: Spencer W. Kimball. Salt Lake City: Intellectual Reserve Inc., 2006.

Teachings of the Presidents of the Church: Joseph F. Smith. Salt Lake City: Intellectual Reserve Inc., 1998.

The Joseph Smith Papers: Revelations and Translations Manuscript Revelation Books. Edited by Robin S. Jensen, Robert J. Woodford and Steven C. Harper. Salt Lake City: The Church Historian's Press, 2009.

The Diaries of J. Reuben Clark, Jr., 1933-1961, Abridged. Salt Lake City: Privately Published, 2010

The Diaries of Heber J. Grant, 1880-1945, Abridged. Salt Lake City: Privately Published, 2010

The Complete Discourses of Brigham Young. Edited by Richard S. Van Wagoner. Salt Lake City: Signature Books, 2009.

The Book of the Prophet John Taylor. Chapter 10. Revelation Received Monday, September 17, 1886. John Taylor Papers LDS Archives. www.voiceofzion.webs.com/JTaylor.pdf

The Mormon Church on Trial: Transcripts of the Reed Smoot Hearings. Edited by Michael H. Paulos. Salt Lake City: Signature Books, 2008.

The Diaries of Heber J. Grant ,1880-1945 Abridged. Salt Lake City: Privately published, 2010.

The Discourses of Wilford Woodruff. Edited by G. Homer Durham. Salt Lake City: Bookcraft, 1946.

The Teachings of Lorenzo Snow. Edited by Clyde Williams. Salt Lake City: Bookcraft, 1984

Times and Seasons, Vol. 5, No. 10. Nauvoo Illinois, May 15, 1844. Whole No. 94.

Traditions About the Early Life of Abraham. Compiled and edited by John Tvedtnes, Brian Hauglid and John Gee. Provo: BYU, 2001.

Whitmer, David. *An Address to all Believers in Christ.* Richmond, Missouri, 1887.

Wilford Woodruff's Journal. Edited by Scott Kenny. Salt Lake City: Signature Books, 1983.

A Note About The Author

DENVER C. SNUFFER, JR. is an attorney living in Sandy, Utah. He has an Associates of Arts degree from Daniel Webster Jr. College, Bachelors of Business Administration from McMurry University, and Juris Doctor from the J. Reuben Clark Law School at Brigham Young University. He was admitted to practice law in 1980 in Utah, and remains a practicing attorney. A convert to the LDS faith in 1973 when 19 years old, he has remained an active member of the LDS Church since then. He has served on the High Council, taught Gospel Doctrine and Priesthood classes for twenty-one years in Wards in Pleasant Grove, Alpine and Sandy, Utah. He has instructed Graduate Institute classes at the University of Utah College of Law for two years, and instructed at the BYU Education Week for three years. He is the author of seven earlier books, *The Second Comforter: Conversing With the Lord Through the Veil*, *Nephi's Isaiah*, *Eighteen Verses*, *Beloved Enos*, *Ten Parables*, *Come, Let Us Adore Him*, and *Removing the Condemnation*, all published by Mill Creek Press.

A Note On The Type

This book was set in Garamond. The fonts are based on the fonts first cut by Claude Garamond (c. 1480-1561). Garamond was a pupil of Geoffroy Tory and is believed to have followed the Venetian models, although he introduced a number of important differences, and it is to him that we owe the letter we now know as "old style." He gave to his letters a certain elegance and feeling of movement that won their creator an immediate reputation and the patronage of Francis I of France.

Designed by Mill Creek Press
Cover by David Christensen
Salt Lake City, Utah
Printed and bound by CreateSpace,
Charleston, South Carolina

46531319R00292

Made in the USA
Lexington, KY
06 November 2015